The RobotBASIC Help File

Copyright January 2010-2015 by
John Blankenship & Samuel Mishal

Printed for the Convenience of Our Users
(This file is provided FREE with RobotBASIC)

The RobotBASIC Help File for IDE V4.2.1

The Integrated Development Environment

The RobotBASIC IDE consists of an Editor screen, a Terminal screen, a Help screen, and a Debugger screen. Each screen has many buttons and menus that facilitate the various actions required in each screen. This section will discuss each screen and what actions can be carried out in them.

•The Editor Screen

The Editor screen has various buttons and menu items that facilitate the creation, editing, and running of programs. If you place the mouse cursor on a button and wait for a second, a hint will pop up showing the button's intended function. In addition, each button has an icon that can be helpful in remembering the button's action.

It is also possible to perform any button's action by using drop down menus. Furthermore each menu action has a keyboard combination (Short-Cut) that executes the action by pressing a function key or a combination of *Ctrl* or *Alt* and a key. The edit menu can be dropped down by clicking the **Edit** option on the main menu, or by pressing *Alt+E*. Each sub-action in the menu can be chosen by clicking that action or by pressing the correct *Alt* combination.

Also, as you can see on the right of each option, there is a Short-Cut key that can invoke the menu action without accessing the menu. For example, to invoke the **Find** option, you can press *Ctrl+F*.

Another feature of the Editor screen is the panel at the bottom of the window. This panel contains the name of the file currently being edited. If the file is a new one that has not been previously saved and named, it will hold the name NoName.Bas, otherwise it will have the file's full name. To the left of the area where the file name is displayed is an area that will either hold the word **Modified** if the file has been modified but not yet saved, or it will be blank if the file has not been modified since the last save or since it was loaded.

The first area in the panel at the bottom of the window will show the line number where the cursor is in the editor area. The next area shows the character number where the cursor is. If the cursor is right at the start of the line it will be 0. The next area will either say **Ins** or **Ovr**. Ins means that when you type, the text will be inserted where the cursor is and any text to the right of the cursor will be moved to the right. Ovr means the text will overwrite the text where the cursor is and move the cursor to the right. You toggle between the two modes using the **Insert** key on the keyboard.

1

Below the Speed Buttons panel is a panel that on start up holds one Tab. The tab will also have the name of the file being edited, but only the name of the file without the path. You can open other files and have many files open simultaneously. Each open file will have a corresponding Tab with its name in it. You can swap between the open files by clicking on the Tab corresponding to the file. When you do that the panel at the bottom of the window will reflect the information corresponding to the file you are currently editing, and the text in the edit area will be the one for the file you have chosen. If the file has been changed then the name of the file in the Tab will have a * in front of it to indicate that the file has been modified and not yet saved. This can be helpful to see at a glance how many files have been modified without having to click on each file's tab in turn and observing the status panel at the bottom of the screen.

To run the program currently loaded in the editor area either, click the **Run / Run Program** sub menu, or press the speed button, or use the *Ctrl+R* shortcut on the keyboard. While a program is running the speed button and its corresponding menus are disabled. They will be enabled when you halt the program or the program is ended, or an error occurs during the program run.

Running a program will bring up the Terminal Screen and show any program interaction on this screen (see the Terminal Screen section).

The menu and speed buttons allow for many helpful features. You can save and open files. You can search and "search & replace". You can Cut, Paste, Copy, Undo, and Print. Additionally you can view a help file that contains a full description of all the features of the language.

Also there is a Pop-Up menu when you right click the mouse over the editor area that holds similar options as in the main menu. Also, if you right click the mouse button over any of the Tabs in the panel under the Speed Buttons you will get another Pop-Menu that holds options relating to closing/saving the open files. The same options are also in the main menu and some have a corresponding Speed button and/or Short-Cut key.

When you do a search if you close the search dialog box you can still search for further occurrences of the same search string by pressing the *F3* key. If you want to enter a new search string then invoke the dialog box again using the menu or *Ctrl+F* or by pressing the search speed button.

The default behavior of the editor is to automatically indent the next line you are typing to the level of the previous line's first character. This is useful when typing programs where loop structures are automatically formatted for you as you are typing. You can change this behavior where no automatic indenting is performed, with the menu option **Edit / Auto Indent** *(F5)* (which checks and un-checks).

The sub-menu option **Edit / Smart Tabbing** *(F4)* allows you to swap between Fixed and Dynamic Tabbing. When smart tabbing is on, the Tab keyboard key will move the cursor either 4 characters to the right, or to inline with the word in the line above if there is a text that has been previously tabbed in the line above. When smart tabbing is off then the cursor will move a fixed distance of 4 spaces regardless of the text above it. The number of spaces is by default 4 spaces but you can change this through the *Edit / Preferences (F6)* sub-menu option.

Two menu items *Indent Block* (or *F8*) and *Un-Indent Block* (or *F7*) from the *Edit* menu are very useful for formatting programs. These allow for indenting a highlighted block of text or un-indenting it one space at a time. The text will not un-indent if the first character of a line is not the space character (or a tab). That means you will not lose any text. This is useful for lining up entire blocks to fit within indented formatting of program structures. If you are using the normal tab then the indenting process may not show an indent until enough spaces have been added to cause a tab to the next tab stop (see above about tabs).

The sub-menu item *File/ Merge* (*Ctrl+G*) facilitates the creation of subroutine libraries. It allows you to select a RobotBASIC (or any text) file which will be merged to the end of the file currently residing in the editor. If the merged file contains a set of subroutines they will become part of your program. *File/ Merge At Cursor* does the same action but *inserts* the text at the current cursor position.

The menu option *File / Set Directory* allows you to select a directory as a working directory. Normally when you save or open a file (.BAS) the directory where the file is becomes the working directory. So when you run the program currently in the IDE you will be running within this directory. This menu option allows you set a working directory without having to open or save any files. However, whenever you Run a file RB will automatically set the File's directory as the working directory. If in your programs you wish to change the default directory then use DirSet().

Note: The *Set Directory* dialog allows you to select a directory by **double-clicking** the mouse over it and will let you see the files contained in the directory, *however*, the selected directory will *not be set* as the working directory *until* you click the *Ok* button.

Note: When you try to run a file within the Editor Screen that has been loaded from a disk file, and the file on disk has been changed since you have loaded it into the editor, say, due to another edit program, then RobotBASIC will **automatically** load the newer file from disk into the Editor Screen and then run the file. This way you will be running the latest version of the program even if you have modified it with another editor program outside of the RobotBASIC IDE. This action can be stopped from being automatic with the *File / Auto Load Newer File* sub-menu option. This option is checked to signify that automatic loading is performed. If you uncheck it RB will display a warning message that allows you the option of either loading the newer file or not.

Note: All the optional stuff mentioned above and much more can be configured using the *Edit / Preferences* dialog (*F6*). See The Preferences System section below.

•The Terminal Screen

The Terminal Screen is where the program input and output take place. This screen has various buttons, a prompt panel, an input box and a display screen. The display screen is where all the output from the program will be displayed. Commands such as Print or Circle will display their results on the screen.

The display screen is 800x600 pixels (width x height). If you are using a Windows system where the monitor limits are less than 1024x768 resolution, the Terminal Screen will resize to a smaller size. You can find the limits of the X, Y coordinates by using the ScrLimits. You can also use programming statements to resize the window to smaller than this size. The Terminal screen is not resizable, however you can change this during the running of a program using ScrSetMetrics.

When the program ends the terminal screen will remain on top of the editor. You can close it or move it to the background (see below). There is a short-cut key (*Ctrl+T*) while in the Editor to reopen the terminal screen, or you can use the menu option or the speed button. The display from the previously run program will not be cleared until the current program is executed again or a new program is run.

If a runtime error occurs a message will be displayed indicating the nature of the error and what line number (in the program) it is on. The Terminal screen will go to the background and the Editor screen will come to the foreground with the line where the error has occurred highlighted up to the point where the error has occurred within the line. You can bring the Terminal screen back into view as described above.

The bottom of the screen is where all input is done using Input, Waitkey, GetKey and GetkeyE (see Standard User Interfacing section). The edit box will only be activated when an Input is issued. Any entry in the box must be terminated with an ENTER. The input box has a buffer that holds any previous inputs. To Access a previous input, press *Ctrl+P* or *Ctrl+N* to step through prior inputs. This facilitates easy repetition of inputs.

When you issue an Input e_Prompt,v_Name statement, the *e_Prompt* will be printed just above the Edit box as a prompt. If *e_Prompt* results in a zero length string then character **>** will be printed as a prompt instead of the null string (See Standard User Interfacing section). Inputted data is treated as a number if it is a legal number otherwise it will be returned as a string. You can use functions to manipulate inputs as needed. This behavior can be changed to make Input do its interaction directly within the body of the Terminal screen using InlineInputMode.

The buttons on the bottom right allow certain actions to occur. Each button, just as in the Editor screen, shows a hint when you place the mouse cursor on it. The **Editor** button allows you to view the Editor screen. The editor screen has a **Terminal** button to display the Terminal Screen again. The program will continue to run when you swap between the terminal and the editor screen; it will not stop. The **Print** button causes the screen area to be printed on the default printer. The screen area is printed as a graphic. Only what is visible on the screen will be printed, any output that has scrolled off the screen will not be printed, but see below for how to retrieve any text that has scrolled off the screen. You can also perform this action programmatically using PrintScr (also see PrinterSetup). The **Debug** button will turn on the debugging feature. See Debug.

The **Stop** button allows the user to abort the currently running program and return to the editor screen. You can do the same action by closing the Terminal screen window (using MS Windows methods). The behavior of this button (or closing the window) depends on a parameter that can be set within your program. The standard behavior is for the Terminal screen to close and the editor screen becoming the active window. Within the editor the cursor position will be where it was when you ran the program. However, you can prevent the user from being able to use the **Stop** button or close the Terminal window, or you can have the action cause the entire system to terminate, or you can have the action behave as if a run time error has occurred. The way RobotBASIC will respond to closing the Terminal screen window (or pressing the **Stop** button) can be changed programmatically with AbortMethod.

The buttons **CutToBuffer** and **ClearBuffer** facilitate the use of a special feature of the Terminal Screen that can be a powerful tool:
   Text printed with Print is stored in a buffer, regardless of whether it has scrolled off the screen or not. Once the buffer is full (it holds 8Kb of text) it will clear and start to fill again. If this occurs in the middle of your output the buffer will only be holding part of the output when you use the **CutToBuffer** button.

   The buffer content can be sent to the Windows clipboard using the **CutToBuffer** button. Once you have done this, the text in the clipboard can be used in any Windows program. The **ClearBuffer** button is used to clear the buffer and the Windows clipboard at the same time. This is needed if you do not want any output from previous program runs to be included when you copy the buffer to the clipboard. Remember to clear the buffer between runs if you desire, but before you start the run.

   You can also access the text buffer in a program using GetTextBuff(), TextBuffToCB and SetTextBuff. Also see ClrCB, SetCBText and GetCBText().

Note: Normally the Terminal Screen window is not a sizeable window and the user will not be able to modify the window width or height. However, in version 4.1.0 and later you can allow the user to resize the window manually or move and resize the window under program control using ScrSetMetrics and ScrGetMetrics. Also with these commands you can show/hide the control panel at the bottom of the window.

•The Preferences System

The IDE can be configured in many ways and various options can be set as you like. The Preferences configurations Dialog presents you with 3 different sections where you can set the various colors and so forth as you prefer them. The dialog is self-explanatory. There is also a help feature where if you place the mouse pointer over a field you will get a good explanation in a panel at the bottom of the screen. There is also a page with some more instructions.

All the parameters configurable through the Preferences dialog will be saved to a file every time you terminate RB. The next time you start RB the file will be read so as to set all the preferences as you had set them. The file is called RobotBASIC.INI and must reside in the same directory as the RobotBASIC.EXE. If this file does not exist or is corrupted RB will default to a default configuration. You can also set this default setup through the Preferences dialog. Also if the .INI file exists you will not be presented with a Licensing Screen since it would be obvious that you have accepted the licensing the first time you ran RB.

Another thing saved in the .INI file is a list of the most recent files you have opened or saved during the last session. The number of files on the list is also configurable through the Preferences dialog.

The position and the height and width of the Editor Screen when you terminated RB will be save to the INI and if you have chosen to do so the next time RB starts the Editor Screen will have the same setting. The option to do so is again configurable through the Preferences dialog. The same also applies to the Help screen.

The Preferences dialog can be invoked by pressing *F6* or the ***Edit/Preferences*** menu option or the Speed button on the Tool Bar. If you change any parameters in the dialog you would be able to either abandon the changes and exit (*Cancel* button) or Apply all the changes and exit (*Apply* button). You can also set **_all_** the parameters to the RB defaults by pressing the button at the bottom of the dialog. You can also set a subset of the parameters (each section) to the defaults by pressing the *Set All To Default* button in each section.

•The Help Screen

The Help Screen provides explanations about the use of RobotBASIC's commands, functions and various other aspects of the entire system. On the left side of the screen there is an expandable table of contents of the headings in the help text displayed on the right side of the screen. When you select a heading in the TOC by clicking on it the section on the right will jump to that particular location in the help file. These sections cover every aspect of the system. The help text can be selected and copied to the Windows clipboard using the **Copy** button (or *Ctrl+C*). The **Search** button (or *Ctrl+F*) allows you to search the text in the help file.

The search dialog will remain open after it has found an occurrence of the search string. This is so that you can keep searching for more occurrences. However, if you do remove it you can still use the *F3* key to search further just like in the editor screen.

In the Help Screen on the left side there is an expandable/collapsible Table of Contents that you can use to click on any of the headings to jump to that heading's area in the help files text (right). Also at the top of the screen are 4 drop down list boxes. These boxes contain all the Commands, the Functions, the Commands & Functions, and the final one has the Constants. You can click on elements of these lists to jump to the verb's main entry in the help file where the verb is described in detail.

The TOC panel's width can be changed by clicking and dragging the separator between the panels. This size will also be saved to the Ini file so that when you start the next session the panel will have the size you prefer. If the panel is too small to display all the text you can scroll it using the scroll bars. Also if you rest the mouse cursor on any of the entries and it is too long to display in the panel then the text will show like a hint text showing the full text. When you click inside the panel it will keep the focus so that you can use the Up/Dn arrows to scroll through it and the Help text will move to the selected topic area.

The help system utilizes a customizable separate file called RobotBASIC_HelpFile.RTF. This is an RTF formatted file that has to reside inside the same folder where the RobotBASIC.exe is contained. The file can be modified to include special help catered to your requirements in a section called Customized Help. RobotBASIC has a reference to this section and as long as you maintain the section name you can have it anywhere in the help file and RB will jump to that position whenever the user requests the section.

This feature can be of utility to teachers. A teacher may customize the help file to the needs and level of the students. Moreover, the help file may be used to give extra information to students regarding coursework materials.

Note: This file is best modified using the WordPad program provided in all MS Windows systems. It must be saved as an RTF format file. MSWord can read and write RTF format files but it may not save using the version of the RTF format required by RobotBASIC. If you find that the file is garbled when you read it in the RobotBASIC help screen, then load and save the file again using the WordPad program. The headings in the file have the character • next or surrounding them. This is important and the headings must remain as is for RB to be able to locate them within the help file.

•The Debugger Screen

The debugging feature of RobotBASIC is discussed in detail under the descriptions for Debug and Stepping. The buttons are self-explanatory. Refer to Debug and Stepping for more detailed information.

The debugger screen buffer will become full if there is too much output. To prevent this from causing an error, use the *Clear* button to occasionally clear the buffer. You can resize and move the Debug Screen, and you can swap between it, the Terminal screen and the Editor screen. The Debugger screen will always stay on top of other windows. If you wish to see other windows in full then drag it to the side while viewing other windows.

Another useful debugging feature is the ability to view a list of all the variables (Type, Name and Value) that have been created during the execution of the code. The value will be whatever it was when the program terminated (whether normally, due to an error or by a user initiated abort). The string values will be surrounded by the characters "" (double quotes). If the string contains the character " it will still be there. Surrounding the string with quotes enables you to see whether the string value has leading or trailing spaces and whether it is an empty string.

You can view the variables by using the menu option *Run / View Variables Table* or by pressing *Ctrl+B*. Also if the debugger screen is active you can see this same table by pressing the *View Variables Table* button. The table shows ***all SIMPLE*** variables in the current running session, it does not show Array elements. To view the values of array elements use the Expression Evaluation system provided at the top of the Debug Screen.

At the top of the screen you will see an text box in which you can enter any valid RobotBASIC expressions. You can enter more than one expression by separating them with the \ character just as in an RB program. In the expression you can use any of the simple variables and/or array elements that have been declared during the run of the program up to that point. The expression can be ***any valid*** RB expression using functions and variables.

Each expression will be evaluated then, it and its value, will be displayed on a separate line in the Debug Screen output area. If the expression cannot be evaluated you will get an error message and the display in the debug area will also show a message saying that the expression could not be evaluated.

You can evaluate the expressions immediately by pressing the *Evaluate Now* button. You also can have the expressions evaluated every time you press the *Step* button, but the expressions will be evaluated the next time the Debug Screen becomes active. This would be immediately after executing the pending line if you are in Stepping mode. However in Debug mode it won't be until the next Debug statement is encountered. Check the check box labeled *Evaluate On Stepping* to activate this mode.

•Creating, Saving And Running Programs

•Creating The Program
To create a program use the editor to type in the program according to the syntax covered in the Overview Of The Language section and referring to the various other sections for details on how to use the commands and functions and flow control statements.

•Saving The Program (Text)
While writing your program you ought to save it as often as you can so that you won't lose your hard work in the case of some mishap. To save the program use the menu option *Save* under the *File* main menu, or the speed button or *Ctrl+S*. There is another menu option called *Save as Binary*. This option is used to save a file as a binary file and will be described later below. During the development stage do not use this option.

•Running The Program
The next step is to run the program using *Ctrl+R* or the speed button or the menu options. Your program may have errors and you may have to iterate through the process until you are satisfied the program is running correctly

•Running Finalized Programs
Once a program is a fully functional program and saved as a text .Bas file (or binary file, see later), there are two ways you can run it. If you share your program with others they also have the same two ways to run the program (the second method might be preferable). You can share your programs by giving the text .Bas file. Another way you can share your program is by giving a binary version of the program (binary .Bas). This method has an advantage in that your source code will be hidden. This method will be described later below. In both cases the other party will have to have their copy of RobotBASIC.Exe. A third way to share your programs is as a compiled stand alone executable which has the advantage of not requiring the RobotBASIC interpreter to be running on the target machine. See later for how to do this.

To run a program you can use either of the following two methods (**also see Sharing an Executable below**) :

•From within the IDE
This method requires that you run the RobotBASIC.exe, then use the editor to load the program (.Bas file) you want to run then use *Ctrl+R* or other methods to run the program. This method is the same as when you were developing a program and has the advantage of being able to view the program code and be able to modify it if needed (if the text .Bas is being used).

•Directly From Windows OS
Using this method you will be able to run the .Bas file directly without having to run

RobotBASIC first. The program will run and when terminated you will be back to the operating system (except in certain cases).

This method is useful for people who want to run the program but without having to know about RobotBASIC and all the actions required to load and run programs within the IDE. Also this method is convenient since you do not have to go through the steps of running RobotBASIC, loading the .Bas, then after running it having to close the RobotBASIC IDE to go back to the OS.

To be able to use this option the OS has to be setup (one time process) before the first time you perform the action. The OS has to be told to use the RobotBASIC.exe to execute the .BAS file every time you double-click on a .BAS file. This setup process has to be performed only once for your computer. Once performed you will be able to double-click on any file with the extension .BAS and the OS will first run RobotBASIC and tell it to load and run the .BAS file all automatically. Also when the program terminates RobotBASIC will automatically close up and return you to the OS (except in certain cases). The process of how to do this will be described later below.

•<u>Sharing Finalized Programs</u>

Once a program is fully functional there are three ways you can share it with others:

    <u>Note:</u> If your program uses additional files like bitmaps, wavs, or other files then you will also have to share these files.
    <u>Note:</u> If your program makes use of the TWAIN image capture functions or the USBmicro functions then you will also have to distribute the required DLLs.
    <u>Note:</u> Other than with the Executable method of sharing your programs, the end user will have to have the RobotBASIC.exe program on their system.

•<u>Sharing a text .Bas file</u>

During the process of creating your program, you have been saving it all along as a text file with the .BAS extension. This text file can be given to any person you wish to use your program (they need to also have a copy of RobotBASIC.exe). This method of sharing your programs has the advantage that the users can read your program and can learn from it and can also edit it, do modifications or improvements or can cut and paste routines for use while making their own programs.

•<u>Sharing a binary .Bas file</u>

If you wish to share your programs with other people but do not wish to allow them to view your source code, you need to save your program as a binary file and distribute this file instead of the text file. They also need to have a copy of RobotBASIC.exe.

This binary file will still have the .Bas extension and will be used in exactly the same manner as the text file. As far as the end user is concerned the process of running the binary file or the text file is exactly the same with no difference whatsoever. The only variation is that if the user executes the binary file from within the IDE (see above) she/he will not be able to view the file, edit or modify it. Instead a message will be visible within the editor screen that explains that the file is a binary file, but that it can be otherwise executed as any other text file.

To save your program as a binary file, load it within the editor and use the menu option *Save as Binary* from under the *File* main menu. The system will show you a dialog box that has a suggested name for the file. This suggested name is the same name as the loaded text file with the character '_' added at the end of the file name (just before the **.**). You can accept this suggested name or enter your own name. For example if the text file name is MyFile.Bas then the suggested name will be MyFile_.Bas.

The naming method suggested by the system is useful for you to be able to distinguish binary files from text files. When you see files named WhatEver.Bas and WhatEver_.Bas you will know that the first one is the text version and the second is the binary version without having to look inside the files. If you do not like this standard create your own but do stick to a standard that makes it easy for you to identify the files without having to load and inspect them.

The file saved must still have the .Bas extension and for all intents and purposes it is the same as the text version except that it cannot be viewed by any programs since it is a binary file and if viewed it will contain nothing but garbled characters. You can now share your program with others assured that no one can discern your algorithms.

•Sharing a compiled Executable (.EXE) file

RobotBASIC allows you to compile your program to a standalone executable (EXE) file. The sub-menu option *File / Create EXE* will compile the .BAS program (text not binary) you currently have active in the Editor and create a standalone Windows Executable program (EXE). You will be given the option to change the name of the program, but as a default it will have the same name as the .BAS file but with the .EXE extension.

The resulting EXE will run on any Windows OS (95 onwards). If your program makes use of the TWAIN functions then you will need to distribute the EZTW32.DLL with your program. Also, if your program makes calls to the USBmicro functions then you will also need the USBm.dll.

If your program expects WAV, BMP or other files to also be there then you should also distribute these with the program. The RobotBASIC_HelpFile.rtf help file will of course ***not*** be needed.

Distributing an executable will alleviate the need to have a version of RobotBASIC on the

11

target PC. This is a major advantage when end users are not programmers, also the setup should be a lot simpler since the executable can run without any setup required.

If you have a web site you can post the executable on it where it can also be run directly from your web site, unless you make use of the DLLs or other additional files (bitmaps or wavs etc.).

Another advantage of creating an executable of your program is that it will always run as when it was compiled regardless of what version of RobotBASIC there is out there.

•Setting up the Operating System

To be able to run .Bas files directly from the operating system you need to tell the OS that RobotBASIC.exe is the file to use to execute .BAS files.

You have been using this method of running files all along with other systems. For example, if you double click on any file with the .TXT extension the OS automatically executes NotePad.exe and gives it the .Txt file. You can setup the OS to do the same with .BAS files and RobotBASIC.exe.

Note: You may have other programs that use the .BAS extension and your OS may have been setup to use these with the .BAS extension. You have to decide whether you want to override this or not. There are other methods (described later) to still be able to run RobotBASIC with a .BAS file without doing these steps. However, this is the most convenient and preferred method.

The process described below assumes you know how to use windows tools such as the Windows Explorer and you know how to navigate around your hard drives and directory structure. If you do not, recruit someone who knows how to do this to assist you.

1- Navigate (using Windows Explorer) to any file that has the .BAS extension (either one you created or one given to you).
2- Use the mouse to right-click on the file (click using the right mouse button).
3- A popup menu will show. This menu has an option *Open With*. Put the mouse pointer on this option. This option may have a sub menu or it may not. If it **does not** have a sub menu click on it. If it has a sub menu then the submenu will have an option called *Choose Program...* or *Setup Default Program...* or something to the effect (usually the last option). Click on that.
4- The previous step will now have you presented with a dialog box that has some program names and some buttons and a check box. The check box will have the title *Always Use This Program To Open these files*, or some equivalent. Click on this check box to check it.
5- One of the buttons at the bottom will have the title *Browse* or *Other*. Click on this button. This will present you with an explorer screen that enables you to navigate to the location where the RobotBASIC.exe file resides. Use this screen to do so and select the

RobotBASIC.exe file. For example the RobotBASIC.exe may be sitting in the directory on your *C:* drive called **Programs Files** in a sub directory called **RobotBASIC**. So navigate to the C: drive then to the Program Files then RobotBASIC. In there you will see the file RobotBASIC.exe. Double click on it.

6- When you come back from selecting RobotBASIC.exe you will be at the dialog box you saw in step 4. Now the button labeled *OK* will be enabled. Ensure that the file RobotBASIC.EXE is highlighted in the list above and that the check button in step 4 is checked then press the OK button.

7- That is all. Your OS is now setup to run any .BAS automatically with RobotBASIC.exe. To test this go back to where you have some .BAS files and double click any of them. You should see the program running.

Once you setup the system to automatically run .Bas files, you can also create shortcuts to the .BAS file so that you won't have to navigate to the location of the file to double click on it and run it. The shortcut can be placed in a convenient location (such as the desktop). Also shortcuts can have a nice Icon that indicates what the file is.

•Other Methods

There are two alternatives to the above. However the above is the best and most convenient method. The first alternative given is the second preferred alternative and also has an additional advantage of using shortcuts, which are a convenient way to run programs rather than navigating to a location of where .Bas files might reside. With these alternatives you can have RobotBASIC automatically load and run the .BAS file without the end-user having to explicitly run the exe then load and run the program from within the IDE. Also these two methods do not require that the OS know that the RobotBASIC.exe is the default executer for the .BAS extension files.

•Using Shortcuts

1- Right click on your desktop and select the menu option called *New*. This option will show a submenu. One option in the submenu is called **Shortcut.** Select this option.

2- You will be presented with a dialog box that allows you to use the Browse button to navigate to where the RobotBASIC.exe file resides. Do so and then press *Next*.

3- Give a name to the shortcut that reflects the name of the .Bas file you want to eventually have run through this method.

5- The shortcut will now be on the desktop. Right click on it.

6- Select the Properties option (at the bottom).

7- You will now have a dialog box that shows the details of the shortcut. The box labeled Target will have the RobotBASIC.exe file name and path highlighted. Use the arrow keys to go to the end of this text.

8- Right after the .exe type a space then type in the name of the .BAS file you wish to have run when this shortcut is executed. You have to type the name of the .BAS file including its directory path. If you do not know this you can find it out by using the Windows Explorer to navigate to it. The Caption at the top left of the window of the windows explorer program will have the exact path and file name once you have the .BAS file highlighted. You can use this information to type the text required.

10- A little lower there is an edit box labeled Start In:. Delete what is already there and type in the same path as the .BAS file. This is the directory where the .BAS resides (without the file name).

11- Press OK and you will now have a shortcut on your desktop that will execute the .BAS file using RobotBASIC.exe any time you double click on it.

12- If you do not want the shortcut to be on your desktop you can use Windows Explorer to navigate to where you want it and then drag and drop the shortcut from the desktop to that location.

You can also edit the icon of the shortcut. If an .ICO file is available you can change the default icon of the shortcut so that it uses the available .ICO file instead. This has the advantage of making the shortcut have a visual cue to what the program does and is pleasing to the end user.

As a programmer you can share shortcuts with your end-users, but unfortunately the shortcuts have absolute path information and cannot be made relative. So you still have to make sure that the paths in the shortcut are correct if you want to share them. You also may have to control where the end-user places the RobotBASIS.exe file and the .BAS files.

•Using Drag and Drop
Use the above procedure to create a shortcut to the RobotBASIC.exe (just the exe no .BAS) and have this shortcut available on the desktop. The user can then drag any .BAS file and drop it onto the shortcut. This will execute RobotBASIC and automatically load and run the .BAS file.

•Controlling How Your Programs Terminate
There are 4 combinations for how to run RobotBASIC programs:

    1- A Text .BAS file from within the IDE

    2- A Binary .BAS file from within the IDE

    3- A Text .BAS file from the Operating System (OS)

    4 - A Binary .BAS file from the OS.

Note: The information in this section does not apply to compiled files. Compiled standalone executables will always terminate back out to the OS.

Each one of the options will have a different behavior in how the system will startup and terminate. RobotBASIC gives you three statements for terminating a program (**End**, **Terminate** and **Exit**). Also it is possible for the user to close the program window while running, effectively aborting the program. RobotBASIC gives you five methods for controlling the abortion procedure (see **AbortMethod** for details). Additionally, it is possible for your program to generate an error and the way the system will terminate again depends on which running style (one of the above 4) is being used.

Thus to summarize, you have 3 program termination statements, 5 program abortion methods and the error condition, for each one of the 4 program execution styles. In addition you also have the condition where you do not give a specific way to exit the program or to handle abortion (i.e. two more default conditions). All together there are 50 possibilities. Do not fret though; most of these will be the same. See the table below while following the description that follows. Also refer to **AbortMethod**, and the **End**, **Terminate**, **Exit** and **onAbort** statements in the Flow Control Statements section, as well as **AbortFlag()**.

	From The IDE		From the OS	
	Text	**Binary**	**Text**	**Binary**
Termination Statements				
None	See Note 1	See Note 1	Goes Back To Editor	Exits To OS
End	Stays in the Terminal Screen See Note 2	Stays in the Terminal Screen See Note 2	Goes Back To Editor	Exits To OS
Terminate	Goes Back To Editor	Goes Back To Editor	Goes Back To Editor	Exits To OS
Exit	Goes Back To Editor	Goes Back To Editor	Exits To OS	Exits To OS
Abortion Control				
None	Goes Back To Editor	Goes Back To Editor	Goes Back To Editor	Exits To OS
am_Normal	Goes Back To Editor	Goes Back To Editor	Goes Back To Editor	Exits To OS
am_Exit	Goes Back To Editor	Goes Back To Editor	Exits To OS	Exits To OS
am_Error	See Note 3	Goes Back To Editor	Exits To OS	Exits To OS
am_NoAbort	No Action (Note 5)	No Action (Note 5)	No Action	No Action
am_Flag	No Action (Note 6)	No Action (Note 6)	No Action	No Action
Runtime Error	See Note 4	Goes Back To Editor See Note 4	Exits To OS See Note 4	Exits To OS See Note 4

Note 1: If you do not have a specific termination statement for the program the termination method will follow the specified abortion method. If there is no specified abortion method then the interpreter will assume an **End** statement. However, you should always have a specific termination statement; End, Terminate or Exit. It is also advisable to also specify an abortion handling method.

Note 2: When the program terminates and the Terminal screen stays visible, you can close the window using the X on the top right corner (or other OS methods). This option is useful to continue seeing the program output even after it terminates. Also even when the Terminal screen

15

is closed (as occurs in other combinations) you can still see the program output again by redisplaying the Terminal screen by pressing *Ctrl+T* from the Editor (or use the menu or speed button). You can do this any time to see what the output of the last executed program. The Terminal screen is not erased after the program terminates until a new program is executed or you exit the IDE.

Note 3: RobotBASIC provides many methods for debugging programs. This is one additional way you can find errors in a program. You can have the program running and at some point during the execution manually abort the program. Normally the system will just go back to the editor if you are running from within the IDE. However, if you use this abort capturing method the system will also highlight and locate for you the line of code which was about to be executed just before you aborted. This can be useful in locating the area of code that may be causing trouble but is not causing an error that stops the program. This feature is only possible though if you are not running binary files nor running from the OS rather than the IDE.

Note 4: If an error occurs during the execution of a program (not using OnError trapping) and it is not a binary file or is not being run from the OS, the system will highlight and locate the line in the source code that caused the error. In all cases however an error message is given that indicates the type and nature of the error and the line number in the code that caused the error. If you are running a text .BAS within the IDE you will also have the added benefit of seeing the line that caused the error. If you are running a binary file from within the IDE the system will just go back to the editor. If you are running the program from the OS (binary or text) the system will go back to the OS. Also see the OnError flow control statement.

Note 5: The am_NoAbort abortion capture method will prevent the user from being able to abort the program and prevents the closing of the Terminal screen window by any method. This is a useful option if you need to always have the user terminate the program using an option you provide programmatically. This option can be a button or any other user interface method. If the user tries to close the window a message will be given to the user using a dialog box that explains that it is not possible to close the window and that another method should be used. See **AbortMethod**.

Note 6: The am_Flag method performs exactly the same function as the am_NoAbort option except for two differences. No message will be given to the user and a flag within the system will be set every time the user tries to close the window. It is possible to interrogate the status of this flag to find out whenever the user tries to abort and take action programmatically. See the **AbortMethod** and **AbortFlag()**. Also see the onAbort statement.

•Running from within the OS

The intent of the above mechanisms is to give you control on how to terminate the program. In all cases, other than when you prevent program abortion, running a binary file from within the OS will exit back to the OS once the program is terminated regardless of what method you use. If a text file is being run from the OS the interpreter will exit back to the OS if you specifically request an Exit or an error occurs. Otherwise, the interpreter will go back to the editor screen within the IDE.

If you run programs from within the OS, the editor window will not be available and will not be shown. So only the Terminal screen will be showing. The editor will be revealed when the program terminates and is a text file and there was no error, nor a specific Exit termination method.

•Running from within the IDE

When you run programs from the IDE, it is assumed that you want to stay within the IDE when the program terminates. Also the Editor window will be visible but will be behind the Terminal screen. You are able to view the contents of the editor.

In most cases, when the program terminates, you will be back inside the Editor screen and the cursor will be where you had left just before running the program. However, in the case of the am_Error abort capture method and in the case of a real error a line will be highlighted (see Note 4 above).

If you do not specify a specific termination or abortion method or you use the End statement the Terminal window will remain active above the Terminal screen (see Note 1 above).

Study AbortMethod and AbortFlag() and also the End, Terminate, Exit, OnError and OnAbort flow control statements.

Overview Of The Language

RobotBASIC is a line-oriented programming language. A program is a set of lines, where each line is either a blank line or contains a Statement. A line ends at the end of the line i.e. a line ends with a CR+LF (Carriage Return + Line Feed).

Therefore a program is a collection of statements like this:

    Statement
    Statement

    Statement
    Statement
    ....

•Statements

A statement is what makes a RobotBASIC program achieve the tasks it is designed to accomplish. There are various types of statements:

- Assignment Statements
- Command Statements
- Flow Control Statements
- Labels
- Comments
- Function call

Labels and Comments can be combined on the same line with other statements (see below).A statement contains various other elements that help in achieving the functionality of the statement. These elements are:

- Simple Variables
- Array Variables
- Expressions

    Expressions contain further elements that constitute the expression. These elements are:

    - Simple Variables
    - Array Variables
    - Constants
    - Strings
    - Numbers

        Which are of the following types:
        - Integer Numbers
        - Floating Point Numbers
    - Operators

Which are of the following types:
- Parenthesis
- Mathematical Operators
- Comparison (Relational) Operators
- Logical Operators
- Bit-wise Operators
• Functions
Which can contain expressions.

•Line Comments

Comments are an important part of any programming language. Without good comments a program can be hard to understand. Without good comments, even the person who wrote the program may not be able to follow the program's logic when reading the program at a later time.

Comments are not executable statements. They are used to annotate a program and format the text of the program to look nice and to make the logic of the program understandable by someone trying to read the program. Comments can also divide the program in sections, making it easy to see where various operations begin and end.

Comments can be in a line on their own, or they can be in line with a statement. Any text in a line after and including the comment indicator will be ignored and not considered as part of the statement. RobotBASIC allows for two methods of indicating a comment. The character combination // is one and the character ' is another. For example:

```
//this is a comment on a line by itself
'this too is another comment
d = 9      //this is a comment in line with a statement
b = d*2    'so is this comment
```

•Block Comments

Sometimes you need to block off a whole block of code so as to try out the program without the code or maybe you need to remove the code but do not want to delete it yet. One way you can do that is to comment each line with the // symbol (or '). This definitely works but you may have many lines and going through each one to put a // is a lot of typing and also if you need to reinstate the code later you have to do a lot of work to delete all these previously typed //.

This is why the block comment will save you a lot of typing. However there are a few rules you need to follow.

A comment block is started with a /* and ended with a */ . But there are conditions on using

19

these.

1- You can put the /* anywhere in a line of code.
2- ALL code from that point until a */ is encountered becomes a comment and is not executed as code.
3- The **/*** symbol **MUST BE the last thing in a line**. So no other code or text can come after it (not even a comment).THIS IS IMPORTANT it has to be the absolute last two characters on a line. If the */ is not the last thing in a line it will not be taken into account and thus causing the whole rest of your program to become a comment. This can be useful. If you want to comment the whole of the rest of the program from a certain point onwards then just put a /* from the point you need and do not put a */ anywhere later as the last thing on a line.
4- **You cannot nest block comments**. So you cannot have /* ....../*.......*/.....*/. RobotBASIC will see the first /* and start looking for a */. The second /* will not be considered. So later it will see the first */ and will think that this is the end of the comment block. Later when the second */ is encountered it will cause a syntax error. So you cannot nest comment blocks. If you want to nest a larger block that would include a previous comment block then just uncomment the inner comment block, or use the // to comment out the first */.

Example:
```
For i= 0 to 5
    print i
    //blocked off code with */ as the last thing in a line
    /*print 3
    print 4*/
    /********************
    this is also a comment block
    this text will not be taken as code
    ********************/
    /******this is a comment ******/
    print /*5    notice the 5 is now part of the comment block
    *****/
    /*
    print 20
    */
next
```

•Assignment Statements

An assignment statement is where you assign a value to a variable. **Variables** are storage spaces for values that will be used in the program logic. Variables can be simple variables or **Array elements**. See the sections below on Variables and Arrays for more detail on what a variable or array is and how to use it. In the discussion below *Var* means a simple variable and *VarA[...]* means an array element. Also see the section below on **Expressions** for further details of what an expression is. Assignment statements are like this:

Var = *Expression*

OR   **Note:** **Also see the Assignment Operators in the Operators Section.**

VarA[…] = *Expression*

For example:
```
Distance = 5.4   //--assigns the variable Distance the
                 //--value 5.4
TimeTaken = 2.1
Speed = Distance/TimeTaken //--Speed will be assigned
                           //--the result of the
                           //--expression
Dim MailBoxes[20,10] //--see later for what this means
MailBoxes[5,3] = 9   //--assign an array element
```

Note: You can place multiple assignment statements on the same line by using the \ character. So instead of saying:
```
a = 1
b = 2
c = 3
```
you can say:
```
a = 1 \ b = 2 \ c = 3
```
This helps for making more compact code (see the Line Break Operator description below).

RobotBASIC is a versatile language in that you do not have to specify the type of a variable. The type of the variable is determined by the data being stored in it. Also the type of a variable can change if you reassign it a different type value. *However you can change this and make RB become a strict typing language with the use of* **Declare.**

Variable names cannot include %,$ or # as in other BASIC implementations. You **cannot** use these characters as part of variable names. These characters are used as operators (see Operators section below).

A variable does not have to have been specified prior to the assignment. But if you use this format a = a+4 then the variable must be previously specified because otherwise the interpreter will not know what the original value was and will give an error.

If the resulting expression is a string/integer/float the variable will be created and assigned that value and type. If the variable already exists but is of a different type and/or value it will be erased and assigned the new type and value. *However also see* **Declare** *that prevents this.*

The Array must have been created using Dim or Data. The element specification has to be legal for the array dimension specified in Dim. The array element is treated as if it is a variable name and the above information regarding variables is applicable.

•The line break operator

RobotBASIC is a line-oriented language. This means that assignment, command as well as flow control statements have to occur on lines by their own. Also a statement must keep going on the same line no matter how long the statement may be.

However, the \ operator allows you to modify these to restrictions. Think of \ as acting as a line break substitute in certain cases and as a line break canceller in other places.

•As a line break substitute

In this case the \ character allows you to put multiple statements on the same line and thus will act as if it were a line break. For example you normally have to do this

```
x = 30+a
b = 5
d = x+b
```

But with using the \ operator you can do the following: (notice how the \ character acts as if it is a line break)

```
x = 30+a \ b = 5 \ d = x+b
```

This is a useful *space saving* and also can help put *logically related* actions on the same line as a grouping.

•As a line Continuation operator

In this case the \ character allows you to break up a lengthy line into two or more lines so as to keep the code from going too far to the right and thus forcing scrolling off the screen. So normally instead of saying:

```
circlewh Centroids[i,0]-5,Centroids[i,1]-5,120,120,black,black
//draw triangular centroid of each face
```

You can now do this:

```
circlewh Centroids[i,0]-5,Centroids[i,1]-5,\
    10,10,black,black  //draw triangular centroid of each face
```

There are conditions for where you can use the \ character to break a line of code:
   1- It *must be* the absolute last thing on the line followed *immediately* with line feed (i.e. cr/lf i.e. Enter).
      So you cannot do

```
      circlewh Centroids[i,0]-5,Centroids[i,1]-5,\    //this is
```

```
                     illegal
                              120,120,black,black
```

2- You cannot break up _PRIMITIVES_. Primitives are numbers, variable names, command names, function names and strings, So you cannot break a line of code in the middle of a variable name or a numeric value or a string (i.e. between the "").

So you cannot do

```
circlewh Centroids[i,0]-5,Centr\
         oids[i,1]-5,120,120,black,black //this is illegal in middle of a variable/array
name
circlewh Centroids[i,0]-5,Centroids[i,1]-5,1\
         20,10,black,black              //this is illegal in the middle of a number
circlewh Centroids[i,0]-5,Centroids[i,\
         1]-5,10,10,black,black //this is allowed but not advisable due to readability
print "this is a lengthy string primitive that cannot \
         be broken up over multiple lines" //this is illegal in the middle of a string
print "this is a lengthy string primitive that cannot"+\
         "be broken up over multiple lines" //this is one you can do it legally
print 456+sin(cos(tan(sqrt(p\
         i()))))  //this is illegal in the middle of a function name
pri\
   nt 456+sin(cos(tan(sqrt(pi())))) //this is illegal in the middle of a command name
print 4;\
      5;\
      sin(\
      pi()\
      )                //perfectly legal....but WHY would you do that???
```

3- You cannot break the line after an inline comment operator (// or ')

So you cannot do

```
circlewh Centroids[i,0]-5,Centroids[i,1]-
5,120,120,black,black //this is \

illegal
```

•Command Statements

RobotBASIC has an extensive set of commands that achieve a variety of tasks like drawing lines on the screen, accepting input from the user, printing results on the screen and so on. These commands are the heart of RobotBASIC and are what makes the language achieve most of its actions.

Some commands have parameters and some do not. Some commands require a specific number of parameters and some have optional parameters. Parameters are how values are passed to the command and results obtained from it. A comma must separate all parameters. Commands look like this:

CommandName _parmater1, parameter2..._

If the parameter is a value to be _passed_ to the command then it must be an **Expression** that results in the value (see Expressions section below). Some parameters may have to be numeric (**float or integer)** and some may have to be **strings**. In either case the Expression must result in the appropriate value.

If the parameter is a value to be *obtained* from the command, then that parameter must be a simple **variable** (see Variables section below). The command will use the values (expressions) passed to it, perform its action and then assign values to the variables passed to it (when appropriate).

Some commands act on an entire array; in that case the parameter must be an array name (see Arrays section below for details on **arrays).** For a list of commands and a description of their action see the various sections below.

New in version 4.1.0 and above:

Some commands have optional parameters which you do not have to specify. In previous versions, if you wished to specify an optional parameter that comes after preceding optional parameters you had to specify values for all these preceding parameters. However, now you can skip these preceding parameters and use a space (or many or none) without specifying any value at all and just go on to the next parameter (you still need the commas though). For example in the command Circle the last two parameters are optional. Say you want to specify the second parameter and accept the default value for the first one. You would say:

```
Circle 10,10,100,100, ,red    //notice the missing parameter in all four
lines
Circle 10,10,100,100,,red      //you can use one space or none
Circle 10,10,100,100,   ,red  //or many
Circle 10, ,100,100,    ,red  //This line will cause an error since the
second
                              //parameter is required but it is not
specified
```

Commands *__are not__* case sensitive, so Print and print are the same. Here are some examples of commands in action:

```
rLocate 100,100,90 //initializes the robot and puts it
                   //at location 100,100 with heading 90
rForward 20 //make the robot go forward 20 pixels
rTurn 40   //make the robot turn 40°
```

•Labels

A Label is a marker to mark a certain location in the program. This marker is given a name and can be used within certain statements to refer to that location in the program. You can see how this is done in the Flow Control Statements section.

A label can be in a line by itself, or can be in line with another statement, but must be first in the line. A label must end with the character **:** and must start with a letter but after the first letter any combination of numbers and letters can be used (read below for other label styles).

Labels **_are_** case sensitive, so `Label1:` and `label1:` are not the same. Here are some examples of the use of labels:

```
ProgramStart:  //this is a label on its own
 Input "Enter a number ",n
 Print "You have entered ",n
 If n < 5 then goto ProgramStart //goes to the position
                                  //marked by the label
                                  //if input is less than 5
 If n > 30 then goto Pos1 //so does this one if the
                           //input is greater than 30
 K = n*2
 Print K
End                              // stops the program here
Pos1: Print "Too high a number" // this shows a label in
                                 // line with another statement
```

There are three styles for labels:

•Alpha-Numerical Style 1

This is the clearest style of all the other styles and is the easiest to pick out while scanning the source code of a program. In this style of labels you must begin the label with a letter followed by any combination of digits and letters and finally ended with the **:** character. You must end this label style with the **:** character and commence with a letter. Example:

```
//this is a label on its own
Label_1:
          print 20
//a label in line with another statement
Label_23: print 40
        goto Label_1
//when you refer to the label do not use the :
```

Note

- When referencing a label in a statement like **Gosub** or **Goto** do not include the **:** character. The **:** is put as part of the label only at the label position to define the label and is not be used in statements referring to the label.
- Labels **_are_** case sensitive. So Loop:, loop:, and _LOOp:_ are all different.
- Labels can be up to 255 characters long, so **do use** meaningful names for Subroutines and looping labels.

•Alpha-Numerical Style 2

This style is similar to programming languages other than BASIC and is supported by RobotBASIC for people who like this style. A label of this style must begin with the character **:**

followed by any combination of digits and letters. For example:

```
//this is a label on its own
:Label_1
        print 20
//a label in line with another statement
:2_Label  print 40
//when you refer to the label do not use the :
        goto Label_1
```

•Numerical Style

This style supports the standard BASIC line numbers and is not a recommended style. You can use any combination of digits that are the first thing in a line or the only thing in the line. A variation to this style is supported where after the first digit you can use a combination of letters and digits, but you must start the label with a number. For example:

```
//10 is the numerical label in line with another statement
10    print 4
20    print 9
//4A2C is the other style inline with another statement
4A2C print 100
//200XYZ1 is the other style in a line on its own
200XYZ1
    print "Hi there"
//30 is the numerical label in a line on its own
30
goto 10
```

•Expressions

An expression is a formula that manipulates numbers, strings or other expressions and returns a result. You can use numbers, strings, variables, constants and/or functions in an expression (See below for details on each of these elements). An expression results in any of the three basic elements of RobotBASIC, an **integer number,** a **floating-point number** or a **string** (see below for details).

In many statements, parameters are needed for the statement to function. Anywhere a parameter is needed an Expression can be used that would result in the correct type required by the statement.

Operators are used in an expression to manipulate the sub-parts of an expression. These operators are parenthesis, comparison operators, math operators, logical operators and bitwise operators (see below for details).

There are many functions in RobotBASIC that accept parameters and return a value. These functions can be used within expressions, are themselves expressions and are given expressions as parameters (see below for details).

Expressions can contain previously assigned variables and/or array elements. If an array element is specified then it must have been assigned and be within the range of the array's dimensional constraints as specified in Dim. Expressions can also contain functions (see Functions section below). Expressions also can contain Bitwise, Logical, Comparison and Math operators (see Operators section below)

```
print sin(4+5/3.0)*(3|4)+ ((a>b)&(c<5))
n = "this{"+b+"} = "+c
```

Note: If all the numbers involved in an expression are integers the result will be an integer. If any of the numbers is a float then the result will be float. For example `B =` `sin(pi(2*Theta^2))/(3+4*Acceleration)` results in a float even though all the numbers are integer since **sin()** returns a float.

•Numbers

Numbers are used in all computer programs. There will hardly ever be a program that does not use numbers. In RobotBASIC there are four types of numbers:

•Integer Numbers (whole numbers)

The range for Integer numbers is from -2,147,483,648 to +2,147,483,647
For Example:
```
Age = 46    //assigns the variable Age the
            //integer value 46
```

•Hexadecimal Integer Numbers (whole numbers)

The range for Hexadecimal Integer numbers is from 0x00 to 0xFFFFFFFF
For Example:
```
n = 0xAF    //assigns the variable n the integer value 175
print n         //prints 175
print Hex(n) //prints AF
print ToNumber("0x"+Hex(0xAF)) //prints 175
print 0xFFFFFFFF //prints -1
print Hex(-1)     //prints FFFFFFFF
```

Note: Hexadecimal numbers are stored internally as integers. If you specify a hexadecimal number larger than 0xFFFFFFFF you will get 0.

Note: 2's compliment applies to the Hexadecimal numbers. If the MSBit is set then the number will be a negative number.

•Binary Integer Numbers (whole numbers)

The range for Binary Integer numbers is from 0%00 to 0%1111111..... up to 32 bits

For Example:
```
n =  0%100010    //assigns the variable n the integer value 34
print n          //prints 34
print Bin(n)     //prints 100010
print ToNumber("0%"+Bin(0%100010)) //prints 34
```

Note: Binary numbers are stored internally as integers. If you specify a binary number larger than 32 bits you will get 0.

Note: 2's compliment applies to the Hexadecimal numbers. If the MSBit is set then the number will be a negative number.

Note: The % sign is also the Percent operator. If it is preceded immediately by only one digit which is a zero and followed immediately by a 0 or 1 it will be considered as the binary number indicator, otherwise it will be considered as the Percent operator. *If you want to use the Percent operator and are not sure then just add spaces between the numbers and the operator.*
```
print 0 % 1  //prints 0   (i.e. 0 percent of 1)
print 0%1    //prints 1   (i.e. binary number with
only LSBit set)
print 10%11  //prints 1.1 (i.e. 10 percent of 11)
print 0%11   //prints 3   (i.e. binary number 11 =
3)
print 1%11   //prints 0.11(i.e. 1 percent of 11))
```

•**Floating Point Numbers** (numbers with decimal fractions)
The range for Floating Point Numbers is from +/-2.23 10^{-308} to +/-1.79 10^{308}
You can use the letter **e** or **E** with a + or - to indicate powers of 10 as shown in the example below.
For Example:
```
//assigns the variable Distance the floating
// point value 5.78
Distance = 5.78
C = 3.1e+8     //speed of light is 3.1 * 100000000
M = 0.1E-6     //  M = 1/10000000
```

RobotBASIC has many functions and commands that require and/or return numbers. There are functions to convert numbers and manipulate them. *When an Integer number is required, if you pass a float instead, the system will truncate the number into an integer by removing the decimal fractional. If float is too large to be converted into an integer (see Integer limits above) an error will be issued.*

When RobotBASIC evaluates mathematical operations with a mixture of floats and integers the result will be a float. However, if all the numbers involved in an expression are integers

then the result will be an integer. This is especially important when performing division.
For example:

```
A = 5 \ B = 6 \ C = 4.2
Print A/B       //prints 0
Print C/B       //prints 0.7
Print 1.0*A/B   //prints 0.83333
```

•Strings

Strings are text and must be enclosed within quotes. In many programs strings are required to communicate with the user. Any time you need to give results to the user in a friendly fashion, or prompt the user regarding what to do next or how to use your program, strings will be required.

For Example :

```
Print "Hello World" // Hello world is a string
```

RobotBASIC has many functions and commands that require and/or return strings. There are functions to convert strings and manipulate them. Strings can be as long as required, there is no limitation on the string size.

You define a string within your program by using the quote **"** character. A string is surrounded by a pair of quote characters. If you need to use the quote character within the string as part of the string you must make it a double **""**.

For Example:

```
Print "Hello ""World""" // will print Hello "World"
```

You can add two strings

```
temp = "test" + "ing"    //temp will be "testing"
```

You can add a string and a variable that is string

```
temp = "test"
print "I'm "+temp+"ing"       //will print I'm testing
```

You can add a string and a number as long as the string resulting expression comes before the number. The number will be converted to a string. Use **ToString()** to do the same regardless of order.

```
a = 12.3 \ b = "Result = " \ c = b+a
print "The "+c     //prints The Result = 12.3
print "The ",b,a   //prints The Result = 12.3
print "The ",b+a   //prints The Result = 12.3
print "The ",b+ToString(a) //prints The Result = 12.3
print a+b          //Gives An Error
```

You can compare two strings for equality. But be careful about > and < since capital and lower case letters will affect the result. You can also use the $ operator

```
if  "tin"  $ "testing" then print "yes"   //prints yes
//ExprS1 $ ExprS2 will test to see if ExprS1
//occurs within ExprS2
```

You can use InString() to do a similar action
```
if InString("Testing","tin") > 0 then print "yes"
//will print yes
```

•Simple Variables

A Variable is a named storage area to keep numbers or strings. Variable names must start with a letter but then any combination of letters and numbers can be used. Variable names *__are__* case sensitive, so *Distance* and *distance* are different.

The length of a variable name can be up to 255 characters, so you can use names like *DistanceToBeacon_1*. It is important to use meaningful names in your programs because this makes your programs easier to follow and understand.

A variable can be used anywhere a number or string is used. As long as the variable has been assigned a value before using it, it can substitute for its value. A Variable is assigned a value in an Assignment Statement (see above) or by passing it as a parameter to a command that will assign it a value.

Unlike standard BASIC or most programming languages, variables in RobotBASIC do not have to be predefined as being of a specific type. Any variable can be of any value type (Float, Integer or String). Additionally you can reassign a value of a different type to a variable that already holds a certain type. If a variable exists when it is being assigned a value, it does not matter what the old value is and of what type it is, the new value will replace the old one. If the original value is an integer and the new value is a string the variable type will be changed to a string, and vice versa. The same is true for floats and integers and floats and strings.

In certain operations RobotBASIC will convert between variable types as necessary if it can. For example if you add an integer to a string the integer will be converted to its string representation and concatenated to the string. If the operation cannot be performed the system will issue an error.

Note: See Declare to see how to convert RB to perform strict typing of variables

The name of a variable cannot contain any operators such as %,$ or # . You **cannot** use these characters as part of variable names. These characters are used as operators (see Operators section below). You can use the underscore character '_'.

For Example:

```
Message="Hello World" //assigns a variable a value
Today=Date(1) //assigns a variable the value of a function
Print Message // will print Hello World
Print "Today is ",Today //will print Today is 2007/03/01
rLocate 400,500
rGps X_Pos,Y_Pos  //will assign X_Pos the robot's x
                  //position and Y_Pos the y position
Distance=PolarR(X_Pos,Y_Pos) //calculates using a
                             //function using variables
Message = 8+4  //change Message to a number
```

- Variables are case sensitive. So *Theta* and *theTa* and *theta* are all different. This can cause logical errors if you miss-type the names. Take care.
- Variable names can be up to 255 characters long so **_do use_** meaningful names to avoid variable clashes. For example for a counter in a subroutine called Delay use *Del_1, Del_2* etc.
- **_Do Not Use_** variables with the same name as Commands/Functions/Constants or Labels **_An error will occur if you do_**.
- All variables **_are_** global **_(except ones created within Call/Sub subroutines)_**. This means that once a variable has been defined and assigned a value it is accessible from any statement in the program from that **_time_** onwards **_(except within Call/Sub subroutines)_**. So if you use a counter inside a subroutine in a For/Next statement like *For I= 1 to 6* and I is being used in a counter in the calling section, unpredictable logical errors may occur. **_So be careful in variable naming assignments and especially within GoSub subroutines. You may want to use Call/Sub subroutines to take advantage of Local Scoped variables._**

Global and Local Scoping:
Once a program starts, any variables created during the progress of the program are **_Global_** variables that can be accessed anywhere in the program. However there is an exception to this rule. In RB there are two ways you can create a Subroutine (see later).

One way uses a Label to mark a section of code and uses the statement GoSub to branch to that section and returns once a Return is encountered. These are called Gosub subroutines. Variables created within this type of subroutine are still considered to be global variables and are available in other parts of the program after the return from the subroutine, also variables created elsewhere are available within the GoSub subroutine and can be changed within the subroutine and the change will be in effect outside the subroutine.

The other method for creating subroutines is with the use of the Sub statement and to call the subroutine using the Call() statement. These are called Call/Sub subroutines. Within the body of this type of subroutine variables have **_Local scoping_**. These subroutines act as if they were an independent program and any variables created during the progress of the subroutine will not be available outside the subroutine (i.e. after the Return). Also the subroutine will not be able to access any Global variables (there is an exception see the details in the Call/Sub definition in the Flow Control Statements section). This can be very helpful in avoiding

31

unintentionally affecting variables and having to come up with variable names that are different from variables elsewhere. There are many benefits to Local Scoping.

•<u>Arrays</u>

An array is a collection of variables all given one name. Each variable is an element in the array. Each element in the array is referenced by its position in the array. Array names *<u>are</u>* case sensitive, so *Dist[ ]* and *dist[ ]* are different.

Each element in an array can be of any data type (Float, Integer or String). Additionally you can reassign a value of a different type to an element that already holds a certain type. If an element has previously been assigned and it is being reassigned, it does not matter what the current value is and of what type it is, the new value will replace the old one. If the original value is an integer and the new value is a string the element type will be changed to a string, and vice versa. The same is true for floats and integers and floats and strings.

Remember the elements of the array do not have to be all of the same type. Each element can be of any type. Also, all the simple variable naming restrictions mentioned above apply to naming arrays.

Think of an array of mailboxes. They are collectively called MailBoxes. To access the 3rd one from the left on the 2nd row we would say MailBoxes[1,2]. The reason we have 1,2 not 2,3 is because we start counting at 0 (not 1) so the first is 0, second 1 and so on.

RobotBASIC allows you to have arrays of any dimension with as many elements in each dimension as you want. The dimension of the array is the number of indexes it has. For example Array_1[5,7,8] is a three dimensional array while Array_2[4,6,7,8] is four-dimensional. The dimensional constraints of an array are the extent of each dimension. For example Array_3[5,7] is a 2 dimensional array with constraints of 5 rows and 7 elements in each row (or 7 columns). **Remember that even though we have 5 rows the 5th row is row number 4 since the 1st row is row number zero.**

Once an array is defined each element in the array can be used as if it were a simple variable. Anywhere a simple variable can be used an array element can be used. And just like a simple variable the array element needs to be assigned a value before it is used.

Note: In Commands that require a variable to be passed, so as to be assigned a value, you cannot substitute an array element, you must use a simple variable. The simple variable can be later stored in the array element if needed.

Note: RobotBASIC has a powerful array structure seldom found in other languages. In addition to a versatile **Data** command, you can have almost limitless (only limit is memory) dimensional arrays and limitless elements in each dimension. You can manipulate and do operations on arrays that include inversion, multiplication and more. There is also a set of statistical operations like variance, regression and more.

Note: Arrays are ***Global scoped*** and are accessible within Call/Sub subroutines and any changes made to an array within the body of a Call/Sub subroutine will continue to be in effect after the routine returns.

Some commands and functions in RobotBASIC act on the entire array at once. These commands require the array name as a parameter. An array is created by using Dim or Data. Here are some examples of array manipulation:

```
Dim Array1[3,4]
Array1[1,1] = "testing"
Array1[0,0] = 9
Array1[0,1] = 8.4
Print Array1[1,1];Array1[0,0]
Array1[2,2] = Array1[0,0]+Array[0,1]*4
```

•Functions

Functions are expressions that use expressions as a parameter and return a number or string. A function can be used anywhere a number or string resulting expression can be used. The form of a function is as follows:

FunctionName(*parameter,parameter,...*)

The parameters are expressions and can also be other functions, since a function is an expression. If the function does not take parameters then you only have the parenthesis and nothing in between them, for example rFeel().

RobotBASIC has many functions that return strings or numbers and accept strings or numbers as parameters. There are functions to get the sine of an angle, to convert a string to uppercase, to convert a float to an integer, to convert a number to a string and many more. Some functions operate on an entire array. In those functions you pass the array name as a parameter to the function.

For Example:

```
Print sin(40*pi(1)/180)
B = ToUpper("test") + Spaces(30)
A = Left(B,20)+ "__"
If !(rFeel() & 2) then rTurn 3
```

NEW in version 4.1.0 and above:

In versions of RobotBASIC before 4.1.0 you could not place a function call as a statement in a

line on its own. That is you could not do:
```
Sin(30)
```

which is of no use anyway since most of the time you need the value returned from the function and thus you have to do:
```
x = Sin(30)
```

However, with version 4.1.0 and above you can place a function call on a line as a statement. This is useful when you are not interested in the value returned by the function and rather the action of the function is what is important. In this case you can use the function as if it were a subroutine and ignore the return value. For example MsgBox() displays a dialog box with text in it. It will also return a value to indicate what button the user pushed to exit the dialog box. However, you may not require this information and you just want to use the function to display information to the user and you are not interested in which button the user pushed to exit. In this situation you would do:
```
data a;"This is line one", "This is line two","etc."
MsgBox(a,"Information box")
//notice how the function is on a line by itself just
//like a statement and there is no need to assign its
//return result to a variable since you do not need it
```

whereas in versions prior to 4.1.0 you would have HAD to do:
```
data a;"This is line one", "This is line two","etc."
x = MsgBox(a,"Information box")
//notice how you HAD to assign the function
//to a scratch variable even though you did
//not actually need the return result
```

There are MANY functions in RobotBASIC that do actions while the function is doing its work and in many situations you are more interested in its actions rather than its return results. Of course you may also need the return results in other situations to verify that it actually worked or as such. Examples of functions whose return value may not often be needed are FileClose(), TCPC_Connect(), TCPC_Close(), DirCreate(), re_Setup() and many more.

•Operators

Expressions are formulas that manipulate expressions. Expressions are manipulated using operators. **Some operators have precedence over other operators**. For example multiplication has precedence over addition. So 4+5*3 result in 19 not 27. That is because the numbers 5 and 3 are multiplied first then the 4 is added. If you want to do the addition first you must write (4+5)*3 which will result in 27. There are six types of operators **(listed in order of precedence)**:

•Parenthesis ( )

Any expression surrounded by parenthesis will be evaluated before it is passed on for further evaluation outside the parenthesis. Thus Parenthesis are used to override any **operator precedence rules** (see above). You can think of any combination of expressions within the parenthesis as an expression in itself just as if it were a single number or string in itself.

Use parenthesis around operations when you are not sure how they would evaluate due to operator precedence, or to make the intent of the formula more clear, or to override the operator precedence.

Examples:
```
Print 3*4+5    //prints 17
Print 3*(4+5) //prints 27
print 3#2*4    //prints 4
print 3#(2*4) //prints 3
```

•Math Operators (Listed in order of precedence)

Unary Negate -

Put in front of a numeric expression makes the result a negative if it is positive and positive if it is negative. For example:
```
a = 5
print -a  //print -5
print  -(a-7)  //prints 2
```

Raise to the power ^ (exponentiation)

Raises an expression to the power of another (the exponent)
Example:
```
Print 4^2+1        //prints 17
Print 4^(2+1)      //prints 64
Print (3+1)^(2+1) //prints 64
Print 4^-2.0       //prints 0.0625
Print 4^-2         //prints 0
Print 4.0^-2       //prints 0.0625
```

Divide / Multiply * Percentage % Modulus

/ divides a number expression by another.
* multiplies a number expression by another.
% the percentage of a number expression
# the integer remainder of dividing an integer number expression by another

In all the above operations, if either expression is not a number an error will occur. All these operators have the same precedence and will be evaluated from left to right if they are in sequence.

Note: **When you divide two integers you will get the result of an integer division not a floating point division so 2/3 is 0 not 0.6666. If you want to make sure the result is a floating point make sure that at least one of the expressions is a floating-point result, so you can do 2.0/3 to get 0.666**

Note: *The Percent operator (%) is an exception to the rule of all Integer operands giving an integer result. The result of a percent operation is always a float regardless of what combination of integer and float operands are used.*

Note: *The Modulus is an integer operation only. If any of the operands is a float it will be truncated to an integer.*

Examples:
```
Print 5/6          //prints 0
Print 4/3          //prints 1
Print 4.0/3        //prints 1.333333
Print 4*3          //prints 12
Print 40%3         //prints 1.2
Print 5* 8 # 5     //prints 0
Print 5* (8 # 5)   //prints 15
Print 8.3 # 5.3    //prints 3
Print "ttt"/3      //ERROR
```

Add +   Subtract -

+ adds an expression to another. If the two expressions are numbers then addition will occur. If the two expressions are strings then concatenation will take place. If the first expression is a string and the second is a number then the second expression will be transformed into a string and concatenated to the first expression. If the first expression is a number and the second is a string an error will occur.

- subtracts a number expression from another. If either operand is not a number an error will occur

Both operators have equal precedence and will be evaluated from left to right if they are in sequence.

Examples:
```
Print "Test"+"ing"     //print Testing
Print "Test"+5         //prints Test5
Print 5+"test"         //ERROR
Print 7+5              //prints 12
Print 7-5              //prints 2
Print "Test" - ""ing"  //ERROR
```

36

•Comparison (Relational) Operators

Comparison operators compare an expression to another and return the value 0 if the result is false and 1 if the result is true. For example 5 > 4 results in 1 (true) but 5 > 10 results in 0 (false).

The result of this type of operation is usually used in Flow Control Statements to determine whether to take action or not. But the result of a comparison operation can be used anywhere an expression can be used, just as if it were a number, which it is (the number 0 or 1).

Comparison operators have the same precedence as each other and will be evaluated from left to right. But it is very confusing if you combine comparison operators in an expression. If you do need to do so use Logical operators (see below) for better clarity and use parenthesis to clarify the meaning. Many operators have multiple formats that perform the same operation. This is so that you can use any style you might be familiar with from other programming languages.

All operators will operate on string or number expressions but both expressions must be the same. Except, for the $ operator where expressions can only be strings.

Note: *If you compare two string expressions beware of lower and upper case letters. Letters are compared in order of their ASCII codes. Upper case letters have less value than lower case letters. Comparing strings with other than the $ operator may give unexpected results depending on the length of strings and letters in the strings. For example "Test" is not equal to "test" but is less than it.*

In the following list True = 1 and False = 0.

$	To see if the left string expression is contained within the right string expression. Both expressions have to be strings or an error will result. e.g. "st" $ "testing" returns true.
>	To see if the left expression is Greater Than the right expression. e.g. 5 > 4 returns true.
<	To see if the left expression is Less Than the right expression. e.g. 4 < 3 returns false.
= or ==	To see if the left expression Equals the right expression. e.g. 4 = 7 returns false.
>= or =>	To see if the left expression is Greater Than Or Equal to the right one. e.g. 5 >= 7 returns false.
<= or =<	To see if the left expression is Less Than Or Equal to the right one. e.g. 5 <= 7 returns true.
< > or > < or !=	To see if the left expression is Not Equal to the right one. e.g. 5 != 4 returns true.

•<u>Logical Operators</u>

Logical operators are usually used to combine results from comparison operators. A Logical Operator will consider the expressions it operates upon as False if the expression results in a zero, or True if the expression results in other than zero (negative or positive). So you can do logical operations on any numerical resulting expressions. If any of the expressions results in a string an error occurs.

All logical operators have equal precedence and will be evaluated from left to right if they occur in sequence. *Use parenthesis* if you are not sure how the combination will perform.

There are two formats for each operator. This is so that you can use the style you are familiar with. The letter formats *<u>are not</u>* case sensitive. So AND, and, AnD are the same.

Logical AND
And   &&

    e.g. (5 > 4) and (4 < 3)   results in false
    e.g. (5 > 4) && (4 < 3)   results in false
    e.g. (5 > 4) and (4 >= 3) results in true
    e.g. (5 > 4) && (4 >= 3) results in true

Logical OR
Or ||

    e.g. (5 < 4) or (4 < 3) results in false
    e.g. (5 < 4) || (4 < 3)   results in false
    e.g. (5 > 4) or (4 < 3) results in true
    e.g. (5 > 4) || (4 < 3)   results in true

Logical XOR
XOR   @@

    e.g. (5 < 4) xor (4 < 3)   results in false
    e.g. (5 < 4) @@ (4 < 3)   results in false
    e.g. (5 > 4) xor (4 < 3)   results in true
    e.g. (5 > 4) @@ (4 < 3)   results in true

Logical NOT
Not   !

    e.g. !(5 < 4)   results in true
    e.g. not(5 < 4)   results in true
    e.g. !(5 > 4)   results in false
    e.g. not(5 > 4)   results in false

Here is a table of how the various operators will do the logic:

Operator	Left Expression	Right Expression	Result
And	0	0	0
	0	1	0
	1	0	0
	1	1	1
Or	0	0	0
	0	1	1
	1	0	1
	1	1	1
Xor	0	0	0
	0	1	1
	1	0	1
	1	1	0
Not		0	1
		1	0

•Bitwise Operators

Bitwise operations only work with numeric resulting expressions. If either the right or left expression results in a string an error will be issued. Bitwise operations will do the equivalent logical operation on each bit of the numbers that result from the expressions. So for example if we do *9* bAnd *4* then since 9 is 01001 and 4 is 00100 then the result will be 00000 which is zero. If we do *9* bOr *4* the result will be 01101 which is 13. Just remember that bAnd, for instance is an And but performed on a bit-by-bit basis.

All the bitwise operators have the same precedence and are evaluated from left to right if they are in sequence. There are two formats for each operator. This is so that you can use the format you are familiar with. The letter formats **_are not_** case sensitive so *bAnd*, band, *BAND* are the same.

Bit-wise AND
    bAnd   &
      7 & 2   equals 2
      7 bAnd 2   equals 2

Bit-wise OR
bOr |
  6 | 1   equals 7
  6 bOr 1   equals 7

Bit-wise XOR
bXOR   @
  6   @   2   equals 4
  6 bXor 2   equals 4

Bit-wise NOT
bNot   ~
  ~ 1   equals -2
  bNot 1 equals -2
  ~ 0   equals -1
  bNot 0 equals -1
  ~ 5   equals -6
  ~ (-6)   equals 5

Shift Right
bShiftR   >>
  514 >> 1   equals 257
  514 bShiftR 1 equals 257

Shift Left
bShiftL   <<
  5 << 4   equals 80
  5 bShiftL 4   equals 80

Rotate Right
bRotR
  514 bRotR 1   equals 1

> **Note:** Operates only on a byte. If the number is greater than 255 the lowest byte alone is used and all other bytes are zeroed.

Rotate Left
bRotL
  5 bRotL 4   equals 80
> **Note:** Operates only on a byte. If the number is greater than 255 the lowest byte alone is used and all other bytes are zeroed.

•<u>Assignment Operators</u>

These are *shortcut* assignment operators. For example instead of saying **Var = Var+1** you can say **Var++**. Statements involving Assignment Operators are just like an assignment statement and have to be in a line by themselves. All of the operators work on a simple variable or an array element just like a normal assignment statement. These are mathematical operators will perform just like their long version. That is if both the variable and expression hold an integer then the resulting operations is an integer one and the new value assigned to the variable will be an integer. However, if either is a float then the value assigned to the variable will be a float regardless of the original type of the variable.

<u>Note:</u> The operators use a double symbol, but the two symbols have to <u>**always**</u> be together and not separated by any spaces. However, the operator can be separated from its operands. So you can say Var   ++ but not Var +   +.

Increment ++

This is equivalent to Var = Var+1 or VarA[...] = VarA[...]+1. The variable (or array element) has to exist and has to hold a numeric value. See examples below.

Decrement --

This is equivalent to Var = Var-1 or VarA[...] = VarA[...]-1. The variable (or array element) has to exist and has to hold a numeric value. See examples below.

AddAssign +=

This is equivalent to Var = Var+Expr or VarA[...] = VarA[...]+Expr. The variable (or array element) has to exist and has to hold a value. If the variable holds a string value then the expression can be a numeric or string result. However, if the variable holds a numeric value then the expression has to result in a numeric value. See examples below.

SubtractAssign -=

This is equivalent to Var = Var-NExpr or VarA[...] = VarA[...]-NExpr. The variable (or array element) has to exist and has to hold a numeric value. See examples below.

MultiplyAssign *=

This is equivalent to Var = Var*NExpr or VarA[...] =

41

VarA[...]*NExpr. The variable (or array element) has to exist and has to hold a numeric value. See examples below.

DivideAssign /=

This is equivalent to Var = Var/NExpr or VarA[...] = VarA[...]/NExpr. The variable (or array element) has to exist and has to hold a numeric value. See examples below.

Examples:
```
data a;10,20.3,8   \ s = "test" \  I = 6   \  F = 3.4
I++  \  F-- \   a[0]  += I  \ a[1]  /= I  \ s+=F \ a[2]*= 3
print I;F;a[0];a[1];s;a[2]
//7    2.4   17   2.9    test2.4    24   .. notice the result test2.4
a[0] /= 6  \ I /= 4.
print a[0]    //prints 2   since both are integers the result is an
integer
print I       //prints 1.75 since one was a float the result is a
float
F   ++        // notice operator is separated from the operand
print F       //prints 3.4
s++           //causes an error
s -= 4        //causes an error
I += "ggg"    //causes an error
F +  +        //causes an error   since the ++ is separated
F+  = 10      //causes an error   since the += is separated
J = F++/4     //causes an error. You cannot use the
increment/decrement
              // operator in an expression
```

42

Flow Control Statements

Flow control statements allow RobotBASIC to:
- Take actions depending on certain condition.
- Repeat actions a number of times.
- Repeat actions until a certain condition is fulfilled.
- Repeat actions while a certain condition is fulfilled.
- Go to a sub-part of the program and return from there and continue execution from where the program branched off.

Flow control statements ***are not*** case sensitive, so While and while are the same. Here is a simple program that shows three different flow control structures:

```
rLocate 100,100
for I = 1 to 5  //forward the robot 5 pixels
    rForward 1
next
Input "Enter a number",N
if N < 5 then print "too small"
if N > 30 then print "too large"
while N > 0 // make the robot turn N times
    rTurn 1
    N = N-1
wend
End
```

Subroutines in RobotBASIC are created by surrounding a group of statements with a Label and the **Return** statement like this *(these are called GoSub subroutines)*:

```
SomeRoutineName:
    Statement
    Statement
       . . .
    Return
```

You can then, anywhere in you program, branch off to the subroutine. The subroutine's statements will be executed and when **Return** is executed the program flow will go back to the line right after the line that called the subroutine. Here is an example:

```
Statement
Statement
   . . .
gosub SomeRoutineName
Statement
Statement
End
```

43

```
SomeRoutineName:
     Statmenet
     Statement
        . . .
  Return
```
Note: The statement **End** in the above code is needed to stop the program from flowing into the area where the subroutine is. Without the **End** statement the program will execute the subroutine as if it were part of the program.

Note: There is another method for creating a more advanced type of subroutine called Call/Sub subroutine. See below.

IF *ExprN* THEN *statement*

The **in-line-if style**. If *ExprN* results in a number not equal to zero (*true*), then the statement after the THEN will be executed. Otherwise (*false*) the program flow will go to the next line ignoring the statement after the THEN. *ExprN* can be any expression that results in a number. If the result is Zero then the condition is redeemed to be *False*. If the result is other than Zero (positive or negative) then the condition will be redeemed to be *True*. See Operators section in the Overview Of The Language section for comparison and logical operators. You can have multiple statements on the same line using the \ operator. These multiple statements will only be executed if the condition is true because when the statement is false the program flow will skip to the next line and therefore misses any statements on the same line separated with the \ operator. For a better method of controlling conditional multiple statements execution see the **structured-if** flow control below.

```
a = 3 \ b = 4 \ c = 5 \ d = 1 \ e = 0
if a then print "true"   // prints true
if d then print "true"   // prints true
if e then print "true"   //will not print
if a > b then print "true"      // will not print
if !(a > b) then print "true"   // prints true
if  !(a > b) && (c < 9) then print "true" //prints true
if "es" $ "test" then print "true"   // prints true
if InString("test","es") then print "true"  // prints true
if a < b then print a \ n=b+c \ print n //prints 3 then 9 on the next
line
if a > b then print a \ n=b+c \ print n //does nothing
```

If *ExprN1*
statement
statement

...

{ElseIf *ExprNn*}
statement
statement

...
.
.
.

{Else}
   statement
   statement
...
EndIf

This is the **Structured-If** style. Notice that there is no **Then** after the IF. This is how it should be. The interpreter will distinguish between the above and this style by this one difference. The conditions are evaluated as above.

This **Structured-If** style is made up of blocks of lines. There is the If-block, the ElseIf-block and the Else-block. You can have multiple ElseIf-blocks or none. You can have only one Else-block or none and it has to be the last block.

If *ExprN1* evaluates to true then the If-block lines will be executed. All the other blocks will be ignored.

If *ExprN1* evaluates to false then the interpreter will evaluate the ElseIf conditions (*ExprNn*) in sequence until the first one that evaluates to true. If none evaluate to true then the Else-block lines will be executed (if used).

The lines of the first ElseIf-block to evaluate to true (if *ExprN1* is false) will be executed and all other blocks (including the Else-block) will be ignored.

This If-style can be nested in any combination. **In-Line-IF** does not count as a nested one. You can nest other IF/.../ENDIF structures within any block of the structure.

For *Var = ExprN1 To ExprN2 {Step ExprN3}*
   statement
   statement
...
Next

The interpreter will repeat the statements between the FOR/NEXT a number of times equaling Abs*(ExprN2-ExprN1)/ExprN3+1*. The interpreter will put *ExprN1* result into Var. The statements between the For/Next structure will be executed. The interpreter will then increment *Var* by *ExprN3* if given or 1 if not. The interpreter will then check if the result is greater than *ExprN2*. If it is, the program flow will continue with the statement after the Next (i.e. Exit the For/Next loop). If not, the flow will go back to the statement right after the FOR and repeat the whole process.

You can optionally give a Step size. *Var* must be a variable but it does not need to have been previously defined. **EprN1, 2 and 3 must result in Integer numbers. ExprN3 must be greater than 0. If it is 0 then it will be made 1. If it is less than 0 then it will be made positive.**

If *ExprN1* is greater than *ExprN2* the interpreter will decrement *ExprN1* until it is less than *ExprN2*. You can nest For loops. An error will be issued if you try to nest too deep.

<u>**Note:**</u> *Normally RB is a free typing language and the variable used for the counter does not have to exist and if it does it will be converted to an integer. However, if RB has been made to become a strict typing system (see Declare) then the counter variable has to have been declared as an Integer variable*.

<u>**Note:**</u> You can modify the *Var* counter within a For/Next loop, just as if it were any other variable. But *beware* of your logic. Use Break/Continue along with If/Else/ Endif or IF/Then to force an early abort or re-loop of the loop (i.e. before reaching the end-count).

ExprN1/2/3 are only evaluated upon entering the loop. They are not revaluated again during the execution of the loop. If for instance ExprN2 is the variable A and you vary the value of A in the body of the loop, there will be no effect. The limit of the loop will be whatever the value of A was upon entering the loop regardless of what its value becomes later. However the value of Var (the counter) will always be reevaluated so if you change it in the body of the loop you may affect the number of times the loop is executed.

Example:
```
For I = 0 to 10 step 2
    Print I
Next //will print 0 2 4 6 8 10
For I=10 to 0 step 2   //even though you said 2, I will be decremented
by 2 not incremented
    Print I
Next //will print 10 8 6 4 2 0
A = 5
For I=A/2 to A+7 step -3    //even though you said -3, I be will
incremented not decremented
   print I
   A = 90   //changing the value of A will not affect the looping count
Next   //will print 2 5 8 11
For I=0 to 10^2
   print I
   if I > 3 then I = 100  //changing the value of the counter will
affect the loop count
next //will print 0 1 2 3 4
```

Repeat
Statement
Statement
...
Until *ExprN*

Will execute the statements between the Repeat-Until as long as *ExprN* evaluates to zero (*false*). The lines within the loop will be executed at least one time, since *ExprN* will not be evaluated until the loop has been executed the first time.

You can use Break within the loop, which will force the loop to terminate immediately ignoring any lines after the Break. You can use Continue within the loop, which will force the loop to re-loop immediately ignoring any lines after the Continue.
Example:
```
I = 0
repeat
  Print I
  I = I+1
  If I # 2 <> 0
     I = I+1
     If I > 10 then break
     continue
  Endif
until I > 20   //will print 0 2 4 6 8 10
```

While *ExprN*
Statement
Statement
...
Wend

Will execute the statements between the While-Wend as long as *ExprN* evaluates to other than zero (*true*). The lines within the loop may never execute if *ExprN* evaluates to zero (*false*) on entry into the loop.

You can use Break within the loop, which will force the loop to terminate immediately ignoring any lines after the Break. You can use Continue within the loop, which will force the loop to re-loop immediately ignoring any lines after the Continue.
Example:
```
I = 0
while I < 20
   Print I
   I = I+1
   If I # 2 <> 0
      I = I+1
```

47

```
      If I > 10 then break
      continue
   Endif
wend  //will print 0 2 4 6 8 10
```

Break

Used inside a FOR/NEXT,REPEAT/UNTIL,WHILE/WEND loops to break the loop immediately. The lines beyond the **Break** statement will not execute and the current level of the FOR/REPEAT/WHILE loop will be abandoned to the line following NEXT/UNTIL/WEND line associated with the current level. This is useful if a loop needs to be abandoned before reaching the end of the loop.

Continue

Use inside a FOR/NEXT,REPEAT/UNTIL,WHILE/WEND loop to re-loop the loop immediately. The lines beyond the **Continue** statement will not execute. The program flow will go to the end of the loop (NEXT/UNTIL/WEND). Execution will continue on that statement. The loop will be executed as per normal. This is useful if a loop needs to be repeated before reaching the end of the loop.

Case Construct

The Case Construct is not implemented in the language. However, you can **emulate** a Case Construct using the Structured-If.

```
If ExprN1 //Case_1 condition here
   //Do stuff
   .
   .
   .
ElseIf ExprN2 //Case_2 condition here
   //Do stuff
   .
   .
   .
ElseIf ExprN3 //Case_3 condition here
   //Do stuff
   .
   .
   .
Else
   //Do Stuff that will be done if no case is true
   .
   .
   .
Endif
```

Gosub *Label*
Gosub *Expr*

Return

Flow will go to the statement directly following the *Label* and will continue until a RETURN statement is encountered after which the flow will go back to the line following the line that called the subroutine. A subroutine is marked by a *label* and the Return statement as the last line. You can use other **returns** within the logic of the subroutine, but always have the last line of the subroutine as a Return, just in case your logic gets there. If you do not do so any program lines following the subroutine would be executed as part of the subroutine.

You can call a subroutine from within another subroutine. An error will be issued if you try to nest too deep. Be careful when you do this that you do not inadvertently create a circular endless loop. Recursion can also cause trouble if you do not have the correct windup conditions.

If you use the format Gosub Expr, then Expr must result in a number or string that is a name of a valid label. If Expr results in a number then it will be converted to a string. So saying Gosub 1000, Gosub 100*10 or Gosub "1000" are all equivalent and would cause the program flow to branch to the label 1000.

The second format is useful if you want to branch to a subroutine name that will be calculated depending on some logic. For example you may have an array of labels and you want the program flow to go to one of the labels depending on some number that is used to index into the array. Example:

```
Data Labels; "L1",100,"1000"
while true
  Input "Enter a number 0 to 2",I
  If !Within(I,0,2) then continue
  Gosub Labels[I]
wend
End
L1:
  print "I am In L1"
  Gosub Substring("I'm going to Test_Sub, Bye",14,8)  //notice this line
calculates the
Return                                          //subroutine name
using functions
100
   print "I am In 100"
   Gosub Labels[I]*10 //notice this line how it goes to a subroutine
name
Return                   //that is mathematically calculated
1000
   print "I am In 1000"
   a = "Test"+"_Sub"
   Gosub a    //notice this goes to a subroutine name defined by a
variable
Return
Test_Sub:
```

49

```
          print "I am in Test_Sub"
    Return
```

Note Returns within IF-Structures inside subroutines have to be carefully considered, be extra careful when using Returns out of subroutines within If-Structures. *Check your logic.*

Sub SubName({{&}var1{,{&}var2{,...}}})
Return {expr}
Call SubName({expr1{expr2{,...}}})

Sub/Return is used to delineate a Subroutine mechanism more advanced than the GoSub mechanism described above.

You define a subroutine using the Sub statement. **The word Sub is _not_ case sensitive however the subroutine name is case sensitive**. You must then have an opening Parenthesis and then you can have as many parameter variables as needed then a closing Parenthesis. You can have many parameters or none. If the subroutine does not need any parameters then use ( ). The parameter variables' naming follows the same rules as apply to naming simple variables (**parameter names are case sensitive**). Any of the parameters may be preceded with an **&**. This indicates that the parameter is by *reference* as opposed to by value. See later for details on this.

A very important aspect of Call/Sub subroutines is that they have *Local Scoped* variables. That means that the subroutine will be as if it were a brand new program with its own set of variables. It starts out with the variables in its parameter list set to the values specified in the Call to the subroutine. The subroutine may create other variables but they will not be visible to other routines outside the body of the subroutine. Only parameters with the & will be visible outside the subroutine by the caller area (see later). Also the subroutine *cannot* see variables previously created outside its scope. (except for Arrays which are Global).

To invoke a Call/Sub subroutine use the Call statement followed by the subroutine's name as defined in the Sub statement then a '(' and then as many expressions as are needed by the subroutine separated by commas then finally a closing ')'.

You cannot specify more expressions than the number of parameters as specified in the Sub statement but you can specify less. Also if you wish to skip a parameter then just do not specify an expression but you still need the comma to mark its place (see examples later). The expressions follow all the rules of Expressions as described above. Also if any of the parameters in the Sub's definition is by reference than the value passed in the Call statement in the position that corresponds to it *has to be* a variable (but also see later).

The Call statement will calculate all the provided expressions and will assign the corresponding variables as specified in the Sub statement the resulting value and then will jump to the body of the subroutine and begin executing. The subroutines will only see those variables that have been assigned. Any ones that have not been assigned will not exist as variables as far as the subroutine is concerned. Use vType() to determine if and which parameter variables have been assigned and to what type. Also you may assign any unassigned variables initial values as needed (see examples later). Other than these variables the subroutine will not be able to access any other variables that may have been assigned outside the body of the routine. Also any variables created or changed in the routine will not be reflected back to the outside (except for by reference parameters i.e. with &).

The subroutine's execution ends when a Return statement is issued. This return statement is similar to but different from the one used with the GoSub statement in that it can have an optional return expression. This expression again follows the normal expressions' rules. It will be calculated and assigned to a variable that will be sent back to the calling area and will become visible to the caller area. This variable will have a name made up of the name of the subroutine and then __ (i.e. two _) and then the word Result. So if the subroutine is called MyRoutine then the variable name would be **MyRoutine__Result** (case sensitive). If you do not specify a return value then MyRoutine__Result will be assigned an empty string (i.e. "").

So there are two methods that can be used to return values to the calling area. One is to use by reference parameters (using &) and the other is to use the xxxx__Result (xxxx is the routine's name) by returning a value. You may also explicitly assign xxxx__Result a value before returning with a Return without a parameter.

By Reference Parameters

Let's say that the Sub has been defined as follows ***Sub XXX(A,B,&C,X)*** then later you call the subroutine using ***Call XXX(10,30,LocalVar,X)***. Then upon entry into the subroutine C will hold the value of the variable *LocalVar*, but then upon return from the call the variable *LocalVar* will have whatever value the subroutine has assigned its variable C since C is a By Reference parameter (&). But X will not be changed even though it has the same name as the parameter in the Sub definition since it is not a By Reference parameter (no &).

The above is what is normal for most languages. However, RobotBASIC goes a little beyond that. RB allows you to say *Call XXX(10, , ,7)* and since there is no value being passed to put in B and C then both will not be defined (use vType() to ascertain if a parameter has been assigned a value and of what type). If you say *Call XXX(,30,55*2)* then in this case C will be assigned the value 110 while A and X will not be defined. Also since what was passed to the subroutine is a value rather than a variable name then no variable will be changed in the caller area when the subroutine changes C.

Access to Global variables

When the program first runs before any calls to subroutines are performed you can create variables and assign them values. These are called **Global Variables.** These variables are accessible to the whole program throughout (and in GoSub subroutines). However, since Call/Sub subroutines act as if they were stand alone programs they do not have ready access to Global variables nor do other parts of the program have access to the subroutine's variables. The proper way to pass values between the subroutine and the caller part of the program is to use the by value and by reference parameters.

However, it is desirable in certain situations to have access to some Global variables. RB allows you to do this but you have to **prefix** the global variable's name with an underscore character _. This will indicate to RB that the desired variable is not a local variable but rather a global variable. Within a Call/Sub subroutine you can therefore access global variables just like any local variable by using the global variable's name prefixed with the _ and you can use it normally in an assignment statement or in an expression. However, you cannot use a global variable:

As a counter for a For-Next loop	an error will be issued
As a variable in a Command that requires variables as parameters	"
In a Declare statement	"
As a variable for a by reference parameter in a Call statement	**no** error will be issued, but the variable's value will be used as if it were an expression.

Note: All arrays created outside or inside a subroutine will be visible inside and outside the subroutine. **Arrays are global. Scoping only applies to simple variables**. This can be useful in that you can use an array as a **shared memory** between different subroutines to exchange data other than using by reference parameters and the return value. Also see Access to Global Variables above.

Note: Ensure that the normal program flow will never run into a Sub statement since that will cause an error. Use an End statement.

Examples:
```
Main:
    V1 = 10 \ V2 = "Test" \ Temp = 0
    Call MySwap(V1,V2)
    Print V1;V2            //Test   10
    Call MySwap(20,V2)
    Print V1;V2            //Test   20
    Call MySwap(V1)
     Print V1;V2           //0      20
    Call MySwap( ,V2)
    Print V1;V2            //0      0
    Call MyTest(30,40,V1)
    Print V1;V2;MyTest__Result   //0    0    40   //notice the use of the
                                           // return result facility
    Print Temp            //prints 4   ...it has been incremented in every
                                //call to MySwap()
```

```
End   //this is important
Sub MySwap(&A,&B)
     if !vType(A) then A = 0
     if !vType(B) then B = 0
   Temp = A \ A = B \ B = Temp
   _Temp++                              //notice here we are using the Global Temp
                                              //not the local Temp
                                        //also see how it is affected in Main
   //GetColor pc,_Temp                  //causes an error Global not allowed as command variables
   //Swap _Temp,A                       //causes an error    "              in the Swap command
   //for _Temp = 0 to 5                 //causes an error    "              as For-loop counters
   //Next
Return
Sub MyTest(V1,A,B)
   V2 = 50 \ V1 = 60
Return A+B    //notice the return ability
//=========================second example============
n=8 \ call Fact(n) \ print factorial(n);Fact__Result
end  //this is important
sub Fact(i)   //recursively calculate the factorial
  if i= 1 then return i
  call Fact(i-1)    //recursion occurs here by the subroutine calling itself
return i*Fact__Result    //makes use of the return result
```

OnError *Label*
OnError *Expr*
OnError

If an error occurs during the run of a program the system will direct the flow to an error handler routine as defined by *Label* or the label resulting from *Expr* (see the description of the use of the *Expr* format in the GoSub statement above). No error message will be issued and the program be directed to the error handler routine that is specified by *Label* or the label that results from *Expr*. In the handler routine you can use GetError to find out the error number, message, line number, and character number. It is up to you to handle the error and how to redirect the program flow accordingly. If you issue a Return the program flow will go back to the line just after the line that caused the error.

Note: **When a jump occurs the OnError event is turned off. In the error handler you need to reissue an OnError statement again before you return out of the error handler subroutine if you wish to continue trapping errors after you return from it.**

Note: **When a jump occurs due to an OnError event, the OnTimer is also turned off. If you need to continue handling timer events you need to reissue OnTimer again <u>inside the error handler routine</u> before returning from it. See example below.**

You can issue this statement with different labels at different times to change the routine that will be used if an error occurs. You can also issue the statement without *Label* (or *Expr*) to turn off the feature and have the interpreter handle errors as normal.

53

Also see AllowEvents.

Example:
```
addtimer "t",250
ontimer tHandler \ onerror eHandler
i = 0 \errcnt = 0
while true
   if !(i#100) then n = n+1  //this causes an error every 100 count
   xystring 10,10, i \ i = i+1
wend
eHandler:
  errcnt = errcnt+1
  xystring 100,130,errcnt," Errors handled"
  onerror eHandler //--notice this line and the next. Comment
  ontimer tHandler //--either or both and see what happens
return
tHandler:
   xystring 100,100,"Timer = ",gettimerticks(lasttimer())
   ontimer tHandler
return
```

OnAbort *Label | SubName*
OnAbort *Expr*
OnAbort

If the user closes the Terminal Screen, using any of the Windows methods, during the run of a program the system will direct the flow to an abort handler routine as defined by *Label* or the label resulting from *Expr* (see the description of the use of the *Expr* format in the GoSub statement above). Also see the AbortFlag() and AbortMethod.

This statement will be as if you have issued an AbortMethod am_Flag statement. This statement will set no aborting allowed with flagging (read about it in the Controlling How Your Programs Terminate sub-section in the IDE section). Later when the user tries to abort the program, the event will be flagged and the program flow will go to the correct handler routine as defined by *Label* or *Expr*.

In the handling subroutine you can take actions to determine if the program should be terminated or not. To terminate issue an Exit or Terminate statement, otherwise, issue a Return statement to return to the original program execution.

You can issue this statement with different labels at different times to change the routine that will be used if an abort is attempted. You can also issue the statement without *Label* (or *Expr*) to turn off the feature.

<u>Note:</u> **If you use a Label or Expr then the Event handler will act as a normal Gosub subroutine and will have global scoping variables. If you instead use a Call/Sub subroutine then the jump will be as if a Call has been issued and the subroutine will have local scoping variables. However when you give the name of the Call/Sub**

subroutine do not specify any parameters nor the ( ). No parameters will be passed or returned from an event handler, it will act just like a normal subroutine but with the benefit of Local Scoping of variables.

Also see AllowEvents.

On[CONTROL] *Label | SubName*
On[CONTROL] *Expr*
On[CONTROL]

If a [control] is changed or clicked (depending on the control) (see later for list) during the run of a program the system will direct the flow to a handler routine as defined by *Label* or the label resulting from *Expr* (see the description of the use of the *Expr* format in the GoSub statement above). In the subroutine you must use Last[CONTROL]() to get the name of the control that caused the jump.

RobotBASIC will reset the ON[CONTROL] to being off once the jump is executed. You must reissue the ON[CONTROL] statement again within the handler routine before you RETURN from it if you wish for RB to continue to capture the ON[CONTROL] event.

You must also make a call to Last[CONTROL]() relating to the control. If you do not do this then the next time you issue the ON[CONTROL] there will be an immediate jump.

You can issue this statement with different labels at different times to change the handler routine that will be jumped to if the control event occurs. You can also issue the statement without *Label* (or *Expr*) to turn off the event handling.

On[CONTROL] can be one of 15 words:

OnKey	occurs when a keyboard key is pressed.
OnMouse	occurs when a mouse button is clicked.
OnSerial	occurs when there are bytes in the serial buffer.
OnTCPC	occurs when there are bytes in the TCP *client* buffer.
OnTCPS	occurs when there are bytes in the TCP *server* buffer.
OnUDP	occurs when there are bytes in *any* activated UDP socket buffer.
OnButton	occurs when a push button is clicked.
OnEdit	occurs when the text in the Edit box has changed.
OnListBox	occurs when an item in the list box is selected.
OnRBGroup	occurs when a radio button from the group is clicked.
OnCheckBox	occurs when the check box is checked.
OnSlider	occurs when the slider position is changed.
OnSpinner	occurs when the spinner is clicked.
OnMemo	occurs when the text in the Memo box is changed.

OnTimer   occurs every time the Timer clicks (every period).

Also see OnAbort statement above and AllowEvents.

Note: If you use a Label or Expr then the Event handler will act as a normal Gosub subroutine and will have global scoping variables. If you instead use a Call/Sub subroutine then the jump will be as if a Call has been issued and the subroutine will have local scoping variables. However when you give the name of the Call/Sub subroutine do not specify any parameters nor the ( ). No parameters will be passed or returned from an event handler, it will act just like a normal subroutine but with the benefit of Local Scoping of variables.

Note: If you have a timer that has a period of a few milliseconds it will trigger the handler quite frequently and it may not give time for other timers which have a bigger period to trigger the event handler. You may want to check *all* timers' status in a timer event handler if you have multiple timers.

Note: When a jump occurs due to an OnError event, the OnTimer is also turned off. If you need to continue handling timer events you need to reissue OnTimer again inside the error handler routine before returning from it. See the example under the OnError statement.

Note: You must read the buffer in the handler for an OnSerial, OnUDP, OnTCPS, OnTCPC which also clears it. If you do not then the moment the event handling is enabled again there will be a jump back to the handler and since the handler does not clear the buffer then you will end up doing nothing more than repeatedly executing the event handler for the event.

Note: For *ALL* the control event handlers you must make a call to Last[control]() so as to clear the flag that caused the event. If you do not, then the moment the event handling is enabled again there will be a jump back to the handler and since the handler does not clear the flag then you will end up doing nothing more than repeatedly executing the event handler for the event.

Warning!!! Exercise great care using Event driven programming. If there are errors in your program things may not be easy to debug using the Debug and Stepping methods since the program does not flow in a sequential manner. Also be very careful with VARIABLES, you must make sure that the variables in the event handler are not going to be changed while handling the event due to another event occurring. The best way to accomplish this is to use unique variable names in the handler routine. Also is you do need to change variables that are shared then maybe you need to implement a semaphore

mechanism. Furthermore, the use of AllowEvents Off to disable all even handling will help in _critical sections_ of code.

<u>Warning!!!</u> Event driven programming can cause perplexing results when there are errors. It may seem that errors are occurring in a different place than where they actually occur.

<u>Warning!!!</u> If you do not reactivate the event trapping of the event before you exit out of the handler, the event will not be activated again. This may cause a program behavior that looks like there is an error when in reality there are none.

Example: Also see the examples under AddSlider and AddMemo for an example of the usage of these flow control statements.

```
MainProgram:
   GoSub Initialization
   while true
       //do nothing just wait for events to be handled
   wend
end
Initialization:
   AddTimer "t1",30
   for i=0 to 2
       n = i+1
       addbutton "But"+n,10,10+30*i
       AddEdit "Edit"+n,60,10+30*i,80,0,," "
       addlistbox "List"+n,150,10+30*i,100,"test1"+n+crlf()+"test2"+n
       addrbGroup "Radio"+n,280,10+60*i,100,50,1,"test1"+n+crlf()+"test2"+n
       if i != 1 then addCheckBox "Check"+n,410,10+30*i
       if i == 1 then addCheckBox "Check"+n,410,10+30*i,"test"
       addSlider "Slider"+n,480,10+40*i,200
   next
   onbutton bHandler \  onedit eHandler \ onlistbox lHandler
   onrbgroup rHandler \ oncheckbox cHandler \ onslider sHandler
   onAbort aHandler \ OnTimer tHandler \
   OnKey kHandler    //you can either use a lable or a Subname this one uses a
subname.
   onMouse mHandler //this one also uses a subname
Return
Sub kHandler()    //this is a Sub subrotuine with local variable scoping
   n = LastKey()
   if n == kc_Esc then gosub aHandler
   OnKey kHandler
Return
Sub mHandler()
   n = LastMouse()
   if n == 2 then gosub aHandler
   OnMouse mHandler
Return
tHandler:    //this is a normal gosub subrotuine with global scoping
   n = LastTimer()
   xyText 10,110,gettimerticks(n),,25,fs_Bold
   ontimer tHandler
Return
```

```
bHandler:
    xystring 10,200,"Button:";lastbutton()
    onbutton bHandler
return
eHandler:
    n = lastedit()
    xystring 10,230,n,":",getedit(n),spaces(50)
    onedit eHandler
return
lHandler:
    n = lastlistbox()
    xystring 10,260,n,":",getlistbox(n),"=",getlistboxtext(n),spaces(50)
    onlistbox lHandler
return
rHandler:
    n = lastrbgroup()
    xystring 10,290,n,":",getrbgroup(n),"=",getrbgrouptext(n),spaces(50)
    onrbgroup rHandler
return
cHandler:
    n = lastcheckbox()
    xystring 10,320,n,"=",getcheckbox(n);getcheckboxcaption(n),spaces(50)
    oncheckbox cHandler
return
sHandler:
    n = lastslider()
    xystring 10,350,n,"=",getsliderpos(n),spaces(50)
    onslider sHandler
return
aHandler:
    an=ErrMsg("Do you want to abort?","Test",MB_YESNO|MB_QUESTION)
    if an==MB_YES then Exit
    onAbort aHandler
Return
```

End

Will cause the program flow to terminate and return to the editor. The Terminal Screen will remain on top but you can close it or use the button on the bottom right corner to switch to the editor window. Or use Windows methods to do so. You can review the terminal screen if you close it, by using *Ctrl+T* or the menu or speed button on the editor window. This option is useful for terminating the program but continue to view the program's last output Also see **Terminate** and **Exit**. This option is the preferred way while you are still editing your programs. Also see AbortMethod below. If you are running a binary file or from within the OS the termination behavior is different. See the IDE section for a table and more details on how this statement will respond in the various cases.

Note: Do ***not*** use End inside If/Else/ElseIf/Endif structures. You should use Terminate (preferably) or Exit.

Terminate

Will cause the program flow to terminate and return to the editor. The Terminal Screen will be closed. You can still view it by using *Ctrl+T* or the menu option or the Speed button on the buttons panel. This option can be useful for terminating programs and remove the Terminal screen where certain program logic requires you to return to the editor screen immediately. Also see **End** and **Exit**. Also see AbortMethod. If you are running a binary file or from within the OS the termination behavior is different. See the IDE section for a table and more details on how this statement will respond in the various cases.

Exit

Will cause the program flow to terminate and will exit RobotBASIC IDE if you are running from within the OS. If you are running from within the IDE the interpreter will close the Terminal screen and go back to within the Editor screen. This option is useful when you are distributing your programs to users who do not need to see the editor screen. It alleviates having to close the Terminal screen then the Editor screen to terminate a program. The non-programmer user can run your programs and press a menu option within the program to terminate the program but also exit the RobotBASIC IDE all in one go, as opposed to **End** or **Terminate**. Also see AbortMethod. See the IDE section for a table and more details on how this statement will respond in the various cases.

Goto *Label*

Program flow will branch to the statement directly following the *Label*. The label can be anywhere in the program.

Be very careful using this flow control. Most of the time you can avoid using GOTOs by using good structured programming logic techniques with the help of the structured flow control constructs detailed above.

The main use for GOTOs is to create loops, but it is more advisable to use REPEAT/ UNTIL,WHILE/WEND loops and FOR/NEXT loops along with Break, Continue and the appropriate If/Else/Endif combinations.

Certain precautions must be taken if you use *Goto* within If/Else/Endif, Repeat/Until, While/Wend or Subroutines.
- When a GOTO statement is executed, the interpreter will reset any IF nesting and any For/Next,REPEAT/UNTIL, WHILE/WEND nesting. It would be as if there are no pending If/ELSE/ENDIF anymore and likewise no more FOR/NEXT, REPEAT/ UNTIL, WHILE/WEND loops. So if you use a GOTO within an IF to go beyond the entire nested IF structure you would be OK, but if you GOTO within the next IF/ELSE or ELSE/ENDIF etc. you will get an error. Likewise if you are within a *FOR/NEXT*, REPEAT/UNTIL, WHILE/WEND use a goto to go out of the entire nested structure, otherwise you will get an unbalanced NEXT/ WEND/UNTIL error.
- It is not a good idea to use Goto within *looping-structures*. If you need to do so, make sure your program logic accounts for it.

- In a Subroutine, try to use goto to branch within the Subroutine. Make sure that somewhere within the subroutine a Return is eventually issued. Using GOTO to get entirely out of the subroutine is legal, but beware of the logic of your program.
- You can use Goto to go beyond an END statement but check your logic.

Try to avoid using Goto. Use of Goto makes the program flow hard to understand, hard to follow, hard to debug and can cause logical and semantic errors that are hard to locate. However, Goto can be useful in handling errors to redirect the program flow to one place in the code to handle all errors. However, even then, it is advisable to use onError.

Flow Control Directives

Note: See the notes at the top of the Standard User Interfacing section.

•AllowEvents {on|off}

Will turn Event handling off if *off* is given or on if *on* is specified or not given. This can be useful for preventing other events from causing jumps when in certain ***critical sections*** of your program. ***Do not forget to turn it back on again when finished with the critical section or else no further event handling can occur.***

•AbortFlag()

In order to use this function you have to have issued the **AbortMethod am_Flag** statement within your program. The function returns true (1) if the user has tried to abort the program by closing the Terminal screen window using any of the methods provided or operating system methods such as pressing the X on the top right hand corner. Every time you use this function the flag will be reset to false. So if the user has not tried to abort since the last time you interrogated the flag a false (0) will be returned. If the user tries to terminate, the flag will be set to true and will remain set until you interrogate the flag status using this function. See AbortMethod, and also the IDE section for more details on aborting and termination behaviors as well as the OnAbort statement.

•AbortMethod {ne_AbortCode}

While a program is running the user can use the **Stop** button to abort the currently running program and return to the editor screen. The same action can be achieved by closing the Terminal screen window (using MS Windows methods). The standard response for doing this action is for the Terminal screen to close and the Editor screen becoming the active window. Within the editor the cursor position will be where it was when the program was run (unless you are running a binary file or from within the OS, see the IDE section for more details).

This command changes how the interpreter will respond to the user trying to terminate a program using the **Stop** button on the Terminal Screen or closing the Terminal screen (also see thestatements Terminate and Exit and AbortFlag() as well as OnAbort). If you do not use this command the standard behavior is as described above (close Terminal screen and return to Editor Screen where you were before the program was run, also see the IDE section for more details on this). But, there are situations were a different response may be required and this command allows you to select the response you desire from among five choices. ne_AbortCode defines the type of response and it should be one of the following: **am_Normal, am_Exit, am_Error, am_NoAbort,** and **am_Flag** (see RobotBASIC Constants section). If it is not given then **am_Normal** will be assumed.

am_Normal

Causes the interpreter to behave normally. The terminal screen will be closed and the Editor screen becomes the active window with the cursor position where it was before the program was run. Also see the Terminate flow control statement and the IDE section for more details on how running binary files or from within the OS will affect this.

am_Exit

Causes the interpreter to close the Terminal Screen and go back to the Editor screen. However in the case of running from within the OS the interpreter will terminate the RobotBASIC system and go back to the OS. This option is useful when you are distributing your programs and do not want a user of your program to have to close the Terminal screen then the Editor screen. The user closes the Terminal screen and the entire system is closed in one action. Also see the Exit flow control statement and the IDE section for more details.

am_Error

Causes the interpreter to close the Terminal screen, activate the Editor screen window and highlight the last line executed before the abort was executed. The highlighted line will be highlighted up to the point where the interpreter was just before aborting the execution. This is similar to a run time error but without the error message, since there was no real error. This option is useful during program development where you may want to terminate a program at a certain point during the execution and see where in the code that action was taking place. This action takes place only if you are running a text file from within the IDE, otherwise the system will behave according to the table described in the IDE section.

am_NoAbort

Causes the interpreter to ignore any attempt by the user to close the Terminal screen or pressing the Stop button. This is useful when you are distributing your programs and do not want users to terminate the program just anywhere. You, of course, have to provide a method for the user to be able to Quit your program (maybe by pressing a button or key press, or mouse press...see AddButton, GetKey, ReadMouse etc.). **Use this option with great precaution**. A user will not be able to abort the program if you have not provided a method for doing so within your program. **Also if the user does try to abort the program a message dialog box will be revealed explaining the fact and directing the user to use the options you have provided within the program to be able to terminate the program.** Also see the option below and the OnAbort statement.

am_Flag

Causes the interpreter to trap any attempt by the user to close the Terminal screen or pressing the Stop button. This is useful when you are distributing your programs and do not want users to terminate the program just anywhere. If the user does try to abort, the interpreter will set a flag to true. This flag can be interrogated using AbortFlag(). If the function returns true then you know that the user has just tried to abort. You then can take any action you wish using the programming language. *No automatic message will occur as in the above option.* If you wish to give a message do so in your program. Also if you wish to abort use the termination statements (Terminate or Exit) as you desire. You, the programmer, have the control. **Use this option with great precaution**. A user will not be able to abort the program if you have not provided a method for doing so within your program. Also see the option above and the OnAbort statement.

•Stepping {On|Off}

From the moment this command is issued until you turn it off, RobotBASIC will execute the program one line at a time. Before each line to be executed the Debug Screen will be shown with a message showing what line is about to be executed.

If you issue the command with *On* or without a parameter, stepping will be turned on. To turn off stepping issue the command with *Off* as a parameter.

You can interact with this screen and use the *View Variables Table* and *Evaluate Now* to get information about the status of variables and array elements and even to do calculations involving these. You can also swap between the Debug Screen, Terminal Screen and Editor Screen. *In the Editor Screen you will notice that the line about to be executed is highlighted, however, the highlighting will only become visible if you bring the Editor Screen to the forefront*. Use the *Show Editor Screen* button to bring the Editor Screen to the forefront, also use the *Show Terminal Screen* button to bring up the Terminal Screen to view the result of the last line to be executed.

If you use the mouse to click on the Editor Screen window to bring it to the forefront then make sure you click on the border frame of the window or else the highlighting of the line about to be executed will be removed due to your clicking inside the Editor. *It is best to use the buttons on the Debug Screen to bring whichever screen you need to the forefront.*

If you press *Step* the current line will be executed and its effects will be shown on the Terminal Screen and then the Debug Screen will become active again showing what line is about to be executed next. The data displayed in the Debug Screen will be:

```
      About to execute (L,C):Code in the line that is about to
be executed
```

L is the line number where the command to be executed is within the program. C is the character number in the line where the command about to be executed starts. The text after the colon is the actual code that is about to be executed.

Stepping will ignore any empty lines in the program and also any comment lines. You can override either of these actions and have stepping not ignore them by un-checking the appropriate check box at the top left of the Debug Screen.

If you press ***Stepping Off*** the stepping mechanism will be turned off and program execution will resume as before until another Stepping On is encountered. Also stepping can be turned off programmatically using Stepping Off. You can also turn Stepping back on again from within the Terminal Screen by pressing the **SteppingOn** button (bottom right hand of the screen, see note below).

<u>Note:</u> Stepping can be turned on/off anywhere in the program. So if you place the Stepping On statement at a particular area of interest you can avoid having to step through the entire program before you get to the area of concern.

<u>Note:</u> Another way stepping can be turned on is through the **SteppingOn** button on the Terminal Screen (lower right). Pressing this button is as if you have issued a Stepping On programmatically, and stepping will remain on until either a Stepping Off statement is encountered or you turn off stepping using the ***Stepping Off*** button on the Debug Screen. The advantage of this method is that you can turn stepping on even though there are no program lines relating to stepping and also you can do it at a particular action situation so that you can start stepping only when you need it.

<u>Note:</u> You can use DebugOn and Stepping On simultaneously. When a Debug {} statement is executed the debug data will be displayed on the next line below the Stepping data. Also the ***Stepping Off*** button will become a ***DebugOff*** button so that you can turn off the debugging if desired. When you step you will be back to the stepping mode of the Debug Screen until the next Debug{} statement if you have not turned debugging off.

<u>Note:</u> See the Debug Screen section in the IDE section for explanations of the Expressions Evaluation feature and controls provided at the top of the Debug Screen.

<u>Note:</u> *This command is deactivated if you save your program as a binary file or if you compile it. No stepping will occur while running a compiled program or a binary program even if you leave the Stepping statements in the program.*

•DebugOn
•DebugOff
•Debug {Expr1,Expr2;Expr3...}
    Outputs the values of *expr....* to a debugging screen. This only takes place if DebugOn has been issued any prior time, or the **DebugOn** button has been pressed on the Terminal Screen. The DebugOff command will turn debugging off again. The debug screen will pause the program execution and display the result of *Expr...* and wait for you to press the ***Step*** button to execute the rest of the program.

If Debug{} is in a loop it will be executed every time the command line is encountered. To stop any further execution use the ***DebugOff*** button on the debug screen. This will be the same as issuing a DebugOff. Or you can close the Debug window using the window close icon on the top right-hand corner; this is the same as pressing the ***DebugOff*** button.

To remain in the debug mode just press the ***Step*** button. To eliminate any further program pausing and debugging press the ***DebugOff*** button or close the debug window, or issue a DebugOff within the program code. To turn on further debugging you must issue a DebugOn again within the program flow, or press the ***DebugOn*** button on the bottom right hand side of the Terminal Screen. This button allows you turn debugging on at any time during the program flow as if a DebugOn has been issued. Subsequently any Debug will be executed. This can be useful to turn the debugging on at a certain stage in the program rather than having to step through until you get to a point of interest.

If you keep the Debug{} lines in the program but do not wish them to be executed next time you run the program, make sure that DebugOff is issued before any Debug{} is issued or that any prior DebugOn are commented out.

{*Expr1,Expr2;Expr3...*} are printed as described in Print in the Standard User Interfacing section.

This combination of commands help in stepping the program and viewing variables while doing so. The ***Clear*** button is to clear any previous printed debug data, but also, every time you run the program from the start the debug screen will be cleared. You can swap windows back and forth between the editor/terminal/debug windows. Use the ***Show Terminal Screen*** and ***Show Editor Screen*** buttons to do so.

Note: Another way debugging can be turned on is through the **DebugOn** button on the Terminal Screen (lower right). Pressing this button is as if you have issued a DebugOn programmatically, and debugging will remain on until either a DebugOff statement is encountered or you turn off debugging using the ***DebugOff*** button on the Debug Screen.

Note: See Stepping above and the second note there regarding having Debugging and Stepping being activated simultaneously.

Note: See the Debug Screen section in the IDE section for explanations of the Expressions Evaluation feature and controls provided at the top of the Debug Screen.

Note: ***This command is deactivated if you save your program as a binary file or if you compile it. No stepping will occur while running a compiled program or a binary***

program even if you leave the Debug statements in the program.

•GetError vn_ErrNo{,vs_ErrMessage{,vn_LineNo{,vn_CharNo}}}

Will fill the variable vn_ErrNo with the last error number (-1 if no error), vs_ErrMessage will be filled with the description of the error (blank if no error), vn_LineNo will be assigned the line number where the error occurred (-1 if no error) and vn_CharNo will be assigned the character number in the line where the error occurred (-1 if no error). Issuing this command will retrieve the details of the **last** error to have occurred and then will clear the data. If an error occurs and you do not issue this command before another error occurs, issuing this command will get the details of the *last* error, the previous details will not be retrievable. If an error occurs and you have not issued an OnError *Label* (see Flow Control Statements section) statement then the error will halt the program and you won't be able to use this command.

•#Include "FileName.Ext"{,...}

This statement allows you to *incorporate* other RobotBASIC files within your file (with conditions). #Include statements are **Directives** to RB to fetch the files named and to **Append** them to the end of the **program being run**. *They are not executable statements*. RB will **pre-scan** the program for any #Include statements and will fetch the named files one by one. Each file may also have #Include statements too, so again these files will also be fetched and appended to the end of the program (and so forth recursively). Once all #Include statements in all files have been processed it will be as if you have merged all the named files together in one file. Then RB will execute the program as if it were one big program but with one difference. RB will insert an End statement right before each included file. This prevents your program's flow from running into the included programs prevent them too from running into each other.

Notice the # is part of the statement. It is **all one word** with # at the beginning. The word Include is not case sensitive just like all commands and statements. But you must have the # in front of it and **no spaces** are allowed.

1- The list of names of the files given in the statement have to be within Quotes ("") and separated by commas (,). You can use a simple expression to create the name...BUT no variables can be used since the #Include statements are processed by the preprocessor and variables are not available to that process.
2- The file names have to be specified with the extension even if it is a .Bas file. Also if the file is not in the same directory as the program being run then you have to give the full path name.
3- If the file cannot be found or cannot be read then an error will be issued. If the file is not a valid RB text or binary program you will get all sorts of problems. So do not include other than valid RB programs.
4- An RB program can have as many include statements as you wish and you can specify multiple files in the same statement.

5- All files will be appended one after the other to the end of the file that has the #Include statement (recursively).

6- Included files may themselves have included files. This however may cause a circular referencing in certain situations. RB will do its best to detect the fact and prevent it, nevertheless you should do your best to prevent it as well.

7- You may include RB Binary files just the same as normal RB files....but not compiled RB EXEs....only Binary RB files (ones saved with the menu option "*Save As Binary*").

8- Include files can be any RB programs. Nevertheless, you should in fact consider the Included files as libraries of either Label subroutines (i.e. to be called with a GoSub) or Sub subroutines (i.e. to be called with a Call).

9- You can have #Include statements anywhere in your program. However, the included files will not be included at the position where the include statements occurs. ALL include files will be *APPENDED* to the end of the file that has the include statement.

10- When you compile a program that has #Include statements, RB will create an EXE out of ALL the files *together* as if they were all merged into one program. Thus the EXE will not require any of the included files again.

11- If you create a Binary file from your program then it will still need to have the Include files. Binary programs will run as if they are text programs. Thus you will still need the included files to be available in the directory along with the main program (or the directory they should be in according to the path in the file name).

12- If an error is encountered within the code of an included file you will see an error statement (as normal) that will indicate the line number and the nature of the error. However, when the program halts the IDE will not highlight the offending line within the editor since it is not in the editor's text (it is an external file). Therefore you will get an extra error warning telling you of the fact and obviously **_no_** line will be highlighted in the editor as per normal. It is assumed that include files have been thoroughly debugged and tested before they are used as include files.

13- Make sure that **ALL** Labels and Call/Sub names are *unique* in the included files. If two Include files have the same Label or Call/Sub name an error will be issued. If you are designing a library of subroutines then ensure that you use a naming convention to minimize the possibility of other libraries or programs using your library having the same names (labels or Subs) as your routines. Also it is *strongly* advised that you use Call/Sub subroutines because they have local scoped variables as opposed to GoSub subroutines that will have global scoping variables.

14- If you are going to distribute your code as include libraries then please make sure that you thoroughly debug and test your code, especially if you distribute them as binaries (RB binaries not EXEs).

•Undeclare

This will cancel the effect of a Declare and will revert RB to be a free typing language. All variables previously created using Declare statements will *remain* and will continue to be of the same type and to hold the same value. However, they will become free again and they can be reassigned any value again.

•Declare v_Name {{=}e_InitialValue} {, ...}

RobotBASIC is by default a free typing system. That is variables do not have to be declared and typed before they can be used. Also if a variable already exist and is being assigned a value of a different type than its current value type then it will be converted to the new type and assigned the new value.

With this command you can force RB to become a strict variable typing system. From the first time a Declare statement is executed RB will become strict and will require that from that time onwards all variables must have either been previously created or that they must be declared using a Declare (see note later for an exception to this). Also from that time onwards variables will not change their type and you won't be able to assign a string to a numeric type or a numeric to a string (but a float can be assigned to an integer if it can be truncated and an integer to a float and RB will do the conversion automatically) and you won't be able to use any variable in an assignment statement or an Input or a For-Next statement unless you have already declared the variable as an appropriate type.

<u>Note:</u> **Variables given to commands (except for Input and also see VarSet) that require variables do not have to have been declared even when strict typing is in effect and if they have they *will* be retyped during the execution of the command to be of the type of the value the command will set them to.**

You can cancel strict typing by issuing an Undeclare.

You can declare as many variables as needed in the Declare statement and you can use as many Declares as you need. If you declare a variable in multiple statements then the last one will be the one that determines the type of the variable *(no error will be issued...this can be useful in changing a variable's type if you wish)*.

After the variable name you can optionally specify an equals sign (=) and an expression or just an expression by itself without the = (the = may be clearer for beginners even though it is more typing). The optional expression must result in a value that will determine the type of the variable and at the same time will set its initial value. Thus achieving the declaration of the variable to be of a certain type (the same type as the result of the expression) and also at the same time initializing the variable to a desired value (the result of the expression). **The expression assignment is optional and if not given then the variable will be assigned the same type and value as the variable *just before* it in the same Declare statement. If the first variable in the list of the same Declare statement is not assigned an expression value then it will be assumed to be of type *Integer* and it will be initialized to 0.**

To summarize:

1- You can have many Declare statements any where in a program.

2- The first statement to be encountered will make RB perform strict type checking and to require that all variables have to exist before they can be assigned values and have to be assigned an appropriate value for their type.

3- Variables that have been created while RB was in the free type mode (i.e. before the first Declare statement is executed) will remain available and to hold the value they do. However, they will become as if they have been declared as of the type.

4- In each Declare statement you can specify as many variables as you wish.

5- You can specify a variable in multiple Declare statements and that will change its type and value accordingly. That is, the last Declare will determine the type of a variable. This is useful if you wish to *explicitly* change the type of a variable from one section of the program to another.

3- Variables in the Declare statement must be separated by commas.

4- Any of the variables can be followed by either an = then an expression or just an expression without the equal separated from the name of the variable by a space.

5- This expression must result in a value of the same type as you wish to make the variable and the value of the expression will be assigned to the variable as an initial value.

6- If no expression is given then the type and value of the variable will be **the same as the one that preceded** it in the same list.

7- If the first variable in the list is not given an expression then it will be assumed to be an integer of value 0.

8- You can have different variables being of different types and of different initial values in the same Declare statement. Just remember that the **last type and value in the list will be applied to all the variables that follow that are not given an expression** until one is encountered with an expression after which the new type and value will become the new defaults. The list starts off with Integer 0 being the default until you change it.

9 - There are many commands in RB that use a variable as a parameter and will set the variable to a value. These commands (except Input and also see VarSet) will not respect the strict typing and will continue to behave as if no Declare statement has been issued.

The following examples illustrate these rules. Examples:

```
Declare i,j,k          //make RB strict typer and also declare i,j
                       //and k as integers initialized to 0
Declare x=0.,y .1,z,W  //declare x as a float with initial value 0.0
                       //then y as a float with initial value 0.1
                       //and z and w as floats with initial value 0.1 since they are
not given expressions
                       //and the last default is that given to y
                       //(i.e. 0.1)
Declare a "",b,c       //declare a,b,and c as strings and initial
                       //value of empty strings
Declare r,p 1.,q,s,t 5,xx,yy "test",zz  //declare r as integer
                //and 0 initial value.
                //p,q and s as floats with 1.0 as initial value,
                //t and xx as integers with initial value of 5 and
                //yy and zz as strings with "test" as initial value.
Declare f=0, g 1. , h="test", aa 9.3 //declare f as an integer with value
                            // 0, g as float with value 1.0
        //h as a string with value "test" and aa as a float with value 9.3
```

69

```
print i;j;k;x;y;z              //prints  0   0   0   0    0.1    0.1
print "-",a,"-";b,"-";c,"-"    //prints  --      -      -
print r;p;q;s;t;xx;yy;zz
        //print    0   1   1   1   5     5    test    test
i = 3.6            //is allowed but i will be 3 (i.e. truncation of 3.6)
print i            //prints 3
i = "test"         //causes an error since i is an integer it
                   //is not allowed to assign it a string
a = 5              //causes an error since a is a string and
                   //only strings can be assigned to it
x = 3              //x will be 3.0 since x is a float and even though 3 is
                   //an integer it will be converted to a float
for K = 0 to 10    //causes error since K is not declared
next
for x = 0 to 10    //causes and error since x is a float only integers
                   //are allowed as For-Loop counters
next
Undeclare          //turn strict typing off
for x=0 to 10      //no error since strict typing is now off and x will
                   //be changed to become an integer
next
Declare i "", j 3.4, k=0  //strict typing back on and i is now
                          //a string with initial value of ""
                          //and j is a float with initial value of
                          //3.4 and k an integer with value 0.
Input i,j,k  //you can enter anything for i, even numbers
             //since they will be converted
             //to strings. But only a numeric entry is allowed
             //for j and k. If you enter a string
             //an error will be issued. If you enter an integer
             //for j it will be made into a float.
             //if you enter a float for k the value will be
             //truncated before assigning it to k.
Print i;j;k
```

70

RobotBASIC Constants

Constants are numerical values defined within RobotBASIC, but instead of using the number you can use a name for the number. This is the same as using a simple variable. The names have been defined within RobotBASIC and you can either use the number if you can remember what it is or use the name anywhere the number is needed.

Constants can be used anywhere a numerical expression is required. Constant names **_are not_** case sensitive so **Red** and **red** are the same. There are constants that define 16 colors and constants to define things like true and false and so forth.

•Color Constants
•Black	= 0
•Blue	= 1
•Green	= 2
•Cyan	= 3
•Red	= 4
•Magenta	= 5
•Brown	= 6
•Gray	= 7
•Darkgray	= 8
•Lightblue	= 9
•Lightgreen	=10
•Lightcyan	=11
•Lightred	=12
•Lightmagenta	=13
•Yellow	=14
•White	=15

Note:
See the discussion about colors in the Screen & Bitmap Graphics section.

•Variable & Array Element Type Constants
•NoType	= 0
•Float	=102
•Integer	= 105
•String	= 115

•Serial Port Settings Constants
Parity:
•pNone	= 0

71

•pOdd	= 1
•pEven	= 2
•pMark	= 3
•pSpace	= 4

Stop Bits:

•sbOneAndHalf	= 0
•sbOne	= 1
•sbTwo	= 2

FlowControl:

•fcNone	= 0
•fcXonXoff	= 1
•fcHardware	= 2

BaudRate:

•br110	= 0
•br300	= 1
•br600	= 2
•br1200	= 3
•br2400	= 4
•br4800	= 5
•br9600	= 6
•br14400	= 7
•br19200	= 8
•br38400	= 9
•br56000	=10
•br57600	=11
•br115200	=12
•br128000	=13
•br256000	=14

•ErrMsg() Dialog Icon Codes And Return Values

Buttons Codes:

•MB_Ok	= 0
•MB_OkCancel	= 1
•MB_AbortRetryIgnore	= 2
•MB_YesNoCancel	= 3
•MB_YesNo	= 4
•MB_RetryCancel	= 5

Icon Codes:

- •MB_NoIcon   = 0 there will be no icon.
- •MB_Error   = 16 will cause a **Stop** icon.
- •MB_Warning   = 32 will cause a **!** icon.
- •MB_Question   = 48 will cause a **?** icon.
- •MB_Information   = 64 will cause an **i** icon.

Default Button Codes:

- •MB_Button1   = 0
- •MB_Button2   = 256
- •MB_Button3   = 512

Returned Value Codes:

- •MB_Ok   = 0
- •MB_Cancel   = 1
- •MB_Abort   = 2
- •MB_Retry   = 3
- •MB_Ignore   = 4
- •MB_Yes   = 5
- •MB_No   = 6

•Mouse Cursor Constants

- •cr_Default   = 0   this is the default system shape (usually a pointer the same as cr_Arrow)
- •cr_None   = -1   this will effectively remove the cursor. ***Beware of this format!***
- •cr_Arrow   = -2
- •cr_Cross   = -3
- •cr_IBeam   = -4   **Note**: -5 is not used and will be the same as -1 if you use it
- •cr_NESW   = -6
- •cr_NS   = -7
- •cr_NWSE   = -8
- •cr_WE   = -9
- •cr_UpArrow   = -10
- •cr_HourGlass   = -11
- •cr_DragPoint   = -12
- •cr_NoDrop   = -13
- •cr_HSplit   = -14
- •cr_VSplit   = -15

•cr_MultiDrag	= -16
•cr_WaitSQL	= -17
•cr_Stop	= -18
•cr_WaitPoint	= -19
•cr_HelpPoint	= -20
•cr_HandPoint	= -21

•Font Style Constants

•fs_Bold	= 1
•fs_Italic	= 2
•fs_Underlined	= 4

•AbortMethod Constants

•am_Normal	= 0
•am_Exit	= 1
•am_Error	= 2
•am_NoAbort	= 3
•am_Flag	= 4

•Some Key Code Constants

These codes should be used only with KeyDown() but they can be used with GetKeyE if the user does not press Shift, Ctrl, or Alt along with the key since GetKeyE will append 1000, 4000, or 2000 correspondingly to the actual code.

The codes for 0 *to* 9 are 48 *to* 57, the codes for A *to* Z are 65 *to* 90. There are no codes for lower case letters the same key is lower and upper. You can detect if shift is pressed also to distinguish (if you need to), however in GetKeyE the code returned will have 1000 added to the normal code if shift is pressed.

•kc_LMouseB	= 1
•kc_RMouseB	= 2
•kc_MMouseB	= 4
•kc_Esc	= 27
•kc_F1 *to* kc_F12	= 112 *to* 123
•kc_LArrow	= 37
•kc_UArrow	= 38
•kc_RArrow	= 39
•kc_DArrow	= 40
•kc_Shift	= 16
•kc_Ctrl	= 17
•kc_Alt	= 18
•kc_Ins	= 45

•kc_Del	= 46	
•kc_Home	= 36	
•kc_End	= 35	
•kc_PUp	= 33	
•kc_PDn	= 34	
•kc_Enter	= 13	
•kc_BkSpace	= 8	
•kc_Space	= 32	

•Spawn Modes

•P_WAIT	= 0
•P_NOWAIT	= 1

•File Low Level I/O Constants

•fo_BEGIN	= 0
•fo_CURRPOS	= 1
•fo_END	= 2
•fo_READ	= 0
•fo_WRITE	= 1
•fo_READWRITE	= 2
•fo_EXCLUSIVE	= 16
•fo_DENYWRITE	= 32
•fo_DENYREAD	= 48
•fo_DENYNONE	= 64

•Conversion Codes Constants

•cc_DCTODF	= 0	Celsius to Fahrenheit
•cc_DFTODC	= 1	Fahrenheit to Celsius
•cc_DTOR	= 2	Degrees to Radians
•cc_RTOD	= 3	
•cc_NMTOR	= 4	Nautical miles to Radians
•cc_RTONM	= 5	
•cc_MITONM	= 6	Miles to Nautical miles
•cc_NMTOMI	= 7	
•cc_KMTONM	= 8	Kilometers to Nautical miles
•cc_NMTOKM	= 9	
•cc_KMTOMI	= 10	Kilometers to Miles
•cc_MITOKM	= 11	
•cc_FTTOMI	= 12	Feet to Miles
•cc_MITOFT	= 13	
•cc_YRDTOMI	= 14	Yards to Miles

•cc_MITOYRD	= 15	
•cc_FTTOYRD	= 16	Feet to Yards
•cc_YRDTOFT	= 17	
•cc_INTOFT	= 18	Inches to Feet
•cc_FTTOIN	= 19	
•cc_YRDTOM	= 20	Yard to Miles
•cc_MTOYRD	= 21	
•cc_INTOM	= 22	Inches to Meters
•cc_MTOIN	= 23	
•cc_M2TOHCT	= 24	Meters^2 to Hectares
•cc_HCTTOM2	= 25	
•cc_M2TOACR	= 26	Meters^2 to Acres
•cc_ACRTOM2	= 27	
•cc_CM3TOCUP	= 28	Centimeters^3 to Cups
•cc_CUPTOCM3	= 29	
•cc_CM3TOGLN	= 30	Centimeters^3 to Gallons
•cc_GLNTOCM3	= 31	
•cc_CM3TOGLNUK	= 32	Centimeters^3 to Gallons UK
•cc_GLNUKTOCM3	= 33	
•cc_CM3TOLTR	= 34	Centimeters^3 to Liters
•cc_LTRTOCM3	= 35	
•cc_CM3TOONC	= 36	Centimeters^3 to Ounces
•cc_ONCTOCM3	= 37	
•cc_CM3TOONCUK	= 38	Centimeters^3 to Ounces UK
•cc_ONCUKTOCM3	= 39	
•cc_CM3TOPNT	= 40	Centimeters^3 to Pints
•cc_PNTTOCM3	= 41	
•cc_CM3TOQRT	= 42	Centimeters^3 to Quarts
•cc_QRTTOCM3	= 43	
•cc_CM3TOTBLSP	= 44	Centimeters^3 to Table Spoon
•cc_TBLSPTOCM3	= 45	
•cc_CM3TOTSP	= 46	Centimeters^3 to Teaspoon
•cc_TSPTOCM3	= 47	
•cc_GTOCART	= 48	Grams to Carrats
•cc_CARTTOG	= 49	
•cc_GTOONC	= 50	Grams to Ounces
•cc_ONCTOG	= 51	
•cc_GTOPND	= 52	Grams to Pounds
•cc_PNDTOG	= 53	
•cc_GTOSTN	= 54	Grams to Stones
•cc_STNTOG	= 55	
•cc_GTOTON	= 56	Grams to Tones

•cc_TONTOG	= 57	
•cc_GTOTONL	= 58	Grams to Long Tones
•cc_TONLTOG	= 59	
•cc_WATTTOHP	= 60	Watts to Horse Power
•cc_HPTOWATT	= 61	

•Regular Expression Mode Codes

•RE_DOTMATCHNEWLINE	=	1
•RE_MULTILINE	=	2
•RE_IGNORECASE	=	8
•RE_RIGHTTOLEFT		= 16
•RE_IGNOREWHITESPACE	= 32	

•Numeric Type Byte Count

•BytesCount_I	= 4
•BytesCount_F	= 8

•Media Player State Codes

•ms_NotReady	=	0
•ms_Stopped	=	1
•ms_Playing	=	2
•ms_Recording	=	3
•ms_Paused	=	5

•DFT/FFT Window Functions Codes

•sw_NoWindow	= 0
•sw_Hamming	= 1
•sw_VonHann	= 2
•sw_Blackman	= 3
•sw_BHarris	= 4
•sw_Bartlet	= 5

•Other Constants

•True	= 1
•False	= 0
•On	= 1
•Off	= 0
•Yes	= 1
•No	= 0

- •Down   = 1
- •Up   = 0

Standard User Interfacing

Note: See the Overview Of The Language section for a discussion on how commands and functions fit within the RobotBASIC language. The commands and functions are listed here in order of functionality. An alphabetical order can be found in another section. Commands and functions **_are not_** case sensitive. ClearScr, clearscr, and *clearSCR* are all the same command also sin(), SIN(), and sln() are all the same function.

Note: In many commands and functions there are **_optional parameters_**. If a parameter is not given RobotBASIC will assume a default value for it. If you need to specify a value for an optional parameter that comes after any preceding optional parameters, you have to put a space (or more or none) in place of any optional parameters that precede the one you wish to specify. For example:

```
//this is how the command to save the screen is specified
//SaveScrWH {ne_X1{,ne_Y1{,ne_Width{,ne_Height}}}}
circlewh 10,10,100,100,red,red
SaveScrWH ,,70    //in this line we have accepted the default
                  //values for the first 2 parameters then
specified
                  //a value for the 3rd and again accepted the
default
                  //value for the last parameter
//this is how the function to obtain a substring from a string
is given
//Substring(se_Text{,ne_StartChar{,ne_NumCharacters}})
s = Substring(ss)        //useless but allowed start from
beginning to the end
s = Substring(ss, ,5)    //get 5 characters from the beginning
s = Substring(ss,3)      //get all the rest of the string from
the 3rd character
s = Substring(ss,7,2)    //get 2 characters from the 7th
```

Note: The following prefixes are used to describe the type of the parameter to be given to a command or function:

ne_	= An expression resulting in a numeric (integer or float).
se_	= An expression resulting in a string.
e_	= An expression resulting in a numeric **or** string.
vs_	= A simple variable that will be set by the command to a string value.
vn_	= A simple variable that will be set by the command to a numeric value.
v_	= A simple variable that will be set by the command to a numeric or string.
a_	= An array variable that will be used by the command or function as a whole

array.

Expr   = An expression that **can** result in a numeric or string but no easy description can be given.

ExprN = An expression that **mus**t result in a numeric but no easy description can be given.

{Expr} implies that it is optional and {Expr...} means many can be optionally given. If a simple variable is expected in any of the commands, then if it exists it will be assigned the result otherwise it would be created and assigned the result.

If an array is expected then it must be a previously dimensioned array, but in some cases where the array is created by the command, it does not have to be previously dimensioned.

The character | means or. So if you see on | off, it means you can use either on, or off.

v_Name | a_Name[...] means you can specify a simple variable or an array element.

•<u>Standard Output</u>

•**Print {Expr,Expr;Expr...}{;|,}**
•**Write {Expr,Expr;Expr...}{;|,}**

Outputs the values of *expr....* to the screen. A **,** between the expressions makes them print with no space between them a **;** prints them with a tab space between them. If there are no expressions then a line feed is printed.

If the list of expression ends with a **,** or **;** there will be no line feed after printing. So the next print will start from where the current printed text ends on the screen. Using a comma as the last thing after the expressions will cause the next print statement to print immediately where the current printed text ends, while a semicolon will put a tab first. If there is no comma or semicolon then a line feed will be issued at the end of the printing. If the expressions result in text that is longer than would fit on one line then the text will wrap around to the next line (***not word wrap***).

Print and Write do the exact same thing. Both syntaxes provide compatibility with most systems and you can either in exactly the same manner.

If you want to issue a linefeed after a series of print statements that end with a semicolon or comma, then issue a Print/Write statement on its own (no parameters).

The first time Print is used the text will print at the top of the screen and then will print on subsequent lines until the screen is filled. When this happens the screen will be cleared and printing will start at the first line again. See the IDE section for more on this and a special feature for retrieving the text that scrolled off the screen. Also see TextBuffToCB, and SetTextBuff and GetTextBuff().

The color of the text is according to the current default colors. If you desire to use different colors then use SetColor and GetColor. Also see ErrMsg() and MsgBox().

Note: In RobotBASIC the ; creates a tab between the printed elements of the Print command while , is used as a no spaces separator. In other versions of BASIC it is the other way around. You can tell RobotBASIC to be like other BASICs using CommaTab (see below).

Note: If the resulting string to be printed contains within it the character 13 (CR) or the combination of characters 13 and 10 (CR/LF) the part of the string after the CR or CR/LF will be printed on a new line. This feature was not in versions earlier than V4.0.1. See HonorCRLF if you need to maintain compatibility with earlier versions.

•CommaTab {true|false}

In RobotBASIC the ; creates a tab between the printed elements of Print while , is used as a no spaces separator. In other versions of BASIC it is the other way around. You can tell RobotBASIC to behave like other BASICs using this command. If true is given or not given then RB will behave like other BASICs and will use , as a tab separator and ; as no spaces separator. If false is given then RB will behave normally and the ; will be the tab separator. Issue this command anytime (only once) before you use any Print statement and you can make RB behave as desired.

•HonorCrLf {true|false}

In RobotBASIC versions earlier than V4.0.1 Print did not effect a Line Feed if the string to be printed contained within it the CR/LF characters [char(13)+char(10)]. Version 4.0.1 onwards will cause a line feed if the string being printed contains either a CR (char(13)) alone or a CR/LF (char(13)+char(10)) combination. This will be done by default.

This command allows you to turn off this feature to maintain compatibility with earlier versions if you need it. If there is no parameter or the parameter is *true* then the feature is on. If the parameter is *false* then the feature is turned off. By default it is on if the command is never issued.

•SetPromptArea {se_Text}

Puts text in the Prompt area at the bottom of the Terminal Screen just above the input area. This can be useful for prompting the user or for displaying status without interfering with the display in the main Terminal Screen area. If se_Text is not given then it will be "", effectively clearing the prompt area.

•SetInputArea {se_Text}

Puts text in the Input area at the bottom of the Terminal Screen. This can be useful for prompting the user or for displaying status without interfering with the display in the main Terminal Screen area. Also it is a way to set default input as a response to an Input. If se_Text is not given then it will be "", effectively clearing the input area.

•xyString ne_X,ne_Y,Expr{;expr,expr;...}

Outputs the result of Expr... at ne_X,ne_Y position on screen. The **,** between expression makes them print with no spaces between them and **;** prints them with tab separation. The color of the text is according to the current default colors. If you desire to use different colors then use **SetColor**. Also see **GetColor** and **GetXY**. If either ne_X or ne_Y is -1 then the current corresponding X or Y screen position will be used. Also see ErrMsg(), TextBox and MsgBox(). Also see TextWidth() and TextHeight().

•xyText
{ne_X{,ne_Y{,e_Text{,se_FontName{,ne_FontSize{,ne_FontStyle{,ne_PenColor{,ne_Backgr oundColor}}}}}}}}

Outputs the result of Expr at ne_x,ne_Y position on screen. se_FontName specifies the font name of the font to be assigned to the printed text. ne_Size specifies a size and ne_FontStyle is a bitwise map of the style.

e_Text can be any valid expression that results in a number or string. If it is a number it will be converted to a string. If it is not given it will be "".

If either ne_X or ne_Y is -1 or is not given then the current corresponding X or Y screen position will be used. The font name size and style are optional. If the font name is not specified or is an empty string then the default font (Courier New) will be used. If the size is not specified or is less than 1 then the default size will be 11. If the style is not specified or is 0 then no style is applied. If ne_PenColor is not given or is less than 0 then the current default Pen Color will be used. If ne_Background color is not given or is less than 0 then the current background color will be used.

The size of the font can be any number and the system will apply the closest allowable size.

ne_FontStyle is a bitwise map of the desired styles to be applied. You can bit wise OR (bOr or |) the values given in the RobotBASIC Constants section to apply multiple styles. So for example if you want bold and italic use fs_Bold | fs_Italic.

Different machines may have different fonts and if the name you specify is invalid the system will apply a default (not necessarily Courier New). To find out what names are available on your machine use the *Fonts* menu option from within the *Help* menu on the Editor screen. This will bring up a dialog that shows all fonts available and what sizes are available for each. You can select a font and when you exit the dialog the font's name will be copied to the clipboard. You can then use *Ctlr+V* (paste) to insert the name into your program. Remember different machines may not have this font. So try to choose fonts that are universally available on most machines.

Many fonts have characters of varying widths. These fonts will not print within a consistent an overall width depending on the number of characters in the string, since different characters have different widths. The font "Courier New" has all characters of the same width. Text written with a font that does not have the same width characters will be hard to line up from line to line.

Also see **GetColor**, **GetXY**, TextWidth() and TextHeight().

•OverlayText
{ne_X{,ne_Y{,e_Text{,se_FontName{,ne_FontSize{,ne_FontStyle{,ne_PenColor}}}}}}

Performs the exact same action as xyText but the text will not have a background color. Both xyText and xyString draw the text over the screen with the default pen color and a rectangular area surrounding the letters with the background color. So when the text is drawn the area under the text will be overwritten. This command draws the text letters with the default pen color, but no background is drawn. So only the letter itself is drawn and any details under the rectangular area surrounding the letter will not be obliterated.

All the parameters are exactly the same as for xyText except that there is no background color since the text with this command will have a transparent background color. Also see TextWidth() and TextHeight().

Example:
```
//makes text look like it is shadowed
s = "Test Words" \ fnt = "Times New Roman"
xyText 65,110,s,fnt,90,fs_Bold,,red
OverlayText 60,100,s,fnt,90,fs_bold,blue
```

•<u>Standard Input</u>

•InlineInputMode {on|off}
By default InlineInputMode is set to off. This command allows you to set it on or off. If on is specified or no parameter is given then RobotBASIC will be put into Inline Input Mode On. If off is given then the mode will be set to off (which is default mode). This will affect how Input and WaitKey behave. See below

•Input {e_Prompt,} v_Name | a_Name[...] {,...}
Prints the text resulting from e_Prompt above the input box at the bottom of the Terminal Screen, then waits for input inside the input box which must be terminated with a RETURN.

The input will be assigned to the simple variable v_Name or to the array element a_Name[...]. The array element must be within the dimension of the previously dimensioned a_Name array. If e_Prompt results in a blank string or is not given then > is printed as a prompt. If it results in a numeric it will be made into a string.

You can have as many v_Name or a_Name[...] parameters separated with commas as needed. When the user inputs a value and presses RETURN it will be assigned to the next variable in the list. The program will keep prompting the user with the e_Prompt (but see below) for as many times as there are variables and will expect the user to enter values with a RETURN for as many times as there are variables in the list.

If e_Prompt is a string that contains the character | then string will be deemed to have separate sections and the first section will be used to prompt for the first variable in the list and the second section for the second variable and so forth. See examples below.

If the user just presses RETURN then the corresponding variable will be assigned a "".

Note: The above is true by default and if InlineInputMode off has been issued. If InlineInputMode on has been issued then instead of using the input box in the Control Panel at the bottom of the screen and prompting just above it, the program will print the prompt on the screen where the next Print statement would have printed and the input from the user is also printed just after that as the user inputs it. If the command expects multiple inputs then the next user input will be on the next line and will have the prompt > unless the original prompt has a corresponding section in the overall prompt (using the | character). The next Print statement will be on the next line after the inputted text.

Note: Normally RB is a free typing language. The variables in the list of variables of Input do not have to exist and if they do their type does not matter. If the value inputted by the user is an integer or a float it will be made into one and assigned to the corresponding variable and the variable will take on that type. If the value inputted cannot be converted to a numeric then it will be deemed to be a string and assigned to the variable and the variable will become a string. You can then use vType() to find out the type entered and use ToNumber(), ToStirng(), IsNumber(), IsString(), Round() etc. to manipulate the variables as needed.
However, if RB has been made to become a strict typing system (see Declare) then the variables in the list *have to have been previously declared* of a certain type. If a variable has not been declared then there will be an error. Also the input has to be appropriate for the type according to the rules:
  1- If the variable is a string then any input is allowed (numeric or string) and it will be assigned to the variable as a string. If it is a numeric then it will be converted to a string.

2- If the variable is an integer then only integer or float input is allowed. A float will be converted to an integer by truncating it if possible. If the float cannot be converted to an integer (i.e. too large) an error will be issued.

3- If the variable is a float then only integers and floats are allowed. If the input cannot be converted to a float then an error will be issued.

Also see ErrMsg(), MsgBox(), StrInput(),and xyInput.

Example:
```
//InlineInputMode on      //uncomment this line to see how the
program behaves
Input a
print "You entered   ",a
Input "Please enter a number",b
If IsNumber(b)
   Print b,"*",5,"=",b*5
else
   Print "You did not enter a number"
endif
Input "Enter three values a,b,c:",a,b,c
Print "You entered: ",a;b;c
Input "Enter your name|Your age|Are you male
(Y,N)?:",Name,Age,IsMale   //notice the | character
Print "Hi ",Name, " You were born in ",Year(Now()-
ToNumber(Age,0)*365),
Print " and you are a ",
if Upper(IsMale) == "Y"
    Print "Male"
else
   Print "Female"
endif
```

•xyInput v_Input{,ne_X{,ne_Y{,e_Title{,e_Default{,ne_BoxLength}}}}}

This will show an input box with a prompt message and will allow the user to enter data in the input box. The entered data is assigned to the variable v_Input. If the data is numeric then v_Input will be numeric, otherwise it will be string.

All the parameters are optional except v_Input. ne_X and ne_Y will default to the value -2. e_Title and e_Default will default to an empty string. ne_BoxLength will default to -1.

If ne_X or ne_Y is -2 then the input box will be centered (in that axis) on the screen. If they are -1 then the input box will be positioned at the current pen position (for that coordinate that is -1) within the terminal screen. Any other value will be used to position the input box within the terminal screen.

e_Title and e_Default can be numeric or string. e_Title is used for the prompting message above the input box. e_Default is used to initialize the input box. The user terminates the input using ENTER or ESC. If Enter is used the current value inside the box will be assigned to v_Input. If ESC is pressed the initial value will be assigned to v_Input regardless of what is inside the box currently. ne_BoxLength assigns a length to the box in pixels. If it is less than 50 then the greater of the length of the prompt or the initial input value or 50 will be used.

The box cannot be positioned outside the screen or be wider than the screen. It will be sized and positioned such that it will still be fully visible if the given parameters will cause it to be otherwise. The input data will scroll within the input box. Also see ErrMsg(), MsgBox() and StrInput().

•Keyboard Input

•WaitKey {e_Prompt,}vn_KeyCode
Prints the prompt above the input box at the bottom of the Terminal Screen then waits for a key to be pressed. When a key is pressed its ASCII code value is assigned to vn_KeyCode. If the prompt is not given or is an empty string ("") then a `Press Any Key` is printed as a prompt. If e_Prompt results in a numeric it will be made into a string. The code assigned to vn_KeyCode is the ASCII code of the key pressed so if you press 'a' then 97 will be assigned, while Shift-a (i.e. A) will give 65. Other key combinations like Ctrl-a or Alt-a will return non-ASCII codes if valid. Keys like up-arrow, home etc. do not return any values. For these keys see GetKeyE. Also see Ascii() and Char() which convert between the ASCII code and string characters.

Note: If InlineInputMode on has been issued then instead of using the Control Panel at the bottom of the screen the Prompt will be shown where the next Print would have printed. The next Print will then be on the next line.

•GetKey vn_KeyCode
Does **not** cause the program to pause and wait for a key, but if a key is pressed then its ASCII code value is assigned to vn_KeyCode, otherwise a 0 is stored. This is useful in loops that need to be exited if a key is pressed but without halting the loop until a key is pressed. The code assigned to vn_KeyCode is the ASCII code of the key pressed so if you press 'a' then 97 will be assigned, while Shift-a (i.e. A) will give 65. Other key combinations like Ctrl-a or Alt-a will return non-ASCII codes if valid. Keys like up-arrow, home etc. do no return any values. For these keys see GetKeyE, Ascii() and Char() which convert between the ASCII code and string characters. Also see KeyDown(). This function has the added power of allowing you to detect multiple keys pressed together.

If you use this command within a loop you may get too many repetitions of the key due to the speed of the system not giving the user time to release the key before it is read many times as being a new key press. This can be counteracted by using Delay to delay between successive reads of the key (150 to 200 milliseconds might be sufficient). Or you can use looping to wait until the key is released (*vn_KeyCode* will be zero) or you can use WaitNoKey. It depends on your application, but the third or second method should be preferable. Example:

```
rLocate 400,300
while true
    GetKey k
    if k== Ascii("w") then rForward 1
    if k== Ascii("a") then rTurn -1
    if k== Ascii("s") then rTurn 1
    if k== Ascii("z") then rForward -1
    //waitnokey 20 //uncomment this line see the effect
wend
```

•GetKeyE vn_ScanCode

Does **not** cause the program to pause and wait for a key, but if a key is pressed then a code value (**scan code**) corresponding to the key is assigned to vn_ScanCode, otherwise a 0 is stored. This is useful in loops that need to be exited if a key is pressed but without halting the loop until a key is pressed and also for detecting key presses of keys like up and down arrows and so on.

This command will return the scan code of the key pressed (not its ASCII code). The keys Shift, Alt and Ctrl have their own codes if pressed on their own. However, if these keys are pressed in combination with another key then the code of the key alone is added to 1000 (Shift), 2000 (Alt) or 4000 (Ctrl). For Example if you press 'a' alone you will get 65 inside vn_ScanCode (notice that this is the ASCII code for A not a). If you press Shift+a you will get 1065, Alt+a will give 2065, Ctrl+a will give 4065, Alt+Shift+a will give 3065, Ctrl+Alt+a will give 6065 and so on.

This command allows you to examine more keys than in GetKey. Keys like Up-Arrow will return 38. The codes returned by this command may not necessarily be the ASCII codes. Rather, they are codes that represent the key inside the operating system (**scan codes**). The codes for the alphanumerical keys are actually the ASCII codes but only for the upper case. So when the key 'D' is pressed the code will be 68 which is the ASCII code for 'D' regardless of the CapsLock state. If you press Shift-D then the code returned will be 1068 (as discussed above) which is not a valid ASCII code. The Shift, Ctrl, and Alt keys pressed alone will have the code 1016, 4017 and 2018. The actual codes for the keys are 16, 17 and 18 but due to the coding described above the values 1000, 4000 and 2000 also get added to the code. Also see the RobotBASIC Constants section for handy constants that represent various key scan codes. The constants kc_Shift, kc_Ctrl, and kc_Alt cannot be used with this command since the command returns 1000, 4000 and 2000 added to the code.

Also see KeyDown(). This function has the added advantage of allowing you to detect multiple keys pressed together.

This command may not return a value for certain combinations of keys pressed if they correspond to key combination that have a meaning for the operating system. So for example Ctrl+Esc will cause the Window's "Start" menu to fire up and will not be possible to detect within your program.

To find out what key code will be returned for a particular key you can experiment with the keys using the program below:

```
while true
   getkeyE k
   if k then xyString 1,2,"Extended Code=",k;"      "
wend
```

If you use this command within a loop you may get too many repetitions of the key due to the speed of the system not giving the user time to release the key before it is read many times as being a new key press. This can be counteracted by using Delay to delay between successive reads of the key (150 to 200 milliseconds might be sufficient). Or you can use looping to wait until the key is released (*vn_ScanCode* will be zero) or you can use WaitNoKey. It depends on your application, but the third and second method should be preferable. Example:

```
   rLocate 400,300
   while true
      GetKeyE k
      if k== kc_LArrow then rTurn -1    //left arrow
      if k== kc_UArrow then rForward 1  //up arrow
      if k== kc_RArrow then rTurn 1     //right arrow
      if k== kc_DArrow then rForward -1 //down arrow
      //waitnokeyE k,50 //uncomment this to see the effect
   wend
```

•WaitNoKey {ne_MillisWait}

If ne_MillisWait is zero or not given then the program will pause until no key on the keyboard and no mouse button is pressed. If it is given then the program will pause until no key is pressed or ne_MillisWait milliseconds elapse whichever comes first.

This is useful when you want to detect a key press and release. See the example program under GetKey.

To illustrate the need for this run this program then uncomment the commented line and run it again to see the difference in behavior.

```
   while true
```

```
        GetKey k
        readmouse x,y,m
        if k || m
           print "Press";m;k
           //WaitNoKey  //uncomment this and see the effect
        endif
    wend
```

•WaitNoKeyE ne_ScanCode{,ne_MillisWait}

If ne_MillisWait is zero or not given then the program will pause until the key with the scan code ne_ScanCode is not pressed. If it is given then the program will pause until the key with the scan code is not pressed or ne_MillisWait milliseconds elapse whichever comes first.

This is useful when you want to detect a key press and release for a particular key. See the example program under GetKeyE.

This command achieves the same purpose as WaitNoKey, except you are only interested in one particular key scan code. If other keys are pressed but not the key specified the command will not cause a pause. You can use any of the scan codes given in the RobotBASIC Constants section.

•LastKey()

Returns the scan code of the last keyboard key to be pressed. This function is equivalent to GetKeyE. This function is necessary in the body of a OnKey event handler subroutine. You must use this function within the body of the subroutine before you return from the routine. The scan code returned is as described in GetKeyE. If there is no key pressed when this function is called the returned value is 0.

•KeyDown({ne_ScanCode})

WaitKey, GetKey and GetKeyE allow you to obtain the code for the *last* key pressed. However, it may become necessary to test if a certain combinations of keys are pressed. Say you want to fire retrorockets horizontally and vertically and allow both at the same time. If you use the above commands the program will only be able to detect the *last* key pressed and thus if the user presses both the Up and Left Arrow keys together the commands will only report the code of the *last* key pressed. Also see the RobotBASIC Constants section for handy constants that represent various key codes.

Using this function you can interrogate each key separately to see if it is pressed down or not. There are 255 keys on the keyboard and you can find out the state of each separately using this function. For instance if you want to find out if the up arrow key is pressed and also at the same time the left arrow key then you would have a statement like
```
  if KeyDown(kc_LArrow) && KeyDown(kc_RArrow) then GoSub
DoSomething
```

89

Or you can use the numbers directly

```
if KeyDown(37) && KeyDown(38) then GoSub DoSomething
```

The function returns a non-zero number if the key is pressed and zero if it is not. ne_ScanCode is an integer value representing the code of the key you wish to query. The codes of the keys can be determined as described under GetKeyE. There is a program segment given there that enables you to determine the code for any key on the keyboard. Most of the alphanumeric keys have a code that is the ASCII code of the UpperCase letter of the key. The shift, Control and Alt keys have the values 16, 17, and 18 respectively. So for example if you wish to find out if Shift+Ctrl+F2 are pressed simultaneously you would have:

```
if KeyDown(kc_Shift)&&KeyDown(kc_Ctrl)&&KeyDown(kc_F2) then
GoSub DoSomething
```

The Function keys have the numbers 112 to 123 (F1 to F12). Remember the key code is specific for each key even if the key has multiple characters printed on it, it will have one code. So the **9(** key will have the code 57 which is actually the ASCII code for the numeral 9. The Left-Up-Right-Down arrow keys have the codes 37 to 40 in order (see the RobotBASIC Constants section). ***You can also use this function to read the condition of the mouse buttons as if they were keyboard keys***. See the RobotBASIC Constants section for their codes.

The function can be useful in gaming where a response to more than one key pressed together may be necessary. Also refer to GetKey, and GetKeyE for a discussion on how to handle the speed of response when you do not wish to detect one press as multiple presses.

Note: This function will report the scan codes of the keys and mouse buttons. If you have mapped the mouse to left handed operations the reported numbers will not be as you expect since 1 will still be the left button on the mouse regardless of left handed swapping operations (4 will be middle and 2 will be right).

Note: ne_ScanCode is optional. If it is not given or is less than zero then the function will report the scan code of a pressed key instead of looking for a particular key. It will return either 0 if no key is pressed when the function is called or the scan code of the key being pressed. If multiple keys are being pressed the function will return the *LOWEST* scan code.

•Mouse Input

•ReadMouse vn_X,vn_Y{,vn_Buttons}
Reads the current mouse position on the Screen and Sets vn_X and vn_Y to the position of the mouse pointer at the time the command was executed. vn_Buttons is set to a number that indicates a variety of things as follows:

Two digit integer where the ones digit is:
>   1 if Left mouse button is down
>   2 if Right mouse button is down
>   3 if Middle mouse button is down
>   The tens digit is:
>   10 if the Shift key is pressed
>   20 if the Ctrl key is pressed
>   30 if the Alt key is pressed
>   40 if the mouse button was double clicked

For Example: vn_Buttons will be 21 if the Left mouse button was pressed while the Ctrl button was held down.

If you use this command within a loop while detecting for a mouse click you may get too many repetitions of the click due to the speed of the system not giving the user time to release the button before it is read many times as being a new button press. This can be counteracted by using Delay to delay between successive reads of the click (150 to 200 milliseconds might be sufficient). Or you can use looping to wait until the button is released (vn_Buttons will be zero) or you can use WaitNoKey. It depends on your application, but the third or second method should be preferable. Example:

```
rLocate 400,300
while true
    ReadMouse x,y,mb
    if mb==  1 then rForward 1
    if mb==  2 then rTurn 1
    //waitnokey 20 //uncomment this and see the effect
wend
```

•SetMousePos {ne_X{,ne_Y}}

Positions the mouse cursor within the terminal screen to any position specified by the given coordinates. Unspecified parameters are made to be 0.

•SetCursor {ne_CursorShapeCode}

Sets the mouse cursor to a particular shape as defined by the given code. The code is optional and if not defined cr_Default will be assumed. See the RobotBASIC Constants section for a set of possible values. If the given code > 0 it will be made negative and it is < -21 it will be made -21.

•GetCursor vn_Code

Assigns vn_Code the value of the current mouse cursor shape value. See the RobotBASIC Constants section for possible values.

•LastMouse()

Returns the code of the mouse button pressed when this function is called. This is the same code returned when ReadMouse is executed. The code is only for the mouse button and any Shift, Alt or Ctrl pressed at the same time as described in ReadMouse. No mouse position is encoded. To get this you must use ReadMouse. If no mouse button (nor shift/alt/ctrl) is currently pressed when this function is called the returned value will be 0.

This function is necessary in the body of a OnMouse event handler subroutine. You must use this function within the body of the subroutine before you return from the routine.

•Joystick Input

•Joystick ne_JoystickNo,vn_XAxisPos,vn_YAxisPos,vn_ThrottlePos,vn_Buttons
Reads the current status of the Joystick and assigns the variables as will be described shortly. You can use up to two joysticks. If ne_JoystickNo is 2 then the second joystick will be interrogated. If it is other than 2 (e.g. 1) then joystick 1 will be interrogated.

Joysticks need to be installed using the operating system and need to be calibrated (also using the OS). If there is no joystick or there is an error in reading the joystick then the variables will all be assigned -1. If there is a joystick in the indicated position and it is successfully interrogated then the variable will be assigned values as follows:

vn_Buttons will be assigned 0 if no button is pressed or a bit wise number representing what combination of buttons are pressed if any are pressed. The first button is the least significant bit (LSB) and the last button is the most significant bit (MSB). So if buttons 2 and 5 are pressed then vn_Buttons will be 10010 i.e. 18, if buttons 3 and 8 are pressed then will 10000100 i.e. 132 will be assigned and so on.

vn_XAxisPos/vn_YAxisPos will be assigned a floating point number 0.0 to 1.0 representing the position of the X-Axis/Y-Axis of the joystick. 0.5 being the center position, 0 all the way to the left and 1.0 is all the way to the right.

Some joysticks only allow the above two axes, however, many joysticks have what is normally called the throttle axis which can be considered to be the Z-Axis. vn_Throttle will be assigned a floating point number 0.0 to 1.0 representing the position of the Z-Axis of the joystick. 0.5 being the center position, 0 will be the fully closed position (usually up) and 1.0 is the fully open position (usually down). Example:
```
While true
    Joystick 1,x,y,z,b
    xyString 10,10,x;y;z;b;spaces(20)
    delay 100
wend
```

•JoystickE ne_JoystickNo,a_ReturnedData

Reads the current status of the *extended* Joystick and assigns values inside the array a_ReturnedData as will be described shortly. You can use up to two joysticks. If ne_JoystickNo is 2 then the second joystick will be interrogated. If it is other than 2 (e.g. 1) then joystick 1 will be interrogated.

Joysticks need to be installed using the operating system and need to be calibrated (also using the OS). If your joystick supports more than three axis and other functionalities then use this command to obtain the extended information about the status of the joystick. You are still able to use Joystick even if you have an extended joystick so long as you do not need the additional controls the extended joystick can give. However, if you need more than three axis and other functionalities then use this command to obtain all the information.

a_ReturnedData will be a two-dimensional array [8x3]. The data will be as follows:

X-axis value	X-axis minimum value	X-axis maximum value
Y-axis value	Y-axis minimum value	Y-axis maximum value
Z-axis value	Z-axis minimum value	Z-axis maximum value
R-axis value	R-axis minimum value	R-axis maximum value
U-axis value	U-axis minimum value	U-axis maximum value
V-axis value	V-axis minimum value	V-axis maximum value
Buttons Pressed	Button number	Number of buttons available
POV value	Type of POV	Number of Axes available

The range for an axis is defined by the maximum and minimum values while the current position is given in the value. There are up to 7 axes supported. The actual number of axes implemented by the joystick is given in a_ReturnedData[7,2].

The Z-axis is usually the throttle. The R-axis is usually the rudder axis and on some joysticks is the twist in the joystick handle. The U and V axis are not common on joysticks but can be available on consoles like driving and flight simulator control consoles.

a_ReturnedData[6,0] holds a value that represents which combination of buttons is pressed (it is a bit map as described in Joystick above). a_ReturnedData[6,1] holds the lowest number (1,2,3, etc) of the buttons pressed. a_ReturnedData[6,2] is the number of buttons available on the joystick.

The POV is a hat button (called Point Of View) that can be pushed in a direction Up, Down, Left, Right and on some joysticks in positions in between. There are two types of POVs. The continuous ones where you can position it at any angle (0 to 359) or the discrete ones which can only be positioned at discrete positions. If a_ReturnedData[7,1] is 0 (false) then the joystick POV is discrete, if it 1(true) then it is a continuous type. a_ReturnedData[7,0] holds the position of the POV in degrees like in a compass. 0° is North, 180° is south, 45° is North

East, and so on. If the POV is not being pushed in any position then the value will be -1.

If the command fails or there is no joystick then all the numbers will be -1. Example:

```
while true
    joysticke 1,a
    for i=0 to 7
        s = ""
        for j=0 to 2
            s = s+format(a[i,j],"##########0")
        next
        xyString 0,i*20, s
    next
    delay 100
Wend
```

•<u>Sound Output & Input</u>

•Beep {ne_Count}

Beeps the Speaker ne_Count times. If ne_Count is not given only one beep will be sounded. Each beep takes 250 milliseconds, so if you beep 4 times the command will be equivalent to a delay of 600 ms.

•PlayWav {se_FileName{,ne_Mode{,ne_Loop}}}

Plays the WAV file specified on the sound card. The value ne_Mode specifies whether it is Synchronous or Asynchronous. If it is false it is Synchronous which means that the program flow will halt until the sound finishes playing. If it is true (the default value) then the file will be played Asynchronously which means that the program will continue without waiting for the sound to finish. ne_Loop specifies whether the sound will play in a loop (i.e. never finish). If ne_Loop is true then wav will continue to play over and over. If it is false or not given the wav will play only once. Looping is only allowed if the wav is being played Asynchronously. So if ne_Mode is false ne_Loop is ignored and is assumed to be false.

To stop a sound before it finishes either issue this command again with no file name specified, or with a new file name to play, which will stop the current file and start the new file. The file must be a WAV file with a ".wav" extension. If you specify a file with no extension or an extension that is not ".wav" then it will be converted to ".wav". If the file is not a valid WAV format or it does not exist then a beep will sound. When the program terminates any sound being played will be terminated also.

If the sound card is playing a sound file asynchronously the program flow will proceed while the sound is playing. You can find out if the sound device is busy playing a sound using

94

WavBusy() which returns true if a sound is playing or false if not. Example:

```
playwav "song"
i=0
while WavBusy()
    print i+1
    delay 10
wend
print "ended"
```

•WavBusy()

Returns true (1) if the sound device is busy playing a sound. Returns false (0) otherwise. This function is useful to enable doing actions until the sound device finishes or while the sound card is still playing a sound file that is being played asynchronously (see **PlayWav**). Example:

```
playwav "song"
i=0
while WavBusy()
    print i+1
    delay 10
wend
print "ended"
```

•MediaPlay ne_DeviceNumber,se_FileName{,ne_Loop}

PlayWav only allows one WAV file to be played at a time. This command allows various media types to be played and many simultaneously. You can play WAV, WMA, MP3 (and others) audio files and AVI, WMV, MPG (and others) video files.

If you specify a file without an extension then it will be assumed to be an Audio WAV file and the extension will be assumed to be ".wav".

You can have multiple media playing simultaneously. You specify a device to play the media on with the ne_DeviceNumber. If ne_Loop is not given or is false then the media will be played once and once finished the device will close. If ne_Loop is true then the media will be played continuously and you have to explicitly stop it with MediaStop. You can also pause and resume the play using MediaPause. You can also find out the state of a device with MediaState().

If the media file to be played is a Video file (see MediaIsVideo()) then use MediaShow, MediaReposition and MediaGetPosition to show a window where the video will be displayed and to control its position and size. See these commands for more details. If you wish to allow the user to Pause/Resume or to Stop the play from within the RB Terminal screen you need to provide Buttons that allow for that using MediaPause and MediaStop.

Example:
```
 Main:
    ScrSetMetrics 650,100,700,250,0
    xyText 10,10,"File To Play:","Times New
Roman",10,fs_Bold,blue
    AddEdit "fn",80,8,200
    ReadOnlyEdit "fn"
    data Buttons;"Choose
&File","&Play","P&ause","&Stop","&Show
Video","&Resume","&Hide Video"
    AddButton Buttons[0],285,6
    for i=0 to 3
       AddButton Buttons[i+1],40+110*i,40,100
    next
    AddCheckBox "Repea&t",60,70,,,0
    fnt = "Times New Roman"
    xyText 150,70,"State:",fnt,10,fs_Bold
    xyText 290,70,"Video Size:",fnt,10,fs_Bold
    EnableButton Buttons[1],false
    onbutton bHandler
    Paused = false
    xyText 20,110,"Press                    to demo how to
Reposition"+\
             " the video window under program
control",fnt,13,fs_Bold
    for i= 0 to 3
       drawshape rotshape("lrrqsaw",i),80+i*11,120,4
    next
    xyText 20,140,"Press - + PgUp PgDn to demo how to "+\
       "Resize the video window under program
control",fnt,13,fs_Bold
    FirstTime = true
    while true
      Call MonitorMediaState()
      Call MonitorKeyPresses()
    wend
 end
 Sub bHandler()
   b = LastButton()
   if b==Buttons[0]
      s = FilePrompt("|All Media Files|*.wav;*.avi;"+\
               "*.wmv;*.mp3;*.mpg;*.mpeg|Others |*.*")
      if s!=""
```

96

```
            SetEdit "fn",s
            EnableButton Buttons[1]
            _FirstTime = true
         endif
   elseif b == Buttons[1]
      MediaPlay 1,GetEdit("fn"),GetCheckBox("Repea&t")
      SetButtonCaption Buttons[2],Buttons[2]
      SetButtonCaption Buttons[4],Buttons[4]
      Call ShowVideoScreen(1)
      _Paused = false
   elseif b == Buttons[2]
      if !_Paused
         SetButtonCaption Buttons[2],Buttons[5]
         MediaPause 1
         _Paused = true
      else
         SetButtonCaption Buttons[2],Buttons[2]
         MediaPause 1,0
         call ShowVideoScreen(0)
         _Paused = false
      endif
   elseif b == Buttons[3]
      MediaStop 1
   elseif b == Buttons[4]
      Call ShowVideoScreen(1)
   endif
   onButton bHandler
Return
Sub ShowVideoScreen(ChangeState)
   if !MediaIsVideo(1) then return
   if !_FirstTime then MediaGetPosition x,y,w,h \
MediaReposition x,y,w,h
   _FirstTime = false
   t = !(GetButtonCaption(Buttons[4]) == Buttons[6])
   if ChangeState
      SetButtonCaption Buttons[4],Buttons[4+2*t]
      MediaShow 1,t
   else
      MediaShow 1
   endif
Return
Sub MonitorMediaState()
   ms = MediaState(1)
```

```
    xyString 185,70,ms,"      "
    ms = (ms !=2 && ms != 5)
    for i=2 to 3
       EnableButton Buttons[i], !ms
    next
    EnableButton Buttons[0], ms
    t = MediaIsVideo(1)
    EnableButton Buttons[4], (!ms && MediaIsVideo(1))
    MediaVideoSize 1,w,h
    xystring 355,70,w,",",h,spaces(10)
  Return
  Sub MonitorKeyPresses()
    if !keydown() then return
    MediaGetPosition ML,MT,MW,MH
    if KeyDown(kc_LArrow) then MediaReposition ML-10
    if KeyDown(kc_UArrow) then MediaReposition ,MT-10
    if KeyDown(kc_RArrow) then MediaReposition ML+10
    if KeyDown(kc_DArrow) then MediaReposition ,MT+10
    if KeyDown(kc_PUp)    then MediaReposition ,,,MH-10
    if KeyDown(kc_PDn)    then MediaReposition ,,,MH+10
    if KeyDown(189)       then MediaReposition ,,MW-10 // -
    if KeyDown(187)       then MediaReposition ,,MW+10 // +
  Return
```

•MediaPause ne_DeviceNumber{,on|off}

Will Pause the media playing on ne_DeviceNumber if on is specified or not given and will Resume play if off is given. Also see MediaState().

•MediaStop ne_DeviceNumber

Will Stop the media playing on ne_DeviceNumber. Also aee MediaState().

•MediaRecord ne_DeviceNumber,se_FileName

This command allows you to RECORD a WAV file. Only WAV files are allowed and if se_FileName has no extension or an extension other than ".wav" it will be changed to ".wav" and the file recorded will have a WAV format. You specify the device that will be recording using ne_DeviceNumber. You must use this same number when later on you use MediaSave to stop recording and save the file. Also see MediaState().

•MediaSave ne_DeviceNumber

Will Stop the Recording and then save the file to the file name specified in MediaRecord. If ne_DeviceNumber does not correspond to a device that is currently recording then no action will be taken. Also see MediaState().

•MediaShow ne_DeviceNumber{,true|false}

> If the media file to be played is a Video file (see MediaIsVideo()) then use MediaShow, MediaReposition and MediaGetPosition to show a window where the video will be displayed and to control its position and size. If you do not call MediaShow you will only be able to hear the Audio. You can move and size the window manually or under program control using MediaReposition. MediaGetPosition returns the window's current position and size. If you close the window manually the video will stop playing. If you stop the video using MediaStop then the window will be closed.
>
> If no second parameter is given or it is true then the window will be displayed. If false is given then the window will be closed but you will still be able to hear the audio. To close the window and stop the video at the same time use MediaStop or the user can close the window manually.
>
> **Note:** Every time you call MediaShow the video window will start at the top left hand corner of the Computer Screen and will be of an initial size according to the size of the video. However, if you specify either the X or Y position of the window (using MediaReposition) *BEFORE* you show the window then it will remain where you specified. If you specify the Width or Height of the window (using MediaReposition) *BEFORE* you show the window then it will remain at the size you specified and will not resize to fit the video. If you wish to keep the window in the same position as it was before it was last closed then use MediaGetPosition to see what the current size and position are *BEFORE* you show the window then use MediaReposition to position and size it according to the returned values *BEFORE* you show the window.

•MediaVideoSize DeviceNumber{,vn_Width{,vn_Height}}

> Will set vn_Width and vn_Height to the video's width and height respectively of the video currently *playing* in ne_DeviceNumber. If the device is not ready or it is playing an Audio then the values are 0. This is related but not the same as the size of the window in which the video is playing. If you call this for a video playing in a window that has not been resized (manually or with MediaReposition) then the width and height will be the video's real width and height as it is save in the file. If the video window has been resized then the values are the current video's width and height as it is playing. Read the notes about the video window under MediaShow.

•MediaReposition {ne_X{,ne_Y{,ne_Width{,ne_Height}}}}

> Can be called while the media window is open or closed. It will cause the window to be placed at a particular X,Y position on the *COMPUTER SCREEN* (not the Terminal Screen). Also you can give the window any width and height desired. The video being played will be resized to fit the window. See the note under MediaShow for important information.

•MediaGetPosition {vn_X{,vn_Y{,vn_Width{,vn_Height}}}}

Will set the specified variables with the values of the current X,Y,Width and Height of the window. See the note under MediaShow for important information.

•MediaState(ne_DeviceNumber)

Returns a number that represents the state the device ne_DeviceNumber is in. See Media Player State Codes in the RobotBASIC Constants section. The codes are ms_NotReady, ms_Stopped, ms_Playing, ms_Recording and ms_Paused. ms_NotReady means the media is either not a valid media or is closed and not playing. ms_Stopped means the media is not playing or paused. MediaStop will close the media and put it in an ms_NotReady mode most of the time but it is possible for it to go into an ms_Stopped state on occasion.

•MediaIsVideo(ne_DeviceNumber)

Returns true if the media *playing* in the device is a video file and false if it is not. Use this function to decide when to use MediaShow.

•Sound ne_Frequency,ne_Duration{,ne_Mode}

Makes the PC speaker make a sound at the frequency for the duration in milliseconds. If ne_Mode is true then the sound is made in the background and if it is false then the sound will stop the system for the duration of the note. Your program will still pause until the note finishes but the Windows OS will not be paused if mode is true. The default mode, if you do not specify it, is True.

Note: *This command may cause an error on machines without a speaker.*

•Speaker {on|off}

This will turn the speaker off or on. The notes played with Sound will play and will take the time required but no sound will be heard if the speaker is turned off. The speaker is on by default upon the start of the program. If no parameter is given it will be on.

Note: *This command may cause an error on machines without a speaker.*

•PlaySong {se_Notes}

This will play a song defined by the string se_Notes. If seNotes is not given then it will be made to be "AA#BCC#DD#EFF#GG#" i.e. all the notes at the default tempo and the default scale (see below). If se_Notes is given it should contain notes and other specs as defined below:

- The Notes are A,A#,B,C,C#,D,D#,E,F,F#,G,G# also P which is a pause.
- You can use lower or upper case. The # must immediately follow a note or it will be ignored
- Immediately after defining the note you can specify a number to define the duration of the note. This number can be any number greater than 0 and is usually 1,2,4,8,16,32,or 64. But you can specify any number you desire. The number will be used to calculate

the duration of the note by dividing into the defined Tempo (see later). The formula is Duration = Tempo/Number. You do not need to define a duration all the time. If a note does not have a duration defined after it then the duration last defined will be used. If you have not previously defined a duration for a previous note then the duration will be 8 by default.

- You define a tempo for the song and can change it at any time by specifying the letter T followed by a number. The number will be in milliseconds. So if you say T1500 then the tempo will be 1 and half seconds. If you never define a tempo then it will be 1000 (i.e. 1 second) by default.
- You can define a scale for the song and can change it any time by specifying the letter S followed by a number. The number must be in the range 0 to 6. This means that there are 7 scales and scale 3 is the Middle C scale. If you never define a scale it will be 4 by default. If you define a number greater than 6 it will be made to be 6.
- The letter P is taken to be a pause of the duration defined as for the notes (see above).
- If the speaker is off (see Speaker) then the song will play but no sound will be heard.

The following example will play a song with the scale being 4 to start with then it will be changed to 3. Also the tempo will start as 1000 and will be changed to 1500 afterwards. The notes A and B will play at 8th and then the rest will be played at 16th

```
PlaySong "abc16dc#T1500dgS3abdg#"
```

Note: *This command may cause an error on machines without a speaker.*

The following will play the song Jingle Bells followed by La Cucaracha. Notice how you have versatility in defining and playing the songs. Also notice how the scale is changed in the La Cucaracha song.

```
data
Jingles;"T1000S4E8EP32E4P32E8EP32E4P32E8GP32C4D16P32E2P16"
data Jingles;"F8FP32F8F16P32F8EP32E8E16P32G8GFDP32C2"
Cucaracha = "T2500S4C16CCP64F8P64A7C16CCP64F8P64A7F16F8P64"
Cucaracha =
Cucaracha+"E16EP64D16DP64C4P32S4C16CCP64E8P64G7"
Cucaracha =
Cucaracha+"C16CCP64E8P64G7S5C8D16P64C16S4A#16AG"
Cucaracha = Cucaracha+"P64F8P4"
playsong Jingles[0]
playsong Jingles[1]
Delay 1000
playsong Cucaracha
```

Graphical User Interfacing

Note: See the notes at the top of the Standard User Interfacing section.

•Dialog Boxes

•StrInput({e_Caption{,e_Prompt{,e_Default}}})

Display a dialog box with a caption (window title), and a prompt and a default input text. The user then can enter any text and press the OK button. If the OK button is pressed the text in the input field will be returned. If the cancel button is pushed then the original default text (se_Default) will be returned. The dialog box will be centered on the screen. The function returns a string regardless of what the input was. If you are expecting a number use the string conversion functions to convert it to a number and test whether it is a valid input and so on.

All the parameter are optional and can be either numeric or strings. If they are numeric they will be converted to the string equivalent. If e_Caption is not give it will be made to be "RobotBASIC:". If e_Prompt is not given then it will be made to be "Please enter a value>". If e_Default is not given it will be "".

•TextBox(se_FileName{,e_Title{,ne_X{,ne_Y{,ne_W{,ne_H{,ne_DoWrap}}}}}})

Shows a dialog box with the content of the text file. The dialog box has two buttons (OK and Cancel). The user can terminate the box by pressing either button. The value returned by the function is 1 (true) if the OK button (or ENTER) was used to close the box, or 0 (false) if the Cancel button (or ESC) was used. The dialog box can also be closed using the Windows methods and the returned value will be 0 (false). se_Title will be used as a title (on the border frame of the box) to the dialog and is optional.

The file can be a simple text file or an RTF formatted file. You must specify the full file name including the extension. If the file is an RTF format then the text formats (color, fonts etc.) will take effect and will be displayed as specified by the formatting codes in the RTF file. If it is a plain text file then it will be displayed as such.

You can override the default width, height and position (X,Y) with the additional parameters. If ne_DoWrap is true then the text will wrap if it is too long for the width of the box and **no** horizontal scroll bar will be shown. If ne_DoWrap is false or is not given then the text will not wrap and a horizontal scroll bar will be shown if needed.

The box will be centered on the screen and there is a scroll bar to scroll the text in the vertical direction. See the commands above for more user interaction commands and MsgBox() below.
 Example:

102

```
if TextBox("Test.RTF")
    print "OK"
else
    print "Cancel"
endif
```

•StringBox(se_Text{,e_Title{,ne_X{,ne_Y{,ne_W{,ne_H{,ne_DoWrap}}}}}})

Shows a dialog box with the content of the string se_Text which is a string with substrings separated with CR/LF character pairs. The box will show each sub string on a line in the box. The dialog box has two buttons (OK and Cancel). The user can terminate the box by pressing either button. The value returned by the function is true if the OK button (or ENTER) was used to close the box, or false if the Cancel button (or ESC) was used. The dialog box can also be closed using the Windows methods and the returned value will be false. se_Title will be used as a title (on the border frame of the box) to the dialog and is optional.

You can override the default width, height and position (X,Y) with the additional parameters. If ne_DoWrap is true then the text will wrap if it is too long for the width of the box and **no** horizontal scroll bar will be shown. If ne_DoWrap is false or is not given then the text will not wrap and a horizontal scroll bar will be shown if needed.

The box will be centered on the screen and there is a scroll bar to scroll the text in the vertical direction. See the commands above for more user interaction commands and MsgBox() below.
Example:

```
SetTextBuff ""
for i=0 to 30
    print "Test"+i
next
clearscr \ s = GetTextBuff()
if StringBox(s,"Testing...")
    print "OK"
else
    print "Cancel"
endif
```

•ErrMsg(se_MessageText{,se_BoxTitle{,ne_Style}})

Shows a message box with the text se_MessageText inside the box and a title on the border. ne_Style is a number that defines the buttons combination and the icon type as well as which button is the default one. If it is zero then the default will be an *OK* button with no icon. The value should be created by ORing the values given in the RobotBASIC Constants section. For example to have a box with the buttons yes and no and the error icon (stop) and to have the no button (second one) as the default button then use:

```
n=ErrMsg("Message here","Title here",MB_YESNO | MB_ERROR |
```

```
MB_BUTTON2)
```

The returned value will be according to the values given in the RobotBASIC Constants section. So in the above example if the user pushes the yes button then the returned value will be MB_YES (5) or the user presses the no button, the value will be MB_NO (6).

When there is a Cancel button the box can be closed using the window close icon on the top right corner and that would be the same as pushing the Cancel button. When there is no cancel button the box close icon is not enabled. If you do not specify a default button then the default will be the first button. Also in the cases where there is a Cancel button then pressing the ESC key on the keyboard will do the same as pushing the Cancel button. Pressing the Enter key will also be the same as pushing the default button.

When creating the value of ne_Style you can either use the constants' names or their values. If you do not want an icon just don't specify it. If you want the default button to be the first button then there is no need to specify one. If ne_Style is 0 then there will only be an OK button and no icon.

If ne_Style is not given the box will have just the "OK" button. If se_BoxTitle is not given it will be "".

•**MsgBox(a_TextLines{,e_Title{,ne_X{,ne_Y{,ne_W{,ne_H{,ne_DoWrap}}}}}})**
Shows a dialog box with text as specified in the one-dimensional array a_TextLines. The dialog box has two buttons (OK and Cancel). The user can terminate the box by pressing either button. The value returned by the function is true if the OK button (or ENTER) was used to close the box, or false if the Cancel button (or ESC) was used. The dialog box can also be closed using the Windows methods and the returned value will be false.

The array a_TextLines has to be a one-dimensional array. Each element will be displayed in the text on a line by itself. If the element is numeric it will be converted to string. If you need to have blank lines use a null string (""). The first element to not have an assigned value will be the end of the text. Use Data to create the array (or Dim).

If e_Title is not given or is an empty string ("") then the first element in the array will be used as a title (on the border frame of the box) to the dialog; it will not show inside the box with the rest of the text. If e_Title is given and is one space (" ") then the title will be "RobotBASIC Message...". If e_Title is given and is anything other than one space or an empty string then that text will be the title. If it is a number it will be converted to a string.

The box will be centered on the screen and will be as wide as needed to display the longest line of text, but will not be wider than the screen. If the box is narrower than any line the line will wrap around. Also there is a scroll bar to scroll the text in the vertical direction. See the commands above for more user interaction. Also see TextBox(), StringBox(), mToString(), ErrMsg(), and mFromString. Also see the buffer functions BuffWrite() and BuffRead().

You can override the default width, height and position (X,Y) with the additional parameters. If ne_DoWrap is true then the text will wrap if it is too long for the width of the box and **no** horizontal scroll bar will be shown. If ne_DoWrap is false or is not given then the text will not wrap and a horizontal scroll bar will be shown if needed.

Example:
```
Data msg;"this is a test message box.",""
Data msg;"the next lines are numerical data displayed as
text"
Data msg;-1,3,5.2,6.1e12
Data msg;"","this is the end."
if MsgBox(msg)
    print "OK"
else
    print "Cancel"
endif
```

•Push Button Components

•Push Button Commands

•AddButton se_Name,ne_X,ne_Y{,ne_W{,ne_H{,se_Hint}}}

Creates a push button in the Terminal Screen at position ne_X,ne_Y. The button will have the name se_Name and will display the given name as a caption inside the button. It will be of height ne_H and width ne_W which are optional and if not given (or are less than 1) the button will be sized to fit the caption. The button will remain active until removed with RemoveButton below. The name is important, is case sensitive, and should be unique for each button you create. The name is used to identify the button using the commands and functions relating to the button.

You can change the name of the button using RenameButton which will also change the caption inside the button. You can change the caption in the button using SetButtonCaption without changing the name as well. See the examples under these commands for a use for these actions.

se_Hint will be a hint text displayed when the user places the mouse cursor over the button and is optional.

Note: In all the functions and commands dealing with push buttons, the name of the button must be exactly the same as se_Name used to create the button with AddButton (case sensitive).

Note: The name is _**case sensitive**_ and _**should be unique**_ for each button.

Once you create buttons in the Terminal Screen, the interpreter will keep track of which button was pressed last. You can find out what button was pushed last with GetButton and LastButton(). If no button has been pushed since the last interrogation, the value returned will be a blank string. The value returned from GetButton and LastButton() will be the name of the last button that was pushed. See example below for details.

If you use the character '&' in the name before any letter then that letter will be displayed as an underlined letter in the caption of the button and pressing Alt+ the letter will be the same as pushing the button. If you desire to have the '&' letter display as is then use a double &&. But remember the caption string will contain these letters and you must take them as part of the string when defining the name for RemoveButton and when checking the returned string from GetButton and LastButton().

See the examples under the RenameButton, AddEdit, AddCheckBox, AddListBox, AddRBGroup, AddSlider and AddMemo)

•RemoveButton se_Name
Removes the button.

•FocusButton se_Name
Sets the focus to the pushbutton. This can be useful for setting the user ready for pushing the button, or for drawing attention to a particular button. The user can also push the button using the _**Enter**_ or _**SpaceBar**_ keys. If se_Name is an empty string "" then focus will be removed from any control in the Terminal screen that may currently have the focus.

Note: You cannot set focus to a disabled or hidden button.

•EnableButton se_Name{,true|false}
Makes the pushbutton enabled if true is given or is not given and disabled if false is given. A disabled button will be grayed out and the user won't be able to push it. It is still visible but won't be pushable. this command is useful in situations where a button should not be used by a user. If you remove a button you have to Add it again if you wish to make it available for use again. This command and HideButton are a more efficient way of making a button temporarily unusable.

•HideButton se_Name{,true|false}

Makes the pushbutton invisible if true is given or is not given and visible if false is given. An invisible button is still a valid button (as opposed to a removed button). But it will not be visible. This is useful in certain situations where you want to make some buttons not available. You can then later make them available. If you remove a button you have to Add it again if you wish to make it available for use again. This command and EnableButton are a more efficient way of making a button temporarily unusable.

•SetButtonCaption se_Name{,e_Caption}

Changes the text displayed inside the push button to e_Caption. e_Caption can be numeric or string. If it is numeric it will be made into a string. If it is not given it will be "".If e_Caption is not given or is "" the button will have no text inside. This command does not change the name of the button. When the button is pushed LastButton() or GetButton will return the name of the button as it was when it was created. Changing the caption does not change the name and any command relating to the button should use the name not the displayed caption. See RenameButton for a contrast. This command can be helpful in changing the text of the button depending on the situation, however you still refer to the button using its name which after this command would be different from the text displayed in it. **See the example under AddRBGroup for an example of the use of this command.**

•SetButtonDim se_Name{,ne_X{,ne_Y{,ne_W{,ne_H}}}}

Sets the position (ne_X, ne_Y) and width and height of the button.

Example:

```
SetColor black,gray \ clearscr
xyText 20,200,"Is RobotBASIC the ","Times New Roman",30,fs_Bold
xyText -1,200,"Greatest","Times New Roman",30,fs_Bold|fs_Underlined|fs_Italic
xyText -1,200," language ","Times New Roman",30,fs_Bold
xyText -1,200,"Ever ?","Times New Roman",30,fs_Bold|fs_underlined|fs_italic
addbutton "Yes",130,300,100 \ addbutton "No",330,300,100
setmousepos 10,10 \ msg = "You ARE a CLEVER and Discerning Person!"
while true
  if LastButton() == "Yes" then Beep\ n =
ErrMsg(msg,"RobotBASIC...",MB_OK|MB_INFORMATION)
  readmouse x,y,mb \ bx = getbuttonx("No") \ by = getbuttony("No")
  if !within(x,bx-20,bx+120) || !within(y,by-20,by+50) then continue
  m = 130+random(20) \ bx = x+m  \ if bx > 700 then bx = x-m
  mm = 60+random(10) \ by = y+mm \ if by > 570 then by = y-mm
  if random(1000) < 500 then bx = x-m \ if bx < 0 then bx = x+m
  if random(1000) < 500 then by = y-mm\ if by < 0 then by = y+mm
  setbuttondim "No",bx,by
wend
```

•SetButtonFont se_Name{,se_FontType{,ne_FontSize{,ne_FontStyle{,ne_FontColor}}}}

Sets the type, size, style and color of the font of the button. The details are the same as in xyText. If the type is not given or is "" then the font type will not be changed. If the size is not given or is < 1 then font size will not be changed. If the style value is not given or is < 0 then the font style will not be changed. If the color is not given or is < 0 then the font color will not be changed. To find out what font details the memo currently has, use GetButtonFont().

•RenameButton se_CurrentName,se_NewName

Renames the pushbutton se_CurrentName to se_NewName. The button will display the new text and will be renamed accordingly. From that point onwards you have to refer to the button using the new name in any commands and functions (see SetButtonCaption for a contrast). This is useful in situations like a toggle switch. The button could be named "Start" and when pushed it becomes renamed "Stop", and vice versa. This command makes it easy to do this kind of action without having to remove the button and adding a new one with the new name. Another way to do a toggle action is to have two buttons occupying the same space on the screen but one is hidden while the other is visible (see HideButton). You then can have the action of pushing the visible button make it hidden and unhide the invisible one.

> **Note: After renaming the button, you have to refer to it using the new name in any further commands or functions. You can accomplish a similar action without renaming the button by using SetButtonCaption to just change the text in the button while maintaining the same name.**

Example: Also see the example under AddRGBGroup.

```
//example for simulating TOGGLE switches with two methods
//RenameButton and HideButton
addbutton "Start",100,100,100
addbutton "Stop",100,100,100
addbutton "On",100,150,100
hidebutton "Stop",true
LED = on \ Runn = false
i = 0 \ xyText 220,100,i,,20,fs_Bold
while true
    getbutton b
    if b=="Start" then hidebutton "Stop",false \ hidebutton "Start",true \ Runn =
True
    if b=="Stop" then hidebutton "Start",false \ hidebutton "Stop",true \ Runn =
false
    if b=="Off" then renamebutton "Off","On"  \ LED = On
    if b=="On" then renamebutton "On","Off" \ LED = off
    circlewh 220,150,20,20,red*LED,red*LED
    EnableButton "Start",LED \ EnableButton "Stop",LED
    if Runn && LED then xyText 220,100,i,,20,fs_Bold \ i=i+1
wend
```

•GetButton vs_Name

Assigns the variable vs_Name the name of the last button pushed. The name returned is the string used to create the button or to rename it if RenameButton was used. If no button has been pushed since the last interrogation using this command or LastButton() the returned string will be an empty string ("").

> **Note:** Once this command has been used (or LastButton()) there will be no more last button value (i.e. an empty string) until another button is pushed again.

Example: Also see the examples under RenameButton, AddEdit, AddCheckBox, AddListBox,

AddRBGroup, AddSlider and AddMemo.

```
for i=0 to 4
    AddButton "Test&"+i,300,20+i*40
next
while true
    GetButton Btn
    if Btn != "" then xyString 10,10,Btn
    if Btn == "Test&3" then RemoveButton Btn
wend
```

•Push Button Functions

•ButtonEnabled(se_Name)
Returns true if the pushbutton is enabled (i.e. you can push on it) and false if it is not.

•ButtonHidden(se_Name)
Returns true if the pushbutton is hidden and false if it is visible.

•GetButtonCaption(se_Name)
Returns the text displayed inside the button.

•GetButtonX(se_Name)
•GetButtonY(se_Name)
•GetButtonW(se_Name)
•GetButtonH(se_Name)
Returns the position (X,Y) and width (W) and height (H) of the button.

•GetButtonFont(se_Name)
Returns a string that has 4 sections separated with CR/LF character pairs. The sections' order is Font Type, Size, Style and Color. The color will be 0-15 if it is one of RobotBASIC's primary colors or the RGB value if it is not. The Style will be 0 if no style, 1 if bold, 2 if italic and 4 if underlined and any binary combination of these. You can AND the number with the constants from the Constants section (fs_Bold etc.). You can extract the different sections using Extract() or you can put them into an array using mFromString. To set the font, use SetButtonFont.

•ButtonHasFocus(se_Name)
Returns true if the button has focus, or false otherwise. This function is useful in finding if the user is able to press the button using the keyboard..

•LastButton()
Returns the name of the last button pushed. The name returned is the string used to create the

button or the new name if it has been renamed using RenameButton. If no button has been pushed since the last interrogation using this function (or GetButton), the returned string will be "" (zero length).

Note: Once this function has been used (or GetButton) there will be no more last button value (i.e. an empty string) until another button is pushed again.

See the use of this function in the example given in the Flow Control Statements section under the On[CONTROL] flow control group of statements. Also see example under AddSlider.

•Edit Box Components

•Edit Box Commands

•AddEdit se_Name,ne_X,ne_Y{,ne_W{,ne_H{,e_Text{,se_Hint}}}}

Creates an Edit Box in the Terminal Screen at position ne_X,ne_Y. se_Name is a name given to the box. This name should be unique and is used to identify the box for other *related* commands and functions. The box will be of height ne_H and width ne_W. The height and width are optional and if not given (or are less than 1) the button will be sized to fit the initial text inside the box (e_Text), but if there is no initial text or it is "" then the width will default to 100. se_Hint specifies a hint for the user when the mouse button is placed over the box (see later for details). The box will remain active until removed with RemoveEdit below.

The name of the box (se_Name) is important and should be unique for each box you create and is *case sensitive*. The name is used to identify the box in related commands and functions. e_Text will be an initial text to be set inside the edit box and if not specified it will be an empty string. If e_Text is a numeric it will be converted to a string.

You can determine if the text inside an edit box has changed with EditChanged(). You can obtain the string of text inside the box with GetEdit(). You can find if the user is still currently inside the box with EditHasFocus().

You can remove the edit box from view and discard it with RemoveEdit. You can set the text inside the box with SetEdit. Additionally, you can disable/enable input in a box using EnableEdit. Also you can highlight a particular edit box with FocusEdit.

Note: In all the functions and commands dealing with edit boxes, the name of the edit box must be exactly the same as the se_Name used to create the box with AddEdit (case sensitive).

Note: The name of the edit box is *case sensitive* and *should be unique* for each box.

110

Note: The end user can change the text inside the box at any time by clicking on it and typing text. If the user presses *Enter* the edit box will be exited and the new text will remain there. If the user presses the *Esc* button then the editing will be rejected and the box will be exited and the previous text will remain unchanged.

If se_Hint is not given or is an empty text ("") then the edit box will have a default hint displayed when the user places the mouse over the box. The default hint will say:

> *You can enter data in this text box. Esc will cancel any editing. Enter will finish editing.*

If you wish to have a hint other than the default hint, or no hint at all, then you must specify se_Hint. If se_Hint is just one character long (e.g. " " or "a") then there will be no hint displayed. If se_Hint is longer than one character then the text in se_Hint will be displayed as a hint.

Upon creation of the box, the color of the background will be white and the color of the font will be black. You can use SetEditColor and SetEditFont to change these colors and also the font size, type and style.

Example: Also see the examples under AddCheckBox, AddRBGroup, AddListBox, AddSlider and AddMemo.

```
for i=0 to 4
   if i==0 then AddEdit "Field"+i,10,i*30+10,100,0,"test"+i," " //no hint
   if i==1 then AddEdit "Field"+i,10,i*30+10,100,0,"test"+i,"test hint"
   if i>1  then AddEdit "Field"+i,10,i*30+10,100,0,"test"+i //default hint
next
AddButton "&Exit",10,200
repeat
  n= LastEdit()
  if n != "" then xyString 200,tonumber(right(n,1))*30+10,GetEdit(n)+spaces(100)
until LastButton() != ""
for i=0 to 4
   RemoveEdit "Field"+i
next
RemoveButton "&Exit"
ClearScr \ xyText 100,150,"All Done",,50,fs_Bold
```

•RemoveEdit se_Name

Removes the edit box.

•FocusEdit se_Name

Puts the cursor inside the edit box and highlights the text inside it. This can be useful for setting the user ready for inputting data into the box, or for drawing attention to a particular box. If se_Name is an empty string "" then focus will be removed from any control that may currently have the focus.

Note: You cannot set focus to a disabled or hidden edit box.

•EnableEdit se_Name{,true|false}

If false is specified the edit box will become a display box where the user cannot enter data and the box will be grayed and it will not be possible to select the box or scroll through the text in it. If true is specified or is not given then it becomes possible to enter data in the box.

•HideEdit se_Name{,true|false}

Makes the edit box invisible if true is given or is not given and visible if false is specified. An invisible edit box is still a valid one (as opposed to a removed one). But it will not be visible. This is useful in certain situations where you want to make some edit boxes not available. You can then later make them available. If you remove an edit box you have to Add it again if you wish to make it available for use again. This command and EnableEdit are a more efficient way of making an edit box temporarily unusable.

•ReadOnlyEdit se_Name{,true|false}

If true specified or no value is given the edit box will become a display box where the user cannot enter data. If false is given then it becomes possible to enter data in the box. A read only box will not be grayed and it will still be possible to select the box and to scroll through the text in it, but no text entry or changing will be possible.

•SetEdit se_Name{,e_Value}

Assigns the text inside the edit box a new string (e_Value). e_Value can be a numeric or a string. If it is numeric it will be made into a string. If it is not given it will be "".

•SetEditColor se_Name{,ne_Color}

Sets the boxes background to the color ne_Color. If the color value given is 0 to 15 then the RobotBASIC primary colors will be used (see RobotBASIC Constants section). If the value is an RGB color value then it will be used. If ne_Color is not given then it will be Blue. See ConsToClr().

•BorderEdit se_Name{,true|false}

If true is specified or is not given, the Edit box will have a border around it and will make the edit box appear slightly sunken into the screen. If false is given there will be no border.

•SetEditDim se_Name{,ne_X{,ne_Y{,ne_W{,ne_H}}}}

Sets the position (ne_X, ne_Y), width (ne_Width) and height (ne_H) of the edit box.

•SetEditFont se_Name{,se_FontType{,ne_FontSize{,ne_FontStyle{,ne_FontColor}}}}

Sets the type, size, style and color of the font of the edit box. The details are the same as in xyText. If the type is not given or is "" then the font type will not be changed. If the size is not given or is < 1 then font size will not be changed. If the style value is not given or is < 0 then

112

the font style will not be changed. If the color is not given or is < 0 then the font color will not be changed. To find out what font details the box currently has, use GetEditFont().

Note: Setting the font size may change the height of the box. If you wish to keep it to a specific height then use SetEditDim **_after_** setting the font size.

•**IntegerEdit se_Name{,true|false}**

Restricts the input in the edit box to a valid integer (**_decimal, hexadecimal or binary_**) value. Any key stroke that makes the text in the box an invalid integer will be rejected. If true is specified or is not given then the Edit box will be restricted to input that can be converted to a valid integer or to an empty string. If false is given then the Edit box will become free format. See the Numbers sub-section in the Overview Of The Language section for a definition of a valid integer.

The text in the box is still text and GetEdit() will return a string, but it is a string that can be conveted to a number by ToNumber(), unless it is empty in which case GetEdit() will be a string of zero length (""). You can still use ToNumber() but give it a default [e.g. `n=ToNumber(GetEdit("t"),0)`]. See example under FloatEdit.

Note: If you want to restrict the input in an Edit box to a special format like dates and phone number then use SetEditMask.

•**FloatEdit se_Name{,true|false}**

Restricts the input in the edit box to a valid floating point number value. Any key stroke that makes the text in the box an invalid float will be rejected. If true is specified or is not given then the Edit box will be restricted to input that can be converted to a valid float or to an empty string. If false is given then the Edit box will become free format. See the Numbers sub-section in the Overview Of The Language section for a definition of a valid float.

The text in the box is still text and GetEdit() will return a string, but it is a string that can be converted to a number by ToNumber(), unless it is empty in which case GetEdit() will be a string of zero length (""). You can still use ToNumber() but give it a default [e.g. `n=ToNumber(GetEdit("t"),0)`].

Note: If you want to restrict the input in an Edit box to a special format like dates and phone number then use SetEditMask.

Example: Compare this example to the one under SetEditMask.
```
addedit "Int",10,10,120,0,0 \ IntegerEdit "Int"
addedit "Flt",340,10,130,0,"0.0" \ FloatEdit "Flt"
xytext 10,130,"Try to enter decimal, hex or binary integers on the left",,,fs_Bold
xytext 10,150,"Try to enter floats on the right",,,fs_Bold
while true
```

113

```
      if EditChanged("Int")
          rectangle 0,40,340,100,white,white
          t = getedit("Int")
          xystring 10,40,"Text="""+t+""""
          xystring 10,70,ToNumber(t,0)," - 1 = ",ToNumber(t,0)-1
      endif
      if EditChanged("Flt")
          rectangle 340,40,800,100,white,white
          t = getedit("Flt")
          xystring 340,40,"Text="""+t+""""
          xystring 340,70,ToNumber(t,0)," - 1 = ",ToNumber(t,0)-1
      endif
  wend
```

•SetEditMask se_Name,se_MaskSpecs

Assigns a mask to the edit box. The mask specifies what kind of characters are allowed and can be used to format the input given to fit a desired format (e.g. phone numbers etc.). The specification of the mask is as follows:

Use this command to restrict the characters a user can enter into the Edit box to valid characters and formats. If the user attempts to enter an invalid character, the Edit box does not accept the character. Validation is performed on a character-by-character basis.

A mask consists of three sections with semicolons separating them. You have to specify the first section. The other two can be left out and will default as described below. The first section of the mask is the mask itself. The second part is the character that determines whether the literal characters of a mask are saved as part of the data. The third part of the mask is the character used to represent un-entered characters in the mask.

Note: A mask is a strict format for how text is entered in the Edit box. You can use it to restrict the input text to numeric but it is not a free form format. If you want a free form numeric Edit box you would be better off to use IntegerEdit or FloatEdit.

These are the special characters used in the first field of the mask:

Character	Meaning in mask
!	If a ! character appears in the mask, optional characters are represented in the text as leading blanks. If a ! character is not present, optional characters are represented in the text as trailing blanks.
>	If a > character appears in the mask, all characters that follow are in uppercase until the end of the mask or until a < character is encountered.
<	If a < character appears in the mask, all characters that follow are in lowercase until the end of the mask or until a > character is encountered.
<>	If these two characters appear together in a mask, no case checking is done and the

114

data is formatted with the case the user uses to enter the data.

\	The character that follows a \ character is a literal character. Use this character to use any of the mask special characters as a literal in the data.
L	The **L** character requires an alphabetic character only in this position (A-Z, a-z).
l	The **l** (lower case L) character permits only an alphabetic character in this position, but doesn't require it.
A	The **A** character requires an alphanumeric character only in this position (A-Z, a-z, 0-9).
a	The **a** character permits an alphanumeric character in this position, but doesn't require it.
C	The **C** character requires an arbitrary character in this position.
c	The **c** character permits an arbitrary character in this position, but doesn't require it.
0	The **0** character requires a numeric character only in this position.
9	The **9** character permits a numeric character in this position, but doesn't require it.
#	The **#** character permits a numeric character or a plus or minus sign in this position, but doesn't require it.
:	The **:** character is used to separate hours, minutes, and seconds in times. If the character that separates hours, minutes, and seconds is different in the regional settings of the Control Panel utility on your computer system, that character is used instead.
/	The **/** character is used to separate months, days, and years in dates. If the character that separates months, days, and years is different in the regional settings of the Control Panel utility on your computer system, that character is used instead.
;	The **;** character is used to separate the three sections of the mask.
_	The _ character automatically inserts spaces into the text. When the user enters characters in the box, the cursor skips the _ character.

Any character that does not appear in the preceding table can appear in the first section of the mask as a literal character. Literal characters must be matched exactly in the edit control. They are inserted automatically, and the cursor skips over them during editing. The special mask characters can also appear as literal characters if preceded by a backslash character (\).

The second section of the mask is a single character that indicates whether literal characters from the mask should be included as part of the text returned by GetEdit(). For example, the mask for a telephone number with area code could be the following string:

    (000)_000-0000;0;*

The 0 in the second section indicates that GetEdit() will return the 10 digits that were entered, rather than the 14 characters that make up the telephone number as it appears in the edit box.

A 0 in the second section indicates that literals should not be included; any other character indicates that they should be included.

The third section of the mask is the character that appears in the Edit box for blanks (characters that have not been entered). By default, this is the same as the character that stands for literal spaces (_). The two characters appear the same in an Edit box. However, when a user edits the text in a masked Edit box, the cursor selects each blank character in turn, and skips over the space character. You can change this to any character. If it is not given or is a blank then the default character (_) will be used.

Setting the Mask to an empty string removes the mask and there will be no formatting.

When the user enters text not in accord with the mask and presses enter there will be a message telling the user that the text entered is not valid and should be reedited or ESC pressed to cancel any changes.

See GetEditMasked() and GetEdit().

Example:

```
data Masks;"#9999;1","#9999;0; ","(000)-000-0000;0; ","(000)-000-0000;1;*"
for i=0 to 3
    addedit "t"+i,10,50+40*i,200 \ SetEditMask "t"+i,Masks[i]
next
m = "Masked"+spaces(12)+"UnMasked"+spaces(5)+"Calculation"
n=LastEdit() \ xyText 265,10,m,,15,fs_Bold|fs_Underlined
onedit eHandler
while true
wend
eHandler:
    le = LastEdit() \ n= tonumber(right(le,1))
    rectangle 230,53+n*40,800,93+n*40,white,white
    m =  Center(""""+GetEdit(le)+"""","",20)
    um = Center(""""+GetEditUnMasked(le)+""""," ",20)
    x = "" \ xx = NoSpaces(GetEdit(le))
    if n < 2 then x = "5*"+xx+"="+ToNumber(NoSpaces(GetEdit(le)))*5
    xystring 230,53+n*40,m;um;x
    onEdit eHandler
Return
```

•Edit Box Functions

•EditEnabled(se_Name)
Returns true if the edit box is enabled (i.e. you can enter text in it) and false if it is *not* enabled (i.e. you cannot enter text in it and cannot select it and is grayed).

•EditHidden(se_Name)
Returns true if the edit box is hidden and false if it is visible.

•EditReadOnly(se_Name)

Returns true if the edit box is a read only box (i.e. you cannot enter text in it but is still selectable and is not grayed) and false if it is *not* read only.

•EditHasFocus(se_Name)

Returns true if the user is inside the edit box entering text, or false otherwise.

When the user enters the edit box and starts typing text in the edit box, the cursor will be inside the box until the user presses *Esc* or *Enter*. This function is useful in finding if the user is inside a particular edit box.

•EditChanged(se_Name)

Returns true if the text inside the edit box has changed since the last time you have interrogated its status using this function. If it has not changed the function will return false.

•GetEdit(se_Name)

Returns the text inside the edit box. If the box has a mask then the text retuned will be formatted as specified by the mask. If you want the text before formatting then use GetEditUnMasked().

If you set a mask for the edit box (SetEditMask) then the text returned will not have the formatting characters and will have spaces for any un-entered characters in the template. Use NoSpaces() or Substitute() to remove these spaces. If the required text is a number then also use the ToNumber() to convert it to a number. Also see IntgerEdit and FloatEdit if you want purely numeric inputs.

•GetEditUnmasked(se_Name)

Returns the text inside the edit box without being formatted by the mask. That is all mask characters and formatting characters are part of the text. If you want the text formatted by the mask then use GetEdit().

•GetEditColor(se_Name)

Returns the color of the edit box's background. If the color is one of RobotBASIC's primary colors then its number will be returned (0-15), otherwise the number will be the RGB code of the color.

•EditBorder(se_Name)

Returns true if the Edit box has the border turned on, and false if not.

•GetEditX(se_Name)
•GetEditY(se_Name)
•GetEditW(se_Name)

•GetEditH(se_Name)
Returns the position (X,Y) and width and height (W,H) of the edit box.

•GetEditFont(se_Name)
Returns a string that has 4 sections separated with CR/LF character pairs. The sections' order is Font Type, Size, Style and Color. The color will be 0-15 if it is one of RobotBASIC's primary colors or the RGB value if it is not. The Style will be 0 if no style, 1 if bold, 2 if italic and 4 if underlined and any binary combination of these. You can AND the number with the constants from the RobotBASIC Constants section (fs_Bold etc.). You can extract the different sections using Extract() or you can put them into an array mFromString.

•LastEdit()
Returns the name of the last edit box to have been changed since the last call of this function. If no edit box has been changed since the last interrogation using this function the returned string will be "" (zero length).

Note: Once this function has been used there will be no more last edit value (i.e. an empty string) until another edit is or the same one changed again.

See the use of this function in the example given in the Flow Control Statements section under the On[CONTROL] flow control group of statements. Also see the example under AddSlider.

•List Box Components

•List Box Commands

•AddListBox se_Name,ne_X,ne_Y{,ne_Width{,se_Items{,se_Hint}}}
Creates a List Box in the Terminal Screen at position ne_X,ne_Y with a width ne_W. The height is not changeable. If the width is not given or is less than 1 it will be assumed to be 100. se_Name is a name given to the box. This name should be unique and is used to identify the box for other *related* commands and functions.

A list box has a list of items one of which can be selected by the user. When the user clicks on the arrow of the box a list will be displayed (drop down/up). The user is then able to scroll to the required item and click on it to select it. The box will then close and the selected item text will be displayed in the box.

You specify the list of items all in one string (se_Items). This string will have to have CR/LF pairs separating the strings for each item in the list. You can use CrLf(). If the items string is not given then the list will have no items. You can add items programmatically using AddListBoxItem. You can also remove an item or clear all the items with RemoveListBoxItem and ClearListBox.

118

If se_Hint is given then the text will be displayed as a hint whenever the user rests the mouse over the box.

When the list is first created there will be no selected item and there will be no text in the box. You can force an item to be selected using SetListBox. Once the user selects an item there will be no way to select NO item. However, you can force a no item selection programmatically using SetListBox with an index of less than 1.

The color of the box's border and the color of the text will be according to the current default foreground and background colors. Use SetListBoxColor to change the color, and SetListBoxFont to set the font color and type.

The box will remain active until removed with RemoveListBox below.

You can determine the index number of the currently selected item using GetListBox() the text of the selected item can be obtained using GetListBoxText() and the entire list of items can be recovered using GetListBoxList(). You can obtain a particular item from the list with GetListBoxItem().

You can make the items in the box a sorted list with SortListBox and any item subsequently added will be positioned correctly in the list. However, this will make the index number meaningless. But you can always obtain the text of the selected item instead of the index.

You can remove the box from view and discard it with RemoveListBox. You can set the selected item programmatically with SetListBox.

You can disable/enable the user from selecting items from the box with the mouse using EnableListBox. Also you can highlight a particular list box with FocusListBox.

Note: **In all the functions and commands dealing with List boxes, the name of the box must be exactly the same as the se_Name used to create the box with AddListBox (case sensitive).**

Note: The name of the List box is ***case sensitive*** and ***should be unique*** for each box.

See mToString(), CrLf(), Substitute() and mFromString. Also see the buffer functions BuffWrite() and BuffRead().

Example:
```
ListName = "Test" \ s="" \CurrIndex = 0
data CBoxes;"Hidden","Enabled","Sorted"
for i=1 to 50
   if i < 4 then AddCheckBox CBoxes[i-1],250,45+i*25
```

```
            s=s+"Item"+i+crlf()
    next
    addlistbox ListName,10,100,200,s,"select one of these items"
    setlistbox ListName,1 \ setListBoxColor ListName,Black
    SetListBoxFont ListName,,,,white
    SetCheckBox CBoxes[0],ListBoxHidden(ListName)
    SetCheckBox CBoxes[1],ListBoxEnabled(ListName)
    SetCheckBox CBoxes[2],ListBoxSorted(ListName)
    data Buttons;"Set Selection","Add Item","Show List"
    AddButton Buttons[0],10,280,100 \AddButton Buttons[1],410,280,100
    AddButton Buttons[2],250,150,100
    xyText 10,220,"Index     Selected Text          Item To Add",,15
    AddEdit "Index",10,250,50,,CurrIndex \ AddEdit "Text" ,100,250,200
    IntegerEdit "Index"
    AddEdit "Item" ,400,250,140,,"Item To be Added"
    ReadOnlyEdit "Text",true
    while true
        n = GetListBox(ListName)
        setedit "Text",GetListBoxText(ListName)
        if n != CurrIndex then CurrIndex = n \ SetEdit "Index",n
        hidelistbox ListName,GetCheckBox(CBoxes[0])
        enablelistbox ListName,GetCheckBox(CBoxes[1])
        sortlistbox ListName,GetCheckBox(CBoxes[2])
        getbutton b
        n = tonumber(getedit("Index"),0)
        if b == Buttons[0] then setlistbox ListName,n
        if b == Buttons[1] then Addlistboxitem ListName,getedit("Item")
        if b == Buttons[2] then n=StringBox(GetListBoxList(ListName),"Testing..")
    wend
```

•RemoveListBox se_Name

Removes the List box and discards it.

•FocusListBox se_Name

Puts the focus on the List box and highlights the text in it if there is any. This enables the user to select items using arrows. If se_Name is an empty string "" then focus will be removed from any controls in the window that may currently have the focus.

Note: You cannot set focus to a disabled or hidden box.

•ClearListBox se_Name

Deletes all the items in the list box.

•EnableListBox se_Name{,true|false}

If false is given the List box will become disabled and the user cannot select items. If true is specified or is not given then it becomes possible to select items.

•HideListBox se_Name{,true|false}

Makes the List box invisible if true is specified or is not given and visible if false is given. An invisible List box is still a valid one (as opposed to a removed one). But it will not be visible. This is useful in certain situations where you want to make some boxes not available. You can then later make them available. If you remove a box you have to Add it again if you wish to make it available for use again. This command and EnableListBox are a more efficient way of making a box temporarily unusable.

•SortListBox se_Name{,true|false}

If true is specified or is not given, the items in the list box will be sorted and will stay sorted when items are added later. The list will not be unsorted when false is given, but, any items added later will be added to the bottom of the list. **Once the list is sorted it will not be unsorted to the original order when sorting is turned off.**

Beware of sorting and using GetListBox(). The index of the selected item will be according to the position of the selected item in the list of items as it is currently. If the list is sorted it may not be the order in which you added the item to the list in the original AddListBox or later with AddListBoxItem. You can use GetListBoxText() to get the actual selected item text. You can also obtain the entire list with GetListBoxList() and then the index will be meaningful since you now have the up to date list.

•SetListBox se_Name{,ne_Index}

Forces the selected item in the list to item number ne_Index. If ne_Index is not given it will be assumed to be 1. Beware of sorted lists since the item index may not be the item you expect. If ne_Index is greater than the number of items in the list then the last item will be selected. If ne_Index is less than 1 then no item will be selected and the text in the box will be blank.

•SetListBoxColor se_Name{,ne_Color}

This sets the box's background to the given color. If it is 0 to 15 then the RobotBASIC primary colors will be used (see the Constants section). If it is an RGB color value then it will be used. If ne_Color is not given then it will be Blue.

•SetListBoxDim se_Name{,ne_X{,ne_Y{,ne_W}}}

Sets the position and width of the list box.

•DeleteListBoxItem se_Name{,ne_Index}

Deletes an item from the list of items in the list box. ne_Index is the index of the item to be removed. If it is not given then it will be assumed to be 1. Beware of sorted lists since the item index may not be the item you expect. If it is greater than the number of items in the list then the last item will be removed. If it is less than 1 then no item will be removed.

•AddListBoxItem se_Name{,e_NewItem}

Will add an item (e_NewItem) to the list box. The item will be added to the bottom of the list unless the list has been set to be a sorted list using SortListBox. e_NewItem can be numeric or string. If it is numeric it will be made into a string. If it is not given it will be "".

•SetListBoxItems se_Name{,e_ItemsList}

Will set the whole items list in one go also replacing any previous items in the list. The list will be the CR/LF separated list of items as specified in e_ItemsList. e_ItemList can be numeric or string. If it is numeric it will be made into a string. If it is not given it will be "". If it is "" or is not given then there will be no items in the list, effectively erasing all the items in the list.

•**SetListBoxFont se_Name{,se_FontType{,ne_FontSize{,ne_FontStyle{,ne_FontColor}}}}**
Sets the type, size, style and color of the font of the list box. The details are the same as in xyText. If the type is not given or is "" then the font type will not be changed. If the size is not given or is < 1 then font size will not be changed. If the style value is not given or is < 0 then the font style will not be changed. If the color is not given or is < 0 then the font color will not be changed. To find out what font details the box currently has, use GetListBoxFont().

•<u>List Box Functions</u>

•**ListBoxEnabled(se_Name)**
Returns true if the List Box is enabled (i.e. the user can select items from it) and false if it is not.

•**ListBoxHidden(se_Name)**
Returns true if the List Box is hidden and false if it is visible.

•**ListBoxHasFocus(se_Name)**
Returns true if the list box has focus, or false otherwise. This function is useful in finding if the user is able to select items using the keyboard.

•**ListBoxSorted(se_Name)**
Returns true if the List Box is a sorted list and false if it is not.

•**ListBoxItemsCount(se_Name)**
Returns the number of items in the list box.

•**GetListBox(se_Name)**
Returns the index number of the selected item from the List Box. The number returned starts with 1 as the first button and 2 as the second and so on. The function returns 0 if no item is selected.

•**GetListBoxText(se_Name)**
Returns the text of the selected item from the List Box. The function returns an empty string if no item is selected.

•**GetListBoxItem(se_Name,ne_ItemIndex)**

Returns the text of item number ne_ItemIndex from the list box. If the index is less than 1 or there are no items in the list then an empty string will be returned. If it is more than the items count then the last item will be returned.

•GetListBoxList(se_Name)
Returns the entire list from the List Box. The list is one string with the items in the list separated with Cr/Lf pairs of characters.

•GetListBoxColor(se_Name)
Returns the color of the box's background. If the color is one of RobotBASIC's primary colors then its number will be returned (0-15), otherwise the number will be the RGB code of the color. Use ConsToClr() to convert RB color constants to RGB values.

•GetListBoxX(se_Name)
•GetListBoxY(se_Name)
•GetListBoxW(se_Name)
Returns the position (X,Y) and the width (W) of the box.

•GetListBoxFont(se_Name)
Returns a string that has 4 sections separated with CR/LF character pairs. The sections' order is Font Type, Size, Style and Color. The color will be 0-15 if it is one of RobotBASIC's primary colors or the RGB value if it is not. The Style will be 0 if no style, 1 if bold, 2 if italic and 4 if underlined and any binary combination of these. You can AND the number with the constants from the Constants section (fs_Bold etc.). You can extract the different sections using Extract() or you can put them into an array using mFromString. To set the font, use SetListBoxFont.

•LastListBox()
Returns the name of the last list box to have been clicked since the last call of this function. The name given is as given to the box when added using AddListBox. If no box has been clicked since the last interrogation using this function the returned string will be "" (zero length).

Note: Once this function has been used there will be no more last box value (i.e. an empty string) until another box or the same one is clicked again.

See the use of this function in the example given in the Flow Control Statements section under the On[CONTROL] flow control group of statements. Also see example under AddSlider.

•Radio Button Components

•Radio Button Commands

•AddRBGroup
se_Name,ne_X,ne_Y{,ne_Width{,ne_Height{,ne_Columns{,se_Buttons{,se_Caption{,se_Hint }}}}}}

Creates a Radio button Group in the Terminal Screen at position ne_X,ne_Y, with a width ne_W and height ne_H. The group will be set out in ne_Columns and as many rows as needed to list all the buttons. If the width and height are not given or are less than 1, they will be set to 100. If ne_Columns is not given or is less than 1 it will be set to 1.

se_Name is a name given to the group. This name should be unique and is used to identify the group for other *related* commands and functions.

A radio button group has a collection of buttons that can be checked. However, only one of the buttons from the group can be checked at a time. When the user checks a button, any previously checked button will be automatically unchecked.

There will be a text to the right of each button. You specify the number of buttons and their texts all in one string (se_Buttons). This string will have to have CR/LF pairs separating the strings for each button. You can use CrLf(). The number of buttons is automatically determined from the number of sub-strings in the overall string. You can add and remove buttons with AddRBGroupButton and DeletRBGroupButton or you can remove all with ClearRBGroup.

The group will have a border around it and a title that is the same as the name of the group (se_NAme), unless you override this with se_Caption. If se_Caption is not given or is an empty string ("") then the group box will have the title as the name. If it is given and is a space (" ") then the box will not have a title. If it is given and is not a space nor is an empty string then the title of the box will be se_Caption.

If se_Hint is given then the text will be displayed as a hint whenever the user rests the mouse over the group.

The color of the group's border and the color of the caption text will be according to the current default foreground and background colors. Use SetRBGroupColor to change the color. You cannot change the font size or style.

The group will remain active until removed with RemoveRBGroup below.

You can determine which radio button is selected with GetRBGroup() which returns the number of the button selected from among the list of buttons. If no button is selected then it returns 0.

You can remove the group from view and discard it with RemoveRBGroup. You can select a button programmatically with SetRBGroup.

Note: **In all the functions and commands dealing with radio button groups, the name of the group must be exactly the same as the se_Name used to create the group with AddRBGroup (case sensitive).**

Note: The name of the group is *__case sensitive__* and *__should be unique__* for each group.

See mToString(), CrLf(), Substitute() and mFromString. Also see the buffer functions BuffWrite() and BuffRead().

Example:
```
s="" \rbgName = "Testing" \ edName = "Index" \CurrIndex = 0
AddEdit edName,10,250,100,,0
data Buttons;"","Hide","Disable","Unhide","Enable"
xyText 2,220,"Select a Button or type its number below","Ms San Serif",15,fs_bold
for i=1 to 10
   if i < 3 then AddButton Buttons[i],250,50+40*i,100
   s=s+"Button"+i+crlf()
next
addrbgroup rbgName,10,10,230,200,3,s," ","select one of these options"
while true
   n = GetRBGroup(rbgName)
   if n != CurrIndex
      CurrIndex = n \ SetEdit edName,n
      xytext 120,250,GetrbGroupText(rbgName)+spaces(20),,20,fs_Bold
   endif
   if EditHasFocus(edName) && EditChanged(edName)
      n = Tonumber(GetEdit(edName),0)
      setrbGroup rbgName,n
   endif
   getbutton b
   if b == Buttons[1]
      hiderbgroup rbgName,!rbgrouphidden(rbgName)
      setbuttoncaption b,Buttons[rbgrouphidden(rbgName)*2+1]
   elseif b == Buttons[2]
      enablerbgroup rbgName,!rbgroupenabled(rbgName)
      setbuttoncaption b,Buttons[!rbgroupenabled(rbgName)*2+2]
   endif
wend
```

•RemoveRBGroup se_Name
   Removes the radio button group.

•FocusRBGroup se_Name
   Puts the focus on the group. This enables the user to check buttons using the keyboard. If se_Name is an empty string "" then focus will be removed from any controls in the window

that may currently have the focus.

Note: You cannot set focus to a disabled or hidden group.

•ClearRBGroup se_Name
Deletes all the buttons in the radio button group.

•EnableRBGroup se_Name{,true|false}
If false is given the radio button group will become disabled and the user cannot select a button from it. If true is specified or is not given then it becomes possible to select a button from the group.

•HideRBGroup se_Name{,true|false}
Makes the radio button group invisible if true is specified or is not given, and visible if false is given. An invisible group is still a valid one (as opposed to a removed one). But it will not be visible. This is useful in certain situations where you want to make some groups not available. You can then later make them available. If you remove a group you have to Add it again if you wish to make it available for use again. This command and EnableRBGroup are a more efficient way of making a group temporarily unusable.

•SetRBGroup se_Name{,ne_Index}
Checks one of the radio buttons in the group. If ne_Index is less than 1 then no button will be selected. Button numbering starts with 1, so the first button in the list is 1 and the second is 2 etc. If ne_Index is larger than the number of buttons in the group then the last button will be selected. If it is not given then it will be assumed to be 1.

The user can only select one of the buttons. There is no way to select NONE once the user has selected one. You can, however, select NONE programmatically using this command by making ne_Index a zero.

•SetRBGroupColor se_Name{,ne_Color}
This sets the group's background to the given color. If it is 0 to 15 then the RobotBASIC primary colors will be used (see the Constants section). If it is an RGB color value then it will be used. If it is not given then it will be Blue. You can change the font of the text next to the buttons using SetRBGroupFont.

•SetRBGroupColumns se_Name{,ne_NumColumns}
This sets the number of columns in the group. If ne_NumColumns is not given or is less than 1 then it will be 1.

•SetRBGroupDim se_Name{,ne_X{,ne_Y{,ne_W{,ne_H}}}}
Sets the position and width and height of the group.

•AddRBGroupButton se_Name{,e_ButtonCaption}
 Adds a button with the text e_ButtonCaption to the group. The button will be added as the last one in the group. e_ButtonCaption can be numeric or string. If it is numeric it will be made into a string. If it is not given it will be "". If it is "" then the button will not have a caption but there will still be a button.

•DeleteRBGroupButton se_Name{,ne_Index}
 Deletes the button with the index ne_Index from the group of buttons in the radio buttons group. If the index is not given then it will be assumed to be 1 If it is greater than the number of buttons in the list then the last button will be removed. If it is less than 1 then no button will be removed.

•SetRBGroupButtons se_Name{,e_ButtonsList}
 Will set the whole buttons list in one go also replacing any previous buttons in the list. The list will be the CR/LF separated list of button names as specified in e_ButtonsList. e_ButtonsList can be numeric or string. If it is numeric it will be made into a string. If it is not given it will be "". If it is "" then there will be no buttons in the group, effectively removing all the buttons.

•SetRBGroupFont se_Name{,se_FontType{,ne_FontSize{,ne_FontStyle{,ne_FontColor}}}}
 Sets the type, size, style and color of the font of the group. The details are the same as in xyText. If the type is not given or is "" then the font type will not be changed. If the size is not given or is < 1 then font size will not be changed. If the style value is not given or is < 0 then the font style will not be changed. If the color is not given or is < 0 then the font color will not be changed. To find out what font details the group currently has, use GetRBGroupFont().

•Radio Button Functions

•RBGroupEnabled(se_Name)
 Returns true if the radio button group is enabled (i.e. the user can select buttons from it) and false if it is not.

•RBGroupHidden(se_Name)
 Returns true if the radio button group is hidden and false if it is visible.

•RBGroupHasFocus(se_Name)
 Returns true if the group has focus, or false otherwise. This function is useful in finding if the user is able to check buttons using the keyboard..

•GetRBGroupCaption(se_Name)
 Returns the caption of the box around the radio button group.

•GetRBGroup(se_Name)

Returns the index number of the selected button from the radio button group. The number returned starts with 1 as the first button and 2 as the second and so on. The function returns 0 if no button is selected.

•GetRBGroupText(se_Name)

Returns the text of the checked button from the radio button group. The function returns an empty string if no button is selected.

•RBGroupItemsCount(se_Name)

Returns the number of buttons in the group.

•RBGroupNumColumns(se_Name)

Returns the number of columns the group is set to.

•GetRBGroupX(se_Name)
•GetRBGroupY(se_Name)
•GetRBGroupW(se_Name)
•GetRBGroupH(se_Name)

Returns the position (X,Y) and width (W) and height (H) of the group.

•GetRBGroupButton(se_Name,ne_Index)

Returns the text associated with button number ne_Index from the radio button group. If the index is less than 1 or there are no buttons in the list then an empty string will be returned. If it is more than the buttons count then the last button's text will be returned.

•GetRBGroupItems(se_Name)

Returns the entire list of buttons' text from the radio button group. The list is one string with the buttons' texts in the group separated with Cr/Lf pairs of characters.

•GetRBGroupColor(se_Name)

Returns the color of the group's background. If the color is one of RobotBASIC's primary colors then its number will be returned (0-15), otherwise the number will be the RGB code of the color.

•GetRBGroupFont(se_Name)

Returns a string that has 4 sections separated with CR/LF character pairs. The sections' order is Font Type, Size, Style and Color. The color will be 0-15 if it is one of RobotBASIC's primary colors or the RGB value if it is not. The Style will be 0 if no style, 1 if bold, 2 if italic and 4 if underlined and any binary combination of these. You can AND the number with the constants from the Constants section (fs_Bold etc.). You can extract the different sections using Extract() or you can put them into an array using mFromString. se_Name must be a valid radio button group name and is case sensitive. To set the font, use SetRBGroupFont.

•LastRBGroup()

Returns the name of the last radio button group to have been clicked since the last call of this function. The name given is as given to the group when added using AddRBGroup. If no group has been clicked since the last interrogation using this function the returned string will be "" (zero length).

Note: Once this function has been used there will be no more last group value (i.e. an empty string) until another group or the same one is clicked again.

See the use of this function in the example given in the Flow Control Statements section under the On[CONTROL] flow control group of statements. Also see example under AddSlider.

•Check Box Components

•Check Box Commands

•AddCheckBox
se_Name,ne_X,ne_Y{,se_Caption{,ne_Checked{,ne_LeftOrRight{,se_Hint}}}}

Creates a Check Box in the Terminal Screen at position ne_X,ne_Y. se_Name is a name given to the box. This name should be unique and is used to identify the box for other *related* commands and functions.

If se_Caption is not given or is an empty string ("") then the text that appears next to the box will be the same as the name of the box. If it is a space (" ") then there will be no text next to the box. Otherwise, se_Caption will be the text next to the box.

ne_Checked is optional and if not given or is false then the box will not be checked. If it is true then the box will be checked. se_Hint is an optional hint text. If given the text will appear when the user rests the mouse pointer over the box.

ne_LeftOrRight is optional and if not given or is false the text next to the box will be to the right of the box. If it is true then the text will be to the left of the box.

The color of the box's border and the color of the caption text will be according to the current default foreground and background colors. Use SetCheckBoxColor to change the color. You cannot change the font size or style. If you want to have more control over the caption then use no caption and use xyText to write the caption next to the box as desired.

The box will remain active until removed with RemoveCheckBox below.

129

You can determine if the check box is checked or not with GetCheckBox(), which returns true or false.

You can remove the box from view and discard it with RemoveCheckBox. You can check and uncheck the box programmatically with SetCheckBox.

You can disable/enable the box with the EnableCheckBox. If the box is disabled the user cannot check or uncheck the box. Also you can highlight a particular check box with FocusCheckBox.

Note: In all the functions and commands dealing with check boxes, the name of the box must be exactly the same as the se_Name used to create the box with AddCheckBox (case sensitive).

Note: The name of the check box is *__case sensitive__* and *__should be unique__* for each box.

Example: Also see the examples under AddSlider, AddMemo and AddListBox

```
data bx;"Option 1","Option 2","Option 3","Option 4"
addcheckbox bx[0],10,10 \addcheckbox bx[1],10,30,,false,true
addcheckbox bx[2],10,60,"testing",true,false,"Test hint"
addcheckbox bx[3],10,100," "
xyText 30,93,"Option 4","Times New Roman",20,fs_bold
data bt;"Check 1","Hide 2","Disable 3","Uncheck 1","Unhide 2","Enable 3"
for i=0 to maxdim(bt,1)/2-1
  addbutton bt[i],10+120*i,200,110
next
while true
    n = LastButton()
    if n==bt[0]
        SetCheckBox bx[0],!GetCheckBox(bx[0])
    elseif n==bt[1]
        HideCheckBox bx[1],!CheckBoxHidden(bx[1])
        setbuttoncaption bt[1],bt[checkboxhidden(bx[1])*3+1]
    elseif n==bt[2]
        EnableCheckBox bx[2],!CheckBoxEnabled(bx[2])
        setbuttoncaption bt[2],bt[!checkboxenabled(bx[2])*3+2]
    endif
    setbuttoncaption bt[0],bt[getcheckbox(bx[0])*3]
    m = MakeBit(0,0,getcheckbox(bx[0])) \ m = MakeBit(m,1,getcheckbox(bx[1]))
    m = MakeBit(m,2,getcheckbox(bx[2])) \ m = MakeBit(m,3,getcheckbox(bx[3]))
    xyText 250,10,"Status = "+bin(m,4),,20
wend
```

•**RemoveCheckBox se_Name**
    Removes the check box.

•**FocusCheckBox se_Name**
    Puts the focus on the check box and highlights the associated caption text if there is any. This enables the user to check/uncheck the box using the Space Bar. If se_Name is an empty string "" then focus will be removed from any control that may currently have the focus.

Note: You cannot set focus to a disabled or hidden box.

•**EnableCheckBox se_Name{,true|false}**
>If false is given the check box will become disabled and the user cannot check/uncheck it. If is true is specified or is not given, then it becomes possible to check/uncheck the box.

•**HideCheckBox se_Name{,true|false}**
>Makes the check box invisible if true is specified or is not given, and visible if false is given. An invisible check box is still a valid one (as opposed to a removed one). But it will not be visible. This is useful in certain situations where you want to make some boxes not available. You can then later make them available. If you remove a box you have to Add it again if you wish to make it available for use again. This command and EnableCheckBox are a more efficient way of making a box temporarily unusable.

•**SetCheckBox se_Name{,true|false}**
>Checks the check box if true is specified or is not given, and un-checks it if false is given.

•**SetCheckBoxDim se_Name{,ne_X{,ne_Y}}**
>Sets the position of the check box.

•**SetCheckBoxCaption se_Name{,e_NewCaption}**
>Changes the text next to the check box to e_NewCaption. e_NewCaption can be numeric or string. If it is numeric it will be made into a string. If it is not given it will be "". If it is not given or is "" the box will have no text next to it.

•**SetCheckBoxColor se_Name{,ne_Color}**
>This sets the box's background color. If it is 0 to 15 then the RobotBASIC primary colors will be used (see the Constants section). If it is an RGB color value then it will be used. If it is not given then it will be Blue.

•Check Box Functions

•**CheckBoxEnabled(se_Name)**
>Returns true if the check box is enabled (i.e. the user can check or uncheck it) and false if it is not.

•**CheckBoxHidden(se_Name)**
>Returns true if the check box is hidden and false if it is visible.

•**CheckBoxHasFocus(se_Name)**
>Returns true if the check box has focus, or false otherwise. This function is useful in finding if

the user is able to check the box using the keyboard..

•GetCheckBox(se_Name)

Returns true if the check box is checked and false if it is not.

•GetCheckBoxCaption(se_Name)

Returns the text next to the check box.

•GetCheckBoxColor(se_Name)

Returns the color of the box's background. If the color is one of RobotBASIC's primary colors then its number will be returned (0-15), otherwise the number will be the RGB code of the color.

•GetCheckBoxX(se_Name)
•GetCheckBoxY(se_Name)

Returns the position (X,Y)of the box.

•LastCheckBox()

Returns the name of the last check box to have been clicked since the last call of this function. The name given is as given to the box when added using AddCheckBox. If no box has been clicked since the last interrogation using this function the returned string will be "" (zero length).

Note: Once this function has been used there will be no more last check box value (i.e. an empty string) until another box or the same one is clicked again.

See the use of this function in the example given in the Flow Control Statements section under the On[CONTROL] flow control group of statements. Also see example under AddSlider.

•Slider/Progress Bar Components

•Slider/Progress Bar Commands

•AddSlider
se_Name,ne_X,ne_Y{,ne_Width{,ne_Min{,ne_Max{,ne_Vertical{,ne_TickFreq{,ne_BigIncr{, se_Hint}}}}}}}

Creates a Slider in the Terminal Screen at position ne_X,ne_Y with a width of ne_W. The height is not changeable. If ne_W is not given or is less than 1 it will be 100. se_Name is a name given to the slider. This name should be unique and is used to identify the slider for other *related* commands and functions.

A slider allows the user to indicate a required number or setting by sliding a dial. The slider can be vertical if ne_Vertical is true or horizontal (default) if it is not given or is false.

The slider will have a minimum and maximum as its limits and are specified by ne_Min and ne_Max respectively. If ne_Min is not given then 0 will be assumed. If ne_Max is not given 100 will be assumed. You can change these limits after creating the slider using SetSliderMax and SetSliderMin. You can also obtain their values using GetSliderMax() and GetSliderMin() (**see note below**). Both or either can be negative or positive.

The slider has a dial that can be moved by the user using the mouse. The dial can also be moved using the arrow keys when the slider has the focus, by increments of 1. Another way to move the dial is by clicking on the bar area to the left and right of the dial, or pressing the PgUp/Dn keys. This will cause the dial to move by increments as specified by ne_BigIncr. If ne_BigIncr is not given or is less than 1 then this increment will be set to 20% of the range (Max-Min).

The slider will have incremental ticks at the Top (Left if vertical) of the bar. The frequency of the ticks will be determined by ne_TickFreq. If it is not given or is less than 0 then the frequency of the ticks will be set at 10% of the range (Max-Min). If it is 0 there will be no ticks.

Note: The tick frequency and big increments quantity do not change once the slider is created. If later you change the Maximum and Minimum limits using SetSliderMax and SetSliderMin the tick frequency does not change nor does the big increment.

se_Hint if given will be displayed as a hint when the user rests the mouse over the bar.

When the slider is created the dial position will be at the minimum value. You can read the dial position using GetSliderPos() and you can set it using SetSliderPos.

You can make the dial visible/invisible using HideSliderDial. If the dial is invisible the user can still change its position using the Arrows and Page keys on the keyboard when the slider has the focus (you can indicate the dial position using the progress bar see later). You can also hide/unhide the slider and also enable or disable it using HideSlider and EnableSlider. A disabled slider cannot be used by the user to slide the dial neither with the mouse nor the keyboard, but it can be changed programmatically.

The slider can also be used as a **progress bar**. The inside area of the bar can display a colored area whose limits are set by SetSliderBarStart and SetSliderBarEnd. These limits will be set to within the Max and Min values if you specify values outside the range. You can aslo read the values of these limits with GetSliderBarStart() and GetSliderBarEnd().

You can also have the bar track the dial automatically by using ShowSliderBar. This will set the bar start to the minimum value and will set the end at the position of the dial and will track it automatically when the dial position is change by the user or programmatically even when the dial is not visible.

If the bar is not automatic you can still use it by setting its start and end values. This can be useful to, say, indicate an optimal range where the dial should be positioned. If the bar's start and end values are set to 0 the bar will be invisible.

The color of the slider's border will be as if it is a Button and you cannot change this.

The slider will remain active until removed with RemoveSlider below.

Also you can set the focus to a particular slider with FocusSlider.

Note: **In all the functions and commands dealing with Sliders, the name of the slider must be exactly the same as the se_Name used to create the slider with AddSlider (case sensitive).**

Note: The name of the Slider is ***case sensitive*** and ***should be unique*** for each slider.

Example: Also see the example under the On[Control] description in the Flow Control Statements section.

```
MainProgram:
    GoSub Initialization
    while true
        //wait for events
    wend
End
Initialization:
    SliderName = "Test"
    addslider SliderName,100,100,200,-20,300
    data CBoxes;"Hidden","Enabled","Hide Dial","Show Bar"
    data Buttons;"Set Dial Position","Animate","Stop"
    data Edits;"BSt",10,"BEn",130,"Pos",250
    AddButton Buttons[1],150,50,110
    AddButton Buttons[0],250,190,110
    for i=0 to 3
        AddCheckBox CBoxes[i],10+100*i,150,,0%0010 & 2^i
        if i < 3 then AddEdit Edits[i*2],Edits[i*2+1],220,110,0,0 \ IntegerEdit Edits[i*2]
    next
    Tmr = "Animate" \ AddTimer Tmr,150 \ SetTimer Tmr,off
    AddTimer "t2",100
    Pos = GetSliderPos(SliderName) \ FocusSlider SliderName
    xyText 90,180,"Type In","Time New Roman",10,fs_Bold
    xyText 20,200,"Bar Start"+spaces(15)+"Bar End","Time New Roman",10,fs_Bold
    xystring 90,80,GetSliderMin(SliderName)
    xystring 285,80,GetSliderMax(SliderName)
    OnButton    BHandler \ OnCheckBox  CBHandler \ OnEdit EdHandler
    OnTimer TmHandler \ OnAbort AbHandler
Return
TmHandler:
    lt = LastTimer()
```

```
     if lt=="t2"
        nn = GetSliderPos(SliderName)
        if nn != Pos then SetEDit "Pos",nn \ Pos = nn
     endif
     if lt==Tmr
        np = GetSliderPos(SliderName)+10
        if np > GetSliderMax(SliderName) then np = GetSliderMin(SliderName)
        SetSliderPos SliderName,np
     endif
     onTimer TmHandler
   Return
   EdHandler:
     le = LastEdit()  //must be done at least once before returning
     v = ToNumber(GetEdit(le),0)
     if le == Edits[0] then SetSliderBarStart SliderName,v
     if le == Edits[2] then SetSliderBarEnd SliderName,v
     OnEdit EdHandler  //must always be done before returning if
   Return              //you want to continue the event handling
   BHandler:
     lb = LastButton()    //must be done at least once before returning
     n =ToNumber(GetEdit("Pos"),0)
     if lb==Buttons[0] then SetSliderPos SliderName,n
     if lb==Buttons[1] then SetTimer Tmr \ RenameButton Buttons[1],Buttons[2]
     if lb==Buttons[2] then SetTimer Tmr,off \ RenameButton Buttons[2],Buttons[1]
     OnButton BHandler  //must always be done before returning if
   Return               //you want to continue the event handling
   CBHandler:
     lc = LastCheckBox()     //must be done at least once before returning
     cc = GetCheckBox(lc)
     if lc == CBoxes[0] then HideSlider SliderName,cc
     if lc == CBoxes[1] then EnableSlider SliderName,cc
     if lc == CBoxes[2] then HideSliderDial SliderName,cc
     if lc == CBoxes[3] then ShowSliderBar SliderName,cc
     OnCheckBox CBHandler  //must always be done before returning if
   Return                  //you want to continue the event handling
   AbHandler:
     ab = ErrMsg("Do you want to abort?","Test",MB_YESNO|MB_QUESTION)
     if ab == MB_YES then exit
     onabort AbHandler
   Return
```

•RemoveSlider se_Name

Removes the Slider.

•FocusSlider se_Name

Puts the focus on the slider and allows the user to slide the dial using the arrow and page keys. If se_Name is an empty string "" then focus will be removed from any controls in the Terminal Screen that may currently have the focus.

Note: You cannot set focus to a disabled or hidden slider.

•EnableSlider se_Name{,true|false}

If false is given the slider will become disabled and the user cannot change the dial position. It can still be changed using SetSliderPos. If true is specified or is not given then it becomes possible to slide the dial.

•HideSlider se_Name{,true|false}

Makes the slider invisible if true is specified or is not given, and visible if false is given. An invisible slider is still a valid one (as opposed to a removed one). But it will not be visible. This is useful in certain situations where you want to make some sliders not available. You can then later make them available. If you remove a slider you have to Add it again if you wish to make it available for use again. This command and EnableSlider are a more efficient way of making a slider temporarily unusable.

•SetSliderPos se_Name{,ne_PositionValue}

Forces the dial to the position even if it is not visible. This is how the dial can be controlled by the program. If it is not given then the position will be zero.

•SetSliderMin se_Name{,ne_NewValue}
•SetSliderMax se_Name{,ne_NewValue}

Sets the slider's maximum and minimum ranges. If it is not given then the minimum will be zero and the maximum 100.

•SetSliderBarStart se_Name{,ne_Value}
•SetSliderBarEnd se_Name{,ne_Value}

Sets the start and end positions of the progress bar. If you specify values outside the Maximum and Minimum of the slider then they will be overridden to stay within the range. If the value is not given it will be zero. If the start and end are both zero then the bar is not visible.

•HideSliderDial se_Name{,true|false}

If true is specified or is not given the dial will become invisible and the user cannot change the value of the position by using the mouse. However the user can still change the value of the position with the keyboard. You can also do it programmatically. There will be no indication of the position since the dial is not visible but if the progress bar is visible and is automatic then you will see it changing in response to the programmatic or keyboard changing of the position value. If false is given then it becomes visible again.

•ShowSliderBar se_Name{,true|false}

If true is specified or is not given then the inside of the slider will be highlighted from the minimum up to the current dial position. This effectively makes the bar into a progress bar that can follow with the user input or can be changed programmatically. If false is given then the bar will be removed and it will stop being automatic and will be reset to 0 on both limits.

•SetSliderDim se_Name{,ne_X{,ne_Y{,ne_W}}}

Sets the position and width of the slider.

•<u>Slider/Progress Bar Functions</u>

•SliderEnabled(se_Name)
Returns false if the slider is disabled and true if it is enabled.

•SliderHidden(se_Name)
Returns true if the slider is invisible and false if it is visible.

•GetSliderPos(se_Name)
Returns the value of the current position of the slider's dial.

•GetSliderMin(se_Name)
•GetSliderMax(se_Name)
Return the slider's maximum and minimum range values.

•GetSliderBarStart(se_Name)
•GetSliderBarEnd(se_Name)
Returns the progress bar high light range start and end values.

•SliderDialHidden(se_Name)
Returns true if the slider's dial is not visible and true if it is.

•SliderBarHidden(se_Name)
Returns true if the progress bar follows the dial's position automatically and false if not.

•GetSliderX(se_Name)
•GetSliderY(se_Name)
•GetSliderW(se_Name)
Returns the position (X,Y) and width (W) of the slider.

•SliderHasFocus(se_Name)
Returns true if the slider has focus, or false otherwise. This function is useful in finding if the user is able to move the slider using the arrow keys.

•LastSlider()
Returns the name of the last slider to have been changed since the last call of this function. The name given is as given to the slider when added using AddSlider. If no slider has been changed since the last interrogation using this function the returned string will be "" (zero length).

Note: Once this function has been used there will be no more last slider value (i.e. an empty string) until another slider or the same one is clicked again.

See the use of this function in the example given in the Flow Control Statements section under the On[CONTROL] flow control group of statements. Also see example under AddSlider.

•Spinner Components

•Spinner Commands

•AddSpinner
se_Name,ne_X,ne_Y{,ne_W{,ne_H{,ne_Min{,ne_Max{,ne_Incr{,ne_Vertical{,ne_Wrap{,se_Hint}}}}}}}}

Creates a Spinner in the Terminal Screen at position ne_X,ne_Y with a width of ne_W and height ne_H. ne_Name is a name given to the Spinner. This name should be unique and is used to identify the Spinner for other *related* commands and functions. If ne_W and ne_H are not given or are less than 1 then the spinner will have a default width of 17 and height 25.

A Spinner allows the user to increment/decrement a value by a certain incremental value (ne_Incr) between a minimum (ne_Min) and a maximum (ne_Max). The maximum value can be +32767 and the minimum -32768. You cannot exceed these values. The increment defaults to 1 if not given or is less than 1. The maximum and minimum values are set to 100 and 0 respectively if not given.

The Spinner can be vertical if ne_Vertical is true or horizontal (default) if it is not given or is false.

The value of the spinner cannot be incremented beyond the limits, but if ne_Wrap is set to true then wrapping around will happen (min → max, max → min). If it is not given or is false then no wrapping will occur and when a limit is reached the value of the spinner stays at the limit.

se_Hint if given will be displayed as a hint when the user rests the mouse over the bar.

When the spinner is created the value of it will be the minimum limit. You can change the value of the spinner using SetSpinner, you can also change the minimum, maximum, increment and wrap using SetSpinnerMin/Max/Incr/Wrap.

You can also hide/unhide or enable/disable the control using EnableSpinner and HideSpinner. And you can remove it with RemoveSpinner.

You can also interrogate the spinner for its min, max, increment, wrap and current value using GetSpinner(), GetSpinnerMin/Max/Incr/Wrap(). Also you can find out if it is hidden or enabled using SpinnerHidden() and SpinnerEnabled().

The color of the Spinner will be as if it is a Button and you cannot change this.

A spinner can be easily associated with a particular Edit box by using the OnSpinner event trapping and then in the event handler you can set the edit box to the current value of the spinner. Also in the Edit box's handler you can set the spinner value to reflect any editing of the edit box to keep the spinner and the edit box in synchronization (see example).

Note: **In all the functions and commands dealing with Spinners, the name of the Spinner must be exactly the same as the se_Name used to create the Spinner with AddSpinner (case sensitive).**

Note: The name of the Spinner is *case sensitive* and *should be unique* for each Spinner.

Example: Also see the example under AddMemo.
```
addedit "ed1",10,10,90,0,0,"0" \ IntegerEdit "ed1"
addspinner "sp1",100,10,0,0,-100,300,1
addspinner "sp2",120,10,25,25,-100,300,10,1
SetSpinner "sp1",0 \ SetSpinner "sp2",0
onspinner spHandler \ onedit eHandler
while true  //wait on events
   xystring
10,100,"VSpinner=",getspinner("sp1"),spaces(20)
   xystring
10,120,"HSpinner=",getspinner("sp2"),spaces(20)
wend
end
spHandler:
   v = getspinner(LastSpinner())
   setedit "ed1",v
   setspinner "sp1",v
   setspinner "sp2",v
   onspinner spHandler
return
eHandler:
   vv = tonumber(getedit(LastEdit()),0)
   setspinner "sp1",vv
   setspinner "sp2",vv
   onedit eHandler
return
```

•RemoveSpinner se_Name
Removes the Spinner.

•FocusSpinner se_Name

Puts the focus on the spinner. This enables the user to increment/decrement the value using the keyboard. If se_Name is an empty string "" then focus will be removed from any controls in the window that may currently have the focus.

Note: You cannot set focus to a disabled or hidden spinner.

•EnableSpinner se_Name{,true|false}

If false is given the Spinner will become disabled and the user cannot click it. It can still be changed using SetSpinner. If true is specified or is not given then it becomes possible to click on it.

•HideSpinner se_Name{,true|false}

Makes the Spinner invisible if true is specified or is not given and visible if false is given. An invisible Spinner is still a valid one (as opposed to a removed one). But it will not be visible. This is useful in certain situations where you want to make some Spinners not available. You can then later make them available. If you remove a Spinner you have to Add it again if you wish to make it available for use again. This command and EnableSpinner are a more efficient way of making a Spinner temporarily unusable.

•SetSpinner se_Name{,ne_Position}

Forces the value of the spinner position even if it is not visible or disabled. If ne_Position is not given it will be zero.

•SetSpinnerMin se_Name{,ne_NewValue}
•SetSpinnerMax se_Name{,ne_NewValue}

Sets the Spinner's maximum and minimum ranges. If the value is not given then the minimum will be zero and the maximum will be 100.

•SetSpinnerIncr se_Name{,ne_Value}

Sets the increment by which the value of the spinner is incremented/decremented when the spinner is clicked. If it is not given then it will be assumed to be 1.

•SetSpinnerWrap se_Name{,true|false}

Sets whether the value of the spinner will wrap around when it is incremented/decremented beyond the limits. If true is specified or is not given then wrap is enabled, if false is given then no wrapping will occur.

•SetSpinnerDim se_Name{,ne_X{,ne_Y{,ne_W{,ne_H}}}}

Sets the position and width and height of the spinner.

•<u>Spinner Functions</u>

•SpinnerEnabled(se_Name)
   Returns false if the Spinner is disabled and true if it is enabled.

•SpinnerHidden(se_Name)
   Returns true if the Spinner is invisible and false if it is visible.

•SpinnerHasFocus(se_Name)
   Returns true if the spinner has focus, or false otherwise. This function is useful in finding if the user is able to change its value using the keyboard..

•GetSpinner(se_Name)
   Returns the value of the current value of the Spinner.

•GetSpinnerMin(se_Name)
•GetSpinnerMax(se_Name)
   Return the Spinner's maximum and minimum range values.

•GetSpinnerIncr(se_Name)
   Return the Spinner's increment value.

•GetSpinnerWrap(se_Name)
   Return true if the Spinner is set to wrap around when limits are reached and false if it is not.

•GetSpinnerX(se_Name)
•GetSpinnerY(se_Name)
•GetSpinnerW(se_Name)
•GetSpinnerH(se_Name)
   Returns the position (X,Y) and width (W) and height (H) of the spinner.

•LastSpinner()
   Returns the name of the last Spinner to have been clicked since the last call of this function. The name given is as given to the Spinner when added using AddSpinner. If no Spinner has been changed since the last interrogation using this function the returned string will be "" (zero length).

   Note: Once this function has been used there will be no more last Spinner value (i.e. an empty string) until another Spinner or the same one is clicked again.

   See the use of this function in the example given in the Flow Control Statements section under the On[CONTROL] flow control group of statements. Also see example under AddSpinner.

•Memo Box Components

•Memo Box Commands

•AddMemo se_Name,ne_X,ne_Y{,ne_W{,ne_H{,se_Text{,se_Hint}}}}

Creates a Memo box in the Terminal Screen at position ne_X,ne_Y with a width of ne_W and Height ne_H. ne_W or ne_H are not given or are less than 1 then they will be set to 100. se_Name is a name given to the box. This name should be unique and is used to identify the box for other *related* commands and functions.

A memo box is an edit box that allows multiple lines and can have horizontal and vertical scroll bars to scroll the box to see text longer than the width and/or the height of the box. The box has no scroll bars by default but you can add vertical, horizontal, or both using SetMemoScrollBars.

The color of the box's background and the color of the text will be according to the current default foreground and background colors. You can change them using SetMemoFont and SetMemoColor. You can change the type, size, style and color of the font of the text using SetMemoFont. The box has a border by default but can be turned off with BorderMemo.

If there is no horizontal scroll bar the text will word wrap around if it reaches the width limit of the box. Word wrap is on by default and you can turn it off using WrapMemo. If the horizontal scroll bar is set on then no word wrap will occur regardless of wrap is set on or off.

The user can type text in the box, but you can also populate it programmatically using AddMemoLine and you can remove any line using DeleteMemoLine or clear all the lines with ClearMemo. Also when you create the box you can have text in it by specifying se_Text. This is a string with all the lines in one string separated with CR/LF character pairs.

se_Hint is a hint text that will be displayed when the user rests the mouse over the box. It is an empty string by default.

The memo box can be made to be a display box with either EnableMemo or ReadOnlyMemo. A disabled memo cannot be entered, while a read only one can be entered and scrolled and text can be copied from it. You can also hide a memo with HideMemo.

You can get information about the memo with functions like GetMemoFont(), GetMemoColor(), MemoLinesCount(), etc.

You can get the whole text content as one string with the lines as substrings separated with CR/LF character pairs with GetMemoText() and GetMemoLine() allows you to get a particular line.

The box will remain active until removed with RemoveMemo below.

Note: **In all the functions and commands dealing with Memos, the name of the box must be exactly the same as the se_Name used to create the box with AddMemo (case sensitive).**

Note: The name of the memo is *case sensitive* and *should be unique* for each box.

See mToString(), CrLf(), Substitute() and mFromString. Also see the buffer functions BuffWrite() and BuffRead().

Example:
```
MainProgram:
    GoSub Initialization
    while true
        //wait for events
    wend
End
Initialization:
    addmemo "m",20,20,500,400
    bordermemo "m",0 \ setmemocolor "m",RGB(204,204,255)
    setmemoscrollbars "m",1 \ setMemoFont "m",,13,fs_Bold
    Rectanglewh 18,18,510,520,black,black
    Rectanglewh 15,15,510,520,black,darkgray
    Line 19,425,519,425,3,gray
    AddMemoLine "m","Enter text here" \ FocusMemo "m"
    SetColor Black,DarkGray
    AddCheckBox "Wrap",22,430,,1
    AddCheckBox "Vert. Scroll Bar",22,450,,1
    AddCheckBox "Horz. Scroll Bar",22,470
    SetCheckBoxColor "Wrap",darkgray
    AddButton "Clear Memo",440,430,80 \ AddButton "Memo Color",440,460,80
    AddEdit "fntS",150,450,50,0,13 \ IntegerEdit "fntS"
    AddSpinner "fntS",203,450 \ setspinner "fntS",13
    xyText 150,435,"Font Size","Ms Sn Serif",8,fs_Bold
    data Fonts;"Courier New","Times New Roman","MS Sans Serif","Arial"
    AddListBox "fntT",225,430,120,mToString(Fonts)
    SetListBox "fntT",3 \ SetListBoxColor "fntT",white
    AddCheckBox "Bold",350,430,,1
    AddCheckBox "Italic",350,450
    AddCheckBox "Underlined",350,470
    AddButton "Font Color",230,465,100
    AddButton "Read From File",120,505,120
    AddButton "Save To File",260,505,120
    onSpinner sHandler \ onButton bHandler \ onCheckBox cHandler
    onEdit eHandler \ onListBox lHandler
Return
lHandler:
    ll = LastListBox() \ fntT = GetListBoxText("fntT")
    setmemofont "m",fntT
    onListBox lHandler
Return
eHandler:
    le = LastEdit() \ fntS= ToNumber(getedit(le),1)
```

```
      setspinner le,fntS \ setmemofont "m",,fntS
      OnEdit eHandler
   Return
   cHandler:
      lc = LastCheckBox() \ nn = getcheckbox(lc)
      if lc == "Wrap" then wrapmemo "m",nn
      if left(lc,1) == "V"
          if nn then setmemoscrollbars "m",setbit(memoscrollbars("m"),0)
          if !nn then setmemoscrollbars "m",clrbit(memoscrollbars("m"),0)
      endif
      if left(lc,1) == "H"
          if nn then setmemoscrollbars "m",setbit(memoscrollbars("m"),1)
          if !nn then setmemoscrollbars "m",clrbit(memoscrollbars("m"),1)
      endif
      if Left(lc,1) == "B" || Left(lc,1) == "I" || Left(lc,1) == "U"
          fntSt = getCheckBox("Bold")|(getCheckBox("Italic")*2)
          fntSt = fntSt |(getCheckBox("Underlined")*4) \ setmemofont "m",,,fntSt
      endif
      onCheckBox cHandler
   Return
   bHandler:
      lb = LastButton()
      if lb == "Clear Memo" then clearmemo "m"
      if lb == "Memo Color" then setmemocolor "m",promptcolor(constoclr(getmemocolor("m")))
      if lb == "Font Color"
          fc = promptcolor(constoclr(tonumber(extract(getmemofont("m"),crlf(),4))))
          setmemofont "m",,,,,fc
      elseif lb == "Save To File"
          fln = FileSave("*.txt")
          if fln !=""
              flh = FileCreate(fln)
              x = FileWrite(flh,GetMemoText("m"))
              x = FileClose(flh)
          endif
      elseif lb == "Read From File"
          fln = FilePrompt("*.txt")
          if fln !=""
              flh = FileOpen(fln,fo_Read|fo_DenyNone)
              x = FileRead(flh,FileSize(flh))
              SetMemoText "m",x
              x = FileClose(flh)
          endif
      endif

      onButton bHandler
   return
   sHandler:
      ls = LastSpinner() \ fntS = GetSpinner(ls)
      setedit ls,fntS \ setmemofont "m",,fntS
      onSpinner sHandler
   return
```

•RemoveMemo se_Name
Removes the memo.

•FocusMemo se_Name
Puts the focus on the Memo. This enables the user to start typing lines. If se_Name is an empty string "" then focus will be removed from any controls in the window that may currently have the focus.

Note: You cannot set focus to a disabled or hidden memo.

•ClearMemo se_Name

Deletes all the lines in the memo.

•EnableMemo se_Name{,true|false}

If false is given the Memo will become disabled and the user cannot type or select text from the memo. If true is specified or is not given then it becomes possible to type lines.

•HideMemo se_Name{,true|false}

Makes the Memo invisible if true is specified or is not given and visible if false is given. An invisible Memo is still a valid one (as opposed to a removed one). But it will not be visible. This is useful in certain situations where you want to make some memo not available. You can then later make it available. If you remove a memo you have to Add it again if you wish to make it available for use again. This command and EnableMemo are a more efficient way of making a memo temporarily unusable.

•ReadOnlyMemo se_Name{,true|false}

If true is specified or is not given, the Memo will become disabled and the user cannot type text. But the user can still scroll through the text in the memo and select and copy parts of it. If false is given then it becomes possible to type lines.

•WrapMemo se_Name{,true|false}

If true is specified or is not given, *and the memo does not have a horizontal scroll bar* then when the user types text that will make a line longer than can be displayed in the width of the memo, then a word wrap to the next line will occur. This is on by default. If false is given *or there is a horizontal scroll bar* then the text will go beyond the width of the memo and will not be visible. You can of course scroll the memo box using the scroll bar if there is one.

•BorderMemo se_Name{,true|false}

If true is specified or is not given, the Memo will have a border around it and will make the memo appear slightly sunken into the screen. If false is given there will be no border.

•SetMemoColor se_Name{,ne_Color}

This sets the memo's background color. If it is 0 to 15 then the RobotBASIC primary colors will be used (see the Constants section). If it is an RGB color value then it will be used. If it is not given then it will be Blue.

•SetMemoDim se_Name{,ne_X{,ne_Y{,ne_W{,ne_H}}}}

Sets the position and width and height of the memo.

•DeleteMemoLine se_Name{,ne_LineNumber}

Deletes a line of text from the memo. ne_LineNumber is the index of the line to be removed. If it is not given then it will be assumed to be 1. If it is greater than the number of lines in the list then the last line will be removed. If it is less than 1 the no line will be removed.

•SetMemoScrollBars se_Name{,ne_Value}

If ne_Value is 0 there will be no scroll bars. If it is 1 there will be a vertical one, if 2 a horizontal one and if 3 there will be both. If it is not given it will be set to 1.

•AddMemoLine se_Name{,e_Text}

Adds a line of text to the end of the current text in the memo. e_Text can be numeric or string. If it is numeric it will be made into a string. If it is not given it will be "". If it is "" the line will be added but will have no text.

•SetMemoText se_Name{,e_Text}

Deletes any text in the memo and replaces it with se_Text. e_Text can contain substrings separated with CR/LF character pairs. If it does then each substring will occupy a line in the Memo. e_Text can be numeric or string. If it is numeric it will be made into a string. If it is not given it will be "". If it is "" then the memo will not contain any text effectively erasing all the text in the memo.

•SetMemoFont se_Name{,se_FontType{,ne_FontSize{,ne_FontStyle{,ne_FontColor}}}}

Sets the type, size, style and color of the font of the memo. The details are the same as in xyText. If the type is not given or is "" then the font type will not be changed. If the size is not given or is < 1 then font size will not be changed. If the style is not given or is < 0 then the font style will not be changed. If the color is not given or is < 0 then the font color will not be changed. To find out what font details the memo currently has use GetMemoFont().

•SetMemoSelection
se_Name{,ne_LineNumber{,ne_CharacterNumber{,ne_SelectionLength}}}}

Set the cursor inside the memo to the Line number ne_LineNumber at character number ne_CharacterNumber. Then it highlights ne_SelectionLength characters in that line starting at the ne_CharacterNumber character.

If the line number or the character number is not given or is less than 1 then it will be set to 1. Character and line numbering start with 1. If selection length is not given or is less than 1 then there will be no highlighted characters.

If ne_LineNumber is larger than the number of lines then the cursor would be positioned past the last line. If ne_CharacterNumber is greater than the number of characters in the line then the cursor would be positioned after the last character in the line. Also there would be no highlighted characters.

If the ne_CharacterNumber+ne_SelectionLength is longer than the length of text in the line then highlighting will only be to the last character in the line.

•SetMemoSelected se_Name{,ne_StartCharPosition{,ne_NumCharacters}}

Sets a section of text as highlighted text. ne_StartCharPosition specifies the char number in the OVERALL memo text. ne_SelectionLength specifies the number of characters to be selected.

As opposed to SetMemoSelection this command treats ALL of the text in the Memo as one string and rather than selecting the text by line number and character position within the line. This command will select text over multiple line as well.

If the ne_StartCharPosition is not given or is less than 1 it will be made to be 1. Character counting starts at 1.
If ne_NumCharacters is less than 0 or is not given it will be made 0.
If ne_NumCharacters is 0 then there will be no selected text but the cursor will be positioned just before the character indicated.

•Memo Box Functions

•MemoChanged(se_Name)

Returns true if the text inside the memo box with the name has changed since the last time you have interrogated its status using this function. If it has not changed the function will return false.

•MemoEnabled(se_Name)

Returns true if the Memo is enabled (i.e. the user can type in it) and false if it is not.

•MemoHidden(se_Name)

Returns true if the Memo is hidden and false if it is visible.

•MemoWrap(se_Name)

Returns true if the Memo has word wrap set and false if not.

•MemoReadonly(se_Name)

Returns true if the Memo is set to read only and false if not.

•MemoBorder(se_Name)

Returns true if the Memo has the border turned on, and false if not.

•MemoScrollBars(se_Name)

Returns the code for what combination of scroll bars are turned on. 0= none, 1=Vertical, 2=Horizontal and 3= Both.

•GetMemoColor(se_Name)
Returns the color of the memo's background. If the color is one of RobotBASIC's primary colors then its number will be returned (0-15), otherwise the number will be the RGB code of the color.

•GetMemoX(se_Name)
•GetMemoY(se_Name)
•GetMemoW(se_Name)
•GetMemoH(se_Name)
Returns the position (X,Y) and width (W) and height (H) of the memo.

•MemoLinesCount(se_Name)
Returns the number of lines in the memo.

•GetMemoText(se_Name)
Returns the text in the Memo. The various lines will be separated with a CR/LF character pair.

•GetMemoSelection(se_Name)
Returns the text in the Memo that is currently highlighted. If there is none then "" will be returned.

•GetMemoLineNo(se_Name)
Returns the number of the line where the cursor currently is inside the memo.

•GetMemoCharNo(se_Name)
Returns the number of the character in the line where the cursor currently is inside the memo.

•GetMemoCharPos(se_Name)
Returns the number of the character just after the position of the cursor or the number of the first character in the selected text. First character is .

•GetMemoLine(se_Name,ne_LineNumber)
Returns the text in line number ne_LineNumber from the Memo. If it is less than 1 or there are no lines in the memo then an empty string will be returned. If it is more than the lines count then the last line will be returned.

•GetMemoFont(se_Name)
Returns a string that has 4 sections separated with CR/LF character pairs. The sections' order is Font Type, Size, Style and Color. The color will be 0-15 if it is one of RobotBASIC's

primary colors or the RGB value if it is not. The Style will be 0 if no style, 1 if bold, 2 if italic and 4 if underlined and any binary combination of these. You can AND the number with the constants from the Constants section (fs_Bold etc.). You can extract the different sections using Extract() or you can put them into an array using mFromString. To set the font, use SetMemoFont.

•MemoHasFocus(se_Name)

Returns true if the user is inside the memo box entering text, or false otherwise. This function is useful in finding if the user is inside a particular memo box.

•LastMemo()

Returns the name of the last memo to have been changed since the last call of this function. The name given is as given to the memo when added using AddMemo. If no memo has been clicked since the last interrogation using this function the returned string will be "" (zero length).

Note: Once this function has been used there will be no more last memo value (i.e. an empty string) until another memo or the same one is clicked again.

See the use of this function in the example given in the Flow Control Statements section under the On[CONTROL] flow control group of statements.

•Timer Components

•Timer Commands

•AddTimer se_Name{,ne_Period}

Creates a Timer with the given period in milliseconds. If it is not given or is less than 1 it will default to 1000 milliseconds (1 sec). Once created the timer is turned on. You can turn a timer on/off with SetTimer. se_Name is a name given to the Timer. This name should be unique and is used to identify the Timer for other *related* commands and functions.

Once created a timer will start counting every period. So if you set the period to 250 ms then the timer will increment a count (Ticks which is zero when the timer is created) every 250 ms. So if you read the ticks with GetTimerTicks() and it is 20 then you know that $20*250 = 5000$ ms have elapsed since the last time the timer ticks were set to 0 (i.e. 5 seconds). You can set the ticks count to any number at any time using SetTimerTicks.

You can change the period of the timer using SetTimerPeriod. However when you do this the ticks count will be reset to 0 and the timer will be turned off. To use it you have to turn it on with SetTimer.

Every time you turn the timer on using SetTimer the ticks count will be reset to 0. However, the ticks count is not changed when the timer is turned off.

You can discard a timer with RemoveTimer. Also you can interrogate the timer for its on/off status with the TimerIsOn() and you can find out the period with GetTimerPeriod().

Note: In all the functions and commands dealing with Timers, the name of the Timer must be exactly the same as the se_Name used to create the Timer with AddTimer (case sensitive).

Note: The name of the Timer is ***case sensitive*** and ***should be unique*** for each Timer.

Example: Also see the examples under AddSlider and AddMemo.
```
addtimer "t1",100
addtimer "t2",500
addtimer "t3",1000
addedit "t3",10,10,100,0,0
addedit "t2",120,10,100,0,0
addedit "t1",240,10,100,0,0
ontimer tHandler
while true
    //just wait for events
wend
tHandler:
    n = lasttimer() \ setedit n,gettimerticks(n)
    ontimer tHandler
return
```

•RemoveTimer se_Name
Removes the Timer. Once removed the timer is not valid for use any longer.

•SetTimer se_Name{,true|false}
Turns the timer On if true is specified or is not given. If false is given the timer is turned off and it will not increment its ticks count until turned back on again.

•SetTimerPeriod se_Name{,ne_Period}
Sets the Timer's period in milliseconds. If the period is not given it will default to 1000 (1 sec). ***When you use this command the timer will be turned off and the ticks count will be reset to zero. To use the timer you have to turn it back on with SetTimer.***

•SetTimerTicks se_Name{,ne_Count}
Sets the Timer's tick count. If it is not given it will default to 0.

•Timer Functions

•TimerIsOn(se_Name)

150

Returns true if the timer is ticking, false otherwise.

•GetTimerPeriod(se_Name)

Returns the Timer's period (milliseconds).

•GetTimerTicks(se_Name)

Returns the Timer's ticks count.

•LastTimer()

Returns the name of the **_last_** Timer to have incremented its ticks count since the last call of this function. The name given is as given to the Timer when added using AddTimer. If no Timer has ticked since the last interrogation using this function the returned string will be "" (zero length).

Note: Once this function has been used there will be no more Last Timer value (i.e. an empty string) until another Timer or the same one ticks again.

See the use of this function in the example given in the Flow Control Statements section under the On[CONTROL] flow control group of statements. Also see example under AddTimer.

Screen & Bitmap Graphics

Note: See the notes at the top of the Standard User Interfacing section.

Note: With all the commands and functions that require a bitmap file name, if you specify a file extension other than ".Bmp" RB will change this extension automatically to ".Bmp". If you do not specify an extension RB will automatically assume that the extension is ".Bmp". So to work with a Bit Map file it has to have a ".Bmp" extension and when specifying its name in the commands you can give the full name with or without the extension. To convert files of different types to a BitMap format see ToBMP.

•Information About Colors

All the graphics commands that allow for color values or return color values will allow you to enter an integer for the color value. If the value is 0 to 15 then the color from the list of colors in the RobotBASIC Constants section will be used. Also if the color returned is one from the list of colors in the RobotBASIC Constants section then its number (0 to 15) will be returned. Any other color (not in the list of colors in the RobotBASIC Constants section) will be according to an integer value that corresponds to the combination of Red-Green-Blue values. The integer number is actually the integer value of the hexadecimal number 0xBBGGRR where BB is the value of the amount of blue to be used to make the color (00 to FF i.e. 0 to 255), likewise for the green and red. You can make a color number using RGB() or you can get a number (at design time) from the colors dialog invoked from the editor screen from the Help-Colors menu. This dialog will allow you to choose a color and will copy its value to the Clipboard. Use *Ctrl-V* to paste this value within your code. At run time you can obtain a color value from the same dialog by using PromptColor() which will allow the user of your program to choose a color. You can convert the constant color values (0 to 15) to an RGB color number using ConsToClr(). You can obtain the values for the red/green/blue components of any color code (full RGB code or the 0-15 constants) by using RedValue(), GreenValue() and BlueValue().

•Color Manipulation

•RGB(ne_RedValue,ne_GreenValue,ne_BlueValue)

Returns a number that is the color value for the color represented by the intensity combination of ne_Red , ne_Green and ne_Blue. RGB(0,0,0) is the black color. RGB(255,255,255) is the white color. Various shades are created by varying the parameters between 0 and 255. RGB(255,0,0) is red, RGB(0,255,0) is green, RGB(0,0,255) is blue, RGB(255,255,0) is yellow, RGB(0,255,255) is cyan, RGB(255,0,255) is magenta, RGB(128,128,128) is gray and so on. Also see PromptColor() below and also the menu *Help/Color* in the Editor screen menu. Also see the discussion about colors above. See below for an example.

•ConsToClr(ne_ColorConstantValue)

Returns the RGB value of the color constant as specified in the RobotBASIC Constants section. If it is a valid color constant (or the number 0 to 15) the value returned will be the RGB value of that color. If it is not a valid color constant the returned value will be the value given. Also see the discussion about colors above. See below for examples.

•PromptColor({ne_DefaultColor})

Causes a dialog box to pop up and allow the user to select a color. Returns a number that is the color value selected. Also see RGB() above. Also see the discussion about colors above. Example:

```
c = PromptColor(ConsToClr(blue))   //prompt with default blue
color
r = RedValue(c) \ g = GreenValue(c) \ b = BlueValue(c)
Rectangle 100,100,200,200,c, c   //rectangle with color
chosen
c = RGB(r/2,g/2,b/2)               //make color half as bright
Rectangle 300,300,400,400,c,c     //rectangle with color
twice darker than chosen
```

•RedValue(ne_Color)
•GreenValue(ne_Color)
•BlueValue(ne_Color)

Returns the Red, Green or Blue saturation of the RGB (or constant color as defined in the RobotBASIC Constants section) color.

An RGB color is made up of saturation values for the three primary colors Red/Green/Blue. Using RGB() above will allow you to create a color as described above. However, if you read a color from the screen using ReadPixel you will either get a constant value (0-15) if the color is one of the 16 colors defined in the RobotBASIC Constants section, or a number that represents the RGB value. Using this command you can obtain the individual saturations for each primary color from the returned value.

b = RedValue(n) is equivalent to: b = GreenValue(n) is equivalent to: b = BlueValue(n) is equivalent to:

b = ConsToClr(n) & 255   b = (ConsToClr(n) >> 8) & 255   b = (ConsToClr(n) >> 16) & 255

```
print RedValue(RGB(10,20,200))     //should return 10
print GreenValue(RGB(10,20,200))   //should return 20
print BlueValue(RGB(10,20,200))    //should return 200
```

Note: RedValue(RGB(10,20,200)) should return 10 but on some machines it may not. Some machines will change the color value to fit the nearest color that can be displayed and may not be exactly the value you specified. RGB() returns the nearest value for the color and may not be what you specified and thus RedValue() will return the modified red value.

•FactorColor(ne_Color,ne_Factor)

Returns the value of ne_Color made brighter or darker by the factor ne_Factor. ne_Factor can be a floating point number >=0. If it is less than 0 it will be made positive. If it is less than 1 the color will be made darker. If it is greater than 1 the color will be made brighter. ne_Color can be either a RobotBASIC color constant or an RGB value, however the value returned is always an RGB value.

•mCombineClr a_RedValues,a_GreenValues,a_BlueValues,a_RGBvalues

a_Red, a_Green, a_Blue have to be two-dimensional arrays with the exact same dimensions. If they are not, an error will be issued. This command is used to do the same action as RGB() but on entire arrays. a_Red holds the red values, a_Green the green values, and a_Blue the blue values. a_RGBvalues will be created (if it already exists it will be deleted first) to be the same dimensions as the given arrays.

This is the equivalent of doing **a_RGBvalues[i,j] = RGB(a_Red[i,j], a_Green[i,j], a_Blue[i,j])** for all i and all j. See mReadBMP.

•Printing The Screen Graphics

•PrintScr

Sends the Terminal Screen to the printer as a graphic. The entire Terminal Screen will be printed as a graphic on the default printer. You can set the default printer through the Windows OS or through the menu option on the Editor screen or programmatically using PrinterSetup.

•PrinterSetup

Shows a dialog box that allows the user to select the printer and to configure it. This will be the printer that will be used from that point onwards whenever the user pushes the **Print** button from the bottom of the Terminal Screen. It will also be the printer used whenever PrintScr is issued.

•Screen Output Buffer Control

•SetTextBuff {se_Text}

Sets the Terminal Screen text buffer to the given text. If it is "" or not given, the text buffer is cleared. Read about the text buffer in the Terminal Screen subsection of the IDE section. Also see GetTextBuff().

•TextBuffToCB

Sends the Terminal Screen text buffer to the Windows Clipboard. Read about the Text buffer of the Terminal Screen section in The Integrated Development Environment (IDE) section.

•GetTextBuff()

Returns a string that is the text in the Terminal Screen text buffer. If there is no text in the buffer then the returned string will be empty (""). If the text in the buffer has multiple lines then the string will contain the two character combination Char(13)+Char(10) (CR/LF) to indicate the line breaks. You can use Extract() and NumParts() to extract each line separately.

Read about the text buffer in the Terminal Screen section of The Integrated Development Environment (IDE) section.

•<u>Screen Manipulation</u>

•ScrSetMetrics {ne_X{,ne_Y{,ne_Width{,ne_Height{,ne_PanelVisible{,ne_AllowResize}}}}}}

This commands allows you to set the Terminal Screen's position (X,Y) and its width and height. Additionally it allows you to hide or show the Control Panel at the bottom of the Terminal Screen, if ne_PanelVisible is not given or is set to true the Panel will be visible and if set to false the panel will be hidden. Furthermore, you can enable or disable the user to manually resize the window using the mouse. If ne_AllowResize is not given or is set to false then the window is not manually resizable. If it is set to true then the window can be resized using the mouse.

If the Control Panel is hidden RB will automatically revert to InlineInputMode on since now the input cannot be performed using the Control Panel's Input Area. When you set the panel to hidden then the inline input mode is automatically activated. If you set the Panel to visible then the inline input mode is automatically deactivated. If you wish to keep the inline input mode active after setting the panel to visible then you must issue an independent InlineInputMode on (see this command above). As long as the Control Panel is hidden you will not be able to deactivate the inline input mode (i.e. InlineInputMode off will not have any effect).

Resizing the Terminal screen (manually or programmatically) will not allow resizing the Terminal screen to bigger than the original screen width and height on startup. This will usually be 800x600 on most systems but may be smaller on some systems.

Example: (also see the example under MediaPlay).

```
scrsetmetrics ,,,,0,1
print "Press up/Dn Lft/Rt arrows to demo moving the screen"
```

155

```
print "under program control"
print "Press PgUp, PhDn, - +  to demo sizing the screen"
print "under program control"
data Buttons;"Show &Panel","Not Allow &Manual Sizing","Hide &Panel","Allow &Manual Sizing"
b1 = 0 \ b2 = 1
AddButton Buttons[0],1,120,160
AddButton Buttons[1],170,120,160
s = char(kc_LArrow)+char(kc_RArrow)+char(kc_UArrow)+char(kc_DArrow)
s = s+char(kc_PUp)+char(kc_PDn)+char(189)+char(187)
xystring 1,70," X,Y";"";"  Width,Height"
while true
    ScrGetMetrics x,y,w,h,p,r
    xystring 1,90,x,",",y;"";"   ",w,",",h
    getbutton b
    if b==Buttons[0]
        b1 = !b1
        SetButtonCaption Buttons[0],Buttons[2*b1]
        ScrSetMetrics ,,,,b1,b2
    elseif b==Buttons[1]
        SetButtonCaption Buttons[1],Buttons[1+2*b2]
        b2 = !b2
        ScrSetMetrics ,,,,b1,b2
    endif
    if KeyDown()
        if keydown(kc_LArrow) then x -= 5
        if keydown(kc_RArrow) then x += 5
        if keydown(kc_UArrow) then y -= 5
        if keydown(kc_DArrow) then y += 5
        if keydown(kc_PUp)    then h -= 5
        if keydown(kc_PDn)    then h += 5
        if keydown(189)       then w -= 5
        if keydown(187)       then w += 5
        k = KeyDown()
        if InString(s,char(k)) then scrsetmetrics x,y,w,h,p,r
    endif
wend
```

•ScrGetMetrics
{vn_X{,vn_Y{,vn_Width{,vn_Height{,vn_PanelVisible{,vn_AllowResize}}}}}}
Will set the variables to their corresponding screen metrics.

•Flip {on|off}
This command controls how all the screen drawing and manipulations commands will behave. If *Off* then all drawing or printing commands will take place on the visible screen. If *On* then all drawing and printing commands will take place on a non-visible background screen and will not be visible. If no parameter is given or is negative then the non-visible background screen will be ***copied*** to the visible screen, effectively showing any previously drawn images.

This command is useful during animations. If you draw and erase then draw on the visible screen there will be a perceptible flicker. If instead, you activate background drawing using Flip on then only show the final screen by using Flip the animation will be flicker free. To activate background drawing issue Flip on, to deactivate it issue Flip off. To cause the background screen to be copied to the visible screen issue Flip.

You only need to issue Flip on once at the beginning of the program. However you need to issue Flip whenever you need the results of any drawings or printing to show.

The default state upon starting any program is **off**. To make drawing take place in the background you must issue Flip on. Flip without parameters will only take effect if Flip on has been previously issued (i.e. flipping is on).

•ClearScr {ne_Color}

Clears the screen with the given color. If the color is not given, the default color is used (see list of colors in the RobotBASIC Constants section and discussion about colors above). The specified color does not set the default color.

•ScrLimits vn_XLimit,vn_YLimit

Assigns the maximum X coordinate of the screen, and the maximum Y coordinate of the screen. This command allows you determine the extent of the screen X,Y coordinates. Zero is always the lower limit.

This Example will draw a rectangle with a border of 1-pixel all around the screen. You should see all 4 sides just perfectly fitting within the Terminal Screen:

```
ScrLimits X,Y
Rectangle 0,0,X,Y,red
```

•SaveScrWH {ne_X1{,ne_Y1{,ne_Width{,ne_Height}}}}
•SaveScr {ne_X1{,ne_Y1{,ne_X2{,ne_Y2}}}}

Saves a copy of a portion of the screen to memory. If you do not specify any parameters the entire screen will be saved. The Expressions specify the coordinates of the top left corner and coordinates of the bottom right corner of the portion to be saved (in the WH version of the command it is the width and height of the portion to be saved that you specify in the 3rd and 4th parameters). ne_X1 and ne_Y1 default to 0. ne_X2 defaults to the Terminal Screen's maximum x-coordinate and ne_Y2 defaults to the Terminal Screen's maximum y-coordinate (ne_Width defaults to Terminal Screen's width and ne_Height to its height).

This command is useful in animations and in drawing temporary objects on top of existing ones and then erasing them without having to redraw the original screen (See CopyToScr below for an example).

Note: CopyScr provides more versatility than these two commands.

•RestoreScr {ne_X{,ne_Y}}

Restores an already saved copy of a portion of the screen from memory. If you do not specify any parameter then the saved portion will be restored to top left corner of the screen. ne_X and ne_Y default to 0. If you specify parameters then the previously saved rectangle will be restored over the area starting at ne_X, ne_Y coordinate. The width and height are determined by the saved data specified in SaveScr. If a SaveScr has not been previously issued (i.e. the buffer is empty) then this command will have no effect. The buffer is **not** cleared between program runs. The transparent state is disregarded, the bitmap in the memory is always restored as non-transparent.

Note: CopyToScr provides more versatility than this command.

•CopyScr {ne_CopyNumber{,ne_X1{,ne_Y1{,ne_Width{,ne_Height}}}}

Makes copy of a portion of the screen ne_Width wide and ne_Height high starting from the position ne_X, ne_Y and saves it to the memory location ne_CopyNumber. If you do not specify ne_CopyNumber or it is less than 0 then 0 will be assumed.

If you do not specify any parameters the entire screen will be saved. The parameters specify the coordinates of the top left corner and the width and height of the portion to be saved. ne_X1 and ne_Y1 default to 0. ne_Width defaults to Terminal Screen's width and ne_Height to its height.

This command is useful in animations and in drawing temporary objects on top of existing ones and then erasing them without having to redraw the original screen (See CopyToScr below for an example).Also see mScrFromArray, mScrToArray, and CopyToScr.
Example:

```
rectanglewh 100,100,200,200,red,blue
savescrWH 100,100,200,200
savescr   100,100,299,299
copyscr  0,100,100,200,200
mScrToArray A,100,100,200,200

Flip on
for i=0 to 400 step 5
  clearscr black
  //--umcomment the line you want to test from the three lines below
  //--and comment the other two
  //restorescr i,i
  copytoscr 0,i,i
  //copyfitscr 0,i,i
  //mScrFromArray A,i,i    //notice this one is a lot slower
  //mscrfitarray A,i,i     //notice this one is a lot slower
  flip
next
copytoscr 0,300,10,40,50,160,150   //restore a portion of the saved bitmap
mscrfromarray A,300,100,40,50,160,150  //restore a portion of the array
flip
```

•CopyToScr
{ne_CopyNumber{,ne_ScreenX{,ne_ScreenY{,ne_Width{,ne_Height{,ne_MapX{,ne_MapY} }}}}}}

Reads a rectangular portion ne_Width by ne_Height starting at the point ne_MapX,ne_MapY from within the Bitmap that has been previously copied to memory location ne_CopyNumber and places it on the Terminal Screen starting at the position ne_ScreenX,ne_ScreenY within the screen.

Any unspecified parameters will default to 0. Any parameters less than 0 will be made zero.

158

If the width is zero it will become the entire remaining width of the bitmap from the x position. If the height is zero it becomes the entire remaining height of the bitmap from the y position.

When placing the read portion of the bitmap onto the terminal screen it will be clipped if its width or height do not fit the remaining space from the specified x,y position in the terminal screen. If you specify a copy number that does not have a previously save copy then nothing will happen.

All the colors of the bitmap will be copied onto the terminal screen regardless of the transparent state, the bitmap in the copy is always restored as non-transparent. Also see mScrFromArray, mScrToArray, and CopyScr.

•**CopyFitScr {ne_CopyNumber{,ne_X{,ne_Y{,ne_Width{,ne_Height}}}}}**
Reads the bitmap in the copy memory area number specified and fits it into the rectangular area ne_Width wide by ne_Height high starting at the point ne_X,ne_Y onto the Terminal Screen. Any unspecified parameters will default to 0. Any parameters less than 0 will be made zero.

If the width is zero it will become the entire remaining width of the screen from the x position. If the height is zero it becomes the entire remaining height of the screen from the y position. If you specify a copy number that does not have a previously save copy then nothing will happen.

When placing the bitmap within the rectangular area onto the terminal screen it will be resized (enlarged or shrunk) to fit the rectangular area. All the colors of the bitmap will be copied onto the terminal screen unless Transparent on has been issued. In which case the bitmap will be copied but the color of the top left hand (0,0) pixel of the original bitmap will be considered as transparent and any pixels in the bitmap that have that color will not be copied to the terminal screen, effectively becoming transparent. Also see CopyScr, FitBMP.

•**WriteScr {se_FileName}**
Saves the screen to a bitmap file on disk. If you do not specify the file name it will default to "RobotBASICScreen.Bmp". See the note at the top of this section regarding the ".Bmp" extension.

•**ReadScr {se_FileName}**
Restores the screen from a bitmap file on disk. If you do not specify the file name it will default to "RobotBASICScreen.Bmp". See the note at the top of this section regarding the ".Bmp" extension. If the bitmap is smaller or larger than the width and height of the screen it will be resized (enlarged/shrunk) to fit the screen limits. The transparent state is disregarded, the bitmap is always restored as non-transparent.

•mScrToArray a_Pixels{,ne_X{,ne_Y{,ne_Width{,ne_Height}}}}
   Saves a rectangular portion ne_Width by ne_Height starting at the position ne_X,ne_Y from the Terminal Screen as a bitmap to the array a_Pixels.

   Any unspecified parameters will default to 0. Any parameters less than 0 will be made zero.

   If the width is zero it will become the entire remaining width of the terminal screen from the x position. If the height is zero, it will become the entire remaining height of the terminal screen from the y position. Also see mScrFromArray, mReadBMP, mWRiteBMP, CopyScr, and CopyToScr.

   Note: For animation purposes CopyScr and CopyToScr are much faster and should be used.

•mScrFromArray
a_Pixels{,ne_ScreenX{,ne_ScreenY{,ne_Width{,ne_Height{,ne_ArrayX{,ne_ArrayY}}}}}}
   Reads a rectangular portion ne_Width by ne_Height starting at the point ne_ArrayX,ne_ArrayY from the Bitmap that has been previously created (or saved) in the array a_Pixels and places it on the Terminal Screen starting at the position ne_ScreenX,ne_ScreenY within the screen. a_Pixels has to exist and has to be two-dimensional. Any unpopulated elements or non-numeric elements in the array will be assumed to be zero. Floating point values will be rounded.

   Any unspecified parameters will default to 0. Any parameters less than 0 will be made zero.

   If the width is zero it will become the entire remaining width of the bitmap from the x position. If the height is zero it becomes the entire remaining height of the bitmap from the y position.

   When placing the read portion of the bitmap onto the terminal screen it will be clipped if its width or height do not fit the remaining space from the specified x,y position in the terminal screen.

   All the colors of the bitmap will be copied onto the terminal screen regardless of the transparent state, the bitmap in the array is always restored as non-transparent. Also see mScrToArray, mReadBMP, mWRiteBMP, CopyScr, and CopyToScr.

   Note: For animation purposes CopyScr and CopyToScr are much faster and should be used.

•mScrFitArray a_Pixels{,ne_X{,ne_Y{,ne_Width{,ne_Height}}}}
   Reads the bitmap contained in the array a_Pixels and fits it into the rectangular area ne_Width wide by ne_Height high starting at the point ne_X,ne_Y onto the Terminal Screen. Any unspecified parameters will default to 0. Any parameters less than 0 will be made zero.

160

a_Pixels has to exist and has to be two-dimensional. Any unpopulated elements or non-numeric elements in the array will be assumed to be zero. Floating point values will be rounded.

If the width is zero it will become the entire remaining width of the screen from the x position. If the height is zero it becomes the entire remaining height of the screen from the y position.

When placing the bitmap within the rectangular area onto the terminal screen it will be resized (enlarged or shrunk) to fit the rectangular area. All the colors of the bitmap will be copied onto the terminal screen unless **Transparent on** has been issued. In which case the bitmap will be copied but the color of the top left hand (0,0) pixel of the original bitmap will be considered as transparent and any pixels in the bitmap that have that color will not be copied to the terminal screen, effectively becoming transparent. Also see CopyScr, and FitBMP.

•**DeskTopWidth()**
•**DeskTopHeight()**
  Returns the width/height of the computer screen's (Desktop) width and height.

•Bitmap Manipulation

•**Transparent {on|off}**
  This command switches the mode of reading a bitmap onto the terminal screen. If it is on (or not given), the bitmap read will have a transparent color. This color is indicated by the top left hand (0,0) pixel color in the bitmap. Any pixel in the bitmap with this color will not be copied on to the terminal screen, effectively becoming transparent. When the mode is off then all pixels of the bitmap will be copied onto the terminal screen (i.e. no transparent color). This option is useful for creating *sprite* animation.

•**PromptBMP({se_Filter})**
  Opens a file selection dialog box and allows the user to select a bitmap file. se_Filter is optional and if not given will be considered to be a null string. It specifies a filter to select from a similar group of files. Do not include the .Bmp extension, it will be included automatically (if you do you will get an incorrect filter). The difference between this dialog and the one in FilePrompt() is that it is specific for pictures (BMPs) and allows a preview of the bitmaps highlighted.

  If the user selects a file the full file's name including the directory and drive will be returned but without the .Bmp extension. If the user closes the dialog without selecting a file or cancels then the returned value will be a blank string (i.e. "").For Example:
```
        fName = PromptBMP("Tiles_*")
        if fName != "" then ReadBMP fName,10,10,500,500
```

•ReadBMP
{se_FileName{,ne_ScreenX{,ne_ScreenY{,ne_Width{,ne_Height{,ne_MapX{,ne_MapY}}}}}}
}

Reads a rectangular portion ne_Width by ne_Height starting at the point ne_MapX,neMapY from the bitmap file specified and places it on the Terminal Screen starting at the position ne_ScreenX,ne_ScreenY within the screen.

Any unspecified parameters will default to 0 and the file name will default to "RobotBASICScreen.Bmp". Any parameters less than 0 will be made zero. See the note at the top of this section regarding the ".Bmp" extension.

If se_FileName is blank then it will become "RobotBASICScreen.Bmp". If the width is zero it will become the entire remaining width of the bitmap from the x position. If the height is zero it becomes the entire remaining height of the bitmap from the y position.

When placing the read portion of the bitmap onto the terminal screen it will be clipped if its width or height do not fit the remaining space from the specified x,y position in the terminal screen.

All the colors of the bitmap will be copied onto the terminal screen unless **Transparent on** has been issued. In which case the bitmap will be copied but the color of the top left hand (0,0) pixel of the original bitmap will be considered as transparent and any pixels in the bitmap that have that color will not be copied to the terminal screen, effectually becoming transparent. Also see mReadBMP and mWRiteBMP.

•WriteBMP {se_FileName{,ne_X{,ne_Y{,ne_Width{,ne_Height}}}}}

Saves a rectangular portion ne_Width by ne_Height starting at the position ne_X,ne_Y from the Terminal Screen as a bitmap file specified.

Any unspecified parameters will default to 0 and the file name will default to "RobotBASICScreen.Bmp". See the note at the top of this section regarding the ".Bmp" extension. Any parameters less than 0 will be made zero.

If se_FileName is blank then it will become "RobotBASICScreen.Bmp". If the width is zero it will become the entire remaining width of the terminal screen from the x position. If the height is zero, it will become the entire remaining height of the terminal screen from the y position. Also mReadBMP and mWRiteBMP.

•mReadBMP a_Pixels{,se_FileName{,ne_ClrCode}}

This command reads a bitmap file defined into an array a_Pixels. It will be created and populated with the color values of the pixels of the bitmap (see below for details). It will be two-dimensional and the number of its rows will be the height of the bitmap and the number

162

of its columns will be the width. See the note at the top of this section regarding the ".Bmp" extension.

An error will be issued if the bitmap does not exist or could not be read into memory. a_Pixels does not have to exist and if it does it will be erased and recreated as a two-dimensional array and then populated.

If the file name is not given or is an empty string ("") then the image will be read from the Windows Clipboard. If the CB does not contain a valid image then a_Pixels will be a 1x1 array and the value will be the RGB value of white (16777215 = 0xFFFFFF) for the non-color specific option and 255 for the color specific ones.

If ne_ColorCode is not given or is 0 then the array will contain the RGB color values of the pixels. If it is 1 or Blue then the elements will be the Blue component of the colors of the pixels. If it is 2 or Green then the elements will be the Green component of the colors of the pixels. If it is other than 0, 1 or 2 (e.g. 3, 4 or Red) then the elements will be the Red component of the colors of the pixels.

See mCombineClr for a method of combining the separate color arrays back into one array just as with RGB().

•mWriteBMP a_Pixels{,se_FileName}

This command will write the data in the two-dimensional array defined by a_Pixels to a bitmap file se_FileName. a_Pixels has to exist and has to be two-dimensional. Any unpopulated elements or non-numeric elements in the array will be assumed to be zero. Floating point values will be rounded. The bitmap width will be the number of columns in the array and the height will be the number of rows. If the file exists it will be overwritten. See the note at the top of this section regarding the ".Bmp" extension. An error will occur if the array is not the right dimensions or does not exist.

If the file name is not given or is an empty string ("") then the image will be saved to the Windows Clipboard.

•RotateBMP

{se_FileName{,ne_Angle{,ne_ScreenX{,ne_ScreenY{,ne_Width{,ne_Height{,ne_MapX{,ne_MapY}}}}}}}}

This command executes the same action as ReadBMP except with the added parameter ne_Angle (all others are moved over). This parameter is an angle of rotation. The bitmap will be drawn exactly as in ReadBMP but the image will be rotated by the angle given. If it is not given it will default to 90. Positive numbers are counter-clockwise rotations. Negative numbers are clock-wise rotations. The angles are in degrees (integers).

•FlipBMP
{se_FileName{,ne_ScreenX{,ne_ScreenY{,ne_Width{,ne_Height{,ne_MapX{,ne__MapY}}}}}}}}

This command executes the same action as ReadBMP except the bitmap will be upside down. The bitmap will be drawn exactly as in ReadBMP but the image will be flipped upside down (i.e. mirrored about the horizontal axis).

•MirrorBMP
{se_FileName{,ne_ScreenX{,ne_ScreenY{,ne_Width{,ne_Height{,ne_MapX{,ne__MapY}}}}}}}}

This command executes the same action as ReadBMP except the bitmap will be mirrored about the vertical axis. The bitmap will be drawn exactly as in ReadBMP but the image will be flipped left to right (i.e. mirrored about the vertical axis).

•FitBMP {se_FileName{,ne_X{,ne_Y{,ne_Width{,ne_Height}}}}}

Reads the bitmap file specified and fits it into the rectangular area ne_Width wide by ne_Height high starting at the point ne_X,ne_Y onto the Terminal Screen. Any unspecified parameters will default to 0 and the file name will default to "RobotBASICScreen.Bmp". See the note at the top of this section regarding the ".Bmp" extension. Any parameters less than 0 will be made zero.

If the file name is blank then it will become "RobotBASICScreen.Bmp". If the width is zero it will become the entire remaining width of the screen from the x position. If the height is zero it becomes the entire remaining height of the screen from the y position.

When placing the bitmap within the rectangular area onto the terminal screen it will be resized (enlarged or shrunk) to fit the rectangular area. All the colors of the bitmap will be copied onto the terminal screen unless **Transparent on** has been issued. In which case the bitmap will be copied but the color of the top left hand (0,0) pixel of the original bitmap will be considered as transparent and any pixels in the bitmap that have that color will not be copied to the terminal screen, effectively becoming transparent. Also see mReadBMP and mWRiteBMP.

•SizeBMP se_FileName,vn_Width,vn_Height

Assigns the width and height of the bitmap to the variables. See the note at the top of this section regarding the ".Bmp" extension.

•ResizeBMP {se_SourceFileName{,ne_Width{,ne_Height{,se_ToFileName}}}}

Will change the width and height of the bitmap file to the new width and height and save it to a new file name. If the source file name is not given or is "" then the image will be taken from the Windows Clipboard. If destination file name is not given or is "" then the resulting image will be written to the CB. If ne_Width is not given or is <=0 then the new width will be the same as the original width. If ne_Height is not given or is <=0 then the new height will be the same as the original height. See the note at the top of this section regarding the ".Bmp" extension. Any parameters less than 0 will be made zero.

The effect of this command can be achieved with FitBMP (or CbFitBMP) then WriteBMP (or CbToBMP) but this command is much faster and it is one operation.

•ToBMP se_SourceFile{,se_ToFile}

Converts an image file of the type JPG, WMF or ICO to a bit map file (BMP). se_SourceFile is the name of the file to be converted and should be specified in full with the extension and path. se_ToFile is the name of the file to be created as a BMP and if it is not specified then the BMP file will have the same name as se_SourceFile but with the .BMP extension. If it is given then it does not matter if you do or do not give an extension since the extension will always be made .BMP (see the note at the top of this section regarding the ".Bmp" extension). If the source file does not exist or is not of an allowed type an error will occur.

•BmpToGray
se_SourceFileName{,se_ToFileName{,ne_RedRatio{,ne_GreenRatio{,ne_BlueRatio}}}}

Converts the bitmap color image file to a gray scale bitmap file. If the se_ToFileName is not specified or is a blank string ("""") then the gray scale image will be put in the Windows Clipboard. If the source is a blank string ("") then the source image will be obtained from the Windows Clipboard (if there is no image in the CB then no action is taken). See the note at the top of this section regarding the ".bmp" extension.

The ratio numbers if not provided will default to 0.3 for red, 0.6 for green and 0.1 for blue. There is no checking done on the numbers so you can use any numbers to get some interesting effects. However, the default ratios give a good gray scale result and if you wish to maintain normal gray scale results the three ratios must add up to 1. Nevertheless, you can get some curios results if you use numbers that do not add up to 1 or even negative numbers.

The operation multiplies the intensity level of the R/G/B values and then adds the results and then sets the intensity of all of them to the sum value.

Note: This command may take a few seconds to complete processing, depending on the size of the BMP file. You may want to display a message to the user of your program to indicate a wait.

Note: If you require to process an image from the screen, use WriteBMP or ScrToCb to save the portion of the screen you want to process. Also, to see the resultant image use ReadBMP, ScrFromCb, FitCb or FitBMP to read the image into the screen.

•BmpNegative se_SourceFile{,se_ToFile}

Converts the bitmap color image file to its negative and saves it to another file. If the destination is not specified or is a blank string ("""") then the negative image will be put in the Windows Clipboard. If source is a blank string ("") then the source image will be obtained from the Windows Clipboard (if there is no image in the CB then no action is taken). See the note at the top of this section regarding the ".bmp" extension.

Note: See the notes under BmpToGray.

•BmpToBW se_SourceFile{,ne_Threshold{,se_ToFile}}
Converts the bitmap color image file to a black and white bitmap file. If the destination file is not specified or is a blank string ("""") then the black and white image will be put in the Windows Clipboard. If the source file is a blank string ("") then the source image will be obtained from the Windows Clipboard (if there is no image in the CB then no action is taken). See the note at the top of this section regarding the ".bmp" extension. This is a ***black and white*** not gray scale, that is there will only be two color values (white and black), no grays or other colors.

If a pixel in the image when converted to gray scale is below ne_Threshold value it will be made black, otherwise it will be white. If ne_Threshold is not given or is <= 0 then 128 will be assumed. If it is > 255 it will be made 255.

Note: See the notes under BmpToGray.

•BmpEdges se_SourceFile{,ne_Threshold{,se_ToFile{,ne_EdgeType}}}
Converts the bitmap image file to a black and white bitmap file but only the edges of any objects in the image will be defined. If the destination file is not specified or is a blank string ("""") then the edges image will be put in the Windows Clipboard. If source file is a blank string ("") then the source image will be obtained from the Windows Clipboard (if there is no image in the CB then no action is taken). See the note at the top of this section regarding the ".bmp" extension.

If the threshold is not specified or is <= 0 then the file will be assumed to be a black and white image. If it is > 0 then the routine will convert the image to a black white image first (internally, no file created) before it does edge detection using the threshold value given. If it is > 255 it will be set to 255.

If ne_EdgeType is not specified or is 0 then the edges will be black and the rest of the image will be white. If it <> 0 then the edges will be white and the rest of the image will be black.

Note: See the notes under BmpToGray. This command may take much longer time than other image processing commands, and especially if the image has to be converted to BW first.

•BmpRGB se_SourceFile,ne_Rratio,ne_Gratio,ne_Bratio{,se_ToFile}
Increases/decreases the RGB color values in the source bitmap according to the ratios and saves the new bitmap to the file destination file. The ratio has to be a float between -1 and 1,

so for example 50% will be 0.5. If the ratio is positive the color will be increased. If the ratio is negative the color will be decreased. If the ratio is greater than 1 then it will be made 1. If it is less than -1 it will be made -1.

If the destination file is not specified or is a blank string ("''") then the new image will be put in the Windows Clipboard. If the source file is a blank string ("") then the source image will be obtained from the Windows Clipboard (if there is no image in the CB then no action is taken). See the note at the top of this section regarding the ".bmp" extension.

You can also use this command to brighten/darken the image. To do this, use the same ratio increase/decrease for all the colors.

Note: See the notes under BmpToGray.

•BmpContrast se_SourceFile,ne_Ratio{,ne_Threshold{,se_ToFile}}
Increases/decreases the contrast of the source bitmap by the ratio and saves the resultant image to the destination file. The ratio has to be a float between -1 and 1, so for example 50% will be 0.5. If the ratio is positive the contrast will be increased. If the ratio is negative the contrast will be decreased. If the ratio is greater than 1 then it will be made 1. If it is less than -1 it will be made -1.

ne_Threshold specifies a threshold (1-255) value for contrasting. If it is <=0 or is not given, it will be made 128. If it is > 255 it will be made 255.

If the destination file is not specified or is a blank string ("''") then the new image will be put in the Windows Clipboard. If source file is a blank string ("") then the source image will be obtained from the Windows Clipboard (if there is no image in the CB then no action is taken). See the note at the top of this section regarding the ".bmp" extension.

Note: See the notes under BmpToGray.

•BmpCompare se_SourceFile,se_CompareFile{,se_ToFile{,ne_Tolerance}}
Compares the source bitmap file against the compare bitmap file with a tolerance level. The result of the comparison will be saved in the destination file. If the destination is not specified or is a blank string ("''") then the resulting comparison image will be saved to the Windows Clipboard. If the source is a blank string ("") then the source image will be taken from the Windows Clipboard. The compare file has to be a valid bitmap file name. See the note at the top of this section regarding the ".bmp" extension.

ne_Tolerance specifies a percentage to apply to each individual component color. So if it is 0.3 then the Red component of the pixel has to be within the lower value RedValue(color)*0.7 and the upper value RedValue(color)*1.3 (the same for green and blue).

167

ne_Tolerance has to be a float 0 to 1. If it is <0 or is not given then it will be set to 0.1 (i.e. 10%).

The result file will be a black and white image where all pixels that were equal (within the tolerance) in the source and compare files, will be black. Any pixels that were not equal will be set to white. The result file will be the same size as the source file. Any pixels in the source that do not have a corresponding pixel in the compare file due to difference in sizes, will make the corresponding pixels in the output file white.

Note: See the notes under BmpToGray.

•**BmpChangeClr se_SourceFile,ne_FromColor,ne_ToColor{,ne_Tolerance}**

Looks through the source bitmap for any pixels with the ne_FromColor with an optional tolerance ne_Tolerance and changes them to the color ne_ToColor. If the source file name is a blank string ("") then the source image will be obtained from the Windows Clipboard.

The resultant bitmap image will be saved to the Windows Clipboard. If you wish to save it to a file or to display it on the screen then use CBToBmp and ScrFromCB or any of the other Clipboard Bitmap related commands.

The colors can be an RGB color values or one of the constant color values (0-15) from the RobotBASIC Constants section. ne_Tolerance specifies a percentage that defines how far away a color can be from ne_FromColor and still would be considered as a color to change. The larger the tolerance fraction the more the departure of the color can be from ne_FromColor and it would still be considered as similar to the color. ne_Tolerance has to be a float 0 to 1 (i.e. 0 to 100%). If it is <0 or is not given then it will be set to 0.2 (i.e. 20%).

•**BmpFindClr se_SourceFile,ne_Color,vn_Result{,vn_Confidence{,ne_ClrTolerance{,ne_ConfidenceTolerance{,ne_GridSize{a_SectorsCount}}}}}**

Looks through the source bitmap for the given color with an optional tolerance. If the color is not found then vn_Result will be set to -1. If the color is found the variable vn_Result will be set to the number of the sector in which the color was found with the maximum density. If the source file name is a blank string ("") then the source image will be obtained from the Windows Clipboard. See the note at the top of this section regarding the ".bmp" extension.

The color can be an RGB color value or one of the constant color values (0-15) from the RobotBASIC Constants section. ne_ClrTolerance specifies a percentage to apply to each individual component primary color (R/G/B). So if it is 0.3 then the Red component of the pixel has to be within the lower value RedValue(ne_Color)*0.7 and the upper value RedValue(ne_Color)*1.3 (the same for green and blue).

ne_ClrTolerance has to be a float 0 to 1. If it is <0 or is not given then it will be set to 0.2 (i.e.

20%).

vn_Confidence is optional but if specified it will contain a count of how many sectors contain the search color with a density that is within ne_ConfidenceTolerance of the maximum density. This value should normally be 1 if the search color lies wholly within one sector. But if the color spans many sectors in such a way so as to be distributed over these sectors within a tolerance of 1 - ne_ConfidenceTolerance, then vn_Confidence will contain a count of these sectors (not where they are, just how many). You can use this value to get a measure of the confidence in the reported maximum sector. If it is large in comparison to the number of sectors then you may conclude that the color is not a suitable color to be searching for since it is distributed (with the given tolerance) over too many sectors.

ne_ConfidenceTolerance has to be a float 0 to 1. If it is <0 or is not given then it will be set to 0.1 (i.e. 10%).

ne_GridSize is the grid size to divide the bitmap into. If it is < 3 or is not given it will be made 5. It has to be >= 3 and <= 20. If you specify a grid size that results in each sector being <10 pixels high or wide vn_Result will be set to -2. You must specify a grid size that will be correct for the bitmap you are trying to search.

The bitmap will be sectored into an ne_GridSize x ne_GridSize grid (5x5 normally). The number returned in vn_Result will report the sector number where the color was found with a maximum density. Since there are 5x5 = 25 sectors then the 25th sector will be sector number 24 and the first sector is sector number 0. The numbering scheme is starting from top left corner, going along the row to the right then going down to the next row and counting right and so forth. So if the grid size is 5 (i.e. 5x5) and the number reported is 17 then the color was found on the 17/5 = 3 (i.e. 4th row) and 17#5 = 2 (i.e. 3rd column). Row and column numbers start at 0. So a sector on the 2nd row, 3rd column will be sector number 1*5+2 = 7 (i.e. 8th sector).

If you specify a_SectorCount (array name) then the array will be a 2-dimensional array with the size of GridSize x GridSize. The elements will contain a number representing the number of pixels within the sector that are the search color (within the tolerance). You can use this array to look for other sectors that contain the search color if you need to do so.

Note: See the notes under BmpToGray.

Example:
```
FitBmp "SomeFile"    //---fits it on the entire screen
CircleWH 270,170,130,130,red,red
WriteBmp "TempFile"
BmpFindClr "TempFile",red,Sctr,Conf,,.3 //---default tolerance = 0.2, GridSize= 5
Row = Sctr/5
Column = Sctr#5
print "Sector=",Sctr, "   Row=",Row,"   Column=",Column  ,"   Conf = ",Conf
```

```
W = 800/5   //---Sector width
H = 600/5   //---Sector height
eRectangleWH Column*W,Row*H,W,H,3,white  //--outline sector
```

•BmpStats a_Stats{,se_FileName}

Creates statistics about the bitmap file. If the file name is not given or is an empty string ("")
then the image will be taken from the Windows Clipboard area. See the note at the top of this
section regarding the ".bmp" extension.

a_Stats will be deleted if it exists and will be recreated as a one-dimensional array with 10
elements as follows:

a_Stats[0] = Average value for the Red components of the colors of the pixels in the
image.
a_Stats[1] = Average value for the Green components of the colors of the pixels in the
image.
a_Stats[2] = Average value for the Blue components of the colors of the pixels in the
image.
a_Stats[3] = Average of the above three averages.
a_Stats[4] = Standard Deviation of the Red components of the colors of the pixels in the
image.
a_Stats[5] = Standard Deviation of the Green components of the colors of the pixels in
the image.
a_Stats[6] = Standard Deviation of the Blue components of the colors of the pixels in the
image.
a_Stats[7] = Average of the above three Standard Deviations.
a_Stats[8] = Width of the image.
a_Stats[9] = Height of the image.

If there is no image on the clipboard the array will contain all values of 0. If you specify a
bitmap file and it cannot be opened, you will get an error.

•Clipboard Manipulation

•SetCBText {se_Text}

Sets the windows clipboard to the given text. se_Text can contain CR/LF separated substrings.
If se_Text is not given then it will be "", effectively clearing the clipboard. Also see
GetCBText().

•GetCBText()

Returns a string that is the text in the Windows Clipboard. If the Clipboard does not contain
valid text then the returned string will be empty (""). If the text in the Clipboard has multiple
lines then the string will contain the two character combination Char(13)+Char(10) (CR/LF)
to indicate the line breaks. You can use Extract() and NumParts() to extract each line

separately.

•ClrCB

Clears the Windows Clipboard, whether it contains text or an image. The Clipboard will become blank.

•SizeCb vn_Width,vn_Height

Assigns the width and height of the image in the Windows Clipboard area to the variables. If there is no image then they will be assigned 0. Use this command to find if the CB has an image and what dimensions it has.

•ScrToCb {ne_X{,ne_Y{,ne_Width{,ne_Height}}}}

Saves a portion of the screen width by height starting at the ne_X, ne_Y position, to the Windows Clipboard. If you do not specify any parameters the entire screen will be saved. If ne_X or ne_Y is less than 0 or is not given then it will be set to 0. If ne_width or ne_Height is less than 1 or is not given or is > Terminal Screen width/height then it will be set to the Terminal Screen width/height. If the width/height specified exceeds the remaining width/height from the starting point then it will be made to be the remaining width/height (see ScrFromCb).

•ScrFromCb {ne_ScreenX{,ne_ScreenY{,ne_Width{,ne_Height{,ne_MapX{,ne_MapY}}}}}}

Reads a rectangular portion width by height starting at the point ne_MapX,ne_MapY from the image in the Windows Clipboard and places it on the Terminal Screen starting at the position ne_ScreenX,ne_ScreenY within the screen. If there is no image in the CB no action is taken.

Any unspecified parameters will default to 0. Any parameters less than 0 will be made zero. If the width is zero it will become the entire remaining width of the image from the x position. If the height is zero it becomes the entire remaining height of the image from the y position.

When placing the read portion of the image onto the terminal screen it will be clipped if its width or height do not fit the remaining space from the specified x,y position in the Terminal Screen.

All the colors of the image will be copied onto the terminal screen unless Transparent on has been issued. In which case the image will be copied but the color of the top left hand (0,0) pixel of the original image will be considered as transparent and any pixels in the image that have that color will not be copied to the Terminal Screen, effactually becoming transparent.

•FitCb {ne_X{,ne_Y{,ne_Width{,ne_Height}}}}

Fits the image in the Windows Clipboard into the rectangular area width by height starting at the point ne_X,ne_Y onto the Terminal Screen. Any unspecified parameters will default to 0. Any parameters less than 0 will be made zero. If the width is zero it will become the entire

171

remaining width of the screen from the x position. If the height is zero it becomes the entire remaining height of the screen from the y position.

When placing the image within the rectangular area onto the terminal screen it will be resized (enlarged or shrunk) to fit the rectangular area. All the colors of the image will be copied onto the terminal screen unless **Transparent on** has been issued. In which case the image will be copied but the color of the top left hand (0,0) pixel of the original image will be considered as transparent and any pixels in the image that have that color will not be copied to the terminal screen, effectively becoming transparent.

•BmpToCb {se_FileName{,ne_X{,ne_Y{,ne_Width{,ne_Height}}}}}
Reads a rectangular portion width by height starting at the point ne_X,ne_Y from the bitmap file specified and places it in the Windows Clipboard area.

Any unspecified parameters will default to 0 and the file name will default to "RobotBASICScreen.Bmp". Any parameters less than 0 will be made zero. See the note at the top of this section regarding the ".Bmp" extension.

If ne_FileName is blank then it will become "RobotBASICScreen.Bmp". If the width is zero it will become the entire remaining width of the bitmap from the X position. If the height is zero it becomes the entire remaining height of the bitmap from the Y position. All the colors of the bitmap will be copied into the CB regardless of **Transparent on**.

•CbToBMP {se_FileName}
Saves the image in the Windows Clipboard to the bitmap file. If the file name is blank or not given then it will become "RobotBASICScreen.Bmp". See the note at the top of this section regarding the ".Bmp" extension.

•CbFitBMP {se_FileName{,ne_Width{,ne_Height}}}
Reads the bitmap file specified and fits it into the rectangular area width by height starting at the origin (0,0) into the Windows Clipboard. Any unspecified parameters will default to 0 and the file name will default to "RobotBASICScreen.Bmp". See the note at the top of this section regarding the ".Bmp" extension. Any parameters less than 0 will be made zero.

If the file name is blank then it will become "RobotBASICScreen.Bmp". If the width is zero it will become width of the Terminal Screen. If the height is zero it becomes the height of the Terminal Screen.

When placing the bitmap within the rectangular area into the CB it will be resized (enlarged or shrunk) to fit the rectangular area. All the colors of the bitmap will be copied regardless of **Transparent on**.

•FlipCb

Flips the image in the Windows Clipboard and puts it back in the Clipboard.

•MirrorCb

Mirrors the image in the Windows Clipboard and puts it back in the Clipboard.

•RotateCb {ne_Angle}

Rotates the image in the Windows Clipboard by the angle of rotation given. If the angle is not given it will default to 90. Positive numbers are counter-clockwise rotations. Negative numbers are clock-wise rotations. The angles are in degrees (integers). The resulting image will be placed back in the CB.

•TWAIN Image Capture

•CaptureRdy()

Returns a 1 (true) if the TWAIN_32.DLL is available and the EZTW32.DLL is loaded. Otherwise it will return a 0 (false). Use this function to ascertain if the Capture system is available for the capture functions below.

The capture system provided relies on the TWAIN standard for communicating with various devices that can provide images (Scanners, WebCams and the like). Many devices are TWAIN compliant and thus will be usable to RobotBASIC programs through the Capture functions below.

In order for RB to be able to use the devices, your system has to have the Twain_32.DLL file in the Windows directory. If you have installed a TWAIN compliant device then this DLL would be also installed with the device's drivers. Additionally, another file (EZTW32.DLL) will have to be available in the same directory where RobotBASIC.exe resides. This DLL is provided with the downloadable Zip file from **www.RobotBASIC.com**. See example below.

Note: Some devices may cause a "floating point error" when you try to set them to certain resolutions. This error has to do with the devices' drivers and RB has no control over this. However the capture operation may still work if you just accept their default settings.

•CaptureSrc()

Opens a dialog box that allows the user to select from among various devices like Scanners, WebCams, and others, available on the system. The user can select the device that is desired to be the source of images for CaptureImage() and CaptureDlg().

The function will return 1 (true) if the operation succeeded and the user did actually select a device. If the user cancels the dialog or the dialog box did not open then the return value will be 0 (false).

Be aware that the dialog box will show the *drivers* for the devices that are available. However, the selected device may not actually be connected. If that is the case the Capture functions will fail. See example below.

•CaptureDlg({se_FileName})

Opens a dialog box that allows the user to configure the default device [as selected by CaptureSrc()] as desired (resolution, color, etc.). In addition to allowing for configuring the various options, this dialog also allows the user to press a button to capture an image and send it on to RobotBASIC.

If the file name is not given or is a blank string then the image will be put on the Windows Clipboard area. Otherwise, the image will be saved to a file. See the note at the top of this section regarding the ".Bmp" extension.

The function will return 1 (true) if it performed the action successfully and an image was actually saved to the Clipboard or the file. Otherwise the returned value will be 0 (false).

The capture process may not be a speedy one. It depends on your device. If it is a scanner the process may take several minutes. If it is a WebCam then seconds. The program flow in RB will not continue until an image is captured or the operation fails. See example below.

•CaptureImage({se_FileName})

Captures an image from the default device [as selected by CaptureSrc()] and sends it on to RobotBASIC. No dialog will be shown. The capture will occur automatically with the default settings as previously set using CaptureDlg().

If the file name is not given or is a blank string then the image will be put on the Windows Clipboard area. Otherwise, the image will be saved to a file. See the note at the top of this section regarding the ".Bmp" extension.

The function will return 1 (true) if it performed the action successfully and an image was actually saved to the Clipboard or the file. Otherwise the returned value will be 0 (false).

The capture process may not be a speedy one. It depends on your device. If it is a scanner the process may take several minutes. If it is a WebCam then seconds. The program flow in RB will not continue until an image is captured or the operation fails.
Example:
```
data Buttons;"&Select Device","Con&figure Device","&Capture","S&top"
for i=0 to 2
  Addbutton Buttons[i],2+110*i,2,110
next
```

```
        while true
           getbutton btn
           if btn == Buttons[0]
              if !CaptureSrc() then GoSub ErrMsg \ continue
           elseif btn == Buttons[1]
              if !CaptureDlg() then GoSub ErrMsg \ continue
              FitCB 5,30,790,565
           elseif btn == Buttons[2]
              if !CaptureRdy() then GoSub ErrMsg \ continue
              RemoveButton Buttons[2]
              AddButton Buttons[3],222,2,110
              while true
                 GetButton btn
                 if btn == Buttons[3] then break
                 if !CaptureImage() then GoSub ErrMsg \ break
                 FitCB 5,30,790,565
              wend
              RemoveButton Buttons[3]
              Addbutton Buttons[2],222,2,110
           endif
        wend
        End
        ErrMsg:
           n=ErrMsg("No Device Is Available","TwainTest.Bas",MB_OK|MB_ERROR)
        Return
```

•2D Screen Graphics Drawing

•PixelClr(ne_X,ne_Y)

Returns the color of the pixel at the given screen position. See the RobotBASIC Constants section and the discussion about colors at the top of this section. Also see ReadPixel.

•GetXY vn_X,vn_Y

Reads the current pen position on the Screen and the values in the variable parameters

•GotoXY {ne_X{,ne_Y}}

Sets the pen position to a point on the screen. If any of the parameters is not given it will be 0.

•SetColor {ne_PenColor{,ne_BackGroundColor}

Sets the default Pen and Background colors. The color values can be 0-15 (i.e. color constants see RobotBASIC Constants section) or and RGB value. If either of the parameters is not given or is -1 then the corresponding default color will not be changed.

•GetColor vn_PenColor,vn_BkgrndColor

Read pen and background colors and assigns them to the variable parameters.

•ReadPixel ne_X,ne_Y,vn_Color

Reads the Pixel color at the position and assigns it to vn_Color (see the RobotBASIC Constants section and the discussion about colors at the top of this section. Also see FloodFill and PixelClr().

•SetPixel {ne_X{,ne_Y{,ne_Color}}}

Sets the color of the pixel at the position to the color. (see the RobotBASIC Constants section and discussion about colors at the top of this section. Also see FloodFill)

If the color is not given or is -1 then it will default to the current default Foreground (Pen) color.

If ne_X is not given or is -1 then it will default to the current X position as set due to the last graphic command. If ne_Y is not given or is -1 then it will default to the current Y position as set due to the last graphic command.

•LineWidth {ne_Width}

Sets the pen width for drawing lines and other drawing primitives. If ne_Width is not given or is less than 1 then it will be made 1. If it is a float it will be truncated.

•GetLineWidth vn_Width

Assigns the variable parameter with the current pen width for drawing lines and other drawing primitives.

•LineTo ne_X,ne_Y{,ne_PenWidth{,ne_PenColor}}

Draws a line from the current pen position to *ne_X,ne_Y*. If the pen width is given then the pen width will be temporarily set to the given value. If the pen color is given then pen color will be temporarily set to the value.

The pen width and color will only affect the line drawn, not any subsequent lines or other drawings. If you desire to specify the color you must also specify the width but if the width is less than 1 it will be ignored. Also if the color is less than 0 it will be ignored. If you do not specify a width and color the current default width and color will be used.

•Line ne_X1,ne_Y1,ne_X2,ne_Y2{,ne_PenWidth{,ne_PenColor}}

Draws a line from the point ne_X1,ne_Y1 to the point ne_X2,ne_Y2. ne_PenWidth and ne_PenColor will temporarily set the pen width and color while drawing the line and will affect any subsequent lines or other drawings. If you desire to specify the color you must also specify the width, but if it is less than 1 it will be ignored. Also if the color is less than 0 it will be ignored. If you do not specify a width and color the current default width and color will be used.

•Rectangle ne_X1,ne_Y1,ne_X2,ne_Y2{,ne_PenColor{,ne_FillColor}}

Draws a rectangle defined by ne_X1,ne_Y1 and ne_X2,ne_Y2 filled with ne_FillColor and bordered with ne_PenColor. If the colors are not given then the default background color will be used for filling and the pen color for the border. If you want to specify the fill color you must also give the pen color but any color value less than 0 will be ignored. ne_X1,ne_Y1 are coordinates on the screen of the top left corner, and ne_X2,ne_Y2 are of the bottom right corner of the rectangle.

•RectangleWH ne_X,ne_Y,ne_Width,ne_Height{,ne_PenColor{,ne_FillColor}}
Draws a rectangle starting at the screen coordinate ne_X,ne_Y with ne_Width ne_Height filled with ne_FillColor and bordered with ne_PenColor. If the colors are not given then the default background color will be used to fill and the pen color will used for the border. If you want to specify the fill color you must also give the pen color but any color value less than 0 will be ignored.

The width and height values specify the actual width and height in pixels So when you say RectangleWH 100,100,200,150 this will be the same as saying Rectangle 100,100,299,249 since the width will then be 299-100+1 = 200 and likewise the height would be 249-100+1 = 150.

•eRectangle ne_X1,ne_Y1,ne_X2,ne_Y2{,ne_PenWidth{,ne_PenColor}}
The above command (Rectangle) will always draw the rectangle and fill it with the color specified or the default background color. This means the inside of the rectangle will be overdrawn if there happens to be any previous drawings there. This command only draws the perimeter of the rectangle and does not fill the inside. Thus any previous drawings inside the area of the rectangle will still be visible.

The rectangle is defined by ne_X1,ne_Y1 and ne_X2,ne_Y2. ne_PenWidth and ne_PenColor will temporarily set he pen width and color for drawing the rectangle and not any subsequent drawings. If you desire to specify the color you must also specify the width, but if values less than 1 it will be ignored. Also if the color is less than 0 it will be ignored. See the example given under Pie.

•eRectangleWH ne_X1,ne_Y1,ne_Width,ne_Height{,ne_PenWidth{,ne_PenColor}}
The above command (RectangleWH) will always draw the rectangle and fill it with the color specified or the default background color. This means the inside of the rectangle will be overdrawn if there happens to be any previous drawings there. This command only draws the perimeter of the rectangle and does not fill the inside. Thus any previous drawings inside the area of the rectangle will still be visible.

The rectangle is started at the screen coordinate ne_X,ne_Y with ne_Width and ne_Height. ne_PenWidth and ne_PenColor will temporarily set he pen width and color for drawing the rectangle and not any subsequent drawings. If you desire to specify the color you must also specify the width, but if values less than 1 it will be ignored. Also if the color is less than 0 it will be will be ignored. See the example given in Pie.

The width and height values specify the actual width and height in pixels So when you say

177

eRectangleWH 100,100,200,150 this will be the same as saying eRectangle 100,100,299,249 since the width will then be 299-100+1 = 200 and likewise the height would be 249-100+1 = 150.

•Circle ne_X1,ne_Y1,ne_X2,ne_Y2{,ne_PenColor{,ne_FillColor}}

Draws a circle/ellipse inside a rectangle defined as in Rectangle. If the rectangle is a square then it is a circle, otherwise it is an ellipse.

•CircleWH ne_X1,ne_Y1,ne_Width,ne_Height{,ne_PenColor{,ne_FillColor}}

Draws a circle/ellipse inside a rectangle defined as in RectangleWH. If the rectangle is a square then it is a circle, otherwise it is an ellipse.

The width and height values specify the actual width and height in pixels So when you say CircleWH 100,100,200,150 this will be the same as saying Circle 100,100,299,249 since the width will then be 299-100+1 = 200 and likewise the height would be 249-100+1 = 150.

•Arc ne_X1,ne_Y1,ne_X2,ne_Y2{,ne_StartAngle{,ne_ArcLength{,ne_PenWidth{,ne_PenColor}}} }

The above command (Circle) will always draw the circle/ellipse and fill it with the color specified or the default background color. This means the inside of the circle/ellipse will be erased if there happens to be any previous drawings there. This command only draws the perimeter of the circle/ellipse and does not fill the inside. Thus any previous drawings inside the area of the circle/ellipse will still be visible. Additionally this command allows you to draw a fraction of the arc of the circle or ellipse.

The circle/ellipse is defined by the bounding rectangle defined by ne_X1, ne_Y1 and ne_X2, ne_Y2. ne_PenWidth and ne_PenColor will temporarily set he pen width and color for drawing the rectangle and not any subsequent drawings. If you desire to specify the color you must also specify the width, but if values less than 1 it will be ignored. Also if the color is less than 0 it will be will be ignored.

ne_StartAngle and ne_ArcLength are angles in radians that specify the start point of the arc and the length of the arc. The angles are defined counter-clock-wise from the right hand horizontal position (i.e. positive x-axis). If the arc length is zero or an even multiple of Pi() (i.e. 0,360,720 ...degrees) the entire circle/ellipse will be drawn. Both values default to 0 if not given. ne_StartAngle defines the angle (in radians) from the positive x-axis (counter-clockwise) at which to start drawing the arc. ne_ArcLength defines the length of the arc (angle inside the arc in radians). To specify angles in degrees use DtoR().

•Pie
ne_X1,ne_Y1,ne_X2,ne_Y2{,ne_StartAngle{,ne_ArcLength{,ne_PenColor{,ne_FillColor}}}}
This command is very similar to Arc above. The difference is that radials from the center of the bounding rectangle to the start and end points of the arc will also be drawn. Also the inside will be filled with the default background color or the color ne_FillColor if given. This command allows for creating Pie graphs.

The circle/ellipse is defined by the bounding rectangle defined by ne_X1, ne_Y1 and ne_X2, ne_Y2. If ne_FillColor is given the pie is filled with the color value given.

ne_StartAngle and ne_ArcLength are angles in radians that specify the start point of the arc and the length of the arc. The angles are defined counter-clock-wise from the right hand horizontal position (i.e. positive x-axis). If the arc length is zero or an even multiple of Pi() (i.e. 0,360,720 ...degrees) the entire circle/ellipse will be drawn. Both values default to 0 if not given. ne_StartAngle defines the angle (in radians) from the positive x-axis (counter-clockwise) at which to start drawing the arc. ne_ArcLength defines the length of the arc (angle inside the arc in radians). To specify angles in degrees use DtoR().

Example:
```
n = 360/16.0
for i=0 to 15
  Pie 100,100,500,500,DtoR(i*n),DtoR(n),i,i
next
Arc 100,100,500,500,,,3,blue
eRectangle 97,97,503,503,5,lightgreen
```

•mPolygon a_Vertices{,ne_FillColor}
This command is used to draw multiple polygons on the screen with one command rather than use looping and LineTo,GotoXY, and/or Rectangle. The polygons can be filled with a specified color or the default pen color. a_Vertices must be a One-Dimensional array created with Dim or Data. It must contain only numbers. If any element in the array contains non-numbers it will be ignored and will not affect the pairing of data, it would be treated as if it were not there.

The data in a_Vertices is a set of pairs of X,Y coordinates. The command will do a LineTo *X,Y* or GotoXY *X,Y* or FloodFill *X,Y{,ne_FillColor}* depending on the following logic:
- If the X and Y value-pair are both positive then a LineTo *X,Y* is executed.
- If the X is negative and Y is positive then a GotoXY *-X,Y* is executed.
- If the Y is negative and X is positive then a FlooFill *X,-Y,ne_FillColor* is executed. If the fill color is not given then FloodFill *X,-Y* is executed.(see FloodFill below)
- If Both X and Y are negative they are both made positive and LineTo is executed.

If there are not enough pairs then drawing will occur only to the last pair. The array can contain any number of point pairs. For example:

```
data p;-100,100,200,100,200,200,100,200,100,100,120,-120
data p;-500,100,600,100,600,200,500,200,500,100,520,-120
mPolygon p //will draw the above and use default pen color for any filling
mPolygon p,blue //will draw the above and use blue for any filling
```

•mBezier a_Vertices{,ne_PenWidth{,ne_PenColor}}

Used to draw Bezier curves using the endpoints and control points specified by the data in a_Vertices. The first curve is drawn from the first point to the fourth point, using the second and third points as control points. Each subsequent curve in the sequence needs exactly three more points: the ending point of the previous curve is used as the starting point, the next two points in the sequence are control points, and the third is the ending point.

This command draws lines using the pen width specified if given or the default pen width if not or is less than 1. The pen color will be as specified or if not given or is less than 0 the default color will be used. Both values default to -1.

The array a_Vertices is a one dimensional array with pairs of point coordinates (x,y). The minimum number of points needed is 4. Also the number of points used for drawing the curve will be (n*3)+1. So if there are 9 points (i.e. 18 elements x,y) only 4 (i.e. 8 elements) will be used if 11 only 10 will be used. So if the number of element pairs (points x,y) is not a multiple of 3 plus 1 then only the first correct number of pairs will be used. If any element in the array is not a valid number (float or integer) it will be ignored and will not count as part of the elements count.

•mGraphPaper a_Specs

Draws a graph paper area with a border, minor vertical and horizontal lines and major vertical and horizontal lines at a particular location on the screen with a width and height.

a_Specs is a one dimensional array whose elements define the parameters of the graph paper as follows:
   data a_Specs;x,y,width,height,border-forecolor,border-backcolor,border-width
   data a_Specs;x-minor-line-freq ,x-major-line-freq,y-minor-line-freq,y-major-line-freq
   data a_Specs;x-minor-line-width ,x-major-line-width,y-minor-line-width,y-major-line-width
   data a_Specs;x-minor-line-color ,x-major-line-color,y-minor-line-color,y-major-line-color

Anay elements of a_Specs that are not assigned or are not a valid numeric will be assigned as -1. You can also assign an element a -1. Any elements assigned as -1 will be assigned a default value as follows:
   x =200, y =100, w =400, h =400, border-forecolor =Green, border-backcolor =White, border-width =4
   x-minor-line-freq =10, x-major-line-freq =50

y-minor-line-freq = x-minor-line-freq, y-major-line-freq = x-major-line-freq
x-minor-line-width =1, x-major-line-width = 2
y-minor-line-width = x-minor-line-width, y-major-line-width = x-major-line-width
x-minor-line-color = border-forecolor , x-major-line-color = x-minor-line-color
y-minor-line-color = x-minor-line-color, y-major-line-color = x-major-line-color

The frequency values are in pixels. So a frequency of 10 means every 10 pixels.

Example:

```
InlineInputMode \ ScrSetMetrics ,,,,0
Data a;-1
mGraphPaper a  //draws a graph paper with All the defaults
Waitkey k
clearscr
Data b;50,50,700,500
mGraphPaper b  //draws a graph paper area with all the defaults but puts it on 50,50
                    //with width of 700 and height of 500
WaitKey k
clearscr
Data c;100,100,600,,yellow,blue,,5,,20,100
mGraphPaper c  //draws a graph paper with yellow lines on blue background
                    //at position 100,100 width of 600 height of default (400)
                    //with x-axis minor lines every 5 pixels and major lines
                    //every 50 pixels (default) color yellow (as border)
                    //with y-axis minor lines every 20 pixels, and major ones
                    //every 100 pixels, color yellow (as x-axis)
```

•mPlotXY a_Specs,a_Xvalues,a_Yvalues
•mPlotXY a_Specs,a_XYvalues

Plots a graph of Xs vs Ys on the screen. The data points are either in two separate one-dimensional arrays or are combined in one two-dimensional array.

In the two separate arrays format, a_Xvalues and a_Yvalues have to be one dimensional and have to contain at least one element each. Also they have to contain the same number of elements. Any elements not assigned or are not numeric will be considered to be zero. The elements can be integers or floats.

In the combined array format, a_XYvalues has to be two dimensional and has to contain at least one data point (x,y). The first row is the X values and the second row is the Y values. Both rows have to contain the same number of elements. Any elements not assigned or are not numeric will be considered to be zero. The elements can be integers or floats.

a_Specs contains the specification for plotting the graph. It has to be one-dimensional and must contain at least one element. Any elements in a_Specs from a_Specs[0] to a_Specs[5], that are not assigned or are not numeric will be made to be -1. Any elements that are -1 will be assigned a default value as follows:

a_Specs[0]=200, a_Specs[1]=100, a_Specs[2]=400, a_Specs[3]=400, a_Specs[4]=blue, a_Specs[5]=2

181

They are: The X,Y position and the width, height of the square area where the plot is to be placed. The plot will have the color specified in a_Specs[4] and the line will have a thickness in pixels as defined by a_Specs[5].

Once the plot is generated the array a_Specs will be populated with 6 extra elements as follows:

a_Specs[6] = Minimum X value, a_Specs[7] = Maximum X value
a_Specs[8] = Minimum Y value, a_Specs[9] = Maximum Y value
a_Specs[10] = X-Scale Factor,   a_Specs[11] = Y-Scale Factor

Except..... Elements a_Specs[6] to a_Specs[9] will not be assigned calculated values if they already hold a numeric value. This allows you to change the limits (and scaling) of the plot. Elements a_Specs[10] and a_Specs[11] will always be populated with the calculated X-Scale and Y-Scale according to the values in the Mi-Max elements whether calculated or assigned.

So if Any of the elements a_Specs[6] to a_Specs[9] are not assigned or are a string then the command will calculate the maximum or minimum from the Xvalues and Yvalues arrays and assign the elements of a_Specs accordingly. But if any of these elements is a numeric then it will be taken as the min or max accordingly. See the example for how this affects the plot.

If a_Specs contains less than 12 elements (0-11) it will be expanded to do so and elements 6-11 will be populated as above. If it already contains 12 elements or more, it will be kept as is, but elements 6-11 will be populated as above.

The values in elements 6-11 are useful for converting Screen-coordinates to Graph-coordinates and Graph-Coordinates to Screen-Coordinates on a point by point basis. Also see Map().

To convert a Graph-X coordinate to a Screen-X coordinate use the following formula:
Sx = (Gx-a_Specs[6])*a_Specs[10]+a_Specs[0]   or you can use Sx =
Map(Gx,a_Specs[6],a_Specs[7],a_Specs[0],a_Specs[2])
To convert a Graph-Y coordinate to a Screen-Y coordinate use the following formula:
Sy = (Gy-a_Specs[9])*a_Specs[11]+a_Specs[1]   or you can use Sy =
Map(Gy,a_Specs[8],a_Specs[9],a_Specs[3],a_Specs[1])   (notice min is [3] not [1] to make sure graph is right way up)

To convert a Screen-X coordinate to a Graph-X coordinate use the following formula:
Gx = (Sx-a_Specs[0])/a_Specs[10]+a_Specs[6]   or you can use Gx =
Map(Sx,a_Specs[0],a_Specs[1],a_Specs[6],a_Specs[7])

To convert a Screen-Y coordinate to a Graph-Y coordinate use the following formula:
Gy = (Sy-a_Specs[1])/a_Specs[11]+a_Specs[9]   or you can use Gy = Map(Sy,a_Specs[3],a_Specs[1],a_Specs[8],a_Specs[9])   (notice min is [3] not [1] to make sure graph is right way up)

The above formulas can be used once a graph is plotted to allow for converting a selected point on the screen from within the graph area to an X,Y real values and vice versa. You can only use the values from a_Specs after you have invoked the command and a_Specs has been populated with the calculated values.

If you combine this command with mGraphPaper you can plot an X-Y plot and have it all automatically scaled and plotted all in one command. If you wish to label the axis and so forth, you can do so with xyText or xyString. Also if you wish to plot more than one X-Y plot on the same graph paper then repeat the command with different arrays. You can share the same a_Xvalues and the same a_Specs but if you don't wish to use the returned maximums and minimums you may need to use a different a_Specs for each plot, and you may need to change the color (and/or thickness) values (a_Specs[4] and a_Specs[5]).

Example:
```
X = -Pi()
While X < PI()+0.1  //generate Xs from -PI() to Pi() in steps of 0.1*Pi()
  Data Xs;X         //and Ys = Sin(Xs)
  Data Ys;Sin(X)
  X = X+PI(0.1)
Wend
data GP_Specs;""              //accept all default specs for graph paper
Data G_Specs;,,,,,,,-5,,,2 //accept defaults for plot area but override MinX and MaxY
                             //play with different values for minx,maxx,miny,maxy,
mGraphPaper GP_Specs              //plot Graph paper
mPlotXY G_Specs,Xs,Ys            //plot the X-Y data
xytext 200-30,100-10,G_Specs[9]  //YAxis Labels
xytext 200-30,500-10,G_Specs[8]
xytext 200-20,500+20,G_Specs[6]  //X-Axis Labels
xytext 600-20,500+20,G_Specs[7]
xytext 350,100-30,"Y = Sin(X)"   //Title Label
end
```

•FloodFill {ne_X{,ne_Y{,ne_NewColor{,ne_OldColor}}}}

Given a coordinate ne_X,ne_Y the interpreter will start filling the area surrounding this coordinate with color ne_OldColor and replacing it with ne_NewColor. It will do so as long as the pixels have the OldColor, but it will not convert any pixels with a different color from ne_OldColor. So if you have a box that has color white while surrounded by a color blue, doing FloodFill X,Y,Red,White will fill the box with the new color Red, but only the box since it will not flow into the blue areas. (See ReadPixel and SetPixel).

Both colors are optional. If ne_OldColor is not given (or is < 0) then the color of the pixel at the specified position will be used as the ne_OldColor. If the new color is not given (or is < 0) then the current pen color will be used as the ne_NewColor.

If ne_X or ne_Y is not given or is -1 then the current Pen's X or Y position will be used.

•FloodFill2 {ne_X{,ne_Y{,ne_NewColor{,ne_BorderColor}}}}

Given a coordinate ne_X,ne_Y the interpreter will start filling the area surrounding this coordinate with color ne_NewColor stopping when it encounters the color ne_BorderColor. So if you have a box that has a black border and white interior, doing FloodFill X,Y,Red,Black will fill the box with the color Red, but only the box since it will not flow into the border or outside it. (ReadPixel and SetPixel).

Both colors are optional. If ne_BorderColor is not given (or is < 0) then the color of the pen will be used as a ne_BorderColor. If ne_NewColor is not given (or is < 0) then the current background color will be used as the Fill Color.

If ne_X or ne_Y is not given or is -1 then the current Pen's X or Y position will be used.

•DrawShape se_Shape,ne_X,ne_Y{,ne_Scale,ne_Color}

Draws an image specified by the string in ne_Shape, at the screen position ne_X, ne_Y. Optional ne_Scale and ne_Color specify a Scale factor (pixels) and Color correspondingly. If Scale is not given then 1 is assumed and if Color is not given the Default Pen color is used. If you are to specify the color you must specify the Scale. If color is a negative number then the color will be the background color. This is handy in appearing to erase the image. The data in se_Shape indicates how to move (lineTo) from the X,Y position. *Also see* **RotShape().**

Example:
```
ship        = "lllllluullldddddddrrrdlllllllllurrruuuuuuuurrrrr"
ship        = ship+"uuwwwrruurrddrrsssddrrrrrddddddddrrrd"
ship        = ship+"llllllllurrruuuuuulllddllllllUU"
flame1       = "DDDDqqaqqauurrrrrrrlDDDDwwswwsuulllllllDD"
flame2       = "DDDDqqqqlqrrrrrrrrrrrrralaaaaUU"
ShipScale = 10 \ flip on \ XI = 300 \ YI = 200
DrawShape ship, XI, YI ,ShipScale
FloodFill ,,RGB(255,136,0)
savescr 200,200,400,400
while true
   DrawShape flame1, XI, YI+1,ShipScale, red
   FloodFill ,,Red
   flip \ delay 50 \ restorescr 200,200
   DrawShape flame2, XI, YI+1,ShipScale, red
   FloodFill ,,Red
   flip \ delay 50 \ restorescr 200,200
wend
```

The details of the action of this command are as follows:
- This command will draw an image specified by the string.
- At screen position ne_X,ne_Y.
- If Scale is not given then 1 is assumed and if Color is not given the Default Pen color is used. If you are to specify the color you have to specify the Scale.

- If color is a negative number then the color will be the background color. This is handy in appearing to erase the image.
- The data in se_Shape indicates how to move (lineTo) from the X,Y position. It contains a list of letters "UDLRQAWS" or "udlrqaws" and "-0123456789" U=Up, D=Down, L=Left, R=Right, Q=Diagonal to left and up, W= Diagonal to Right and up, A=Diagonal to left and down, S=Diagonal to right and down. If lowercase letter is used then drawing and moving will take place. If uppercase letter is used then only moving will occur.
- Starting at the start coordinate the interpreter will *draw* a line to the next pixel (or scale pixels) up/dn and so on if the letter used is lower case. If it is upper case it will *move* to the position instead of drawing a line, and thus next letter will cause drawing or moving from that new position.
- The pen color will be as given or as specified in the next paragraph. If a number e.g. 4 or 12 is given, it will be taken to indicate a change of color from the specified color in ne_Color, or default pen color if no color is specified. The change will take effect until another number is given or -. If - is given then the color will revert back to ne_Color or default color. This action will only take place if ne_Color is not negative (see above).
- When you specify numbers refer to the Colors Table in the RobotBASIC Constants section. If you specify a number greater than the last color it will revert to the last color. Any other characters will be ignored. This command can be emulated with a combination of GotoXY and LineTo combined with SetColor.

•RotShape(se_ShapeString,ne_Direction)

This will return a string that can be used in DrawShape. The new string will be such that when drawn it will be an (ne_Direction x 90°) rotation of the original string resulting from se_ShapeString. ne_Direction can be a positive integer for clockwise rotations and negative for counter-clockwise rotations of multiples 90°. So if ne_Direction is 3 then that is 270° clockwise and if it is -2 then that is 180° counter-clockwise: Example:

```
Scale = 20 \ X = 400 \ Y = 300
UpArrow = "UUlulwwssldlUU"              //The shape data to draw an up arrow.
drawshape UpArrow,X,Y,Scale
FloodFill
drawshape RotShape(UpArrow,3),X,Y,Scale   //the same string is rotated +270° to make left
arrow.
FloodFill
drawshape RotShape(UpArrow,1),X,Y,Scale   //the string is rotated to +90° to make right
arrow
FloodFill
drawshape RotShape(UpArrow,-2),X,Y,Scale  //the string is rotated to +90° to make right
arrow
FloodFill
for i=0 to 3    //this is a better way to do the same as above
   DrawShape RotShape(UpArrow,i),300,100,20
   FloodFill
next
end
```

•TextWidth(se_Text{,se_FontName{,ne_FontSize{,ne_FonctStyle}}})
•TextHeight(se_Text{,se_FontName{,ne_FontSize{,ne_FonctStyle}}})

Will return the width/height in pixels that the string se_Text will occupy on the screen with the specified font and size and style. See xyText for explanations for the font parameters. If the se_FontName is not specified or is "" then Courier New will be assumed. If ne_FontSize is not given or is < 1 then 11 will be assumed. If ne_FontStyle is not given or is < 0 then 0 will be assumed (i.e. no style).

•3D Screen Graphics Drawing

•ge3Dto2DV
ne_X,ne_Y,ne_Z,ne_Rho,ne_Theta,ne_Phi,ne_Dist,ne_CenterX,ne_CenterY,vn_ScrX,vn_ScrY

This command will convert an X,Y,Z world 3D coordinate point to screen 2D coordinate ScrX,ScrY. All parameters must be integer or float except for the last two which have to be variables that will be assigned float values..

ne_Rho	the distance of the camera from the origin.
ne_Theta	the angle (radians) from the X-axis in the XY-plane, counter-clockwise is positive
ne_Phi	the angle (radians) from the Z-axis, counter-clockwise is positive and positive Z is up towards the camera.
ne_Dist	the distance of the projection plane from the origin
ne_CenterX	the screen X-coordinate of the center point of the window (usually 400)
ne_CenterY	the screen Y-coordinate of the center point of the window (usually 300)

The command will calculate the screen ScrX,ScrY coordinate and assign the variables vn_ScrX and vn_ScrY the values. There will be no clipping if the ScrX,ScrY coordinates are outside the window limits. It is up to you what to do with the data returned. The values will be floats.

•ge3Dto2DVA ne_X,ne_Y,ne_Z,a_CameraSpecs,vn_ScrX,vn_ScrY

This command will convert an X,Y,Z world 3D coordinate point to screen 2D coordinate ScrX,ScrY. This command is similar to ge3Dto2DV but instead of the camera data being specified as 6 parameters this command uses an array (a_CameraSpecs) as in ge3Dto2DA.

•ge3Dto2DA a_3DPoints,a_CameraSpecs

This command will convert an *array* of world 3D coordinates to screen 2D coordinates.

a_3DPoints must be a two-dimensional array with the dimensions being [n,>=5] where n is the number of points that need to be converted. The first 3 elements in each row are X,Y,Z (coordinates of the point), the 4th and 5th elements will be filled by the command with the screen X,Y coordinates. The number of columns has to be a minimum of 5 but can be more if

186

you are going to encode more information about vertices.

a_CameraSpecs must be one-dimensional and must have 6 elements (or more but not less). The elements are parameters that describe the position of the Camera position in space using polar coordinates. The elements in order are as follows:

Rho   the distance of the camera from the origin.

Theta   the angle (radians) from the X-axis in the XY-plane, counter-clockwise is positive

Phi   the angle (radians) from the Z-axis, counter-clockwise is positive and positive Z is up towards the camera.

D   the distance of the projection plane from the origin

Cx   the screen X-coordinate of the center point of the window (usually 400)

Cy   the screen Y-coordinate of the center point of the window (usually 300)

The command will calculate the screen X,Y coordinate for each point using the parameters provided. There will be no clipping if the X,Y coordinates are outside the window limits. It is up to you what to do with the data returned.

Example (also see example under gePlotSurface):

```
data Eye;120,pi(.25),pi(.35),1550,400,300 //rho,theta,phi,d,Cx,Cy
x = 20 \ data points;0,0,0,0,0,  x,0,0,0,0,  0,x,0,0,0,  0,0,x,0,0
x = 15 \ data points;x,0,0,0,0,  0,x,0,0,0,  x,x,0,0,0,  x,x,x,0,0
dim Points[10,5] \ mcopy points,Points  //make appropriate array of vertices
flip on
while true
   ge3dto2da Points,Eye              //calculated screen coordinates
   for i=1 to 3
     line Points[0,3],Points[0,4],Points[i,3],Points[i,4],2,0
     line Points[6,3],Points[6,4],Points[3+i,3],Points[3+i,4],1,red
     if i < 3 then line Points[0,3],Points[0,4],Points[5+i,3],Points[5+i,4],i,blue+i
   next
   line Points[7,3],Points[7,4],Points[6,3],Points[6,4],1,green
   flip \ clearscr \ Eye[1] = Eye[1]+.01
wend
```

•geVisibles a_3DPoints,a_CameraSpecs,a_SurfacesSpecs{,a_Edges{,ne_ColorFactor}}

This command will process an array of surfaces to evaluate which ones are visible. The surfaces are defined by vertex numbers from within a vertices array. The surface must have at least three vertices.

a_3DPoints and a_CamerSpecs are the vertices and camera data arrays as described in ge3Dto2D above.

a_SurfacesSpecs is an array of surfaces. Must be two-dimensional. Each surface is a row. Each row has the following elements (remember 1st element is element number zero):

- 1st element is the color of the surface. This value can be a RobotBASIC constant color (e.g. red) or can be an RGB value.

- 2nd element will be set by this command to true (1) if the surface is redeemed to be visible or false (0) if not.
- 3rd element onwards is a number representing the vertices that define the surface. The vertex numbers are the index within the vertices array a_3dPoints. There must be a minimum of 3 vertices but you can have more. Only the first three vertices will be used by the command. **The order of the vertices has to be <u>counter-clockwise</u> as the surface is viewed from the front**. *The order is very important it is what defines visible and invisible surfaces*.

a_Edges is optional and is an array that will be created by the command if the parameter is defined. The array will be two-dimensional. It is an array of edges that are visible. Each row is an edge. The elements of the row will be as follows:
- 1st element is the vertex number of the first point of the edge. The vertex number is an index within the array a_3DPoints.
- 2nd element is the vertex number of the other point of the edge. The vertex number is an index within the array a_3DPoints.
- 3rd element is a count of how many surfaces share this edge.
- 4th element is an RGB color value that will be 10% darker than the color of the first surface that the edge belongs to. That is it will be a factor of 0.9 of the original color. You can change this factor by specifying the parameter ne_ColorFactor as the value you need as a number between 0 and 1. If a_ColorFactor is not given it will be 0.9. If you give a number less than 0 it will be 0 and if greater than 1 it will be 1.
- 5th element is an RGB color value that will be the color of the first surface that the edge belongs to.

The command uses the vertices and camera data as well as the surfaces data to evaluate which surface is visible inserting the value in the 2nd element of each row (element number 1) of the surfaces array. The command also creates (if desired) an array of edges that are visible. See gePlotEdges and gePlotSurfaces.

•gePlotSurfaces
a_3DPoints,a_SurfacesSpecs{,ne_DoFilling{,ne_LineWidth{,ne_OnlyVisible{,ne_CentroidAl l}}}}
This command will use the array of surfaces and a corresponding array of vertices that have already been processed using ge3Dto2DA and geVisibles to render the surfaces on the screen.

a_3DPoints is the vertices data arrays as described in ge3Dto2D above and **you need to have already called the command to process the array as described in the command details**.

a_SurfacesSpecs is the surfaces array as described in geVisible and **you need to have already have called the command to process the array as described in the command details**.

The command uses the vertices and surfaces data to plot the surfaces on the screen. By default a surface's edges will be plotted and then they will be filled with the color of the surface as specified inside the array (see geVisibles), but if you set ne_DoFilling to off then only the edges of the surfaces will be plotted and no filling will occur. By default the edges will be plotted with a line width of 2, but you can specify any other value >= 1. By default only the surfaces that have been calculated to be visible after calling geVisibles will be plotted. But if you set to ne_OnlyVisible to false then all surfaces will be plotted. During the processing of the command the centroid of the surface has to be calculated to be able to do the filling. Normally only the first three vertices that define the surface will be used to do this calculation. However, you may need in some situations to use all of the vertices to get a better centroid position. This will slow the calculations but will give a more accurate centroid. If ne_CentroidAll is set to true then all vertices that define the surface will be used for the calculation (note that this will slow the command down).

Example:

```
data Eye;120,pi(.25),pi(.25),1550,400,300      //rho,theta,phi,d,Cx,Cy
data points;0,0,0,0,0, 20,0,0,0,0, 0,20,0,0,0, 0,0,20,0,0
dim Points[maxdim(points,1)/5,5] \ mcopy points,Points      //make appropriate array of
vertices
data surfaces;red,0,2,0,3, blue,0,2,3,1, green,0,1,3,0, yellow,0,0,2,1 //surfaces
dim Surfaces[4,5] \ mcopy surfaces,Surfaces   //create surfaces array
flip on
while true
   ge3dto2da Points,Eye                    //calculated screen coordinates
   geVisibles Points,Eye,Surfaces,Edges    //calculated visible surfaces
   gePlotSurfaces Points,Surfaces          //Plot and fill visible surfaces
   gePlotEdges Points,Edges,3,-2
   geCentroids Points,Surfaces,Centroids   //Get Centroids data
   for i=0 to 3 //plot visible centroids
     if Surfaces[i,1] then circlewh Centroids[i,0]-5,Centroids[i,1]-5,10,10,white,white
   next
   flip \ clearscr
   Eye[1] = Eye[1]+.01 \ Eye[2] = Eye[2]+.02  //move the camera
   if keydown(Ascii("X")) then geRotateA Points,.05,1
   if keydown(Ascii("Y")) then geRotateA Points,.05,2
   if keydown(Ascii("Z")) then geRotateA Points,.05,3
   xytext 0,0,"Press X,Y and/or Z to see a nice effect"
wend
```

•geCentroids a_3DPoints,a_SurfacesSpecs,a_Centroids

This command will use the array of surfaces and a corresponding array of vertices that have already been processed using ge3Dto2DA and geVisibles to create an array that contains as many rows as there are rows in the surfaces array and 5 elements per row.

a_3DPoints is the vertices data arrays as described in ge3dto2D above and **you need to have already called the command to process the array as described in the command details**.

a_SurfacesSpecs is the surfaces array as described in geVisible and **you <u>DO NOT</u> need to have already have called the command to process the array as described in the command details**.

The command uses the vertices and surfaces data to calculate the Triangular and Polygonal Centroids as well as the area of the polygon representing the surface as it would be drawn on the screen in response to all the calculations after calling ge3Dto2DA you may have also called the geVisibles too but that is not needed for the calculations of the centroids. The data will be put in the array a_Centroids which if it already exists will be erased and will be recreated and populated with data.

a_Centroids will be two dimensional and will contain as many rows as there are in a_SurfacesSpecs. In each row it will contain TCx,TCy,PCx,PCy,A. Where T means triangular. P means polygonal and Cx means X-Coordinate of the centroid and Cy means the Y-Coordinate of the centroid. A means the area.

So for each surface in a_SurfacesSpecs using the vertices as defined in the array and using the already calculated Screen X,Y coordinates for each vertex in the a_3DPoints array after it has already been processed as described in ge3Dto2DA this command will calculate the Centroid of the Surface using two methods. The first method will use only the first THREE vertices of the surface and calculates the centroid of the TRIANGLE formed by these vertices. The second method will use ALL the vertices and will calculate the AREA and REAL centroid of the surface as it would be drawn on the screen.

These centroid are the same as the ones used in gePlotSurfaces to do a FILLING of the surface after drawing its edges. gePlotSurfaces uses the triangular centroid by default since it is quite an adequate method since the triangular centroid will always lay inside the surface and since it only uses three vertices it is a much quicker calculation than using all the vertices of the surface. But the command can be told to use the polygonal centroid instead. geCentroids gives you the coordinates of these centroids which can be helpful in doing further plotting of the surface other than in gePlotSurfaces.

Note: If the surface is triangular then of course both the triangular and polygonal centroids will be the same.
Note: The centroids and the area are for the surface as it would be drawn on the 2D screen since they are calculated from the 2D coordinates as calculated in ge3Dto2DA from the 3D coordinates of the vertices in the a_3DPoints array and inserted into that array .

•gePlotEdges a_3DPoints,a_Edges{,ne_LineWidth{,ne_LineWidth{,ne_Color}}

This command will use the array of edges and a corresponding array of vertices that have already been processed using ge3Dto2DA and geVisibles to render the surfaces on the screen.

a_3DPoints is the vertices data arrays as described in ge3Dto2D above and **you need to have already called the command to process the array as described in the command details**.

a_Edges is the edges array as described in geVisibles and **you need to have already have called the command to process the array as described in the command details**.

The command uses the vertices and edges data to plot the edges on the screen. The edges will be plotted with the current default line width if ne_LineWidth is not given or is < 1. Also the edges will be plotted with the current default pen color if ne_Color is not given or is -1. You can specify either a RobotBASIC color constant or an RGB color. If ne_Color is -2 then the edge will be plotted using the color as specified in the 4th element of the corresponding row in the edges array. This element is an RGB color value that would have been created by geVisibles as described in the command's details.

•**geRotVx ne_X,ne_Y,ne_Z,ne_RotAngle,vn_X',vn_Y',vn_Z'**
•**geRotVy ne_X,ne_Y,ne_Z,ne_RotAngle,vn_X',vn_Y',vn_Z'**
•**geRotVz ne_X,ne_Y,ne_Z,ne_RotAngle,vn_X',vn_Y',vn_Z'**
These three commands will rotate the point (ne_X, ne_Y, ne_Z) about the X/Y/Z-Axis by the angle ne_RotAngle (radians). Counter-Clockwise is positive. The new coordinates of the point will be assigned to vn_X', vn_Y', vn_Z'. Positive angles are counterclockwise and negative angles are clockwise (using the left-handed rule).

•**geRotateA a_3DPoints,ne_RotAngle,ne_AxisCode{,ne_From{,ne_To}}**
This command will use an array of 3D points and will rotate them by the specified ne_RotAngle (radians) about the specified ne_AxisCode (1=X-Axis, 2=Y-Axis, 3=Z-Axis).

a_#DPoints has to be a 2 two dimensional array with as many rows as there are points and in each row there has to be at least three elements where the first element is the X-Coordinate, the second is the Y-Coordinate and the third is the Z-Coordinate of the point. You may have more elements in each row as would for instance be required for the a_3DPoints array in the above other commands.

The resulting new (X',Y',Z') values. will be placed back over the original (X,Y,Z) values. Positive angles are counterclockwise and negative angles are clockwise (using the left-handed rule).

ne_From specifies the row number (i.e. vertex number) to start from within the a_3DPoints array and ne_To specifies the row number to finish at. If ne_From is not given or is less than 0 it will be set to 0. If ne_To is not given or is less than NumberOfRows-1 or is greater than NumberOfRows-1 then it will be set to NumberOfRows-1.

Note: The original coordinates will be overwritten with the resulting coordinates due to the rotation. Use mCopy to keep a copy of the original array.

Creating & Using Arrays

Note: See the notes at the top of the Standard User Interfacing section. Also see the note at the top of the Screen & Bitmap Graphics section concerning the .BMP extension when specifying a file name for the bitmap functions.

Note: See ge3Dto2DA, ge3Dto2DVA, geVisibles, gePlotSurfaces, geCentroids, mReadBMP, mWriteBMP, BmpFindClr, mPolygon, mBezier and JoystickE.

•Arrays Creation & Manipulation

•Dim a_Name1[ExprN{,ExprN...}]{ , a_Name2[ExprN{,ExprN...}] {, ...}}}...

This will specify that a_Name1 is an Array of the dimensions *[ExprN{,ExprN...}]* the [and] are required and so is the , between each dimension. You can use an array element anywhere as any variable (see the Overview Of The Language section). The **Dim** statement establishes the maximum value for each dimension and the over all dimension of the array. The Index of the dimension starts at 0 and ends at *ExprN-1*. *ExprN* must result in an integer value, otherwise an error will occur. Each element of the array can be any of the data types (String, Float or Integer).

In version 4.1.0 and upwards you can specify multiple arrays' dimensions using the same DIM statement by separating the specifications with commas.

If you try to access any un-assigned element an error will occur. If you try to access outside the specified range in the **DIM** statement an error will occur.

If you have a two dimensional Array **Dim** *N[4,5]* then there are 4 rows and 5 columns i.e. there are 4 rows with 5 elements in each row. If you have **Dim** *N[6,7,8]* then there are 6 rows where each element in the row constitutes a matrix in itself, where those matrices each have 7 rows and 8 columns.

This can go on for as long as you care, but remember that the row count is the first dimension and the second dimension is a count of elements in each row. Each element in the row can be a string, integer, float or another matrix as described above.

```
Dim XY[2,4,5] , AB[3,2]
//means that XY is an array of 3D. The first dimension goes from 0 to 1
//second dimension from 0 to 3 third dimension from 0 to 4
//Also AB is a 2D array with 3 rows and 2 elements in each row (2 columns)
AB[0,0] = 5                 //assigns 1st element in first row in AB the value 5
XY[1,3,2] = sin(pi(2.0/3))+4  //assigns element [1,3,2]
print AB[0,0]; XY[1,3,2]      //prints element [1,3,2]
XY[2,4,5] = 9                      //causes an error because range is XY[1,3,4]
```

```
        Print AB[0,1]                    //causes an error because AB[0,1] was not
        assigned
```

•Data a_Name;Expr{,Expr....}

This command creates an array of 1 dimension named a_Name and puts all the resulting values from the *Expr's* into the array. a_Name is the array name, the **;** after the name is necessary to separate the name from the data. The data is separated by a **,**. *Expr* can result in any value type (String, Integer, or Float). If you specify the same array name in two or more **Data** statements then the data is appended together. If you desire to erase the array, so as to start populating it at the first element, use **Dim** *a_Name[0]* where a_Name is the array name used in the data statement. If you have previously dimensioned a_Name before issuing the **Data** statements, then you must use the **Dim** *a_NAme[0]* before you use the **Data** statements. If you do not the data will not be loaded into the array.

If you do not wish to give a specific value to an element and skip it (i.e. use it as a place holder) then just put a space between the commas for that element. See example below.

```
data test;1,2,"some text",4.5,sin(3/4.6),length("test")
data test;,,,66,44.5,log(3)
print test[10]          //print 44.5
print test[2]           //prints 'some text'
print test[0]+test[3]   //prints 5.5
print test[7]           //causes an error since element 7 is not defined
                        //due to the ,, since no value was given for that
                        //element position
print test[8]           //also causes an error since again this element is
                        //not specified due to the ,,

Dim test[0]             //effectively erases the array data
data test;"again",3     //repopulate the array
print test[0]           //prints 'again'
print test[7]           //gives an error since there are not 7 elements
```

•mDim(a_Name)

Returns the dimension of the array. If it does not exist 0 will be returned. The dimension of the array starts at 1. For example if an array *MyData* has been created with the statement **Dim** *MyData[4,5,6]* then *mDim(MyData)* returns 3.

This function can be useful if you read an array from a file with **mRead** (see above). The array read from a file will have the dimensions of the array that was used to write the file. It may be unknown to you as a programmer and this function and **MaxDim** can be used to determine details of the matrix.

•MaxDim(a_Name{,ne_Dimension})

Returns the limit of the specified dimension. This function can be useful if you read an array from a file with **mRead** (see above). The array read from a file will have the dimensions of the array that was used to write the file. It may be unknown to you as a programmer and this function and **mDim** can be used to determine the details of the matrix. The dimension constraint has a minimum value of 1. If ne_Dimension is not given or is less than 1 it will be made to be 1.

```
    dim MyData[4,5,9]
    gosub populate_mydata  //some routine to put data in the array
    mWrite MyData,"Test.Txt"
    //later on in any program you read the data from a file
    mread NewData,"test.Txt"
    print mDim(NewData)          //=== prints 3
    for i = 1 to mDim(NewData)
        print MaxDim(NewData,i)  // will print 4 then 5 then 9
    next
    //===print out all the data elements
    for i = 0 to MaxDim(NewData,1)-1
        For j = 0 to MaxDim(NewData,2)-1
            for k=0 to MaxDim(NewData,3)-1
                print NewData[i,j,k]
            next
        next
    next
```

•mType(a_Name[...])

This function is used to determine the type of an array element. You specify the array element in the normal way as described in the description for Dim or Data above. The returned values are:

> 102 = Ascii("f") ➜ floating point number
> 105 = Ascii("i") ➜ integer number
> 115 = Ascii("s") ➜ string
> 0   ➜ No Value i.e. has not been assigned a value

The values above are also defined in the RobotBASIC Constants section

> Float   = Floating point number
> Integer = Integer number
> String   = String
> NoValue = Not a defined element

This function can be useful in iterating through arrays where you may need to determine if an element is a valid element before using it. If you try to use an invalid array element an error will occur. This function can be used to prevent this.

•mCopy a_Source,a_Destination

a_Source must be a existing previously dimensioned array, or an array created by Data above. a_Destination does not have to exist. If it does not then it will be created by the command and will be an exact copy of a_Source, including the dimension, and dimensional constraints. If it does exist and has been dimensioned, the data in a_Source will be copied into a_Destination row wise. That is each data element from a_Source will be copied into elements of a_Destination until all the elements of the first row are filled, then it starts with the elements from the next row and so on until a_Destination is filled or a_Source runs out of elements.

194

This command is useful for looking at the data of one array in different row-column dimensions. **Data** can only create 1-dimensional arrays with all the data in one row. But if you want to load the data into a 2-dimensional array then dimension an array according to desired dimensions and copy the array created by **Data** into it.

```
Data a;1,2,3,4,5,6,7,8,9
Print a[5]  //will print 6
Dim b[3,3]
mCopy  a,b
Print b[1,2]  //will print 6
```

•mWrite a_Name,se_FileName

Will write the contents of the array to the specified file. When specifying the file name you can use directory structures for example:

```
"C:\RobotBasic\Programs\MySimulation.sim"
```

The directory must exist. The file does not have to exist, and if it does it will be overwritten. Any error in writing to the file will cause an error to be issued. The array has to be a valid previously dimensioned array or an array created with **Data**. See mTextFW and mTextFR below.

Note: The command in version 2.1.0 and later will not write files compatible with older versions.

•mRead a_Name,se_FileName

Will create a new array (if it already exists it will be erased first) and will populate its elements with the data from the specified file. The file must exist and it must be of the right format written previously with m**Write** (see above). The array will be dimensioned the same as the matrix that was used to write the file in the first place. You can find out the dimensions of a_Name with m**Dim()** and **MaxDim()**. Any elements that were unpopulated in the original matrix will still be unpopulated in the new matrix. You will get an error if the file does not exist or if it is the wrong format. If the file is the correct format but there was an error in reading it an error message will be issued. See mTextFW and mTextFR below.

Note: The command in version 2.1.0 and later is not compatible with files created in older versions. You must convert files created with older versions using mReadOld. Write a program to read the old file with mReadOld and write it again with the new mWrite. There is no mWriteOld; it is not needed. The syntax for mReadOld is the same as for mRead. mReadOld may be removed in later versions.

•mTextFW a_Name,se_TextFileName

Will write the contents of the one-dimensional array to the text file. When specifying the file name you can use directory structures for example:

```
"C:\RobotBasic\Programs\MySimulation.sim"
```

195

The directory must exist. The file does not have to exist, and if it does it will be overwritten. You must specify the file name in full including the extension. Any error in writing to the file will cause an error to be issued. The array has to be a valid one-dimensional array or an array created with **Data**.

The file will be a plain text file with each element of the array written on one line as text. If the element is a number it will be converted to the text representation of the number. Each element will be one line of text in the file. That is a line with a CR/LF at the end of it. The first non-valid element (i.e. not assigned) will be redeemed to be the end of the array.

This command is useful in creating text files that can be easily read by humans. You can use formatting functions and other functions to create elements in the array that are combinations of data from various other arrays and/or variables to create a nice printable (or readable by humans) report file.

This is not like the above mWrite which will create coded unreadable files that can only be read by mRead. mTextFW will create text files that can be easily modified, read or printed.

mWrite and mRead are easier to use if you need to save and read a database. However mTextFW and mTextFR are more suited for creating and reading report files.

•mTextFR a_Name,se_TextFileName

Will create a new array a_Name (if it already exists it will be erased first) and will populate its elements with the text from the text file. The file must exist and it must be plain text file. The array will be one-dimensional and each element will be one line from the text file. Each element will be assigned the line of text as a string regardless if it is a number or text. You can use Extract(), SubString(), ToNumber() and other functions to manipulate the data. So if a line contains multiple fields of data you can use code to separate the fields into individual data and assign them to variables or elements of another (properly dimensioned) array.

You will get an error if the file does not exist. You must specify the file name in full including the extension.

mWrite and mRead are easier to use if you need to save and read a database. However mTextFW and mTextFR are more suited for creating and reading report files.

•mFromString a_Name,se_String{,se_Separator}

se_String is a string that contains substrings separated with the characters in se_Separator. If the separator is not given then it will be a CR/LF pair of characters [char(13)+char(10) = CrLf()]. The string will be parsed into its substrings using the separator characters and each substring is then placed into an element in the array in order. Any substring that can be converted to an integer or a float will be converted and will be placed into the array as an element of the correct type (the numbers in the string must be the string representation of the numbers not binary) .

a_Name will be a one dimensional array. It does not have to exist and if it does it will be deleted and recreated with the new dimension and data.

If se_String is an empty string then the array will have one element with the value being an empty string.

Also see mToString(), Substitute() and CrLf(). Also see the buffer functions BuffWrite() and BuffRead().

Example:
```
data a;10,3.45,"test",2.34e245,0xFFFFF,0%1110001110101,"testing  this"
s = mToString(a)  //by default the separator will be CR/LF
addlistbox "tt",100,100,200,s
SetListBox "tt",1
AddRBGroup "Select One",400,100,350,300,3,s
mFromString b,s  //notice by default the separator is Cr/Lf
for i=0 to maxdim(b,1)-1
    n=b[i]
    xystring 10,200+i*20,n;"          "
    if isnumber(n) then xystring -1,-1,n*2
next
s = "test1,3.4,6,Test2,Test3"
mFromString b,s,","   //now the separator is ,
for i=0 to maxdim(b,1)-1
    n=b[i]
    xystring 10,400+i*20,n;"          "
    if isnumber(n) then xystring -1,-1,n*2
next
```

•mToString(a_TextLines{,se_Separator})

Returns a string that is all the elements in the array put together into one string. If any element in the array is a number it will be converted to a string representation. The elements are separated with the characters in the string se_Separator if given or the character pair CR/LF [char(13)+char(10) = crlf()] if not given. The array has to exist and has to be a one-dimensional array and must not have any non-assigned elements. The returned string will contain the elements up to the first unassigned element if there is one.

Also see mFromString and the example there. Also see CrLf() and Substitute(). Also see the buffer functions BuffWrite() and BuffRead().

•mToCommaText(a_TextLines)

Returns a string that has all the elements in the array put together into one string. If any element in the array is a number it will be converted to a string representation. The elements are separated with a comma. Any strings that contain a comma or a space will be surrounded with quotations (""). If the string contains a quotation already then it will be doubled just like when you want to specify a quotations in an RB normal string (see examples). Also see mFromString and the example there. Also see CrLf(), ToCommaString() and Substitute(). Also see the buffer functions BuffWrite() and BuffRead().

•ObjectGet a_ObjectArray,ne_ObjectNumber   or   •RecordGet a_DataBaseArray,ne_RecordNumber
•ObjectPut a_ObjectArray,ne_ObjectNumber   or   •RecordPut a_DataBaseArray,ne_RecordNumber

These two commands can be useful in creating a pseudo-object based action or a simple database system.

The array a_ObjectArray (or a_DataBaseArray) has to be a 2-dimensional array. The 0th row in the array is assumed to hold the names of the elements (fields) of the instances of the object (records in the database). The next row (row 1) onwards hold the actual values for each instance of the object (record in the data base).

ObjectGet/RecordGet will look into the array and will create as many variables as there are elements in the 0th row and each of these variables will have the name as specified in the element. Then it will go to the row specified by ne_ObjectNumber/ne_RecordNumber (ranging from 1 onwards) and will get the values of each element in that row and assign that value to the variable corresponding to that element. So after invoking this command there will be a collection of variables whose names correspond to the elements of the object (fields of the database) and whose values correspond to the values in the desired instance of the object (record).

ObjectPut/RecordPut will look into the array and will fetch the value of a local variable whose name corresponds to the name in each element in the 0th row and then it will go to the row specified by ne_ObjectNumber/ne_RecordNumber (ranging from 1 onwards) and will put the value of the variable in the corresponding element in that row. So after invoking this command the collection of variables whose names correspond to the elements of the object (fields of the database) will have their values stored in the row that corresponds to the desired instance of the object (record).

Also see varSet and varType() and varValue() as well as vType() and mType().

This is best appreciated with an example:
```
Main:
  InlineInputMode on
  call CreateSTUDENTclass()          // create the class
  STUDENT.Sam =0                     // create three objects
  STUDENT.John=1
  STUDENT.Mary=2
  call CreateSTUDENT(STUDENT.John)   // demo calls to class methods
```

198

```
        call CreateSTUDENT(STUDENT.Mary)
        call PrintSTUDENT(STUDENT.John)
        call PrintSTUDENT(STUDENT.Mary)
        call EditSTUDENT(STUDENT.John)
        call PrintSTUDENT(STUDENT.John)
    End
    Sub CreateSTUDENTclass()
        Dim STUDENT[11,4]        // create a Class of Type STUDENT capable of handling 10 students
        mConstant STUDENT,0      // initialize all to 0 to make all objects inactive
        STUDENT[0,0]="Active"    //create the object's elements in the 0th row
        STUDENT[0,1]="Name"      //they have to be names that can become valid variable names
        STUDENT[0,2]="Gender"    //so when the ObjectGet and ObjectPut commands are called then
        STUDENT[0,3]="Avge"      //variables by these names will be created and will be assigned
    return                       //the values pertaining ot the desired object (i.e. row).
    Sub CreateSTUDENT(n)
        ObjectGet STUDENT,n
        print crlf(),"ENTER DATA FOR NEW STUDENT"
        Input "Enter Name:|Enter Gender:|Enter Grade Average (0-100):",Name,Gender,Avge
        Active=1  // indicate that the object has been created
        ObjectPut STUDENT,n
    return
    Sub PrintSTUDENT(n)
        ObjectGet STUDENT,n
        if Active
          Print crlf()+"Name:",Name,crlf(),"Gender:",Gender,crlf(),"Average:",Avge
        else
          print crlf(),"This object has not been created"
        endif
    return
    Sub EditSTUDENT(n)
        ObjectGet STUDENT,n
        if Active
          print crlf(),"Enter new grade average for: ",Name
          Input "Average = ",Avge
        else
          print crlf(),"This object has not been created"
        endif
        ObjectPut STUDENT,n
    Return
```

Here is another example that uses RecordGet and RecordPut

```
    Main:
        call DB_Initialize(4)
        Call DB_SetVals(1,"Sam",50,"30043")
        Call DB_SetVals(2,"Pam",20,"30055")
        for i=1 to 2
          Call DB_GetVals(i,OName,OAge,OZipCode)
          print OName;OAge;OZipCode
        next
    End
    Sub DB_Initialize(HowMany)
        Dim DB[HowMany,3]
        DB[0,0] = "Name"
        DB[0,1] = "Age"
        DB[0,2] = "ZipCode"
    Return
    Sub DB_GetVals(Which,&Name,&Age,&ZipCode)
        RecordGet DB,Which
    Return
    Sub DB_SetVals(Which,Name,Age,ZipCode)
        RecordPut DB,Which
    Return
```

•Array Math Commands

•mAND a_Name,ExprN
•mOR a_Name,ExprN
•mXOR a_Name,ExprN
•mShiftL a_Name,ExprN
•mShiftR a_Name,ExprN
    Will bitwise AND/OR/XOR/ShiftLeft/ShiftRight each element in the array by the result of the numeric expression *ExprN*. a_Name has to exist. Also all the elements must be numeric. If an element is not numeric it will not be affected. If an element is a float it will be converted to an integer and the operation is performed on the integer and the element will become an integer. Any uninitialized elements will remain so.

•mNOT a_Name
    Will bitwise NOT (invert) each element in the array by the result of the numeric expression *ExprN*. a_Name has to exist. Also all the elements must be numeric. If an element is not numeric it will not be affected. If an element is a float it will be converted to an integer and the operation is performed on the integer and the element will become an integer. Any uninitialized elements will remain so.

•mScale a_Name,ExprN
    Will multiply each element in the array by the result of the numeric expression *ExprN*. a_Name has to exist. Also all the elements must be numeric.

•mConstant a_Name,Expr
    Will fill each element in the array by the result of the expression *Expr*. It has to exist. *Expr* can be numeric or string.

•mDiagonal a_Name,Expr
    Will fill all the diagonal elements in the array by the result of the expression *Expr*. It has to exist. *Expr* can be numeric or string. If *Expr* is numeric then all the other elements will be zero. If *Expr* is a string then all the other elements will be blank. a_Name must be two-dimensional.

•mmAND a_Source,a_Destination
•mmOR a_Source,a_Destination
•mmXOR a_Source,a_Destination
•mmShiftL a_Source,a_Destination
•mmShiftR a_Source,a_Destination
    This equivalent to saying a_Destination = a_Destination (op) s_Source. Where (op) is bitwise AND/OR/XOR/ShiftLeft/ShiftRight. Both arrays must exist and must be of the same

dimension and of the same dimensional constraints. If any element in a_Source that is a string or not initialized will be considered 0. Any element in either array that is a float will be made into an integer to do the operation but only a_Destination's element will be changed to integer type. Any element in a_Destination that is not initialized or is a string will remain so. Remember it is a_Destination = a_Destination (op) a_Source.

•mAdd a_Source,a_Destination

Will Add elements of a_Source to a_Destination. This equivalent to saying a_Source = a_Destination + a_Source. Both arrays must exist and must be of the same dimension and of the same dimensional constraints. If any element is a string and the corresponding element to be added is a numeric then the result will be a string concatenation of the string with the numeric converted to a string. If the elements to be added are both strings then the result is a concatenation. If one element is an integer while the other is a float then the result is a float.

•mSub a_Source,a_Destination

Will subtract elements of a_Source from a_Destination. This equivalent to saying a_Source = a_Destination - a_Source. Both arrays must exist and must be of the same dimension and of the same dimensional constraints. If any element is a string then there will be no operation done. If one element is an integer while the other is a float then the result is a float.

•mMultiply a_Left,a_Right,a_Result

Will multiply a_Left and a_Right and put the result in a_Result. This equivalent to saying a_Result = a_Left x a_Right. The order is important a_Left x a_Right is not equal to a_Right x a_Left. a_Result does not have to exist, but if it does it will be erased and recreated. Both arrays must be two-dimensional. The number of Columns of a_Left must be the same as the number of Rows of a_Right. That is if a_Left has the dimension [R1,C1] and a_Right has the dimension [R2,C2] then multiplication is possible only if C1=R2. The resultant a_Result will have the dimension [R1,C2]. Also, the elements of a_Left and a_Right must be numeric.

•mInvert a_Source,a_Inverse,vn_Determinant

Will calculate the inverse of array a_Source and assign it to a_Inverse, and also the determinant of a_Source will be assigned to vn_Determinant. That is equivalent to saying a_Inverse = a_Source^{-1} and vn_Determinant = |a_Source|. a_Inverse does not have to exist, but if it does it will be erased and recreated. a_Source must be two-dimensional and a square matrix. That is the number of rows must equal the number of columns. All elements in a_Source must be numeric and if it is not invertible then vn_Determinant = 0 and elements of a_Inverse will be all zeros.

•mDet a_Source,vn_Determinant

Will calculate the determinant of the array and assign it to vn_Determinant. That is equivalent to saying vn_Determinant = |a_Source|. a_Source must be two-dimensional and a square matrix. That is the number of rows must equal the number of columns. All elements in the array must be numeric.

•mTranspose a_Source,a_Transpose
Will transpose a_Source and assign the result to a_Transpose which does not have to exist, but if it does it will be erased and recreated. a_Source must be two-dimensional. *a_Source[i,j] = a_Transpose[j,i]*.

•mRegression a_XYdata,vn_Slope,vn_Intercept
Will do a regression analysis (Line Fit) on the data in the array *a_XYdata* which must be two-dimensional and all data must be numeric. The first row contains the X values, and the second row contains the Y values. There must be a Y value for each X value. Any non-numeric or undefined elements will be taken as 0. The line formula is Y=mX+b where m is the slope and b the Y-Axis intercept. *vn_Slope* will be assigned the slope (m). *vn_Intercept* will be assigned the intercept (b).

•mExpFit a_XYdata,vn_Exponent,vn_Factor
Will do an Exponential Curve Fit on the data in the array *a_XYdata* which must be two-dimensional and all data must be numeric. The first row contains the X values, and the second row contains the Y values. There must be a Y value for each X value. Any non-numeric or undefined elements will be taken as 0. The formula is $Y = be^{(aX)}$, where a will be assigned to *vn_Exponent* and b to *vn_Factor*.

Note: e^X is the exponential to the base e, which is Exp() in RobotBASIC.

•mLogFit a_XYdata,vn_Factor,vn_Translation
Will do a Logarithmic Curve Fit on the data in the array *a_XYdata* which must be two-dimensional and all data must be numeric. The first row contains the X values, and the second row contains the Y values. There must be a Y value for each X value. Any non-numeric or undefined elements will be taken as 0. The formula is Y=aLn(X)+b . a will be assigned to *vn_Factor* and b to *vn_Translation*.

Note: Ln() is the natural logarithm, which is NLog() in RobotBASIC.

•mPolyFit a_XYdata,a_Coefficients
Will do a Polynomial Curve Fit on the data in the array a_XYdata which must be two-dimensional and all data must be numeric. The first row contains the X values, and the second row contains the Y values. There must be a Y value for each X value. Any non-numeric or undefined elements will be taken as 0. The formula is $Y = A_0+A_1X+A_2X^2+\ldots\ldots+A_mX^m$. You must specify the required order of the polynomial in a_Coefficients[0]. After the command executes the array a_Coefficients will contain m+1 elements where a_Coefficients[0] = A_0, a_Coefficients[1] = A_1, a_Coefficients[2] = A_2, ...a_Coefficients[m] = A_m. Where m is the number that was originally in a_Coefficients[0] (i.e. polynomial order).

If a_Coefficients[0] is not specified or is less than 1 it will be made 1 (i.e. straight line). The amount of data points in the a_XYdata array has to be appropriate for the desired order of the polynomial required. If you need a quadratic you will need at least 3 data points. For a cubic 4 data points and so on. That is you need m+1 data points to be able to find a polynomial of order m that fits the m points.

Note: Remember that before invoking the command a_Coefficients[0] must be set to the desired polynomial order. After the command is invoked a_Coefficients[0] will be overwritten and set to the value of A_0.

Example:
```
//---y data
data y;.486,.866,.944,1.144,1.103,1.202,1.166,1.191,1.124,1.095,1.122
data y;1.102,1.099,1.017,1.111,1.117,1.152,1.265,1.380,1.575,1.857
n = maxdim(y,1) \ dim Points[2,n]
for i=0 to n-1
  Points[0,i] = i*.05 \  Points[1,i] = y[i]
next
m = 5  \ data Coefficients;m    //change m to 2 and 3 and 4 to see the effects
mPolyFit Points,Coefficients
data GPSpec;-1 \ mGraphPaper GPSpec
data GSpec;-1,,,,0,5 \ mPlotXY GSpec,Points
for i=0 to n-1
  Points[1,i]=0
  for j=0 to m
    Points[1,i] = Points[1,i]+Coefficients[j]*Points[0,i]^j
  next
next
GSpec[4] = blue \ mPlotXY GSpec,Points
xystring 140,100,Max(y)    \ xystring 140,490,Min(y)
xystring 600,520,(n-1)*0.05  \ xystring 190,520,0
xystring 370,520,"X-Axis" \ xystring 130,300,"Y-Axis"
```

•mSortR a_Name{,ne_OnRowNumber{,ne_Descending}}

Sorts the array which can be 1 or 2-dimensional. If it is 2-dimensional sorting will be carried out on the data in the row specified by ne_OnRowNumber. If the row number is not specified it will be performed on the first Row (row 0) (row and column numbering start with 0). The data in the other rows will be moved around to maintain the same association between the rows. That is the columns are moved to fit in the correct sort order depending on the value in the specified row (or first row if it is not given). If ne_Descending is not given or is false then the sort is in ascending order, if it is true then the sort order will be in descending order. The elements in a row must be of the same data type, but the elements in a column can be of different data types. This can be helpful in creating databases, where the elements in a column are the different fields of the database and each column is a record.
Note: You can still use mSort a_Name{,ne_OnRowNumber} which was in versions prior to V4.1.0.
Example:
```
data a;"John","Ted","Pam","Sue"   //names
data a;45   ,55   ,20   ,10       //ages
data a;30045,30067,30045,20022    //zip codes
```

203

```
Dim b[3,4]          //make a 2-d array to hold data
mCopy a,b           //copy the data into it
mSortR b            //sort data by name
gosub print_data    //a subroutine to display the data in a good format
mSortR b,2          //sort data by zipcode
gosub print_data
mSortR b,1          //sort data by age
gosub print_data
mSortR b,,1          //sort data by name again but in descending order
gosub print_data
```

•mSortC a_Name{,ne_OnColumnNumber{,ne_Descending}}

Sorts the array which can be 1 or 2-dimensional. If it is 2-dimensional sorting will be carried out on the data in the column specified by ne_OnColumnNumber. If the column number is not specified it will be performed on the first Column (column 0) (row and column numbering start with 0). The data in the other columns will be moved around to maintain the same association between the columns. That is the rows are moved to fit in the correct sort order depending on the value in the specified column (or first column if it is not given). If ne_Descending is not given or is false then the sort is in ascending order, if it is true then the sort order will be in descending order. The elements in a column must be of the same data type, but the elements in a row can be of different data types. This can be helpful in creating databases, where the elements in a row are the different fields of the database and each row is a record. Example:

```
data a;"John",45,30045    //name,age,zipcode
data a;"Ted" ,55,30067    //name,age,zipcode
data a;"Pam" ,20,30045    //name,age,zipcode
data a;"Sue" ,10,20022    //name,age,zipcode

Dim b[4,3]          //make a 2-d array to hold data
mCopy a,b           //copy the data into it
mSortC b            //sort data by name i.e. column 0 by default
gosub print_data    //a subroutine to display the data in a good format
mSortC b,2          //sort data by zipcode
gosub print_data
mSortC b,1          //sort data by age
gosub print_data
mSortC b,,1          //sort data by name again but descending order
gosub print_data
```

•mDFT a_Samples{,ne_WindowFunction}
•mFFT a_Samples{,ne_WindowFunction}

These two commands will perform a Complex Discrete and Fast Fourier Transform frequency spectral analysis on a set of sample data. The array a_Samples has to be a 2-dimensional array with at least 8 rows and 16 elements in each row so a_Samples has to be [>=8, >=16]. The first and second rows (rows 0 and 1) should hold the sample data. The row 0 hold the REAL part and row 1 the IMAGINARY part of the samples. If the samples are Just REAL values (i.e not Complex) then just leave row 1 empty and do not assign any elements any values. Any elements in the rows that are not valid numbers (integer or float) will be taken to be 0.

ne_WindowFunction specifies a value for one of 5 different Window Functions (or none) to apply to the sample data. If ne_WindowFunction is not given or is sw_NoWindow then no window is applied. See RobotBASIC Constants section for valid window function codes (e.g. sw_Hamming).

For the following discussion N is the number of elements in row 0 (i.e. the number of samples). That is the elements go from 0 to N-1.

If N > 4096 then only 4096 will be taken into account. If N < 16 then an error will be given. If the array is not dimensioned to be 8 rows or more then an error will be given but if it has more rows than 8 then the other rows will be ignored.

For mDFT N can be any number >=16 and <= 4096. However, for mFFT N has to be a power of 2 (e.g. 16, 32, 64 etc.) an if it is not then the remaining elements up to the next power of two will be assumed to be 0. For example if there are 20 elements only, then the remaining 12 (32-20 = 12) will be assumed to be 0.

Rows 2 to 7 (i.e. third to eighth rows) will be filled with N/2+1 values (i.e. from 0 to N/2) in each row as follows:
- Row 2 will be assigned the *amplitude* of the harmonic frequencies (see note below). Element 0 is the DC magnitude. Element 1 will be the magnitude of the first harmonic (f_0) the second will be the magnitude of the second harmonic ($2f_0$) an so on until N/2.
- Row 3 will be assigned the *power* of the harmonic frequencies (see note below).
- Row 4 will be assigned the *real* part of the Complex DFT/FFT result.
- Row 5 will be assigned the *imaginary* part of the Complex DFT/FFT result.
- Row 6 will be assigned the *magnitude* of the Complex DFT/FFT result.
- Row 7 will be assigned the *phase* of the Complex DFT/FFT result.

Note: For mFFT if Actual_N is less than the Assumed_N (i.e. higher number that is a power of two) and Assumed_N/2+1 is > Actual_N then there will only be as many elements in each row as Actual_N. That is the rows will ***not*** be expanded. FFT results are not valid if the number of samples is not a power of two. *Always make sure that the number of samples is a power of two for mFFT.* For mDFT that is not necessary but is *advisable*.

Note: The fundamental frequency's value (f_0) is dependant on the sampling rate and the number of samples. The Nyquist criterion dictates that the maximum possible frequency content is 0.5/sampling rate. The Nyquist criterion dictates that if you have N samples then the DFT/FFT will return N/2+1 results with the 0th value being the DC component. Then value 1 is for the fundamental frequency (f_0) and then value 2 is for $2f_0$ and so on.

Here is an example to calculate the DFT and FFT values for a square wave (+1 to -1 but change it and see how it affects the harmonic contents and verify against a normal Continuous

FT):

```
NDFT = 20 \ NFFT = 32              //change the 32 to none power of 2 and
dim a[8,NDFT], b[8,NFFT]           //see how the results become invalid
for i=0 to NDFT-1
  a[0,i] = 1
  if i >= NDFT/2 then a[0,i] = -1  //change this to 0 and see what happens
next
for i=0 to NFFT-1
  b[0,i] = 1
  if i >= NFFT/2 then b[0,i] = -1  //change this to 0 and see what happens
next
mDFT a,sw_NoWindow \ mFFT b,sw_NoWindow   //change the window types
fmt = "##0.0000   "
data x;center("DFT data"," ",50)
data x;"Amplitude   Power    Real(X)   Imag(X)    Mag(X)     Phs(X)"
data x;sRepeat("=",58)
for i=0 to NDFT/2
  s = ""
  for j=2 to 7
    s += format(a[j,i],fmt)
  next
  data x;s
next
data x;x[2],center("FFT data"," ",50),x[2]
for i=0 to NFFT/2
  s = ""
  for j=2 to 7
    s += format(b[j,i],fmt)
  next
  data x;s
next
msgbox(x,"DFT and FFT calculations:")
for i=0 to NFFT/2
  if i <= NDFT/2 then data dx;i-.05,i,i+.05  \ data dy;0,a[2,i],0
  data fx;i-.05,i,i+.05 \ data fy;0,b[2,i],0
next
data g1;10,10,300,300 \ mGraphPaper g1 \ mPlotXY g1,dx,dy
data g2;400,10,300,300\ mGraphPaper g2 \ mPlotXY g2,fx,fy
xyText 200,50,"DFT",,20,fs_Bold \ xyText 600,50,"FFT",,20,fs_Bold
```

•Arrays Statistical Functions

•Sum(a_Data)
Returns the sum of all the elements of the array which must be one or two-dimensional and contain only numerical data. If it is two-dimensional then the second row must contain the frequencies for the data in the first row. If there is no corresponding frequency for any data value in the first row then it will be considered 1.

•mSum(a_Data)
Returns the sum of all the numeric elements of the array which can be any dimensions and can contain any data. Any string elements will be disregarded and will not contribute to the sum.

•Average(a_Data)
Returns the average of the elements of the array which must be one or two-dimensional and

contain only numerical data. If it is two-dimensional then the second row must contain the frequencies for the data in the first row. If there is no corresponding frequency for any data value in the first row then it will be considered 1.

•mAverage(a_Data)

Returns the average of all the numeric elements of the array which can be any dimensions and can contain any data. Any string elements will be disregarded and will not contribute to the sum or the count.

•Median(a_Data)

Returns the Median value of the elements of the array which must be one-dimensional and contain only numerical data.

•Max(a_Data)

Returns the largest element of the array which must be one or two-dimensional and contain only numerical data. If it is two-dimensional then the second row will be ignored, as it has no bearing on the determination of the maximum value.

•mMax(a_Data)

Returns the value of the maximum numeric element of the array which can be any dimensions and can contain any data. Any string elements will be disregarded.

•Min(a_Data)

Returns the smallest element of the array which must be one or two-dimensional and contain only numerical data. If it is two-dimensional then the second row will be ignored, as it has no bearing on the determination of the minimum value.

•mMin(a_Data)

Returns the value of the minimum numeric element of the array which can be any dimensions and can contain any data. Any string elements will be disregarded.

•Range(a_Data)

Returns the difference between the largest and smallest elements of the array which must be one or two-dimensional and contain only numerical data. If it is two-dimensional then the second row will be ignored, as it has no bearing on the determination of the range value.

•mRange(a_Data)

Returns the difference between the values of the maximum and minimum numeric elements of the array which can be any dimensions and can contain any data. Any string elements will be disregarded.

•Count(a_Data)

Returns the number of elements in the array which must be one or two-dimensional and contain only numerical data. If it is two-dimensional then the first row will be ignored, as it has no bearing on the determination of the count. The count will be the sum of all the frequencies in the second row. If there are data in the first row without a corresponding frequency then the frequency will be considered to be 1.

•mCount(a_Data)

Returns the number of numeric elements in the array which can be any dimensions and can contain any data. Any string elements will be disregarded.

•Variance(a_Data)

Returns the Variance of the elements of the array which must be one or two-dimensional and contain only numerical data. If it is two-dimensional then the second row must contain the frequencies for the data in the first row. If there is no corresponding frequency for any data value in the first row then it will be considered 1.

•mVariance(a_Data)

Returns the Variance of the numeric elements of the array which can be any dimensions and can contain any data. Any string elements will be disregarded.

•StdDev(a_Data)

Returns the Standard Deviation of the elements of the array which must be one or two-dimensional and contain only numerical data. If it is two-dimensional then the second row must contain the frequencies for the data in the first row. If there is no corresponding frequency for any data value in the first row then it will be considered 1.

•mStdDev(a_Data)

Returns the Standard Deviation of the numeric elements of the array which can be any dimensions and can contain any data. Any string elements will be disregarded.

•CorrCoef(a_Data)

Returns the value of the Correlation Coefficient for the data in array which must be two-dimensional. The first row contains the X values, and the second row contains the Y values. There has to be a corresponding Y value for each X value and all data has to be numerical.

Mathematical Functions

Note: See the notes at the top of the Standard User Interfacing section.

•Trigonometric Functions

•Pi({ne_Multiplier})
Returns the value PI i.e. (3.141592654) multiplied by the result of ne_Multiplier which if not given is assumed to be 1.

•RtoD(ne_Radians)
Converts an angle in radians to degrees. This is the same as using the conversion **ne_Radians*180/Pi()**.

•DtoR(ne_Degrees)
Converts an angle in degrees to radians. This is the same as using the conversion **ne_Degrees*Pi()/180**.

•Sin(ne_Radians)
Returns the Sine of an angle in Radians. If you want to specify degrees then use the conversion DtoR().

•Cos(ne_Radians)
Returns the Cosine of an angle in Radians. If you want to specify degrees then use the conversion DtoR().

•Tan(ne_Radians)
Returns the Tangent of an angle in Radians. If you want to specify degrees then use the conversion DtoR(). This function can cause an error if the angle is +/-Pi()/2 (i.e. +/-90 degrees) since the result is infinity. If the angle is slightly more or less than 90° the result is valid but is an extremely large number.

•ASin(ExprN)
Returns the angle in radians whose Sine is *ExprN*. If you want to get degrees then use the conversion RtoD(). This is the inverse of **Sin()**.

•ACos(ExprN)
Returns the angle in radians whose Cosine is *ExprN*. If you want to get degrees then use the conversion RtoD(). This is the inverse of **Cos()**.

•ATan(ExprN)

Returns the angle in radians whose Tan is *ExprN*. If you want to get degrees then use the conversion RtoD(). This is the inverse of Tan().

•ATan2(ne_X,ne_Y)

Returns an angle in radians, given the X and Y lengths. This gives the angle 0 to PI and 0 to -PI. Negative angles are clockwise from the X-Axis, and positive angles are counter clockwise from the X-axis. So atan2(1,1) will give 0.785398 which is 45°, while atan2(1,-1) gives -0.78539816 which is -45°. If x=0 and y=0 the result will be 0.0

•Cartesian To Polar Functions

•PolarR(ne_X,ne_Y)

Returns the Polar Radius from the x,y coordinates both must result in numbers (float or integer), otherwise an error will occur.

•PolarA(ne_X,ne_Y)

Returns the Polar Angle from the x,y coordinates. This is effectively the same as Atan2() above. The angle returned is in radians. Both ne_X and ne_Y must be numeric (integer, or float) or an error will occur.

•Polar To Cartesian Functions

•CartX(ne_Radius,ne_ThetaRadians)

This returns the Cartesian X Coordinate given the polar R, Theta (in radians). Both must be numeric (integer, or float) or an error will occur. This is effectively the inverse of the PolarR() and PolarA() above.

•CartY(ne_Radius,ne_ThetaRadians)

This returns the Cartesian Y Coordinate given the polar R, Theta (in radians). Both must be numeric (integer, or float) or an error will occur. This is effectively the inverse of the PolarR() and PolarA() above.

•Logarithmic & Exponential Functions

•NLog(ExprN)

Returns the Log to base **e** (**e**=2.178281828) of *ExprN*. *ExprN* has to be greater than zero. (ExprN > 0).

•Log(ExprN)

Return the Log to base 10 of *ExprN*. *ExprN* has to be greater than zero. (ExprN > 0).

•Log2(ExprN)

Return the Log to base 2 of *ExprN*. *ExprN* has to be greater than zero. (ExprN > 0).

•LogB(ne_Base,ExprN)

Return the Log to base ne_Base of *ExprN*. Both parameters have to be greater than zero. (ne_Base > 0 also ExprN > 0).

•Exp(ExprN)

Returns **e** raised to the power *ExprN* (**e**=2.178281828).

•Exp10(ExprN)

Returns 10 raised to the power *ExprN*.

•SqRt(ExprN)

Returns the Square-Root of *ExprN*. If *ExprN* is negative an error will occur. (ExprN >= 0).

•CbRt(ExprN)

Returns the Cube-Root of *ExprN*.

•<u>Hyperbolic Functions</u>

•SinH(ExprN)

Returns the Hyperbolic Sine.

•CosH(ExprN)

Returns the Hyperbolic Cosine.

•TanH(ExprN)

Returns the Hyperbolic Tangent.

•ASinH(ExprN)

Returns the inverse of Hyperbolic Sine.

•ACosH(ExprN)

Returns the inverse of Hyperbolic Cosine. ExprN has to be greater than or equal to 1. (ExprN >= 1).

•ATanH(ExprN)

Returns the inverse of Hyperbolic Tan. ExprN has to be greater than -1 and less than 1. (-1 < ExprN < 1).

•Probability Functions

•Random(ExprN)

Returns a value between 0 and *ExprN-1* randomly. If ExprN is not an integer it will be rounded down. If ExprN is negative it will be made positive. If ExprN is zero or one then the result will be a random floating point value between 0 and 0.99999999999. See SeedRandom. ***Do not use SeedRandom if you want purely random numbers. The use of SeedRandom will make the random number generator always generate the same sequence of random numbers and thus not purely random.***

•RandomG(ne_Mean,ne_StdDev)

Returns a random number with Gaussian distribution about the Mean with a Standard Deviation. This is useful for simulating data with sampling errors and expected deviations from the Mean.

•Factorial(ExprN)

Returns the factorial of *ExprN*. *ExprN* must be a number. If it is a float it will be made into an integer. *ExprN* cannot be negative. Mathematically **Factorial(n) = n!**

•nPr(ne_NumElementsAvailable,ne_NumElementsToSelect)

Returns the number of Permutations ne_NumElementsToSelect can be selected from ne_NumElementsAvailable. Both must be numeric and if not integer will be converted to integer. Neither can be negative. Also ne_NumElementsToSelect must be less than or equal to ne_NumElementsAvailable. The formula is **nPr(n,r) = n! / (n-r)!**

•nCr(ne_NumElementsAvailable,ne_NumElementsToSelect)

Returns the number of Combination an ne_NumElementsToSelect set can be selected from a set with ne_NumElementsAvailable elements. Both must be numeric and if not integer will be converted to integer. Neither can be negative. Also ne_NumeElementsToSelect must be less than or equal to ne_NumElementsAvailable. The formula is **nCr(n,r) = n! /(r! *(n-r)!)**

•ProbG(ne_Element,ne_Mean,ne_StdDev)

Returns the Gaussian probability for an element in a bell-shaped (normal) probability distribution. ne_StdDev is the standard deviation (sigma) of the distribution. If ne_Mean (mean=mu=average) is less than 0 an error will be issued. If ne_StdDev is less than or equal to zero then an error will be issued. The returned value will be a float usually between 0 and 1, but if you provide an inappropriate standard deviation value then the returned probability may be greater than 1.

This function uses the formula $P = Exp(-(((ne\_Element-ne\_Mean)/ne\_StdDev)^2)/2)/sqrt(2*pi()*ne\_StdDev^2)$

•ProbGI(ne_Probability,ne_Mean,ne_StdDev)

Returns the element in a bell-shaped (normal) probability distribution whose Gaussian probability and mean is as given. ne_StdDev is the standard deviation (sigma) of the distribution. If ne_Mean (mean=mu=average) is less than 0 an error will be issued. If se_StdDev is less than or equal to zero then an error will be issued. ne_Probability must be a floating point value between 0 and 1, if it is less than 0 it will be made 0. If it is greater than 1 then it will made 1.

Since the bell-curve is symmetrical around the mean, an element with a value above the mean (right side) will have the same probability as a value equally spaced below the mean (left side). This function will always return the element value below the mean (left side). Also, this function uses a numerical solution (approximation) to the Gaussian probability function, so the result may not be the exact inverse of ProbG() above.

•SeedRandom {ne_Seed}

Random() returns a totally random number and no matter how many times you use it the number returned is always random. However, in certain situations you may require to generate a ***repeatable sequence*** of random numbers. That is, even though the numbers in the sequence are random, you want to have the ***same*** sequence to be repeated if you run the program again or repeat the code in a loop. This can be achieved if you always ***seed*** the random number generator with the ***same seed*** just before generating the sequence using Random().

If you want totally random numbers then do not use this command. If you invoke this command then any numbers generated by Random() from that point onwards will be random but repeatable, in that if you issue SeedRandom again with the same seed value and generate more random numbers they will be the same as the previous sequence of generated numbers.

So random numbers generated with Random() after SeedRandom will be the same every time you run the program or even in a loop. In the example below you will get 5 lines of 10 numbers in each line. The 10 numbers in each line are random but the 5 lines are the same sequence. If you comment the `SeedRandom 10` line, you will get 50 totally random numbers instead of 5 lines of just 10 random numbers.

The seed value allows you to generate different sets of numbers, but each seed value will always be associated with the very same sequence. If ne_Seed is not specified then it will be set to 0.

Do not use this command if you want purely random numbers. The use of SeedRandom will make the random number generator always generate the same sequence of random numbers and thus not purely random.

Example:

```
for i=1 to 5
    SeedRandom 2  //comment this line and see what happens
    for j=1 to 10
        print random(100);
    next
    print
next
```

•Financial Functions

All financial calculations involve a periodic payment (PMT) at an interest rate per period (INTR) for a certain number of periods (TERM). There are three possible scenarios:

- -You are making payments into a savings fund. At the end of a certain number of periods (TERM) the account will have a certain amount of money called the future value (FV).
- -You are paying off a loan. Some loans may have a balloon payment (BAL) at the end of the final period (TERM). Also the amount of money borrowed is called present value of money (PV).
- -You have a sum of money (PV) in an interest bearing account that will become a certain value in the future (FV).

The PMT may be made at the end of every period as in paying off a mortgage (TYPE <>1), or at the beginning of every period as in lease payments (TYPE =1).

The period of the INTR, PMT and TERM has to be consistent. So if the interest rate is annual then the period is one year and payments have to be made every year. However, this is not how you usually make payments. Usually the INTR is quoted as yearly, while the PMT has to be made monthly. So in order to make the periods consistent you must make the INTR into a monthly rate and your period becomes a month. Also the TERM will be in months. Additionally, the INTR has to be an actual number not a percentage; so 6% will be 0.06 (6/100.0).

All the amounts (INTR, PMT, TERM, BAL, FV and PV) have to be positive numbers (float or integer), any negative or zero values will cause a "Function parameter is not allowed e.g. Log(-1)" error to be issued (BAL and TYPE are allowed to be zero). Non-numeric entries will cause an error.

As an example:
   You have a loan of $10,000.00 at a 5% annual interest rate for 6 years with a balloon payment of $1,000.00. You want to find out the monthly payments.

```
PV = 10000          //borrowed amount
INTR = 5/100.0/12 //notice we have to use 100.0 to
                    //force floating point division
BAL = 1000          //amount to be paid at end of loan
TERM = 6 * 12       //6 years is 6*12 months
TYPE = 0            //Payments at end of every month
PMT = ff_PVP(PV,INTR,TERM,BAL,TYPE)
```

214

```
print PMT                               //prints 149.11
print "Total paid=",PMT*TERM+BAL
print ff_fv(PMT,INTR,TERM,0)            //prints 12490.18
print ff_pv(PMT,INTR,TERM,BAL,0) //10000
print ff_cifv(PV,INTR,TERM)             //prints 13490.18
```

•ff_FV(PMT,INTR,TERM,TYPE)

Returns the future value of a periodic payment (PMT) into a savings account at a periodic interest rate (INTR) for a number of periods (TERM). If the payments are made at the beginning of the period then TYPE has to be 1. If at the end of every period then TYPE = 0.

•ff_FVT(PMT,INTR,FV,TYPE)

Returns the number of periods required to accumulate a future value (FV) at a periodic payment (PMT) into a savings account at a periodic interest rate (INTR). If the payments are made at the beginning of the period then TYPE has to be 1. If at the end of every period then TYPE = 0.

•ff_FVP(FV,INTR,TERM,TYPE)

Returns the periodic payments required to be made into a savings account at a periodic interest rate (INTR) for a number of periods (TERM) so as to accumulate a future value (FV). If the payments are made at the beginning of the period then TYPE has to be 1. If at the end of every period then TYPE = 0.

•ff_PV(PMT,INTR,TERM,BAL,TYPE)

Returns the present value of a loan you would get if you can make periodic payments (PMT) against the loan at a periodic interest rate (INTR) for a number of periods (TERM) with a final balloon payment (BAL). If the payments are made at the beginning of the period then TYPE has to be 1 (Lease). If at the end of every period then TYPE = 0 (mortgage).

•ff_PVT(PMT,INTR,PV,BAL,TYPE)

Returns the number of periods required to pay off a loan (PV) if you make periodic payments (PMT) against the loan at a periodic interest rate (INTR) with a final balloon payment (BAL). If the payments are made at the beginning of the period then TYPE has to be 1 (Lease). If at the end of every period then TYPE = 0 (mortgage).

•ff_PVP(PV,INTR,TERM,BAL,TYPE)

Returns the value of payments to be made periodically against a loan (PV) for a number of periods (TERM) at a periodic interest rate (INTR) with a final balloon payment (BAL). If the payments are made at the beginning of the period then TYPE has to be 1 (Lease). If at the end of every period then TYPE = 0 (mortgage).

•ff_CIFV(PV,INTR,TERM)

Returns the future value of a compound interest savings account with an initial amount (PV) at a periodic interest rate (INTR) for a certain number of periods (TERM).

215

•ff_CIT(PV,INTR,FV)

Returns the number of periods after which a compound interest savings account with an initial amount (PV) at a periodic interest rate (INTR) will attain a future value (FV).

•ff_CII(PV,FV,TERM)

Returns the periodic interest rate required for a compound interest savings account with an initial amount (PV) to attain a future value (FV) after a number of periods (TERM).

•ff_SLN(COST,SALVAGE,LIFE)

Returns the Straight Line Depreciation of an asset (COST) with a final value (SALVAGE) at the end of its useful life (LIFE). All parameters must be > zero.

•ff_SYD(COST,SALVAGE,LIFE,PERIOD)

Returns the Sum-Of-Years'-Digit depreciation of an asset (COST) with a final value (SALVAGE) at the end of its useful life (LIFE) for a particular period (PERIOD). PERIOD and LIFE have to be of the same period (e.g. years or months). All parameters must be > zero.

Great Circle Navigation

Note: See the notes at the top of the Standard User Interfacing section.

•Great Circle and Rhumb Line Navigation

Notes:

This suite of commands will perform Great Circle (nGC_) and Rhumb Line (nRL_) navigational calculations. All distance are in Nautical Miles. All headings are in degrees and are True headings. All Latitudes (Parallels) and Longitudes are also in degrees.

North Latitudes and West Longitudes are Positive. South Latitudes and East Longitudes are Negative. You specify the values as negative degrees if you need to specify S/E values. Also the returned values will be negative to indicate S/E values.

If any value cannot be calculated it will be set to be -9999 to indicate the failure of the command to calculate the value. The situations that can give rise to errors will be explained in the description for the specific commands below.

Use Degrees() to convert degrees, minutes and seconds to degrees. Also use Convert() to convert other distance scales to nautical miles. Remember that a nautical mile is 1 minute of Longitude. It is **not** 1 minute of Latitude except on the equator.

Remember that the Prime Meridian is the Greenwich Meridian and is considered to be 0°. West of that are Positive Longitudes up to 180° W (=180.000) and East of that are Negative Longitudes up to 180° E (=-180.000).

The Equator is Latitude 0°. North of that are Positive Latitudes up to 90° N (North Pole = 90.000)) and South of the Equator are Negative Latitudes up to 90° S (South Pole = -90.000)

The shortest distance between two points on the Globe is a GC course. However the GC headings have to change continuously along the course. An easier way to navigate is to use the Rhumb Line course. This gives a True heading that you can maintain all along the course. However this will result in a slightly longer course. Also RL courses will not work close to the Poles since they will become tight spirals.

•**ngc_DistanceHeading ne_LatA,ne_LonA,ne_LatB,ne_LonB,vn_Distance,vn_Heading**
•**nrl_DistanceHeading ne_LatA,ne_LonA,ne_LatB,ne_LonB,vn_Distance,vn_Heading**

Given the Latitudes and Longitudes of two points this command will assign the variables vn_Distance and vn_Heading the distance and heading from the first point to the second.

nGC_ gives the Great Circle values. nRL_ gives the Rhumb Line values.

•ngc_RadialPoint ne_LatA,ne_LonA,ne_Distance,ne_Heading,vn_Lat,vn_Lon
•nrl_RadialPoint ne_LatA,ne_LonA,ne_Distance,ne_Heading,vn_Lat,vn_Lon
Given the Latitude and Longitude of a starting point and a distance away along a heading the command calculates the Lat and Lon of the end point.

nGC_ gives the Great Circle values. nRL_ gives the Rhumb Line values.

The Rhumb Line version will return -9999 for both vn_Distance and vn_Heading if the Lat of the starting point is the North or South poles (90 or -90).

•ngc_LatFromLonCrossing ne_LatA,ne_LonA,ne_LatB,ne_LonB,ne_Lon,vn_Lat
Given the Latitudes and Longitudes of both ends of a course and a Lon, this command will calculate the Lat where the course will cross the specified Lon.

If the end points of the course are on the same meridian vn_Lat will be set to -9999. Points are on the same meridian if their Longitudes are the same or 180 apart.

•ngc_LonFromLatCrossing ne_LatA,ne_LonA,ne_LatB,ne_LonB,ne_Lat,vn_Lon1,vn_Lon2
Given the Latitudes and Longitudes of both ends of a course and a Lat, this command will calculate the Lon where the course will cross the specified Lat. There may be two Longitudes or one (two equal values) or none. If there are none then the returned values vn_Lon1 and vn_Lon2 will be -9999. If there is only one value then both variables will be set to that value.

•ngc_FractionDistancePoint
ne_LatA,ne_LonA,ne_LatB,ne_LonB,ne_FractionalDistance,vn_Lat,vn_Lon
Given the Latitudes and Longitudes of two points and a percentage of the total distance between the points the command will calculate the Lat and Lon of the point at that fractional distance between the two points along the track.

The percentage is a fraction. So 40% should be given as 0.4.

•ngc_RadialIntersection
ne_LatA,ne_LonA,ne_LatB,ne_LonB,ne_HeadingFromA,ne_HeadingFromB,vn_Lat,vn_Lon
Given the Latitudes and Longitudes of two points and a heading from the first point and another heading from the second point the command will calculate the Lat and Lon of the point of the intersection of the two tracks.

If there are many intersection points (e.g. tracks are the same or almost the same) then both the vn_Lat and vn_Lon will be assigned the values -8888. If there is no intersection point then they will be assigned -9999.

•ngc_XTrackError
ne_LatA,ne_LonA,ne_LatB,ne_LonB,ne_LatD,ne_LonD,vn_XTrackDistance,vn_AlongTrackDistan ce

Given the Latitudes and Longitudes of two end points of a track as well as of a point off from the track, this command will calculate the Cross Track Distance and Along Track Distance. the XTD is the shortest distance from the off the track point to the track. The ATD is the distance from the starting point to the point abeam the off the track point.

•ngc_TrackPointsFromPoint
ne_LatA,ne_LonA,ne_LatB,ne_LonB,ne_LatD,ne_LonD,ne_DistanceFromPoint,vn_Lat1, vn_Lon1, vn_Lat2, vn_Lon2

Given the Latitudes and Longitudes of two end points of a track as well as of a point off from the track and a certain distance, this command will calculate the Latitudes and Longitudes of the two points on the track that are that distance away from the off the track point.

If the distance given is the XTD then the two points will be the same point. If there are no possible points the given distance away from the off the track point then vn_Lat1 and 2 and vn_Lon1 and 2 will be set -9999.

•Wind or Current Triangle Navigation

Notes:

This suite of commands will solve the Wind/Current Triangle. In the wind triangle there are 6 elements

Wind/Current Direction and Speed. Remember the Wind and Current directions are the True headings where the Wind/Current is coming from.

The Airplane/Ship Heading and Speed. The Plane speed is the True Air speed. The Ship speed is the speed through the water.

The course Heading and Ground Speed. Ground speed is the speed of the plane/ship along the ground not through the air/water.

In the wind triangle we always know 4 values and want to calculate the other 2. Most commonly we know the wind/current speed and direction as well as True speed and desired course and want to calculate the heading to steer to maintain the desired course, this will also result in a Ground speed along the course.

All speeds can be in any units (usually Knots i.e. nautical miles per hour) as long as they are consistent for both the wind/current and plane/ship. All headings are TRUE and are in degrees.

Note: Wind direction is where the wind is coming from. So when you say the wind direction is 270° then that means that the wind is blowing from the west to the east. The commands below will assume that this is the way you will be specifying the wind direction AS WELL AS THE CURRENT direction when using the commands. However, sometimes with current the reported direction is the direction where the current is heading. If that is the case then when using these formulas you need to add180° to make it a direction rather than a heading (it does not matter if the addition results in a value > 360° RB will adjust it automatically).

•**nwt_XWind ne_WindSpeed,ne_WindDirection,ne_RunwayHeading,vn_XWind,vn_HeadWind**
Will calculate the Cross Wind and Head Wind components of the wind along a Runway.

•**nwt_GSpeedHeading**
ne_WindSpeed,ne_WindDirection,ne_TrueSpeed,ne_CourseHeading,vn_GrndSpeed,vn_Heading
Given the Wind/Current speed and direction as well as the desired course heading and the plane/ship speed will calculate the Heading to fly/sail and the resulting ground speed along the course.

The values will be set to -9999 if the course cannot be achieved due to the Wind/Current Speed being to fast.

•**nwt_WSpeedDirection**
ne_GrndSpeed,ne_CourseHeading,ne_TrueSpeed,ne_Heading,vn_WindSpeed,vn_WindDirection
Given the actual ground speed and the course heading as well as the speed of the plane/ship and heading steered will calculate the wind's speed and direction.

•**nwt_GSpeedCourse**
ne_WindSpeed,ne_WindDirection,ne_TrueSpeed,ne_Heading,vn_GroundSpeed,vn_CourseHeading
Given the Wind/Current speed and direction as well as heading steered and plane/ship speed will calculate the resulting course and ground speed.

•**nwt_TSpeedHeading**
ne_WindSpeed,ne_WindDirection,ne_GroundSpeed,ne_CourseHeading,vn_TrueSpeed,vn_Heading
Given the Wind/Current speed and direction as well as the desired ground speed and course heading course heading will calculate the heading to steer and speed to maintain.

•**nwt_TSpeedWSpeed ne_V1,ne_V2,ne_V3,vn_TrueAirSpeed,vn_WindSpeed**
This command helps in calibrating the Speed indicator. If you Fly/sail along three headings

that are 120° apart and record the Ground speed maintained along the courses the command will calculate the True speed of the plane/ship as well as the wind/current speed at the time. You can then compare this value against the indicated value to observe the accuracy of the instrument.

•Navigation Conversion Functions

•Degrees({ne_Degrees{,ne_Minutes{,ne_Seconds}}})
•Degrees(se_FormattedDegrees)

Converts Degrees, Minutes and Seconds to Degrees. Any of the parameters can be Integer or Float. The function always returns a float = ne_Degrees+ne_Minutes/60.0+ne_Seconds/3600.0. You can omit any or all of the degrees, minutes or the seconds. Any one not given will be made 0.

In the alternative format se_FormattedDegrees is a string that can contain 1, 2 or three numbers separated with anything you want. The numbers are considered to be (from left to right) the degrees, minutes and seconds. The string could be for instance the result of Lat_DMS() etc.

se_FormattedDegrees may be for instance "45° 34.34" or "45° 34' 45.3" N" or "-45.2 56.33" or any combination. The numbers have to be separated by any non-numeric character. Only the first three numbers will be considered and they will be treated as in the formula above. Any number that contains digits but is not of a valid number format will be made to be 0 in the formula above.

If the string does not contain numbers that can be converted -9999 will be returned. The FIRST VALID number will be taken as degrees, the second as minutes and the third as seconds. Only the sign of the FIRST number will matter and determines the sign of the result. If the second and/or the third numbers are negative they will be considered as positive. In the formula above all the numbers will be made positive before applying the formula. The final result will have the sign of the first number.

If the LAST letter in the string is E or S the resulting degrees value will be negative, according to the convention used in the navigation suite, where South Latitudes and East longitudes are negative. If you have an E or S as the last letter the number will be negative regardless of the sign used with the first number. If you have N or W as the last letter but the negative sign is used with the first number (degrees) then the number will be negative regardless. Examples:

```
print degrees()            //prints  0
print degrees(,,10)        //prints  0.00277777777777778
print degrees(1,,87)       //prints  1.02416666666667
print degrees(23,87)       //prints  24.45
print degrees(23,87,2)     //prints  24.4505555555556
print degrees(34,-4.54,3.4) //prints  34.0766111111111
```

```
print degrees(54,45.33)            //prints  54.7555
print degrees(-54,45.33)           //prints  -54.7555
print degrees("54 -45.33")         //prints  54.7555
print degrees("-54° 45.33'")       //prints  -54.7555
print degrees("54° 45.33' N")      //prints  54.7555
print degrees("54° 45.33' S")             //prints  -54.7555
print degrees("54° 45.33' 34.3"" N")      //prints  54.7650277777778
print degrees("54:45.33:34.3")            //prints  54.7650277777778
print degrees("54:45.33:34.3 N")          //prints  54.7650277777778
print degrees("54:45.33:34.3 S")          //prints  -54.7650277777778
print degrees("54,   45.33Sabc34.3")      //prints  54.7650277777778
print degrees(",   45.33Sabc34.3")        //prints  45.9016666666667
print degrees("0,   45.33Sabc34.3")       //prints  0.7650277777778
print degrees("sdfsd")                    //prints  -9999
```

•Lat_DMS(ne_Degrees)
•Lon_DMS(ne_Degrees)

Will return a string that looks like this:

    dd° mm' ss.s" N   for the Lat_ version (S if ne_Degrees is negative)

    ddd° mm' ss.s" W   for the Lon_ version (E if ne_Degrees is negative)

The ne_Degrees value is converted to Degrees, Minutes and Seconds and then put into the string as shown above. The seconds field will always have one decimal place. You can convert a formatted string back to a number using Degrees().

•Lat_DM(ne_Degrees)
•Lon_DM(ne_Degrees)

Will return a string that looks like this:

    dd° mm.mmm' N   for the Lat_ version (S if ne_Degrees is negative)

    ddd° mm.mmm' W   for the Lon_ version (E if ne_Degrees is negative)

The ne_Degrees value is converted to Degrees and Minutes and then put into the string as shown above. The minutes field will always have 3 decimal places. You can convert a formatted string back to a number using Degrees().

222

String Functions

Note: See the notes at the top of the Standard User Interfacing section.

•String Manipulation Functions

•CrLf()
Returns a string that is the two characters sequence Carriage Return and Line Feed = char(13)+char(10). This is useful in some commands and functions where a list of strings is incorporated into one string with Cr/Lf pair of characters as a separator between them. Instead of having to remember the sequence and what characters code numbers they are, you can use this function to get the sequence.

•Length(se_Text)
Returns the length of the resulting string from se_Text.

•Trim(se_Text)
Returns se_Text without leading or trailing spaces.

•LeftTrim(se_Text)
Returns se_Text without leading space.

•RightTrim(se_Text)
Returns se_Text without trailing spaces

•NoSpaces(se_Text)
Returns se_Text without any spaces, even within the string not just left and right.

•Substring(se_Text{,ne_StartChar{,ne_NumCharacters}})
Returns a string consisting of ne_NumCharacters from se_String starting at character ne_StartChar. If ne_StartChar is not given or is <1 then first character is assumed. If ne_StartChar is longer than the string then the function will return a null string (""). If ne_NumCharacters is more than there are characters available starting at the given position or is not given or is < 1 then function will return all the remaining characters starting at the ne_StartChar.

•Left(se_Text,ne_NumChars)
Returns a string containing ne_NumChars from the string starting from first character. This is equivalent to *Substring(se_Text,1,ne_NumChars)*.

•Right(se_Text,ne_NumChars)

Returns a string containing ne_NumChars from the string ending with the last character. This equivalent to *Substring(se_Text, Length(se_Text)+1-ne_NumChars,ne_NumChars).* If ne_NumChars < 1 then 1 is assumed. If it is > the length of the string then the length of the string is assumed.

•InString(se_Main,se_Sub{,ne_StartFrom})

Returns the position of the first occurrence of se_Sub within se_Main. if the sub does not occur inside the main then 0 is returned. If ne_StartFrom is specified then the search will start from the character number ne_StartFrom. Character counting starts with 1. So first character is character 1. If ne_StartFrom is not specified or is less than 1 it will be made 1. If it is greater than the length of the se_Main string then the function will obviously return 0.

Example:

```
S = "This is a test"
s = "is"
print Instring(S,s)          //prints 3
print Instring(S,s,99)       //prints 0
print Instring(S,s,3)        //prints 3
print Instring(S,s,4)        //prints 6
print Instring(S,s,9)        //prints 0
```

•Contains(se_Text,se_CharList)

Returns a string that contains the characters in se_charList which occur in the se_Text. The function searches inside se_Text for each character in se_CharList to see if it occurs at least once and if it does it will be part of the returned string. For example:

```
print Contains("this is a test","abcdefghi")    //prints aehi
```

Note: Note the contrast to InString().

•NotContains(se_Text,se_CharList)

Returns a string that contains the characters in se_charList which *do not* occur in the se_Text. The function searches inside se_Text for each character in se_CharList to see if it does not occur at all and if it does not it will be part of the returned string. For example:

```
print NotContains("this is a test","abcdefghi")
//prints bcdfg
```

Note: Note the contrast to Contains().

•Upper(se_Text)

Returns se_Text with all characters converted to upper case.

•Lower(se_Text)
Returns se_Text with all characters converted to lower case.

•Proper(se_Text)
Returns se_Text with the first character of each word in capital and the rest of the characters in the word as lower case. Words are separated with spaces. e.g. print Proper("this is a test") would print This Is A Test.

•Spaces(ne_NumOfSpaces)
Returns a string of ne_NumOfSpaces spaces.

•sRepeat(se_RepeatChars,ne_NumTimes)
Returns a string with se_RepeatChars repeated ne_NumTimes times.

•Center(se_Text,se_PadChar,ne_NumChars)
Returns the string se_Text centered within the length ne_NumChars. The character on the left and right of the string will be the first character in se_PadChar. If se_PadChar is empty then the space character will be used. se_Text will be left and right trimmed before the operation is done. That is all space characters from the left and right will be removed. If the length of se_Text (after trimming) is greater than ne_NumChars then se_Text will be returned unchanged.
Example:
```
print "-",JustifyR("   test   ","",10),"-"   // prints -      test-
print "-",JustifyL("   test   ","",10),"-"   // prints -test      -
print "-",Center("   test   ","",10),"-"     // prints -   test   -
```

•JustifyL(se_Text,se_PadChar,ne_Len)
Returns the string se_Text padded (on the right) up to the length ne_Len with the first character in se_Pad. If se_Pad is empty then the space character will be used. se_Text will be trimmed on the left before padding. If the length of se_Text (after trimming) is greater than ne_Len then se_Text will be returned unchanged. This is useful for left justifying the string within a certain width. See example in Center() above.

•JustifyR(se_Text,se_PadChar,ne_Len)
Returns the string se_Text padded (on the left) up to the length ne_Len with the first character in se_Pad. If se_Pad is empty then the space character will be used. se_Text will be right trimmed before padding. If the length of se_Text (after trimming) is greater than ne_Len then se_Text will be returned unchanged. This is useful for right justifying the string within a certain width. See example in Center() above.

•Insert(se_Text,se_Insert,ne_CharNum)
Returns a string that is se_Text with se_Insert inserted inside it just before the ne_CharNum

225

chararcter. If char number is less than 1 then 1 will be assumed and if it is longer than the length of se_Text then se_Insert will be inserted at the end of se_Text (i.e. concatenated). For example:

```
s = "-test-"
print Insert(s,"hh",-1)              //prints hh-test-
print Insert(s,"hh",1)               //prints hh-test-
print Insert(s,"hh",3)               //prints -thhest-
print Insert(s,"hh",length(s))       //prints -testhh-
print Insert(s,"hh",50)              //prints -test-hh
```

•Replace(se_OriginalString,se_NewSubString,ne_StartingAt)

Returns se_OriginalString with the characters starting at and including the ne_StartingAt character replaced by se_NewSubString. As many characters as there are in replacement string will be replaced. If ne_StartingAt is less than 1 then 1 will be assumed and if it is longer than the length of the original string then the replacement will be ***inserted*** at the end of the original (i.e. concatenated). If the remaining length of se_OriginalString after the neStartingAt character is less than the length of se_NewSubString then the characters starting at the ne_StartingAt character from the original will be dropped and the new substring will be concatenated to the remaining initial part of se_Original. For example:

```
s = "-test-"
print Replace(s,"hh",-1)                  //prints hhtest-
print Replace(s,"hhhhhhhh",-1)            //prints hhhhhhhh
print Replace(s,"hh",1)                   //prints hhtest-
print Replace(s,"hhhhhhhh",1)             //prints hhhhhhhh
print Replace(s,"hh",3)                   //prints -tht-
print Replace(s,"hhhhhhhh",3)             //prints -thhhhhhhh
print Replace(s,"hh",length(s))           //prints -testhh
print Replace(s,"hhhhhhhh",length(s))     //prints -testhhhhhhhh
print Replace(s,"hh",50)                  //prints -test-hh
print Replace(s,"hhhhhhhh",50)            //prints -test-hhhhhhhh
```

•Substitute(se_Text,se_TextToReplace,se_ReplaceWith)

Returns se_Text with all the occurrences of the string se_TextToReplace within it replaced with se_ReplaceWith. se_TextToReplace and se_ReplaceWith do not have to be the same length. For example:

```
s = "a;testing;b"
print substitute(s,";",", ")  //prints a, testing, b
```

•ToCommaText(se_Text)

Given seText which is a string with substrings in it that are all separated with Cr/Lf will returns a string that has all the substrings separated with commas. Any substrings that contain a comma or a space will be surrounded with quotations (""). If the string contains a quotation already then it will be doubled just like when you want to specify a quotations in an RB normal string (see examples).

226

•Extract(se_Text,se_SeparatorChars,ne_Part)

Returns the ne_Part part of se_Text separated by the separator se_Separator. se_Text is a string with data separated by characters specified in se_Separator. Extract() will return the data part number ne_Part. If ne_Part is greater than the number of parts Extract() will return the last part. If se_Text does not contain the separator characters specified in se_Separator then se_Text will be returned. If ne_Part is not a number an error will be given. If it is not an integer it will be made into an integer. If it is less than 1 then it is made into 1.

```
a = "test,5,2.4"
b = ","
print Extract(a,b,2)     //will print 5
print Extract(a,b,3)     //will print 2.4
print Extract(a,b,6)     //will print 2.4
b = ";"
print Extract(a,b,1)     //will print test,5,2.4
```

•NumParts(se_Text,se_Separator)

Returns the number of parts a string se_Text has that are separated by characters specified in se_Separator. This function is used to determine the count of parts to help with Extract(). If se_Text does not contain the separator characters specified then 0 is returned.
Example:

```
s = "test,67,345,abs" \ d = ","
For i=1 to NumParts(s,d)
   print Extract(s,d,i)
next
//will print test then 67 then 345 then abs
```

•Encrypt(se_Text,se_Key)

Returns a string that is the exact same length as se_Text but with all the characters from se_Text encrypted according to the password key se_Key. If se_Key is less than 2 characters then no encrypting occurs and the original text is returned. The text and key can be any lengths and can contain any characters. The key can even be longer than the text. You can encrypt an entire text file by reading it into a string and then encrypting it then saving it back to the file. See the example.

Note: - To decrypt an encrypted text you need to encrypt it with the original key.
- The encrypted text will contain all sorts of un-displayable characters and may even contain the character with ASCII code zero. These characters will not be displayable. The encrypted string is just that, a string and can be manipulated as a normal string. But it contains characters that may not display properly when the string is printed on the screen using Print, xyText, xyString, or in an Edit box or a Memo box etc.

Example:

```
Addedit "Key",10,30,200
xyText 30,5,"Key",,15,fs_Bold
xyText 90,60,"Text",,15,fs_Bold
AddMemo "Text",10,90,350,300
```

```
AddMemo "Text2",370,90,350,300
SetMemoScrollBars "Text",1 \ SetMemoScrollBars "Text2",1
wrapmemo "Text",0 \ ReadOnlyMemo "Text2"
AddButton "Encrypt",220,30
data txt;"This text will be encrypted using the key you specify"
data txt;"in the edit box above.",""
data txt;"The result will be displayed in the memo to the right.",""
data txt;"Then the encrypted text will decrypted and placed back"
data txt;"in this memo.",""
data txt;"If there is any loss in the encryption/decryption action"
data txt;"the result below will be (0 i.e. false). Also you will"
data txt;"see that this text has changed.",""
data txt;"You may notice that the encrypted text's length does not"
data txt;"match the length of this text. This is due to the encrypted"
data txt;"text containing un-displayable characters."
setMemoText "Text",mToString(txt)
while true
   if LastButton() != ""
      s = GetMemoText("Text") \ k = GetEdit("Key")
      t = Encrypt(s,k)
      SetMemoText "Text2",t
      t = Encrypt(t,k)
      SetMemoText "Text",t
      xystring 10,550,"Original = Restored? ",t=s
   endif
wend
```

•Soundex(se_Text{,ne_Length})

Returns a code representing the sound of the string resulting from se_Text. The length of the code will depend on the value ne_Length which if is less than 4 or is not given will default to 4. The Soundex code can be used to search for words that sound the same e.g. Smith and Smyth will give the same code. The first letter of the code is always the first letter of the original string.

Example:

```
print Soundex("Smith")      //prints S530
print Soundex("Smyth")      //prints S530
print Soundex("Smythe")     //prints S530
print Soundex("Smith",6)    //prints S53000
print Soundex("Smyth",7)    //prints S530000
print Soundex("Smythe",8)   //prints S5300000
print Soundex("Lincoln")    //prints L524
print Soundex("lincoln")    //prints L524
print Soundex("lincoln",6)  //prints L52400
```

•Regular Expression String Functions

Regular Expression (RegExp) function allow for an advanced string searching (and replacing) functionality. RegExp is a very involved subject which has entire books dedicated to explaining and teaching how to use RegExps to accomplish tasks as searching strings for numbers, email addresses, HTML tags and much more. A good place to go to start learning about RegExps is the web site listed below. It has a very good tutorial as well as links to books and other resources.

228

You can use RobotBASIC's RegExp functions while studying the tutorial sessions on the site. Also see the example code below:

http://www.regular-expressions.info

RobotBASIC's RegExp engine functions in a similar (not exact) manner to Perl's extended RegExp standards and almost all (almost) of the examples and topics on the above web site can work using RB's functions.

re_SetUp() allows you to specify a template search pattern which will then be used to search through a string of text. re_Match() enables you to see if the ENTIRE string is a match to the pattern. re_Search() allows you to see if the pattern matches a PART of the string. If re_Search() is successful you can use the re_Start() and re_End() to get the character position of the start of the match and the character position just after the end of the match. You can use the re_Search() repeatedly to search for the next occurrence of the pattern.

You can also use re_Replace() to replace any or all matches to the pattern from the string to a different text.

The search template pattern can have *groups* (see the web site tutorial). The re_GrpNumber() allows you to retrieve the numerical order of a *named* group. The re_NumOfGrps() gives the number of groups in the pattern.

When a pattern matches within the search string using re_Search() you can obtain the position of the start and end of a match to any of the groups within the template pattern with re_Start() and re_End() with the group number option.

Note: **It is important that you follow the following order of actions to obtain successful results from RB's RegExp functions:**
  1- You must specify the search template pattern using re_Setup() before you use any other functions.
  2- You must then either use re_Match() to match the Entire string to the pattern, OR, you must use re_Search() to initiate an initial search. Both functions return true if there is a match and false otherwise.
  3- If se_Search() is successful you can obtain the character number within the string where the match occurred and the character number just after the end of the match (Length = End-Start) using re_Start() and re_End().
  4- To get the next match reissue re_Search() but this time specify the ne_StartCharacter parameter to start the matching from a different position other than the start of the string (usually you would use the re_End() returned value). Again if it is successful you can repeat step 3 above.
  5- To perform a replace operation you need to issue re_Replace() after step 1 above.
  6- You can get the number of a named group in the pattern using re_GrpNumber() after

step 1 above.
7- You can obtain the number of groups in the pattern using the re_NumOfGrps() after step 2 above results in a successful match.
8- You can get the character position number of a sub-match to any group using the re_Start(ne_grpnumber) and the end using re_End(ne_grpnumber) after step 2 above.

Note: In RobotBASIC character position numbers start with 1 for the first character 2 for the second and so on. In other languages RegExp functionality may use Zero indexing where 0 is the first character. So you may want to check the numbering if you copy examples from other languages (e.g. Perl).

Note: Group numbering starts with 1 for the first group and so on. However, group number 0 is the ENTIRE RegExp. The order proceeds from Left to Right.

Note: Named Group numbering starts after all unnamed groups have been assigned numbers. So if there are 3 unnamed groups and 2 named groups. Then the first unnamed group will be group 1 the second is group two and the third group 3, REGARDLESS of where the named groups might occur before or between or after these unnamed groups. Also remember that group 0 is the entire RegExp. So the first named group will be group number 4 and the second will be number 5. Also notice that in this example re_NumOfGrps() will return 5 since there are 5 actual groups (remember there is an implicit 6th group which is the entire RegExp and is group 0 always). The numbering is from left to right. But remember that the named groups will start after the unnamed ones even if a named group occurs to the left of an unnamed one (see examples later).

Note: re_Start() and re_End() have a meaningful value **ONLY after** an re_Search() or re_Match() has been issued. If they are not successful in a match then both functions will return 0.
Note: re_NumOfGrps() **only returns the correct number** of groups **after** an re_Search() or re_Match() has resulted in **a successful match**.

Example:
```
//-----example to demo all RegExp functions and how to use them
x = re_Setup("\d[+-]\d")
data s;"3+5","4-7","45+A5","  4+5 "
data a;"Not Match","Match"
for i=0 to 3
   print "'",s[i],"' does ",a[re_Match(s[i])]
next
print srepeat("=",30)
for i=0 to 3
   print "'",s[i],"' does ",a[re_Search(s[i])]," starting at ",re_Start()," ending at
",re_End(),
   if re_Start()
     print " the portion = """,substring(s[i],re_Start(),re_End()-re_Start()),""""
   else
     print
   endif
next
print srepeat("=",30)
```

230

```
s = "In this text we are going to replace all occurences of 'we' and 'is' to XXXX"
x = re_Setup("(we)|(is)")
ss = re_replace(s,"XXXX")
print s,crlf(),ss
print srepeat("=",30)
x = re_Search(s)  //we need to match before we count groups
print "There are ",re_NumOfGrps()," groups in the template"
for i= 1 to re_NumOfGrps()
    n=0 \ print "   Group ",i," matches at :"
    while re_Search(s,n)
        x=re_start(i) \ y = re_End(i)
        if y
            print "";x;y;" = """,substring(s,x,y-x),""""
            n=y
        else
            n = n+1
        endif
    wend
    print
next
print srepeat("=",30)
tmp = "(?<Test>we)|(is)"
x = re_Setup(tmp)
print "In this template    ",tmp,"    there is a named group"
print "The group named 'Test' is group number ",re_GrpNumber("test")
print "notice it is number 2 even though it comes first"
print "notice when we specify the name in re_GrpNumber() the case does not matter"
```

•re_Setup(se_Template{,ne_Mode})

Always returns true. You must invoke this function before you do other actions with other RegExp functions. se_Template is the search pattern required and can be any expression that results in a string. ne_Mode is a numeric expression that modifies how the RegExp functions will behave.

You can use the constants listed below in any combination by ORing them together. Also see the RobotBASIC Constants section. If ne_Mode is not specified or is less than 0 it will be made 0 which makes the RegExp function work in the default mode.

RE_DOTMATCHNEWLINE	normally the . (dot) in a template pattern will match any character in the string except for the new line character (char(13)). By setting this flag in the ne_Mode parameter the dot will be able to match any character including char(13).
RE_MULTILINE	normally the ^ and $ operators in the template pattern will match the beginning and ending of the entire search string regardless if there are cr/lf line breaks or not. By setting this flag in the ne_Mode the ^ and $ will match the beginning and ending of each line in the string when there are multiple lines separated by CR or CR/LF.
RE_IGNORECASE	normally the searching and matching will be case sensitive. By setting this flag in the ne_Mode you

231

will make the matching case insensitive. However characters in a character set (i.e. inside []) will be still case sensitive.

RE_RIGHTTOLEFT   normally the searching will take place from the left to the right if no starting position is specified in re_Search() then the start is the left. If this flag is set the matching will take place from right to left and if no starting position is specified in re_Search() then the start will be the end of the string. ^ will still match the beginning of string and look ahead still goes left to right and group numbering also will still be from left to right.

RE_IGNOREWHITESPACE   normally within the template string a space or CR will be taken as a character to match to the within the string. If this flag is set in the ne_Mode then spaces and other white space characters will be ignore and will no attempt will be made to match them within the string. In this case you have to specifically specify a space to be matched using \x20. Also the # will be taken to indicate a comment from the # until a CR. If you need to use a # as a match character then use \#. However, (?#xxxx) will still be considered as a comment regardless. This is similar to the EXTENDED mode in Perl.

You can use these in combination by ORing them together so RE_IGNORECASE | RE_RIGHTTOLEFT will cause RB to do the matching from right to left and also to ignore the case.

Note: Many of these modes can be specified explicitly in the template itself using meta-characters as described in the RegExp specifications. See the tutorials on the web site given above.

•**re_Match(se_Text)**
Returns true if the *entire* text string can be matched by the template specified in re_Setup(). Otherwise it will return false.

•**re_Search(se_Text{,ne_SartFromPositionNumber})**
This searches *within* se_Text for a match to the template and returns true if there is a match or false other wise. If the function is successful you can use re_Start() and re_End() to obtain the character positions of the start and end of the match or the start and end of a match to group within the template.

232

ne_StartFromPositionNumber if not given or is less than 1 will imply that the search will start from the beginning of the string by default. However if the mode specified in re_Setup() has been specified to be RE_RIGHTTOLEFT then the search will be from the right (i.e. last character) of the string. If the parameter is specified then the search will take place from the specified position.

This is useful for repeated searching of the string. By specifying a start position as the re_End() result from the previous search will cause the search to start right after the previously found match and thus will search for the next match.

•re_Start({ne_GroupNumber})

Returns the character number where a successful search has matched the template. If there is no successful previous search the value returned will be 0. Character 1 is the first character etc. If ne_Group number is specified then the value returned is the character number of a successful match to a GROUP as specified by the number from the search template. If ne_GroupNumber is less than 1 then it will be made 0 which is the entire pattern and thus is the same as not having specified a group number.

•re_End({ne_GroupNumber})

Returns the character number **just after** the substring that successfully matched the template. If there is no successful previous search the value returned will be 0. You can obtain the length of the matched text by using `re_Start() - re_End()`. If you want the character **position** of the last character in the matched sub-string then subtract one from the value returned by this function.

If ne_Group number is specified then the value returned is the character number of the character just after a successful match to a GROUP as specified by the number from the search template. If ne_GroupNumber is less than 1 then it will be made 0 which is the entire pattern and thus is the same as not having specified a group number.

•re_GrpNumber(se_GroupName)

Returns the group number within the template of a named group as specified by the se_GroupName expression. Remember named groups numbering starts after all the unnamed groups have been numbered.

•re_NumOfGrps()

Returns the number of groups in the template pattern. This will be the total of named and unnamed groups.

•re_Replace(se_Text{,se_ReplaceWith{,ne_SartFromPositionNumber{,ne_NumberOfMatchesToReplace}}})

Returns a string with ALL or ne_NumberOfMatchesToReplace occurences of matches to the template pattern from within the se_Text replaced with the se_ReplaceWith text.

If se_ReplaceWith is not specified it will be made into an empty string ("") which means the matched subtext will be deleted. If ne_NumberOfMatches to replace is not given or is less than 1 it will result in ALL matches being replaced. If ne_StarFromPositionNumber is not given or is less than 1 it will cause the matching to the template to start from the beginning of the text (or end if the mode is set to RE_RIGHTTOLEFT).

Conversion Functions

Note: See the notes at the top of the Standard User Interfacing section.

•Scaling And Weight & Measure Conversion

•Convert(ne_ValueToConvert, ne_ConversionTypeCode)

Will return a value that is the conversion of the ne_ValueToConvert multiplied by a factor depending on the ne_ConversionTypeCode given.

See the RobotBASIC Constants section for the conversion codes. The returned result will always be a float.

For example :

```
    print Convert(30, cc_DCtoDF) //prints 86 since 30 celsius is 86
fahrenhite
    print Convert(86, cc_DFtoDC) //prints 30
    print Convert(1, cc_NMtoKM)  //prints 1.852 1nm = 1.852 Km
```

•Map(ne_FromValue, ne_FromMin, ne_FromMax, ne_ToMin, ne_ToMax)

This function returns a value calculated as a mapping from a certain scale to another. ne_FromValue is a value that is according to the scale defined by the range ne_FromMax-ne_FromMin. The value will be scaled to the new scale defined by the range ne_ToMax-ne_ToMin.

The formula is
Returned Value = ne_ToMin + (ne_FromValue-ne_FromMin)*(ne_ToMax-ne_ToMin)/(ne_FromMax-ne_FromMin).

If ne_FromMin = ne_FromMax or   ne_ToMin = ne_ToMax an error will be issued.

It is up to you to ensure that the Min and Max values are in that order. However it also be useful to specify them in the reverse order as when converting the Y-coordinate to Screen Y since the Screen has the 0 at the top and the Max at the bottom. Specifying Min as the high value and Max as the low value will reverse the mapping so as to make the graph appear the right way up. See mPlotXY for how this is done.

It is OK for ne_FromValue to be outside the From_Range, the returned value will also be outside the To_Range but correctly according to scale.

This function can be of use in mapping a value in a certain scale to a value within another scale. For example when plotting a graph of data on the screen this function can be useful in converting a data x-point or y-point to a screen x-point or y-point.

Also see mPlotXY

•Sign Conversion

•Abs(ExprN)
Returns the Absolute value of *ExprN*. Returns *ExprN* as a positive number.

•Sign(ExprN)
Returns -1 if *ExprN* is negative, 1 if positive and 0 if zero.

•Float & Integer Conversion

•Round(ExprN)
Will return the Integer value closest to the Float value ExprN.
Round(3.4) => 3 Round(3.5) => 4 Round(3.6)=> 4
Round(-3.4) => -3 Round(-3.5) => -4 Round(-3.6)=> -4

•RoundUP(ExprN{,ne_Type})
If ne_Type is not specified or is 0 (false) the function will round UP the float ExprN regardless of the sign of the float.
RoundUp(3.4) => 4 RoundUp(3.5) => 4 RoundUp(3.6) => 4
RoundUp(-3.4) => -4 RoundUp(-3.5) => -4 RoundUp(-3.6) => -4
If ne_Type is not 0 (true) the function will round UP the float ExprN if it is positive and Down if it is negative (i.e. higher number).
RoundUp(3.4,1) => 4 RoundUp(3.5,1) => 4 RoundUp(3.6,1) => 4
RoundUp(-3.4,1) => -3 RoundUp(-3.5,1) => -3 RoundUp(-3.6,1) => -3

•RoundDn(ExprN{,ne_Type})
If ne_Type is not specified or is 0 (false) the function will round DOWN the float ExprN regardless of the sign of the float.
RoundUp(3.4) => 3 RoundUp(3.5) => 3 RoundUp(3.6) => 3
RoundUp(-3.4) => -3 RoundUp(-3.5) => -3 RoundUp(-3.6) => -3
If ne_Type is not 0 (true) the function will round DOWN the float ExprN if it is positive and UP if it is negative (i.e. lower number).
RoundUp(3.4,1) => 3 RoundUp(3.5,1) => 3 RoundUp(3.6,1) => 3
RoundUp(-3.4,1) => -4 RoundUp(-3.5,1) => -4 RoundUp(-3.6,1) => -4

•SignExtend8(ExprN)

•SignExtend16(ExprN)

Since RB deals only with 32 bit integers you would have a problem with 8 bit (byte) and 16 bit (word) numbers when stored in RB. The number will be stored in the lower 8/16 bits of the 32 bit integer. However this will obscure the SIGN of the 8/16 bit number. Normally a number is indicated as a negative or positive depending on the HIGHEST Bit of the number. So normally 90 (0x5A) and 23439 (0x5B8F) are positive 8/16 bit numbers while 0x9A and 0x9B8F can be considered as positive (154 and 39823) or negative (-102 and -25713) depending what you need. If you need to consider them to be negative you would have a problem in RB since these numbers are stored in a 32 bit integer and RB only considers a 32 bit number to be negative if the 32nd bit (bit 31) is 1.

So these two functions will Sign EXTEND the 8th (bit 7) and 16th (bit 15) to ALL bits from that bit upwards. So if bit 7/15 is 0 then all bits upwards will be made 0 and if it is 1 then all bits upwards will be set to 1. This will effectively sign extend the number and it will become a negative number in the 32 bit format.

Example:
```
a1 = 0x5A \ b1 = 0x5b8f
a2 = 0x9A \ b2 = 0x9b8f
print a1;a2                                    //prints      90       154
print signextend8(a1);signextend8(a2)          //prints      90      -102
print b1;b2                                    //prints   23439     39823
print signextend16(b1);signextend16(b2)        //prints   23439    -25713
```

•Frac(ExprN)

Returns the decimal fraction of a number. *Frac(12.3456)* => 0.3456

•Mod(ne_Numerator,ne_Denominator)

Returns the remainder of dividing **ne_Numerator** over **ne_Denominator**. If either parameter is not an integer it will be made into one (*RoundDn()*). *Mod(9,4)* => 1

•MaxInteger()

Returns the maximum integer value.

•MinInteger()

Returns the minimum integer value. This is not *quite* the negative of the maximum integer value.

•MaxFloat()

Returns the maximum floating point number value.

•MinFloat()

Returns the smallest floating point value. This not the negative of the maximum. It is rather the smallest value that can be used (negative or positive) that will still result in accurate calculations.

•MaxV(ExprN1,ExprN2)

Returns the maximum of the two values ExprN1 and ExprN2. The values have to be numeric but either can be an integer or a float. The value returned will be a float regardless of either value's type.

•MinV(ExprN1,ExprN2)

Returns the minimum of the two values ExprN1 and ExprN2. The values have to be numeric but either can be and integer or a float. The value returned will be a float regardless of either value's type.

•Within(ne_Value,ne_LowerLimit,ne_UpperLimit)

Checks to see if ne_Value is within the range (inclusive). All the numbers can be floats or integers. If ne_Lower is greater than ne_Upper they will be swapped to do the checking. The function returns True if ne_Value >= ne_LowerLimit AND ne_Value <= ne_UpperLimit otherwise it returns False. The swapping is internal and does not affect the parameters.

•Limit(ne_Value,ne_LowerLimit,ne_UpperLimit)

Checks to see if ne_Value is within the range (inclusive) and returns the value if it is within the limit or the limit value closest to the value if it outside the range. All the numbers can be floats or integers. If ne_Lower is greater than ne_Upper they will swapped to do the checking. If ne_Value is less than the lower limit the returned value is the lower limit. If it is greater than the upper limit the returned value is the upper limit otherwise the returned value is ne_Value. Swapping (if needed) is internal and does not affect the parameters. The returned value will have the type of the original value regardless of the type of the given lower and upper limits. So if the function is going to return one of the limits and its type is float but ne_Value is integer then the returned value will be made into integer, and vice versa.
Example:

```
print Limit(10.2,4,5)/2    //prints 2.5  since returned value is float 5.0
print Limit(10,4,5.5)/2    //prints 2    since the returned value is integer 5
print Limit(10,4,25.5)/2   //prints 5    since the returned value is integer 10
print Limit(10.2,4,25)/2   //prints 5.1 since the returned value is float 10.2
```

•BitSwap(ne_Number{,ne_NumberOfBits})

If ne_NumberOfBits is less than 2 or is greater than 4*8 i.e. 32 or is not given then it will be made 8. This function will return ne_Number with ne_NumberOfBits bits swapped. If ne_NumberOfBits is 8 then bit at position 7 (bit position numbering starts with 0) will be swapped with the bit at position 0 and 6 with 1 and 5 with 2 and 4 with 3.

This is useful in outputting to devices that require shifting the bits of a number a bit at a time with the MSbit first order.

You can swap any number of bits starting from bit 0 to the last bit. An integer has 4 bytes and so 32 bits. If you want to swap the bits of only the first byte then ne_NumberOfBits is 8, the first two bytes then 16 and so on.

•MakeBit(ne_Number,ne_BitPosition,on|off)
Will return the number ne_Number with the bit at position ne_BitPosition set to 1 if true is specified or 0 if false is specified. All parameters have to be numeric and if they are not integers they will be truncated.

The bit count starts at 0 from right to left (LSBit = 0, next one =1 and so on).

```
b = MakeBit(n,x,1) is equivalent to:        b = MakeBit(n,x,0) is equivalent to:
    b = (1 << x) | n                            b = ((1<<x) @ (~0)) & n
```

•MakeByte(ne_Number,ne_BytePosition,ne_ByteValue)
Will return the number ne_Number with the byte at position ne_BytePosition set to ne_ByteValue. All parameteres have to be numeric and if they are not integers they will be truncated. Only the LSByte of ne_ByteValue will be considered.

The byte count starts at 0 from right to left (LSByte = 0, next one =1 and so on).
```
    b = MakeByte(n,x,v) is equivalent to:
        b = (n & ~(0xff << x*8)) | ((v & 0xFF) << x*8)
```

•SetBit(ne_Number,ne_BitPosition)
•ClrBit(ne_Number,ne_BitPosition)
Will set/clear the bit at position ne_BitPosition in the numeric ne_number to 1/0 and returns the resulting new value. Both parameters have to be numeric and if not integers will be truncated.

The bit count starts at 0 from right to left (LSBit = 0, next one =1 and so on). See example in GetBit().
```
    b = SetBit(n,5) is equivalent to:     b = ClrBit(n,5) is equivalent to:
        b = (1 << 5) | n                      b = ((1<<5) @ (~0)) & n
```

•SetByte(ne_Number,ne_BytePosition)
•ClrByte(ne_Number,ne_BytePosition)
Will set/clear the byte at position ne_BytePosition in the numeric ne_Number to 255/0 and returns the resulting new value. Both parameters have to be numeric and if not integers will be truncated.

The byte count starts at 0 from right to left (LSByte = 0, next one =1 and so on). See example in GetBit().
```
    b = SetByte(n,2) is equivalent to:            b = ClrByte(n,2) is equivalent to:
```

```
b = (255 << 2*8) | n                          b = ((255<<2*8) @ (~0)) &
n                                             n
```

•GetBit(ne_Number,ne_BitPosition)
•GetByte(ne_Number,ne_BytePosition)
   Will return the value of the bit/byte at position se_Bit/BytePosition in the number ne_Number.
   Both parameters have to be numeric and if not integers will be truncated.

   The bit/byte count starts at 0 from right to left (LSBit/Byte = 0, next one =1 and so on).
         b = GetBit(n,2) is equivalent to: b = GetByte(n,2) is equivalent to:
              b = (n >> 2) & 1   b = (n >> 2*8) & 255

   Example:
```
         n = (125<<8)+122
         print GetByte(n,2)    //prints 0
         print GetByte(n,1)    //prints 125
         print GetByte(n,0)    //prints 122
         print GetBit(n,12)    //prints 1
         n = ClrBit(n,12)
         print GetBit(n,12)    //prints 0
         n = clrByte(n,0)
         print GetByte(n,0)    //print 0
         n = SetBit(n,12)
         print GetBit(n,12)    //prints 1
         n = SetByte(n,0)
         print GetByte(n,0)    //print 255
```

•Number & String Conversion

•Hex(ExprN{,ne_NumBytes})
   Returns a string that contains the Hexadecimal representation of the integer resulting from
   ExprN. If either parameter is not numeric an error is issued and if it not integer it will be
   converted to integer. The string returned does not include the "0x" indicator. To convert the
   string back to a number use HexToInt() but append the "0x" indicator to it. Optional
   ne_NumBytes specifies the minimum number of bytes and if it is negative it will be made
   positive, and if it is greater than 7 it will be set to 7. If it is not given or is less than the number
   of bytes in the number then the result will be as many digits (nibbles) as needed to render the
   number, but up to a minimum of 2 nibbles unless you specify 0 then a minimum of 1 nibble
   will be returned.

   Example:
```
         print Hex(655)            //prints 28F   notice only 3 nibbles
         print Hex(655,3)          //prints 00028F
         print Hex(655,2)          //prints 028F  notice leading zero
         (2 bytes)
         print Hex(655,1)          //prints 28F
```

```
print Hex(3)                           //prints 03      notice minimum of 2
nibbles
print Hex(3,0)                         //prints 3       notice forced to 1
nibble minimum
print HexToInt("0x"+Hex(655))   //prints 655
print HexToInt("0x"+Hex(655,5))//prints 655
```

•HexToInt(e_HexValue)
<u>Note:</u> This function is left for backward compatibility. It is better if you use ToNumber().

Returns the resulting integer number that is the equivalent to the hexadecimal value given as a string or numeric in Expr. If Expr is not a valid hexadecimal string or integer number then 0 will be returned. The string must have the "0x" indicator to indicate that the string is a hexadecimal representation.

Examples:
```
print hextoint(10)      //prints 10
print hextoint("10")    //prints 10
print hextoint("0x10")  //prints 16
print hextoint("0x1E")  //prints 30
print hextoint("1E")    //prints 0      not a valid hex
print hextoint("0x1N")  //prints 0      not a valid hex
```

•Bin(ExprN{,ne_NumBits})
Returns a string that contains the Binary representation of the integer resulting from *ExprN*. Ig either parameter is not numeric an error is issued and if not integer it will be converted to integer. The Number of bits will depend on ne_NumBits. If it is not given then the number of bits will be up to most significant bit that is not 0 and if is less than the number of significant bits it will be ignored. Use string manipulation functions to eliminate bits if desired. The string returned does not include the "0%" indicator. To convert the string back to a number use BinToInt() but append the "0%" indicator to it.
Example:
```
print bin(10)       //prints 1010
print bin(10,8)     //prints 00001010
print bin(10,3)     //prints 1010 ..... notice 3 is ignored
print bin(2,4)      //prints 0010
print bin(2)        //prints 10
```

•BinToInt(e_BinaryValue)
<u>Note:</u> This function is left for backward compatibility. It is better if you use ToNumber().

Returns the resulting integer number that is the equivalent to the binary value given as a string in Expr. If Expr is not a valid binary string or integer number then 0 will be returned. The string must have the "0%" indicator to indicate that the string is a binary representation.
Examples:
```
print BinToInt(10)      //prints 10
```

241

```
print BinToInt("10")    //prints 10
print BinToInt("0%10")  //prints 2
print BinToInt("0%123") //prints 0     not a valid binary
```

•SFtoDF(ExprN)

ExprN results in a 32 bit hex value in the little-endian order of a IEEE fixed floating point number. The function will convert the 32 bit fixed floating point format to a 64 bit floating point format which is the RB native floating point number. This can be useful when receiving data from a microcontroller such as the Propeller Chip which stores floating point numbers as 32bit fixed floats (Long integer with 4 bytes). This functions helps to convert this format to RB's native 64 bit floats. Also see DFtoSF(). If ExprN is not a valid 32 bit fixed float the result is not a valid result but you will still get a float.

•DFtoSF(ExprN)

ExprN results normal RB native floating point number (IEEE 64 bit float). The function will convert the RB float to the floating point value to the IEEE 32 bit fixed float number. This can be useful when sending data to a microcontroller such as the Propeller Chip which stores floating point numbers as 32bit fixed floats (Long integer with 4 bytes). This function helps to convert RB's floats to a format that can be sent to such microcontrollers as 4 bytes (32 bits) in the little-endian order. Also see SFtoDF(). If ExprN is larger than the limitations of a 32bit fixed float then the result is a meaningless result but is still a 32 bit float.

•ToByte(Expr)

If Expr results in a number the function will convert the number to an integer (if it is not already an integer) then it will bitwise AND it with 0xFF to remove all bytes but the LSByte and then will return a string of one character whose ASCII code is the value of the resulting number i.e. **char(rounddn(ExprN) & 0xFF)**.

If Expr results in a string then the function returns a string with one character which is the first character of the resulting expression. If Expr results in an empty string ("") then the function returns a string with one character whose ASCII code is zero.

•Spell(ExprN)

Returns a string that contains words that say the number ExprN in English. ExprN can be float or integer, but the decimal fraction will be removed. It is up to you to extract the decimal value and use Spell() again to spell it out if you desire (see example). If the number is negative it will be made positive. It is up to you to test if the number is negative and treat the result by adding an additional word if you need to (e.g. "Negative", "Minus", "Outlay", see example). ExprN cannot be larger than 999,999,999,999,999. If it is the function will return the word "Overflow".
Example:
```
n = -678.56
sn = ""
```

242

```
if n < 0 then sn = "Negative "
nf = Round(Frac(Abs(n))*100)
print sn+Spell(n)+" Dollars and "+Spell(nf)+" Cents"
//prints Negative Six Hundred Seventy Eight Dollars and Fifty Six
Cents
```

•IsNumber(Expr)

Returns 1 if *Expr* is a string that can be converted to a numeric or is a numeric, otherwise returns 0.

•IsString(Expr)

Returns 1 if *Expr* is a string (regardless if it can be converted to a number or not), otherwise returns 0.

•ToNumber(Expr{,ne_Default})

If Expr results in a numeric then that value is returned. If Expr results in a string that can be converted to a numeric then it will be converted and the result is returned. If Expr results in a string that is not a legal number then if no default value is given then the string will be returned as is. If ne_Default is specified and the string cannot be converted to a number then ne_Default is returned. ne_Default can be integer or float.

If the string is a valid Hexadecimal or Binary string then it will be converted to an integer. A valid Hexadecimal string is one that starts with 0x and contains only digits and A,B,C,D,E, or F and no other character. A valid binary string is one that starts with 0% and contains only the digits 1 or 0. See Numbers section in the Overview Of The Language section.

Note: This function should be used in preference to the older (but still available) HexToInt() and BinToInt().

•ToString(Expr)

If Expr results in a number it converts the number to a string and returns the value as a string. If *Expr* results in a string then the string is returned.

•Char(ne_AsciiCode)

Returns a string of one character that is the character whose ASCII code is ne_AsciiCode.

•Ascii(se_Text)

Returns the ASCII code of the first character in se_Text.

•GetStrByte(se_String,ne_ByteNumber)

This function will treat the string as an array of bytes. ne_ByteNumber is the index into the string (1 = 1st character and so on). The function will return the ASCII code for the character at the specified position. If the specified position is less than 1 it will be made 1 and if it is greater than the length of the string an error will be issued.

This command is useful with I/O commands and functions that return byte data as a string. With this function you can access the byte data as numbers.

See PutStrByte() below. GetStrByte(S,N) is equivalent to:
```
Ascii(Substring(S,N,1))
```

Also see the Buffer manipulation functions BuffWrite() and BuffRead() etc. that treat a string as a one-dimensional array (0 indexed) and allow you to write integers and floats to the string as binary values rather than just one byte. This function is more compatible with other string manipulation functions in that indexing into the string is 1 based.

•PutStrByte(se_String,ne_ByteNum,ne_Val)

This function will treat the string as an array of bytes. ne_ByteNumber is the index into the string (1 = 1st character and so on). The function will return the string back with the character at the specified position set to ne_Value. If the specified position is less than 1 it will be made 1 and if it is greater than the length of the string the string will be lengthened to that lenght with all the new bytes being set to 0 and then the desired byte will be placed in its correct position. ne_Value can be an integer or a float. If it is a float it will be truncated to an integer. The resulting integer is then ANDed with 0xFF to zero all bytes other than the LSByte.

This command is useful with I/O commands and functions that are passed data as a string of bytes. With this function you can create the string by using the byte value as a number.

See GetStrByte() above. PutStrByte(S,n,V) is equivalent to (almost, the formula below does not work for n=1):
```
S = S+sRepeat(Char(0),n-Length(S))
S = Substring(S,1,n-1)+Char(V&0xFF)+Substring(S,n+1,0)
```

Also see the Buffer manipulation functions BuffWrite() and BuffRead() etc. that treat a string as a one-dimensional array (0 indexed) and allow you to write integers and floats to the string as binary values rather than just one byte. This function is more compatible with other string manipulation functions in that indexing into the string is 1 based.

•StrOfBytes(Expr{,Expr{,....}})

This function has to have at least one parameter, but it can have as many after that as you wish. Each parameter can be a string or an integer or a float.

The function will return a string (buffer) formed from the byte values according to the parameters. If a parameter is a string then all the bytes in the string will be included as they are. If the parameter is an integer value then its Least Significant Byte (LSB) will be taken. If the parameter is a float, it will be converted to an integer (rounded down) and then the LSByte

will be taken. For example:
```
S = StrOfBytes(20,300,"ABC",45,200.76)
For i=1 to length(S)
    print GetStrByte(S,i);
next
//will print 20   44   65   66   67   45   200
//which are the values of the individual bytes. Notice the 2nd value is 44
//not 300 that is because the value 300 is 2 bytes 0x012C and 0x2C = 44
//Also notice the last value is 200 which is the result after truncating 200.76
```

•**Format(ExprN,se_FormatSpecifier)**

Returns a string containing *ExprN* formatted according to the se_FormatSpecifier. The parameters and specifiers are:

Specifier	Represents
0	Digit place holder. If the value being formatted has a digit in the position where the **0** appears in the format string, then that digit is copied to the output string. Otherwise, a **0** is stored in that position in the output string.
#	Digit placeholder. If the value being formatted has a digit in the position where the **#** appears in the format string, then that digit is copied to the output string. Otherwise, nothing is stored in that position in the output string.
.	Decimal point. The first **.** character in the format string determines the location of the decimal separator in the formatted value; any additional **.** characters are ignored. The actual character used as the decimal separator in the output string is determined by the Decimal Separator global variable. The default value of DecimalSeparator is specified in the Number Format of the International section in the Windows Control Panel.
,	Thousand separator. If the format string contains one or more **,** characters, the output will have thousand separators inserted between each group of three digits to the left of the decimal point. The placement and number of ',' characters in the format string does not affect the output, except to indicate that thousand separators are wanted. The actual character used as a the thousand separator in the output is determined by the ThousandSeparator global variable. The default value of ThousandSeparator is specified in the Number Format of the International section in the Windows Control Panel.
E+	Scientific notation. If any of the strings **E+**, **E-**, **e+**, or **e-** are contained in the format string, the number is formatted using scientific notation. A group of up to four **0** characters can immediately follow the **E+**, **E-**, **e+**, or **e-** to determine the minimum number of digits in the exponent. The **E+** and **e+** formats cause a plus sign to be output for positive exponents and a minus sign to be output for negative exponents. The **E-** and **e-** formats output a sign

character only for negative exponents.

'xx'   Characters enclosed in single or double quotes are output as-is, and do not affect formatting.

;   Separates sections for positive, negative and zero numbers in the format string.

Notes:

The locations of the leftmost '0' before the decimal point in the format string and the rightmost '0' after the decimal point in the format string determine the range of digits that are always present in the output string.

The number being formatted is always rounded to as many decimal places as there are digit placeholders ('0' or '#') to the right of the decimal point. If the format string contains no decimal point, the value being formatted is rounded to the nearest whole number.

If the number, being formatted has more digits to the left of the decimal separator than there are digit placeholders to the left of the '.' character in the format string, the extra digits are output before the first digit placeholder.

To allow different formats for positive, negative, and zero values, the format string can contain between one and three sections separated by semicolons.

One section: The format string applies to all values.
Two sections: The first section applies to positive values and zeros, and the second section applies to negative values.
Three sections: The first section applies to positive values, the second applies to negative values, and the third applies to zeros.

If the section for negative values or the section for zero values is empty, that is if there is nothing between the semicolons that delimit the section, the section for positive values is used instead.

File & Directory Functions

Note: See the notes at the top of the Standard User Interfacing section.

•Directory Functions

•DiskSize(ne_DiskNumber)

Returns the size in bytes of the disk specified. If ne_DiskNumber is 0 then the current disk is the one reported upon. Use 1 for A:, 2 for B: etc. If the disk number specified is not a valid disk then the function will return -1 as a result. Remember a Kilobyte is 1024 bytes and a Megabyte is 1024x1024 bytes etc.

•DiskFree(ne_DiskNumber)

Returns the size in bytes of the free space on the disk specified. If ne_DiskNumber is 0 then the current disk is the one reported upon. Use 1 for A:, 2 for B: etc. If the disk number specified is not a valid disk then the function will return -1 as a result. Remember a Kilobyte is 1024 bytes and a Megabyte is 1024x1024 bytes etc.

•DirCurrent()

Returns a string that contains the current directory including the drive name.

•DirSet(se_DirPath)

Set the current default directory to the directory specified. Returns true (1) if successful or false (0) if not.

•DirExists(se_DirPath)

Checks to see if the directory specified is a valid directory. Returns true (1) if successful or false (0) if not.

•DirCreate(se_DirPath)

Creates the directory specified and all parent directories on the path if they do not exist. Always returns true.

•DirRemove(se_DirPath)

Removes the directory specified. It only removes the last directory on the path not any parent directories. Returns true (1) if successful or false (0) if not. The directory can only be removed if it does not contain files or sub-directories.

•DirCount()

Returns then number of the sub-directories in the current directory. The count includes the drive name and directories on the path of the current directory name. See the example given in DirList() below.

•**DirList()**

Returns a string containing the names of the directories in the current directory. The list of directories is separated by the | character (the same one used for the or operator). You can use Extract() along with DirCount() to obtain a particular directory name from the list. For Example:

```
n=DirCount()
s= DirList()
for i=1 to n
    ss = Extract(s,"|",i)
    print ss
    if !(i#35) then waitkey k \ clearscr
next
```

•**DirPrompt()**

Opens a directory selection dialog box and allows the user to select a directory. If the user types a directory that does not exist a prompt for creating the directory will be given and if the user selects to do so the directory will be created and selected. The selected directory will be returned with the full path name.

Note: The dialog allows the user to select a directory by **double-clicking** the mouse over it and will show the files contained in the directory. Pushing the *Ok* button will return the selected directory name. Pushing the *Cancel* button will return a blank string "". The directory selected does not become the current directory, use DirSet() if you wish to do so.

•**File Functions**

•**FileExists(se_FileName)**

Checks to see if the file exists and returns true (1) if it does. If the file does not exist or there is a problem with the operation the function returns false (0).

•**FileSearch(se_FileName,se_DirList)**

Searches for the file in the list of directories given. If the file is found in any of the directories in the list the function returns the fully qualified name of the file including the directory path in which it resides. If the file name is not found a null string ("") is returned. se_DirList is a list of directory paths separated with a semicolon (;).

•**FileRename(se_OldName,se_NewName)**

Renames the file to the new name and returns true (1) if successful. If the file does not exist or there is a problem with the operation the function returns false (0).

•FileSize(se_Name)

Returns the size in bytes of the specified file. The name has to be the full path of the file. If the file is not found or there was a problem in accessing it then -1 will be returned. Remember a Kilobyte is 1024 bytes and a Megabyte is 1024x1024 bytes etc.

If you wish to find the size of a file that has been opened/created using FileOpen() or FileCreate() then use FileSize(ne_FileHandle). Since the use of the name version may fail due to the file being currently in use by your process.

•FileDate(se_FileName)

Returns the date and time of the file as a floating point number just as described in Now(). Use the date and time functions [e.g. DateTime()] to convert this number to Date and/or Time strings for display.

•FileCopy(se_SourceFile,se_DestinationFile{,ne_Mode})

Makes a copy of the source file to the destination file. If ne_Mode is not given or is false then if the file destination file already exists the function will not overwrite it and will return an error code as described below. If true is given then if the destination file exists it will be overwritten unless it is a read only file, in which case an error code will be returned.

The function will return the size of the file copied if it successfully completed the operation. If the source file could not be opened then -1 will be returned. If the destination file could not be created then -2 will be returned. This can occur if the file already exists and ne_Mode is not specified or is false, or if the system could not create the file for any other reason. If the copying operation could not finish copying (e.g. disk full) then -3 will be returned.

Note: *Depending on the size of the file, this function may take a perceptible time to execute. You may want to display a message to the user of your program before you execute this function.*

•FileDelete(se_Name)

Deletes the file and returns true if successful. If the file does not exist or there is a problem with the operation the function returns false.

•FileName(se_Name)

Returns a string containing only the name of the full file specification given (i.e. with no directory or path data).

•FileExt(se_Name)

Returns a string containing only the extension of the file given.

•FileDrive(se_Name)
Returns a string containing only the drive name of the file given.

•FileDir(se_Name)
Returns a string containing only the directory name of the file given.

•FilePath(se_Name)
Returns a string containing only the path name of the file given.

•FileChangeExt(se_FileName,se_NewExtension)
If the file name has no extension or has an extension different from se_NewExtension, it will be modified to have the new extension and the new name is returned. **This function does not actually change the name of the file on the drive. It only changes the string. To rename the file use the new name in FilRename().**

•FilePrompt({Expr})
Opens a file selection dialog box and allows the user to select a file. Expr is optional. If Expr numerical and is not within the range 1-5, or is not given or is an empty string ("") then 1 will be assumed.

If Expr is given and is numerical (integer) and is within the range 1-5 then Expr specifies a filter from a list of file filters as follows:
        1 = All Files (*.*)
        2 = Bitmap Files (*.Bmp)
        3 = WAV Sound Files (*.Wav)
        4 = RobotBASIC Array files (*.Rba)
        5 = Text Files (*.Txt)

The RBA extension is not a standard extension but may be used by you (the programmer) as an extension for files created by mWrite used to save the data of arrays.

If Expr is given and is a string that does not contain the | character then the string will be considered as a Filename to be filled as a default before the File Open dialog box is shown. Also the first filter (*.*) will be assumed.

If Expr is given and contains the | character then it has to follow the following specs:
- The text before the first | character will be a default file name.
- Subsequent text must be in pairs of strings separated with |. The first string is a description of a filter type, the second is the filter specs (see example below).
- You can repeat as many string pairs to specify as many filters as you need.
- The first of these filter specs will be used as default.

An example for a string specification:

"MyFile.RBA|RobotBASIC Arrays (*.RBA)|*.RBA|TextFiles (*.Txt)|*.Txt|Bitmap Files (*.Bmp)|*.Bmp"

It is advisable to have the actual filter as part of the description. You must not have a space before or after the |. If you do not want to specify a default file then just don't but the first | must still be there e.g.

"|RobotBASIC Arrays (*.RBA)|*.RBA|TextFiles (*.Txt)|*.Txt|Bitmap Files (*.Bmp)|*.Bmp"

If the user selects a file the full file's name including the directory and drive will be returned. If the user closes the dialog without selecting a file or cancels then the returned value will be a blank string (i.e. ""). **The file name specified must be an existing file**.

Note: This dialog does not actually open any files it just returns the name of a selected file. The button on the dialog will say "Open", if you need a dialog to allow the user to select a file name for saving see FileSave() below.

•FileSave({Expr})

Opens a file selection dialog box and allows the user to select or specify a file name. Expr is optional. If Expr numerical and is not within the range 1-5, or is not given or is an empty string ("") then 1 will be assumed.

If Expr is given it must follow the specifications given above in FilePrompt().

If the user selects a file the full file's name including the directory and drive will be returned. If the user closes the dialog without selecting a file or cancels then the returned value will be a blank string (i.e. ""). **The file name specified does not have to exist. If it does exist the user will be given a warning and is given the opportunity to cancel or proceed.**

Note: This dialog does not actually save any files it just returns a name of a selected or specified file. The button on the dialog will say "Save", if you need a dialog to allow the user to select a file name for opening see FilePrompt() below.

•FilesCount({se_Filter})

Returns the number of files in the current directory that satisfy the filter. The filter is optional and if not given will be equivalent to "*.*". The specification can be a particular file or can use the characters ? and * as place holders to specify a file names template. See the example given in FilesList() below.

•FilesList({se_Filter})

Returns a string containing the names of files in the current directory that satisfy the filter. The list of files is separated by the | character (the same one used for the or operator). The filter is optional and if not given will be equivalent to "*.*". The specification can be a particular file or can use the characters ? and * as place holders to specify a file names template. You can use Extract() along with FilesCount() to obtain a particular file name from the list. For Example:

```
n=FilesCount("*.bas")
s= FilesList("*.bas")
for i=1 to n
    ss = extract(s,"|",i)
    print ss
    if !(i#35) then waitkey k \ clearscr
next
```

•Byte Buffer Manipulation

RobotBASIC provides a suite of functions that allow you to manipulate a buffer area. You can read and write data to the buffer area. This can be useful in many situations, such as File I/O, Serial I/O, TCP I/O, USBmicro functions and many other situations.

The buffer is considered as a string with special properties. You can use it for all intents and purposes as a string if you wish. But the Buffer Read/Write functions below provide extra abilities that you will find useful.

Note: Position indexing in the buffer manipulation functions starts at 0 for the first byte 1 for the second etc. Just like Arrays. As a matter of fact the buffer is really a one dimensional array of BYTES, but it can also be treated as a string too (a string is also really a one dimensional array of bytes too). However, when you use the buffer with string commands, you will consider the first byte as 1 and so on, just like with other string functions.

Note: When you use the buffer with string functions, you will consider the first byte as 1 and so on, just like with other string functions. Also see GetStrByte(), PutStrByte() and ToByte().

Note: A string representation of a number is just that. So if you have the number 24659 then you will have 5 bytes with the first byte having a value of 50, which is the ASCII representation of the character 2. The next byte will be 52 and so on. This format is good when outputting to text files or to systems that will be able to read numbers as strings. Nevertheless, this format can be wasteful since a number like 147483647 will need 9 bytes. If the number is a float it can be even worse since a number like pi will need 16 bytes. You can convert numbers to strings using ToString(). Also see mToString() and mFromString.

A more efficient way to store integers and floats in a buffer or in a file is to use their BINARY representation. An integer needs 4 bytes and a float needs 8 bytes. See the BytesCount_I and BytesCount_F constants in the Constants section. If you store in integers

252

or floats in the RobotBASIC buffer using the Buffer functions below they will be stored in the buffer as binaries. If you treat the buffer as a string you would not get the numbers correctly if you read the 4 bytes, say, of the integer.

There are functions to convert entire arrays into a string and vice versa, see mToString() and mFromString.

To illustrate the difference do the following:
```
Buffer = BuffWrite("",-1,3456)
print "--",Buffer,"--"          //prints --€    --
print BuffReadI(Buffer,0)*2  //prints 6912    also notice indexing is 0
print hex(Ascii(Substring(Buffer,1,1)));  //notice indexing is 1
print hex(Ascii(Substring(Buffer,2,1)));
print hex(Ascii(Substring(Buffer,3,1)));
print hex(Ascii(Substring(Buffer,4,1)))    //prints 80   0D   00   00
                                // ... notice Little-Endian format
print ToNumber(Buffer,0)*2    //prints 0
print ToNumber(Buffer)*2      //gives an error
```

Notice how the 3456 is not even there but there are garbage 4 characters that have the values 0x80, 0x0D, 0x00, 0x00. These are the backwards representation of the number 0x00000D80 which is the number 3456 in hex. Windows (and Intel) use the Little-Endian order representation; that is why the bytes are in reverse.

What really matters here is that if you BuffWrite() integers or floats to the buffer then you will not be able to use those bytes to get the number back by using the bytes directly, you have to use BuffReadI() and BuffReadF() to do so. But if you do:
```
Buffer = ""+3456
print "--",Buffer,"--"    //prints --3456--
print hex(Ascii(Substring(Buffer,1,1)));  //notice indexing is 1
print hex(Ascii(Substring(Buffer,2,1)));
print hex(Ascii(Substring(Buffer,3,1)));
print hex(Ascii(Substring(Buffer,4,1)))  //prints 33   34   35   36
print ToNumber(Buffer)*2 //prints 6912
```

•BuffPrintT vs_BuffString{,Expr,Expr;Expr...}{;|,}

This command will put data into a Buffer as specified by the string variable vs_BuffString. It can be either an existing buffer variable (string) that already contains data or it can be empty. If it does not exist or does not contain a string, it will be recreated and initialized as an empty string. If it exists and already has a string in it, the new data will be appended to the *end* of the existing string.

The data is specified by the values of *expr*.... Numerical data will be converted to text. A **,** between the expressions causes them to be appended with no space between them a **;** appends them with a tab space between them. If there are no expressions then a Cr/Lf pair will be appended to the buffer.

If the list of expressions does not end with a , or ; there will be a Cr/Lf at the end of the appended data. A , makes the next use of BuffPrintT append data immediately after the previous data, while ; causes the next data to be appended in a tabbed position.

If you wish to populate the buffer with numbers without converting them to text first then use BuffPrintB below. Also see BuffWrite/B().

Note: vs_BuffString has to be a variable name and the data will be appended to the end of the existing data in it if it contains a previous buffer data or a string. If it does not exist or it does and contains a number then it will be erased and recreated as an empty buffer (string). If there are no expressions then it must _not_ be followed by a , or ; . If you do list expressions as data to be appended then you follow vn_BuffString either with a ; or , it does not matter.

Note: Normally the ; creates a tab between the printed elements of BuffPrint while , is used as a no spaces separator. You can tell RobotBASIC to make , the tab indicator and ; the no spaces one by using CommaTab (see Standard User Interfacing section).

•**BuffPrintB vs_BuffString{,Expr,Expr,Expr...}**
This command will put data into a Buffer as specified by the string variable vs_BuffString. vs_BuffString can be either an existing buffer variable (string) that already contains data or it can be empty. If it does not exist or does not contain a string, it will be recreated and initialized as an empty string. If it exists and already has a string in it then the new data will be appended to the END of the existing string.

The data is specified by the values of *expr....* Numerical data will be appended as Binary bytes. You can separate the expressions with a , or a ; it does not matter which. Unlike in BuffPrintT above there is no tabbing or converting numbers to strings. Each expression will either result in a numeric which is appended as its binary representation, or a string which is then appended as is.

Integers will be 4 bytes and floats will be 8 (See the Constants section). If there are no expressions then nothing will be appended to the buffer (no Cr/Lf). If you want to append an integer as a byte value then use ToByte(). If you wish to insert a float as a 32bit format (4 bytes) then use DFtoSF().

The list of expressions must _**not**_ end with a , nor ;. If it does you will get an error.

If you wish to populate the buffer with numbers as strings use BuffPrintT above or use

ToString(). Also see BuffWrite/B(). Also see SFtoDF() and DFtoSF().

Note: vs_BuffString has to be a variable name and the data will be appended to the end of the existing data in it if it contains a previous buffer data or a string. If it does not exist or it does and contains a number then it will be erased and recreated as an empty buffer (string). If there are no expressions then vs_BuffString must *not* be followed by a **,** or **;** . If you do list expressions as data to be appended then you follow it either with a **;** or **,** it does not matter.

•**BuffWrite(se_Buffer,ne_Position,e_Value)**

Will return the new buffer which is the result of e_Value written to se_Buffer starting at the ne_Position. If e_Value is a string then each individual character in the string will be written in the buffer. If e_Value is an integer value then it will be written to the buffer as 4 bytes which is the binary representation of the integer. If e_Value results in a float then 8 bytes (i.e. 64 bits) will be written (see BuffWriteF32 to write a float as 4 bytes i.e. 32 bits).

If the position specified is so that when the value is written it will be longer than the current length of the buffer then the buffer will be lengthened to accommodate the result. Any bytes in the buffer starting at the specified position will be overwritten.

Bytes that are a result of lengthening the buffer will have a value of 0x00 until they are overwritten.

If ne_Position is less than 0 then the position will be just beyond the end of the buffer, that is the written bytes will be concatenated to the end of the original buffer.

•**BuffWriteB(se_Buffer,ne_Position,ne_Value)**

Will return the new buffer which is the result of ne_Value written to se_Buffer starting at the ne_Position. If ne_Value is a float it will be truncated to an integer. The result whether is a truncated float or the original integer will be made into a one byte value i.e. only the LSByte will be used. For example if ne_value is 2345 (= 0x0929) then what is written to the buffer at the ne_Position is a one byte value of 0x29 (=41 decimal). If ne_Value results in 293.56 then what will be written is 0x25 (=37 decimal) which is the LSByte of 293.56 after it is truncated to 293 which is 0x0125.

If the position specified is so that when the value is written it will be longer than the current length of the buffer then the buffer will be lengthened to accommodate the result. Any bytes in the buffer starting at the specified position will be overwritten.

Bytes that are a result of lengthening the buffer will have a value of 0x00 until they are overwritten.

255

If ne_Position is less than 0 then the position will be just beyond the end of the buffer, that is the written bytes will be concatenated to the end of the original buffer.

•BuffWriteF32(se_Buffer,ne_Position,ne_Value)

Will return the new buffer which is the result of ne_Value written to se_Buffer starting at the ne_Position. What is written in the buffer is 4 bytes that represent the IEEE 32 bit float representation of the ne_Value (Little-Endian). If ne_Value is an integer it will be made into a 32bit float. If ne_Value is float (64 bit in RB) it will be made into a 32 bit float and if it exceeds the limitations of 32 bit float values then it will be meaningless. This can be useful if the buffer is to be sent to microcontrollers (e.g. Propeller) that use 32 bit floats. Since RB uses a 64 bit float (8 bytes) you can use this to insert a float from RB that does not exceed limits of the 32 bit format into the buffer and it will be recognized by the receiving microcontroller as a 32 bit float (Little-Endian).

If the position specified is so that when the value is written it will be longer than the current length of the buffer then the buffer will be lengthened to accommodate the result. Any bytes in the buffer starting at the specified position will be overwritten.

Bytes that are a result of lengthening the buffer will have a value of 0x00 until they are overwritten.

If ne_Position is less than 0 then the position will be just beyond the end of the buffer, that is the written bytes will be concatenated to the end of the original buffer. Also see SFtoDF() and DFtoSF().

•BuffRead(se_Buffer,ne_Position,ne_NumBytes)

Will return a string (buffer) that consists of the bytes from the se_Buffer starting at ne_Position and is ne_NumBytes long unless the buffer is shorter than ne_Position+ne_NumBytes then the returned string will be as long as there are characters remaining in the buffer from the specified position.

If ne_Position is less than 0 it will be made 0. If ne_NumByets is less than 1 then the remaining number of bytes from the ne_Position will be read (i.e. all the way to the end). If ne_Position is longer than the buffer then "" will be returned.

•BuffReadB(se_Buffer,ne_Position)
•BuffReadI(se_Buffer,ne_Position)
•BuffReadF(se_Buffer,ne_Position)
•BuffReadF32(se_Buffer,ne_Position)

Will return an RB float (64 bits) or and integer formed from reading the right number of bytes from the buffer.

In the byte version BuffReadB(), the returned value is an integer value with all but the LSByte set to 0. The LSByte will have the value of the one byte read from the buffer.
In the Integer version BuffReadI(), the returned value is an integer value formed from reading 4 bytes from the buffer. The 4 bytes are the bytes that represent a 32 bit integer values in Little-Endian order.
In the Float version BuffReadF(), the returned value is an RB float (64 bits) value formed from reading 8 bytes from the buffer. These 8 bytes are the IEEE 64 bit format for a floating point number representation (Little-Endian)
In the Float32 version BuffReadF32(), the returned value is an RB float (64 bits) value formed from reading 4 bytes from the buffer. These 4 bytes from the IEEE 32 bit float format (Little-Endian). This can be useful if the buffer has been received from a microcontroller (e.g. Propeller) that uses 32 bit floats. The value returned by the function is the 32bit float converted to 64 bit float which is the native RB float format.

If the buffer is too short to read the right number of bytes from the specified position then an error will be issued. If ne_Position is less than 0 it will be made 0.

Also see SFtoDF() and DFtoSF().

•Low Level File I/O

Low level file I/O allows reading and writing data from a disk file with a little more control over the process than is provided by the other commands and functions (e.g. mTextFR, mTextFW, mWrite, mRead and others) which provide much easier and safer file input and output. Nevertheless, there are situations where more control over the process of reading and writing a file is needed. This is when the following function should be utilized to access data from a file a byte at a time or in chunks of bytes or as binary integers or floats or as text. However, more care is needed and error checking should be carried out often.

These functions can cause trouble if not used correctly. There is a sequence of actions that has to be followed precisely for the functions to execute without trouble.

The sequence is as follows (see the examples to see how it should be done):
1- Open the file if it exists, or, create it if it does not exist or if overwriting it is required. A file can be opened for reading, writing or reading and writing. The file being manipulated can be opened with exclusive access and thus denying access to other processes, or only read access can be denied or write access or neither.
2- Insure the file is actually opened by checking the returned file handle.
3- If the file is to be accessed sequentially *sequential* then start reading or writing, if it is a *random access* file then position the pointer to where you want to start the read/write

operation before you do the read/write.

4- Repeat reading and/or writing as desired, always checking the fact that the read/write has succeeded.

5- When done with the file, **ALWAYS** FileClose() the file to release its handle and flush any buffered writes to the disk.

6- After each operation you must check for errors if you do not want to run into trouble.

Note: In regards to numbers you have the choice, you can either treat them as string representations when you write them to the file by converting them to strings using ToString() or you can write them to the file using FileWrite/B() as binary representations. When it is time to read the numbers back, if they have been written as strings then you read them back as strings then you can convert them to numbers using ToNumber() and IsNumber(). If they have been written as binary then you need to read them using FileRead/I/B/F().

There are functions to convert entire arrays into a string and vice versa, see mToString() and mFromString. Also see the buffer functions BufferWrite/B() and BufferRead/I/B/F(). Additionally, see GetStrByte(), PutStrByte() and ToByte() and of course all the string mainpulation functions as well as number conversion functions. Also see CrLf(), Substitute(), Extract() and NumParts().

•FilePrintT vn_FileHandle{,Expr,Expr;Expr...}{;|,}

This command will output data to a file as specified by the numeric variable vn_FileHandle. vn_FileHandle has to be an existing variable and has to contain an integer which is a **File Handle** as returned by FileCreate() or FileOpen().

The data is specified by the values of *expr....* Numerical data will be converted to text. A **,** between the expressions causes them to be outputted with no space between them a **;** outputs them with a tab space between them. If there are no expressions then a Cr/Lf pair will be outputted to the file.

If the list of expressions does not end with a **,** or **;** there will be a Cr/Lf at the end of the outputed data. A **,** makes the next use of FilePrintT output data immediately after the previous data, while **;** causes the next data to be outputted in a tabbed position.

If you wish to output numbers without converting them to text first then use FilePrintB below. Also see FileWrite/B().

Note: vn_FileHandle has to be the name of an already existing variable with a File Handle integer number as returned by a FileOpen() or FileCreate().

Note: Normally the **;** creates a tab between the outputted elements of FilePrint while **,** is used as a no spaces separator. You can tell RobotBASIC to make **,** the tab indicator and **;** the no spaces one by using CommaTab (see Standard User Interfacing section).

•FilePrintB vn_FileHandle{,Expr,Expr,Expr...}

This command will output data to a file as specified by the numeric variable vn_FileHandle. vn_FileHandle has to be an existing variable and has to contain an integer which is a **File Handle** as returned by FileCreate() or FileOpen().

The data is specified by the values of *expr....* Numerical data will be appended as Binary bytes. You can separate the expressions with a **,** or a **;** it does not matter which. Unlike in FilePrintT above there is no tabbing or converting numbers to strings. Each expression will either result in a numeric which is outputted as its binary representation, or a string which is then outputted as is.

Integers will be 4 bytes and floats will be 8 (See the Constants section). If there are no expressions then nothing will be outputted to the file (no Cr/Lf). If you want to output an integer as a byte value then use ToByte().

The list of expressions must __*not*__ end with a **,** nor **;**. If it does you will get an error.

If you wish to output numbers as strings use FilePrintT above. Also see FileWrite/B().

Note: vn_FileHandle has to be the name of an already existing variable with a File Handle integer number as returned by a FileOpen() or FileCreate().

•FileOpen(se_FileName,ne_Mode)

This function opens se_FileName in the mode specified as ne_Mode. If the function succeeds in opening the file then a number is returned which is the *FileHandle* that has to be used with other File I/O commands. If there is an error then the returned value is -1.

The ne_Mode value can be created by ORing the various **fo_** constants in the RobotBASIC Constants section. For example to read the file and still allow others access to it, you use **fo_Read | fo_DenyNone**. To open the file for reading and writing while denying write access to others then use **fo_ReadWrite | fo_DenyWrite**.

Note: If you open a file in one of the denying modes then even your program cannot Open() or Create() the file again until you FileClose() the file first.

The returned value should always be checked for errors. Trying to manipulate a file through a bad handle will result in errors. RobotBASIC will not attempt to do any file operation if the handle given is a -1.

If the file being opened does not exist or is being used by another process (or even the same program elsewhere) then the returned handle will be -1.

Example: This example shows how TEXT files can be created. See the example at the end of FileClose() for an example of BINARY files. After running this program, use NotePad to view the file dBase.txt. Notice how the numbers are readable text as opposed to when you look at the file created whith the other example.
But also view the contents of dBaseEncrypted.txt. Notice how Encrypt() can help make a text file unreadable.

```
data a;"Pam"   ,35,"here and there",60963
data a;"Tammy",45,"over somewhere",80443
s = mToString(a) //uses CR/LF by default
fn = "dBase.txt" \ fn2 = "dBaseEncrypted.txt" \ PassWrd = "Pass
word"
h = Filecreate(fn)  \ FileWrite(h,s) \ FileClose(h)
h = FileCreate(fn2) \ FileWrite(h,encrypt(s,PassWrd))   \
FileClose(h)
h = FileOpen(fn,fo_Read)  \ s = FileRead(h,FileSize(h)) \
FileClose(h)
h = FileOpen(fn2,fo_Read) \ t =
encrypt(FileRead(h,FileSize(h)),PassWrd)
FileClose(h) \ mFromString b,s //default cr/lf
for i=0 to maxdim(b,1)-1 step 4
   For n=0 to 3
     print b[i+n];
   next
   print
next
AddMemo "m",400,10,300,400 \ SetMemoText "m",s
AddMemoLine "m",crlf()+"------Decrypted-----"
Addmemoline "m",crlf()+t
```

•FileCreate(se_FileName)
Creates the file and opens it for reading and writing *in exclusive mode*. If successful then it will return the *FileHandle* to be used later. If it does not succeed the returned value is -1.

Note: **If the file exists and is not locked due to being used by another process (or yours elsewhere) then it will be erased and recreated.** *So be careful with this command since you can erase files without warning. You can use FilExists() to verify if a file already exists and take appropriate action.*

•FileReadField(ne_FileHandle{,se_Separator})
Will read from the file from the current position until it encounters the se_Separator string. All

characters read until then will be returned as a string. If it does not encounter the se_Separator string it will return all the bytes from the current position until the end of the file.

If se_Separator is not specified it will be considered as CR/LF [(char(13)+char(10)]. You can specify any character or combination of characters as the separator string.

The returned string will not contain the se_Separator string. Also the file pointer will be positioned right after the se_Separator string within the file, thus is ready for another read.

This function can be useful in reading FIELDS of data from the file. For instance if the file contains Comma separated data you can use se_Separator of "," to read each field. But also remember that each record is also separated by a CR/LF or maybe CR only. So you need to handle that. One way is to read a whole record at once using CR/LF (default) as the se_Separator string, then handle the various fields using Extract().

•FileRead(ne_FileHandle{,ne_ByteCount})

Returns a string whose individual characters have been read from the file with the handle value ne_FileHandle, as returned by FileOpen() of FileCreate(). The number of bytes read into the string will be according ne_BytesCount, which, if not given or is less than 1, will be made 1.

The reading operation will take place from the current position pointer in the file. If you open the file and do successive reads then the file is accessed *sequentially*. If you open the file and position the position pointer to a particular place along the length of the file using FileSeek() then the file becomes a *random access* file.

The read will either fail and return a blank string "", or it will partially succeed and return a string that is shorter than the specified number of characters to read, or it will succeed and return a string with exactly the number of characters specified. You must check the length of the returned string to determine the situation and act accordingly.

Partial success is usually due to reaching the end of the file before the specified number of character could be read.

•FileReadB(ne_FileHandle)
•FileReadI(ne_FileHandle)
•FileReadF(ne_FileHandle)

Returns an integer value (integer or byte version) or a float from the file with the handle ne_FileHandle as returned by FileOpen() of FileCreate(). If the operation fails then the function will return "" (string with zero length). You must check for this situation before attempting to use the number (see IsNumber()).

261

The reading operation will take place from the current position in the file. If you open the file and do successive reads then the file is accessed *sequentially*. If you open the file and position the position pointer to a particular place along the length of the file using FileSeek() then the file becomes a *random access* file.

The read will either fail and return a blank string "", or it will succeed and return an integer/float value. You must check to see if the returned value is a number.

Note: The byte version will read 1 byte but will convert the byte to an integer, since RB does not have a byte type. The integer will have the LSByte set to the value of the read byte the other bytes will be zero.

Note: The byte version will read 1 byte, the integer version will read 4 bytes and the float version will read 8 bytes from the current position in the file and convert these bytes to an integer/float. If the 1/4/8 bytes read were not written to the file as a byte/integer/float then the value returned is still an integer/float, but it is a meaningless value. Also if you lose synchronization by positioning the file pointer to the wrong place in the file before reading the value, you will get a meaningless value.

Note: Make sure you read numeric values from precisely the same position in the file as they were written. You can also read a chunk of bytes from the file into a buffer and then use Buffer functions (e.g. BuffRead()) to read individual data from the buffer.

•FileWrite(ne_FileHandle,e_Value)
If e_Value results into a string then the entire content of the string will be written to the file starting at the current position. The file is defined by the ne_FileHandle.

If e_Value results in a float then 8 bytes will be written to the file starting at the current position. If e_Value results into an integer then 4 bytes will be written. The function returns the number of bytes written to the file. So you must check to see if the returned number is according to the specified number, if it is not then an error has occurred.

•FileWriteB(ne_FileHandle,e_Value)
If e_Value results in a float it will be truncated to an integer. The resulting integer (or if e_Value is already an integer) is ANDed with 0xFF to zero all but the LSByte and then that byte is written to the file. If e_Value results in a string then the first character in the string will be considered as a byte value and written to the file. The file is defined by the ne_FileHandle. The function returns 0 if an error occurs during the writing operation, otherwise it returns 1.

•FileSeek(ne_FileHandle,ne_FromWhere,ne_OffsetCount)
Positions the file position pointer to a desired position where the next read or write will start

reading or writing. You indicate the desired position as a number of bytes offset from either the beginning (fo_Begin) or the end (fo_End) or the current position (fo_CurrPos) in the file (see the Constants section)

The offset count can be positive to go forwards, or negative to go backwards. If you go beyond the start of the file then the position pointer will be placed at the start of the file. However, you can position the pointer to a position that is beyond the length of the file. If you do so, the file will be lengthened to that length and all the added bytes will be set to 0.

The function returns the position of the pointer relative to the start of the file if it is successful or -1 if there was an error. So if the returned value is 230 then the pointer is placed on 231st character, any read/write operation will start there. A value of 0 means the start of the file (the first character). You can use this function to find the current position pointer by doing:

```
curr_pos = FileSeek(fHandle,fo_CurrPos,0)
```

This function is used to manipulate a file as a random access file. For example, you may have 20 records in a file with each record being 50 bytes long. Let's say you want to read record number 10 (records' count starts with zero). So you would do
`FileSeek(fHandle,fo_BEGIN,50*9)`. Then you would do `s =`
`FileRead(fHandle,50)` or if you know that the record was written as 2 integers 1 float and a 34 character string then you would do `a=FileReadI(fHandle)` then
`a=FileReadI(fHandle)` then `c=FileReadF(fHandle)` then `s =`
`FileRead(fHandle,34)`. See example after FileClose().

Note: **Any file reading or writing operation will always start at the current position pointer and will update the pointer to just after the number of bytes read or written. So you can either use the file as a _sequential_ file by doing successive reads/writes without manipulating the pointer, or you can treat the file as a _random access_ file by positioning the pointer to the beginning of the record before each read/write.**

•**FileSize(ne_FileHandle)**

Returns the size in bytes of the file specified by the handle. The handle has to be a valid one returned by a FileCreate() or FileOpen(). If the file handle is not for a valid opened/created file then -1 will be returned. Remember a Kilobyte is 1024 bytes and a Megabyte is 1024x1024 bytes etc.

If you wish to find the size of a file that has not been opened/created then use FileSize(se_FileName). However, if you have opened the file then you must use the handle version since the use of the name version will fail due to the file being currently in use by your process.

•FileEnd(ne_FileHandle)

Returns *true* (none-zero) if the file position pointer is positioned at the end of the file, and *false* (0) if it is not. This can be useful while iterating through the file to see if the position pointer is at the end of the file indicating no more bytes to read.

•FileClose(ne_FileHandle)

Returns true if the file was closed or false if the file handle was an invalid one. This function must ***always*** be called to close and release an opened/created file. If you open/create a file and never close it, it will not be possible to open it again until the program is terminated. Also other processes cannot access the file too until your program terminates.

Example: Also see the example under AddMemo.

```
MainProgram:
  RecordLength = 25
  n = filecreate("t.tt")
  for i=5 to 0
     fileseek(n,fo_begin,i*RecordLength)
     print filewriteb(n,i);filewrite(n,random(50000));
     print filewrite(n,random(0));filewrite(n,"record no. "+i)
  next
  print fileclose(n)
  gosub SequentialRead
  print
  gosub RandomRead
End
SequentialRead:
  print FileSize("t.tt");
  n = FileOpen("t.tt",fo_Read|fo_DenyNone)
  print FileSize(n)
  for i= 0 to 5
     print FileReadb(n);FileReadi(n);fileredf(n);fileread(n,12)
  next
  print FileClose(n)
Return
RandomRead:
  data order;3,1,4,2,5,0
  print FileSize("t.tt");
  n = FileOpen("t.tt",fo_Read|fo_DenyNone)
  print FileSize(n)
  for i= 0 to 5
     FileSeek(n,fo_Begin,order[i]*RecordLength)
     print FileReadb(n);FileReadi(n);fileredf(n);fileread(n,12)
  next
  print FileClose(n)
Return
```

Time, Date, System & Other Functions

•Time & Date Functions

•Timer( )

Returns a floating point number that represents the time in milliseconds. You can save this value and then after the elapse of some time subtract the stored value from the new value to get the amount of time elapsed in millisecond (i.e. 1000 = 1 second). For Example:

```
StartTime = Timer()
while Timer() - StartTime < 5000
  // do stuff here that can be accomplished within 5 seconds
wend
print "done"
```

•Now()

Returns a floating point number. The integer value of the number is the number of days between the current date as reported by the OS and **December 30th 1899**. The fractional value of the returned number is the fraction of 24 hours that has passed since midnight. So the number 5.23 would mean 5 days from Dec 30, 1899 so that would be Jan 4th, 1900. Also 0.24 is 5 hours 48 minutes and 28.800 seconds since midnight so it would be 5:48:28 AM.

The number returned represents the current date and time and can be used in the functions below to obtain various values and calculations. See this example for details:

```
TD = Now() \ TM = TD+1 \ TY = TD+365
print "Today      =",DateStr(TD)," ",DateTime(TD,"dddd mmmm d,yyyy")
print \ GetXY x,y
print "Tomorrow   =",DateStr(TM)," ",DateTime(TM,"dddd mmmm d,yyyy")," "
print "Today Year =",DateStr(TY)," ",DateTime(TY,"dddd mmmm d,yyyy")," "
print "Current Month=",Month(TD),DateTime(TD," (mmmm,mmm.)")
print "Day =",Day(TD),", Day ",DayOfWeek(TD)," of the week",DateTime(TD,"
(dddd,ddd.)")
print "Year =",Year(TD)
print
n = DateVal(2021,5,25)
print "Difference between Today and May 25,2021 = ",n-rounddn(TD)," Days"
print "It is a ",DateTime(n,"dddd")
print
n1 = TimeVal(10,32,45,0) \ n2=TimeVal(23,11,34,0)
n3 = n2-n1
print DateTime(n2,"  hh:mm:ss")
print DateTime(n1,"-  hh:mm:ss")
print sRepeat("-",13)
print "=  ",hour(n3),":",minute(n3),":",
print second(n3)," = ",n3*24*3600," seconds = ",
```

```
print format(n3*24*60,"#0.0000")," minutes = ",
print format(n3*24,"#0.0000")," hours"
while true
  TD = Now()
  m = DateTime(TD,"hh:mm:ss")+"."+millisecond(TD)
  xystring x,y, "Time=",TimeStr(TD);m
  m = DateTime(TD,"hh AM/PM mm 'minutes' ss")+"."
  xystring 300,-1,"  ",m,Format(millisecond(TD),"000")," seconds"
wend
```

•Hour(ne_DateTimeValue)
•Minute(ne_DateTimeValue)
•Second(ne_DateTimeValue)
•Millisecond(ne_DateTimeValue)
•Year(ne_DateTimeValue)
•Month(ne_DateTimeValue)
•Day(ne_DateTimeValue)
•DayOfWeek(ne_DateTimeValue)

Returns an integer value that represents the value of the Hour/Minute/Second/Milliseconds/Year/Month/Day of the date and time as indicated by the floating point number given which is as described in the Now() function. It can be a number returned by Now() or a calculated number.

The day of the week value is a number 1 to 7 where 1 represents Sunday.

•DateStr(ne_DateTimeValue)
•TimeStr(ne_DateTimeValue)
•DateTimeStr(ne_DateTimeValue)

Returns a string that is the date/time or date and time formatted according to the specifications of the operating system. The date is the Short Date format and the Time is the Long Time format as specified in the operating system.

See DateTime() for more powerful formatting. Also see the example above for an example.

•DateTimeVal(se_DateTimeString)

Returns a floating point datetime value (as described in Now()) that represents the date and time given in the string. The formatting in the string has to be according to the formatting specified in the operating system for the short date. For the time you can use 24 hour format or AM/PM format as specified in the long date format of the OS.

If the string results in an invalid date or time then the value returned will be zero.

•DateVal(ne_Year,ne_Month,ne_Day)

Returns a floating point datetime value (as described in Now()) that represents the date given. Notice the fractional part will be zero since no specific time is given and therefore it is assumed to be midnight.

266

The year can be 1 to 9999, the month 1 to 12 and the day 1 to 28/29/30/31 depending on the month. If the parameters result in an invalid date then zero is returned.

To form a specific date and time, add the result of this function and TimeVal() to get a value that represents a specific date and time.
Example:
```
n = DateVal(2009,1,23)+TimeVal(13,45,36,0)
print DateTime(n,"ddd. mmmm dd,yyyy hh:nn:ss AM/PM")
//prints Fri. January 23,2009 01:45:36 PM
print DateTime(n+5.2,"dddd mmm. dd,yyyy hh:nn:ss")
//prints Wednesday Jan. 28,2009 18:33:36
```

•**TimeVal(ne_Hour,ne_Minute,ne_Second,ne_Milliseconds)**
Returns a floating point datetime value (as described in Now()) that represents the time given. Notice that the whole number part would be zero (since no specific date is given).

The hours have to be 0 to 23. The minutes and seconds 0 to 59. The milliseconds 0 to 999. If the parameters result in an invalid time then -1 is returned.

To form a specific date and time, add the result of this function and DateVal() to get a value that represents a specific date and time. See example above.

•**DateTime(ne_DateTimeValue{,se_Format})**
Returns a string that is the date/time or date and time or day name or month name and so forth formatted according to the specifications of the formatting string. ne_DateTimeValue is a floating point datetime value as specified in Now() that can be the result of a calculation and/or any of the above functions.

If the formatting string is invalid then an empty string will be returned. The formatting string is according to the following: (see above for specific examples) (**Note:** OS means Operating System)

Specifier	Result
c	Displays the date using the OS ShortDate format, followed by the time using the OS LongTime format. The time is not displayed if the fractional part of the DateTime value is zero.
d	Displays the day as a number without a leading zero (1-31).
dd	Displays the day as a number with a leading zero (01-31).
ddd	Displays the day as an abbreviation (Sun-Sat) using the OS ShortDay names.

dddd	Displays the day's full name (Sunday-Saturday) using the OS LongDay names.
ddddd	Displays the date using the OS ShortDate format.
dddddd	Displays the date using the OS LongDate format.
m	Displays the month as a number without a leading zero (1-12). If the m specifier immediately follows an h or hh specifier, the minute rather than the month is displayed.
mm	Displays the month as a number with a leading zero (01-12). If the mm specifier immediately follows an h or hh specifier, the minute rather than the month is displayed.
mmm	Displays the month as an abbreviation (Jan-Dec) using the OS ShortMonth names.
mmmm	Displays the month as a full name (January-December) using the OS LongMonth names.
yy	Displays the year as a two-digit number (00-99).
yyyy	Displays the year as a four-digit number (0000-9999).
h	Displays the hour without a leading zero (0-23).
hh	Displays the hour with a leading zero (00-23).
n	Displays the minute without a leading zero (0-59).
nn	Displays the minute with a leading zero (00-59).
s	Displays the second without a leading zero (0-59).
ss	Displays the second with a leading zero (00-59).
t	Displays the time using the OS ShortTime format.
tt	Displays the time the OS LongTime format.
am/pm	Uses the 12-hour clock for the preceding h or hh specifier, and displays 'am' for any hour before noon, and 'pm' for any hour after noon. The am/pm specifier can use lower, upper, or mixed case, and the result is displayed accordingly.
a/p	Uses the 12-hour clock for the preceding h or hh specifier, and displays 'a' for any hour before noon, and 'p' for any hour after noon. The a/p specifier can use lower, upper, or mixed case, and the result is displayed accordingly.
ampm	Uses the 12-hour clock for the preceding h or hh specifier, and displays the contents of the OS TimeAM string for any hour before noon, and the contents of the OS TimePM string for any hour after noon.
/	Displays the date separator character given by the OS DateSeparator string.
:	Displays the time separator character given by the OS TimeSeparator string.
'xx'	Characters enclosed in single or double quotes are displayed as is, and do not affect formatting.

Note: If se_Format is not given or is a "", the DateTime value is formatted as if a **c** format specifier had been given.

•Time({ne_Type})

Returns a string that has the time in the format "HH:mm:ss" (24 hour format) if ne_Type is not given or is true (1). If it is false (0) then it will return "AM hh:mm:ss" or "PM hh:mm:ss". This function is equivalent to:

```
DateTime(Now(),"hh:mm:ss")              if ne_Type = 1 or is not given
```
and
```
DateTime(Now(),"AM/PM hh:mm:ss")        if ne_Type = 0.
```

•Date({ne_Type})

Will return a string yyyy/mm/dd if ne_Type is not given or is true (1). If it is false (0) then it will return "yyyy/mm/dd Day:Month" where Day is the Day Name and Month is month name. This function is equivalent to:

```
DateTime(Now(),"yyyy/mm/dd")            if ne_Type = 1 or not given
```
and
```
DateTime(Now(),"yyyy/mm/dd dddd:mmmm")  if ne_Type = 0.
```

•ToTime(ne_Seconds)

Converts the number of seconds given (ne_Seconds) to a string of the form HH:MM:SS (i.e. hours:minutes:seconds). The hours field will be as many digits as needed to report the number of hours. It may have more than 24 hours if ne_Seconds results in more than 24 hours. The seconds and minutes fields will always be two digits (e.g. 02 or 45). If you want to format the field further into days, years and so on, you can use further string manipulation and conversion functions to treat the hours field.

It is better to use DatTime() above to do the same work. For example ToTime(5000) gives the same result as DateTime(5000/24.0/60/60,"hh:mm:ss"). But if ne_Seconds exceeds 24 hours (> 86400) then this function will return a number in the hours filed that is > 24 while with DateTime() you can treat the number as days and hours etc.

•<u>Variables Manipulation & Indirection (Pointers)</u>

•vType(v_VarName)

This function is used to find the type of variable. You specify the variable name. The returned values are:

102 = Ascii("f")	➔	floating point number
105 = Ascii("i")	➔	integer number
115 = Ascii("s")	➔	string
0	➔	No Value i.e. has not been assigned a value

The values above are also defined in the RobotBASIC Constants section

```
Float     = Floating point number
Integer   = Integer number
String    = String
NoValue = Not a defined Variable
```

This function can be useful to determine the type of a variable or if it is an un-assigned variable. You can check if a variable is a valid one before you use it. If you try to use an unassigned variable an error will occur. This function can be used to prevent this. Also see varType(), IsString(), IsNumber(), ToString(), ToNumber() and others.

•varType(se_VarName)

This function is used to find the type of a variable by defining the variable name as a string expression which contains the variable's name. Unlike vType() where you give the actual variable as a parameter, this function is passed a *string* that contains the variable name. The string can be a result of a calculation which eventually results in a variable name. This way the string can be used as a *pointer* to the actual variable name and thus providing a level of *Indirection*.

The returned values are as specified in the definition of vType(). Also see varsList(), varValue() and VarSet.

•varValue(se_VarName)

This function is used to find the value of a variable by defining the variable name as a string expression which contains the variable's name. The string can be a result of a calculation which eventually results in a variable name. This way the string can be used as a *pointer* to the actual variable name and thus providing a level of *Indirection*.

Normally you can say b = 2 \ a = b+3 but using this function you can say b = 2 \ a = varValue("b")+3 to get the same result. You may ask but why? Well, the answer is *POINTERS*. This function helps in implementing a pointer in RobotBASIC. se_VarName would be a string that calculates the name of the variable whose value you want to get. This way se_VarName becomes a *pointer* to the variable.

If se_VarName results in a variable that has not been defined you will get an error just like using a variable that has not been defined. Also see varsList(), varType() and VarSet

Example:
```
a = 2 \ b = "test" \ c = 23.456
for i=0 to 2
   s=char(ascii("a")+i)
   print varType(s);varValue(s)
next
print varValue("tt")    //gives an error since the variable tt
                        //has not been defined
```

270

•VarSet se_VarName, e_Value

se_VarName is a string expression that results in a string that represents a Variable's name. The command will then set that variable to the value as results from the expression e_Value. This is like using a pointer to the variable. e_Value can result in a value of any type and the variable by that name as indicated from se_VarName will be set to that value (but see below). If the variable's name is prepended with a _ then it will be a global variable.

***If RB has been put in the Strict Variable Typing mode (by use of* Declare*) then the variable will have to have been declared and e_Value has to result in a value of an appropriate type for the variable's type*.**

This command and varsList(), varType() and varValue() can help in creating **Indirection** (Pointer Like) operations to access variables and set their values using an Expression that results in the name of the variable not by directly giving the variable's name in the program code. Thus the variable's name to be accessed can be determined at at RunTime rather than at design time.

•varsList({ne_Global})

This function will return a list of variable names that have been created (or Declared) up to that point in the programs execution. The list will have the variables names separated with Cr/Lf. If ne_Global is not given or is false then the local variables (if in a Sub subroutine) will be listed. If ne_Global is true then the global variables list will be listed (the names will have a _ prepended to them). This function combined with varType() and varValue() and varSet can help create a dynamic system and provide access to variables in a dynamic way. Also see mFromString.

•Swap v_Left | a_Left[...] , v_Right | a_Right[...]

Swaps the values of the simple variable v_Left or array element a_Left[...] and another simple variable v_Right or the array element a_Right[...]. The array elements can be two elements of the same array or different arrays. The arrays have to exist and the elements have to be valid with assigned values, however, the values can be of different types. The indexing into the arrays has to be within the allowable array dimension and dimensional constraints. Also the simple variables have to have been previously assigned values.

•System Information

•ProgName()

Returns the File name (including Path) of the currently running program. If the program is an EXE then only the File name is returned (no Path), if you wish to get the path as well then use DirCurrent().

- **CommandsList()**
- **FunctionsList()**
- **StatementsList()**
- **ConstantsList()**

Returns a string with all the Syntax Verbs of RobotBASIC. The string will have the verbs separated with Cr/LF.

•<u>Miscellaneous Functions</u>

•Delay {ne_Milliseconds}

Causes a delay in milliseconds i.e. 1000 = 1 sec. If the value is not given then 1000 will be assumed i.e. 1 second.

•MicroDelay {ne_Amount}

Causes a delay in steps of 15 microseconds. So for example to get a delay of 1 second you would issue the statement MicroDelay (1.0e6)/15. Notice that you can use a floating-point numbers also since the ticks are in intervals of 15 microseconds a value of 2 will make a delay of 30 microseconds. ne_Amount is optional and if it is not given or is less than 1 then it is assumed to be 1. This means that the minimum delay is 15 microseconds.

<u>Note:</u> *This command does not work on machines without a parallel port or a speaker.*

•Evaluate(se_Expression)

se_Expression is a string that contains a valid expression (see the Overview Of The Language section on expressions). Depending on the context you can use variables. BUT these must be existing variables for the evaluator to be able to evaluate the expression correctly. This can be useful to have expressions defined at runtime instead of design time.

For example say you are writing a function plotter. Further you want the user to define the function to be plotted at run time. The user would enter a string in response to an Input. For example *sin(x)*. The programmer can then define a loop through all values in the desired range of x and evaluate the expression given by the user as *y* = Evaluate(se_Expression) where se_Expression was given by the user as f(x).

```
 Input "Enter f(x)",fx
 x = 0.1
 if ToString(evaluate(fx))=fx then goto error_handler //handle error
 for x = 0 to 10
   y = Evaluate(fx)
   print y
 next
 End
 error_handler:   //handle errors here
```

```
print "Invalid function"
```

If an error is encountered while evaluating the function given by the user an error message would be given indicating the error, and **Evaluate** will return the se_Expression as it was, i.e. if se_Expression is not a valid expression **Evaluate**(*se_Expression*) will display an error message and return the original input without evaluation. Another error message will also be displayed indicating an error in Evaluate(). However this second error will not halt the program as in other error. This way you can check if the return result is still the same as the input then do any error handling within the program. The error message given by the interpreter is meaningful in that it indicates the type of error, but the line number will always be one because se_Expression is just one line any way. The second error message will not occur if the OnError statement has been issued to cause error trapping. If OnError trapping is in effect the second error will cause the interpreter to jump to the error handler specified by the OnError statement.

•Spawn(se_ProgramName,se_Parameters,ne_Mode)

Will execute the executable program se_ProgramName with the parameters defined in se_Parameters passed to it. This function will run a program (exe, com or bat) and pass it the parameters. The program name including its path is se_ProgramName. The parameters are defined in se_Parameter. ne_Mode defines the mode of execution.

If ne_Mode = P_WAIT (0) then the RobotBASIC program will wait for the termination of the spawned process. If ne_Mode = P_NOWAIT (<>0) then the RobotBASIC program will not wait and will continue to run after the process is spawned.

If se_Parameters is blank then no parameters are passed to the process. If se_Parameters is not blank then the string must contain the parameters separated by spaces. If any of the parameters has spaces in it, you must surround it with two double quotes on either side (see example below).

se_ProgramName defines the name and path of the program to be spawned. If there is no path then the system will search the current directory then the paths on the PATH parameter of the environment.

The function will return a number. If the number is -1 then an error was encountered in spawning the requested program. If the number is <> -1 then the program was run successfully and the value reflects the following:

    -If the P_WAIT mode was used, then the number returned is whatever the spawned process has returned to the operating system when it terminated.
    -If the P_NOWAIT mode was used then the number is meaningless but has to be <> -1 to indicate that the process was successfully spawned.

For example:

```
n = spawn("NotePad.exe","myfile.txt",P_NOWAIT)
   // will run notepad and pass it the parameter and
   // will not wait
n = spawn("D:\tests\Tester.exe","1 2 ""a b c"" X",P_WAIT)
   //will run the program and pass it 4 parameters:
   //1, 2, a b c, and X  (notice ""a b c"" causes
   //a b c to be passed as one parameter not three
   // separate ones due to the spaces
```

Robot Simulator

•General Information

The Robot Simulator is a set of commands and functions that allow for easy programming of a robot to move around a simulated environment. The environment is drawn on the screen using the drawing commands and functions. The Robot is then *Located* in the environment and is made to programmatically move, turn and sense around the screen.

The Robot is equipped with sensors to *feel* around and to *look* for objects and to *sense* for lines on the ground. The view on the screen is as if you are looking at the robot and the environment from vertically above. Objects drawn with LineTo, Rectangle, Circle and other commands will have colors and can be considered as furniture or other objects and obstacles. Additionally, you can draw lines on the floor and have the robot *sense* for them and follow them with the right combination of commands.

To use the Robot you must first rLocate it on the screen. Make sure the environment drawing commands are done first. Once the robot is located you can issue commands to rForward and rTurn the robot. Also you can rSense, rLook and/or rFeel around the environment to avoid objects.

Since the entire environment is two dimensional, you must specify any colors to be considered as invisible to the robot and therefore non-obstacles. Any color on the screen that is not in the list of invisible colors will be considered an obstacle when encountered by the robot while it is moving around (except for the floor color). If you change the color of the floor, you must do so before locating the robot and then locate the robot on the new floor (see rFloorColor below). You specify invisible colors with rInvisible

The first color in the list you specify is special in that it will be used as a default color for rPen and rSense() if you do not specify a color when you issue the command or call the function (see below). The second color in the list is also special in that it will be the default color if you do not specify a color for rDFeel() and rDBumper().

Note: *In older versions of the software (before 1.3.0) there was two commands (now obsolete) rLineColor and rBeaconColor. You can still use these commands for backward compatibility. rLineColor will set the color as if you included it as the first color in the rInvisible command. rBeaconColor will set the second color.*

Note: *The Robot cannot be located or moved off the screen. The screen boundaries are the walls of a room. The robot will not move forward into an object. Any attempt to do so will cause an error. No sensor commands can sense beyond the walls.*

The Robot has a Battery that discharges upon using the commands to move and sense. Moving depletes more charge than sensing. The battery level can be checked and it can also be recharged. The Robot will refuse to move and will return nonsense values from the sensors if the battery is depleted. The default state is to ignore the battery charge level but you can use a command to make the robot heed the charge level.

The Robot Simulator Commands and Functions **_are not_** case sensitive, so rLocate, RLOCATE, and rlocate are all the same.

•**Simulator Commands**

> <u>Note:</u> See the notes at the top of the Standard User Interfacing section. The following lists the commands in a functionality order rather than alphabetical order. See Simulator Command/Functions Listed Alphabetically section for an alphabetized listing..

> <u>Note:</u> *Commands with a * have additional functionality as explained in Ports & Serial I/O section.*

*•**rLocate**
ne_X,ne_Y{,ne_Heading{,ne_Size{,ne_BorderColor{,ne_InsideColor{,ne_ObeyFlip}}}}}
    Creates Robot of specified size and color at a specified position and heading.

    If you need to specify ne_Size, you must also specify ne_Heading and so on. The Heading defaults to 0 (North), Size defaults to 20, BorderColor defaults to Blue and InsideColor defaults to White. The size is limited to between 5 and 50 pixels. The size value is the radius of the robot. A size of 20 means a radius of 20 and a diameter of 40.

    This command must be executed before any other robot functions or command. It is the command that creates the robot, places it on the ground and switches it on. If you issue any commands/functions before this command an error will be issued and the program will halt.

    The size of the Robot should be considered in relation to the screen size. The screen is 800x600 pixels. So if you consider a room of 20 feet then each pixel is 1/3 inch. So a robot of 20 pixels radius is 12 inches in diameter. Which is a reasonable robot size. But you can specify smaller or larger size.

    If you locate the robot over a color other than the floor color, or if you change the floor color from the default screen color you must issue an *rFloorColor* (see below) before you do any movement of the robot.

    Normally the simulated robot will draw on the screen and will not be affected by Flip On.

However, if specify ne_ObeyFlip as true (and Flip has bee turned on with Flip On) then the robot will do its actions on the Back Buffer screen and will not show its actions unless Flip is issued. This can be useful in speeding up the robot *animation* but it may also slow the robot animation if you need to keep watching the robot's action after each move and having to issue a Flip all the time. Therefore you need to exercise prudence in when to use this ability.

Also you need to rLocate the robot *after* you have already issued Flip On for the ne_ObeyFlip property to take place. Also remember that the robot actions will take place in the *invisible* back buffer screen and will not be visible until Flip has been issued. Thus if you issue an rTurn 30 or rForward 40 for instance then issue a Flip then the robot will appear to be jerking around since it has already forwarded/turned a substantial distance/angle before it became visible. Therefore be careful about how you use the rForward and rTurn commands in your simulations if you are also going to use the Flip facility.

The primary use of the flip facility is to really make the simulation go faster since no drawing of the robot will take place until the next time you issue Flip. But since this will make the robot appear to be jerky then it is mostly useful while testing. If you have to keep issuing Flip to keep the animation smooth then the process may go slower than if no flip is being used. Thus, use this feature carefully and only if you need to speed up the robot even more than normal during testing.

•rRelocate {ne_X{,ne_Y{,ne_Heading}}}

This function allows you to simulate picking up and replacing the robot somewhere else. All the properties of the robot will remain the same. This will only relocate the robot on the screen to the new position and heading specified. Other previously set things line the pen. invisible colors, slip, charge and so forth will not be changed.

If any of the parameters is not given then it will remain as it is and will not be changed. You can also use this command to redisplay the simulated robot after a ClearScr which will also clear the image of the simulated robot off the screen. This command without any parameters will redraw the robot exactly where it was and thus helping in allowing for clearing the screen without having to move the robot to redisplay it. This can be useful in certain situations especially during animations.

•rInvisible ne_Color1 {,ne_Color2...}

This command sets the list of colors that will ***not be*** considered as objects when encountered by the robot while moving and also by many of the sensors as specified. You must pass at least one color and a maximum of 15. The colors are according to the colors specified in the RobotBASIC Constants section. The first and second colors in the list are also special as explained in the General Information section above.

•rFloorColor {ne_Color}

Sets the color that will be considered as the floor and thus will not affect sensors and Forward. This is only needed if you are going to place the robot on a surface that is not the default screen color upon creating the robot. If ne_Color is not given then it will be 15 (white).

*•rForward {ne_Pixels}

Moves in the direction of the robot heading *ne_Pixels* forward if the count is positive, or backwards if it is negative. This command will cause an error if the Robot tries to move into objects of any color not listed in the list of invisible colors (see rInvisible below). If nePixels is not given then it will be 1 and if it is a float it will be truncated.

This Command will cause an error if the battery is depleted and the IgnoreCharge *False* has been issued.

*•rTurn {ne_Degrees}

This will cause the robot to turn *ne_Degrees* right (Clockwise) if the count is positive and left (counterclockwise) if it is negative. If ne_Degrees is not given it will be made 1 and if it is a float it will be truncated.

This Command will cause an error if the battery is depleted and the rIgnoreCharge *False* has been issued.

•rHeading {ne_Degrees}

Sets the robot heading (0-359). 0 is facing up (North), 90 is facing right (East) etc. If n

*•rSpeed {ne_Speed}

Sets the robot speed. The larger the number the slower the robot. *ne_Speed* has to be >= 0. If ne_Speed is not given it will be made 0. If it is a float it will be truncated.

*•rGps vn_X,vn_Y

Assigns *vn_X* the Robot's current X position and *vn_Y* the Y position. Effectively giving the robot's position on the screen. This Command will NOT cause an error if the battery is depleted and rIgnoreCharge *False* has been issued, but the values will be zero.

*•rPen ne_State {,ne_Color}

The robot has a pen positioned at its centre and can be put Up or Down using this command. When the pen is down the robot will draw a line using the color specified. If you do not specify a color then the first color specified in the list of invisible colors (rInvisible) is used. If you have not specified a list of invisible colors then the pen will draw using the floor color which means that you will not see the trace if it is over the floor color. Also the width of the line is determined by the current line width as set by the drawing commands (see LineWidth). If *ne_State* is 0 (up) then the pen will be put up. If it is not Zero (Down) then the pen will be set down and drawing will take place. You can use the constants *Down* and *UP* so you can

say:
```
    rPen Down,Cyan   //---will set the pen down and use cyan
  for
                     //   drawing
    rPen Up          //--- will set the pen up
```

Remember the line width is whatever has been set previously by the last **LineWidth** issued. Also the line color will be whatever has been specified or the first color in the invisible colors list. Also note that the color drawn by the pen will be considered as an obstacle unless it is in the list of invisible colors.

•rCharge {ne_Value}

Sets the batteries to percentage charge. *ne_Value* is a percentage value 1-100%. If ne_Value is not given it will be 100 and if it is a float it will be truncated. If it is less than 1 it will be made 1.

•rIgnoreCharge {true|false}

If true is given or no parameter is given then the Battery charge level will be ignored and the robot will continue to operate regardless of the battery charge level. This is the default state. If false is given then the Battery charge level will be heeded and the robot will not operate if the battery is depleted and in some cases will issue an error as specified in the commands.

•rSensor ne_SensorNo,ne_Range,vn_Color,vn_Distance,vn_Found

The robot has a default set of sensors located at 90 and 45 degrees to the left and right of the front and at the front. These sensors can look and return the color of the first object encountered and the distance to that object. *ne_SensoNo* can be one of the following values:

             1 = 90 degrees to the right
             2 = 45 degrees to the right
             3 = Front
             4 = 45 degrees to the left
             5 = 90 degrees to the left

- ne_Range is used to specify the limit of the sensor range (Pixels).
- vn_Color will be set to the first color found directly in front of the sensor that is not on the list of invisible colors. If the range of the sensor is reached or the walls of the room (screen extent) without sensing an object then this color value will be -1, otherwise it will be the color of the object.
- vn_Distance will be set to the distance to the object found. If no object was found then the distance will be the range of the sensor, or the distance to the wall if that was within the sensor range.
- vn_Found will be set to true if an object was found or a wall was seen within the sensor range. If the sensor range was reached without seeing a wall or an object then it will be set

279

to false. Colors on the invisible colors list will be ignored in the process.

This Command will *NOT* cause an error if the battery is depleted and rIgnoreCharge *False* has been issued, but the values will be nonsense.

•rSensorA ne_Angle,ne_Range,vn_Color,vn_Distance,vn_Found

This is the same as rSensor, except that instead of a sensor number you use a sensor angle (0-359) clockwise relative to the robot heading. 90 is 90 degrees to the right, 270 is 90 degrees to the left. So this command can be used to do the same as above but instead of a limit of 5 sensors you have 360 of them.

This command will *NOT* cause an error if the battery is depleted and the rIgnoreCharge *False* has been issued, but the values will be nonsense.

•rSlip {ne_PercentageLevel}

This command defines a percentage for the Slipping feature of the robot.

Real robot motors tend to slip in a random way where going forward/backward can go less than expected. If the motors do not turn exactly the same amount while going forward a slight turning tendency may occur. Also during turning if the motors do not turn as expected less or more turning than commanded may occur.

Issuing this command will cause the robot to behave in this manner. If you do not specify a value the slip will occur 2% of the time. If you want to simulate a different percentage then issue the command with a specified value. A value of zero will turn the slipping off which is the default state. If it is less than 0 then it will be made zero. If it is greater than 100 it will be made 100.

•rSenseType {ne_NumSensors}

This command specifies the mode of operation of rSense() (see below). If ne_NumSensors is not given or is 3 (or less) then rSense() will use 3 line sensors. If ne_NumSensors is 5 (or greater than 3) then 5 line sensors will be used. The default is 3 sensors when the robot is initialized. See the description of rSense() for details.

•rInstError {ne_PercentageLevel}

This command defines a percentage for the Instrumentation Error feature of the robot.

Real instruments are not usually precise and they can report values that are either less or more than the actual value being measured. Electronic compasses and range finders as well as GPS devices report values that are to within a percentage values plus or minus from the actual value. The simulated instruments in RobotBASIC by default report precise values for the rRange(), rBeacon(), rGPS, rGpsX(), rGpsY() and rCompass() functions and commands.

Issuing this command will cause the reported values to be in error by a certain percentage (+/-). If you do not specify a value the error will be up to a maximum of +/-2%. If you want to simulate a different percentage then issue the command with a specified value. A value of zero will turn the error off which is the default state. If it is less than 0 then it will be made zero. If it is greater than 100 it will be made 100.

For instance if the actual X position of the robot is 100 then GpsX() will normally report 100. If rInstError 3 has been invoked then the reported value can be any value from 97 to 103 since 3% of 100 is 3 and thus minimum reported value would be 100-3 and maximum would be 100+3 but since the error is random and up-to the 3% then the reported value can be anywhere between the minimum and maximum (97 to 103).

This command can help you simulate more realistic instrumentation and therefore force you to develop algorithms that are more able to cope with this kind of real situations.

•Simulator Functions

In the following if () is specified then the function does not require a parameter but the () has to still be typed. All functions will NOT cause an error if the battery is depleted and the rIgnoreCharge False has been issued, but the values returned will be nonsense. The functions are listed according to functionality rather than in an alphabetical order. See below for alphabetical order.

Functions that look or sense for colors will not detect the colors on the invisible colors list (see rInvisible above) unless otherwise stated.

Note: Functions with a * have additional functionality as explained in Ports & Serial I/O section.

*•rChargeLevel()
Returns the Batteries Charge % value.

•rPoints()
The Robot keeps a count of the number of times you have used its sensors and have turned its motors (rTurn, rForward) on. Thus this point value can be used as a measure of the efficiency of an algorithm to achieve a task in the minimum possible points. This function returns the current count value.

*•rRange({ne_Angle})
Returns the distance to the first color seen directly in front of the robot. If the walls are seen before any object then the distance to the wall is returned. Colors on the invisible colors list are ignored.

ne_Angle is option and if given it defines an angle relative to the robot's heading. It must be between -90 and +90. Positive is to the right of the robot, negative is to the left of the robot. Pivoting is about the front of the robot not the center of the robot. The ranger is fitted on the front point of the robot and pivots 90 degrees left and right centered on this point.

Specifying an angle places the range finder at any angle relative to the robot's heading. With this sensor you can measure distances relative to the front of the robot from 90 degrees to the right (+90) up to 90 degrees to the left (-90) at intervals of 1 degrees.

*•rBeacon(ne_Color)

Returns the distance to the specified color if it is in front of the robot, even if that color is blocked by other objects between the robot and the color. It returns 0 otherwise.

This is useful for detecting of a "flashing" beacon mounted above obstacles in the room. The command looks for any color specified. It **DOES NOT** ignore colors on the invisible colors list. The result can be treated as true/false (false = 0, true = otherwise) or you can use the number returned **if it is not zero** as the distance to the color specified.

*•rFeel()
*•rDFeel({ne_Color})

Returns a number 0-31 according to the following logic:
There are 5 infrared sensors around the robot. At 90 and 45 degrees to the left and right of the robot and directly in the front. The sensors are able to feel any object within a robot's radius ahead of the sensor (ignoring invisible colors).

The Number returned is a bit map of the condition of the sensors. If any of the sensors feels something then its bit position is set to 1, otherwise 0. So there are 5 bits MSB...LSB 00000. The most significant bit is the sensor 90 degrees to the left, then 45 degrees then 0 degrees then 45 degrees to the right, and the least significant bit is 90 degrees to the right. So if the number is 01110 (14) then the sensors in front and 45 degrees right and left are feeling objects and the rest do not. Use Bit-wise operators (bAnd/bOr etc) to manipulate the result. Colors on the invisible colors list are not considered objects.

The difference between rFeel() and rDFeel({ne_Color}) is that rDFeel({ne_Color}) will draw radials out from the sensors to show the range of feel of the sensors using the color specified. If you do not specify a color then the second color on the invisible colors list will be used. This is a useful feature for debugging the rFeel() result.

Do not use rDFeel({ne_Color}) unless you need to debug since it is a lot slower than rFeel(). You must specify a color or have a valid (not a floor color) in the second item of the invisible colors list. The radial lines will be drawn using this color or the second color on the invisible colors list otherwise the beams will not be visible.

*•rBumper()
*•rDBumper({ne_Color})
  Returns a number 0-15 according to the following logic:
  There are 4 bumpers around the robot. At the front covering an arc of 130 degrees i.e. from 65 degrees to the left to 65 degrees to the right. There is also a bumper at the back just like the front one, that is from 115 to 245 degrees. To the left and to the right there are bumpers that cover an arc of 50 degrees i.e. from 65 to 115 degrees on the right and from -65 to -115 degrees on the left. The bumpers will close (turn on) if there is any object within 2 pixels of the robot's perimeter (ignores invisible colors).

  The Number returned is a bit map of the condition of the bumpers. If any of the bumpers is closed then its bit position is set to 1, otherwise 0. So there 4 bits MSB...LSB 0000. The Least Significant Bit is the back bumper, then the right, front and then the left one.

  If the number is 1110 (14) then the right, front and left bumpers are closed while the rear one is not. Use Bitwise operators (bAnd/bOr etc) to manipulate the result. Floor/Line/Beacon colors are ignored.

  The difference between rBumper() and rDBumper({ne_Color}) is that rDBumper({ne_Color}) will light up an LED where the bumper is touching objects using the specified color or the second color on the invisible colors list. If no color is specified then the second color on the invisible colors list will be used. If that is not specified then the color will be the floor color and the beacon may not be visible. This is a useful feature for debugging the rBumper() result. Do not use rDBumper({ne_Color}) unless you are debugging since it is significantly slower than rBumper().

*•rSense({ne_Color})
  Returns a number 0-7 according to the following logic:
  There are 3 sensors around the robot, at 10 degrees to the left and right of the robot and directly in the front. The sensors see only the color specified or, if you don't specify a color, then the first color on the invisible colors list. If neither is specified then the floor color will be sensed. The sensors only look at the ground directly under the sensor situated directly at the perimeter of the robot. The Number returned is a bit map of the condition of the sensors. If any of the sensors sees the ne_Color then its bit position is set to 1, otherwise it is 0. There are 3 bits MSB.LSB 000. The most significant bit is the sensor 10 degrees to the left, then ahead (0 degrees) and then 10 degrees to the right. If the number is 010 (2) then only the sensor in the front is on the line and the other two are outside of the line. Use Bit-wise operators (bAnd/bOr etc) to manipulate the result.

  The default mode of this function is to use the above mode. That is 3 sensors as described above. However, if rSenseType is issued with a parameter greater than 3 then the above still applies but in addition there are two more sensors that will be reported in the returned number in Bits 3 and 4 (that is 4th and 5th bit positions in the number). Bit 3 will report the status of a sensor 35 degrees to the right of the front of the robot and Bit 4 will be for a sensor 35 degrees to the left of the front.

So if rSenseType 5 has been issued then there will be 2 more sensors (one 35 degrees right and one 35 degrees left) in addition to the 3 standard sensors and their status will be reported in bits 3 (right sensor) and 4 (left sensor) of the value returned by the function.

*•rLook({ne_Angle})

Returns the first color seen directly in front of robot. If the walls are seen before any object then -1 is returned. Colors on the invisible colors list are ignored.

ne_Angle specifies an angle relative to the robot's heading. It has to be between -180 and +180. Positive is to the right of the robot, negative is to the left of the robot. The pivoting center is the center of the robot. Specifying an angle allows you to place the camera at any angle relative to the robot's heading. So with this sensor you can look at objects relative to the robot's heading 180 degrees to the right (+180) up to 180 degrees to the left (-180) at intervals of 1 degrees.

•rGround(ne_SensorNo)

The robot has a default of 3 sensors to look at the ground directly at the perimeter of the robot. ne_SensorNo can be:
>   1 = 10 degrees to the right
>   2 = In front
>   3 = 10 degrees to the left.

It will return the color seen by the sensor. It will not ignore ANY color (i.e. the colors on the invisible colors list **are not** ignored). It is up to you what to make of the value. If you want to ignore any colors use programming logic to do so.

•rGroundA(ne_Angle)

This is the same as rGround, except that instead of a sensor number you specify an angle (0-359) clockwise relative to the robot heading. 90 is 90 degrees to the right, 270 is 90 degrees to the left. So this command can be used to do the same as above but instead of a limit of 3 sensors you have 360 of them.

*•rCompass()

Returns the Robot's current heading (0-359) 0= North.

•rGpsX()

Returns the Robot's current X-position on the screen.

•rGpsY()

Returns the Robot's current Y-position on the screen.

•<u>Simulator Serial I/O Protocol</u>

This protocol uses serial communication (can be Bluetooth virtual serial port) to communicate between RobotBASIC and a real robot with the ability to send and receive serial data. You can create your own protocol using the above serial communications commands. This protocol is provided for convenience.

You can write programs normally using the simulator commands and functions. However if you signal RobotBASIC to use the serial port protocol the same program will run, but instead of simulating the robot on the screen it will send and receive data back and forth between a real robot and RobotBASIC. This allows you to test your simulated algorithms on a real physical robot.

The microcontroller on the real robot receives data representing the commands (like rForward etc.), responds to the commands and returns data to RobotBASIC to tell it that it received the command and acted upon it and that the current state of sensors is as per the data sent.

You can write programs using the commands and function in the Robot Simulator, but the commands will not cause the simulated screen robot to move. Rather, a set of two bytes is sent via the serial port and then RobotBASIC will wait for a set of 5 bytes to be sent back. These 5 bytes are then stored and interpreted to provide data to be returned by the command or function.

To tell RobotBASIC to use the serial communications protocol rather than the simulator, use rCommPort (see below) to make all subsequent commands and function use the protocol in place of the simulator.

The commands and functions will cause RobotBASIC to send two bytes where the first byte is a code for the command and the next byte is the parameter for the command. The receiving microcontroller on the physical robot can make use of these bytes and must respond within the timeout limit (see SetTimeOut above) by sending 5 bytes to be received by RobotBASIC. The first three bytes are the status of the Bumpers, Infrared sensors, and Line sensors (in this order). The last two bytes are the returned values relating to the function/command. The order is MSB first. The first byte is the most significant byte of the number. (rGPS is the exception to the 5 byte rule see below).

The values received in the first three bytes of the 5 bytes are used to update the status of the Bumper, Infrared and Line sensors. These values will be used by rBumper(), rFeel() and rSense(). This means that these functions will still work in the same way as in the simulated situation but instead of returning the values read by the simulated robot off the screen they will return the real physical values received by the protocol from real sensors on the physical robot. The values can be used in exactly the same manner as before (as described in the Robot Simulator section).

Note: The byte corresponding to the rSense() (3rd byte) in the 5 returned bytes will be Bit Anded (masked) with 7 (0%00000111) when received unless an rSenseType 5 has been issued. This is to keep the value returned in accordance with only 3 sensors being rported in bits 0 to 2 (first three). If you wish to send values in this byte that want to receive in full (all 8 bits) then issue an rSenseType 5 statement before using the protocol. This will stop the masking and the whole byte will be kept as it was received. This can be useful for receiving more than 3 line sensors or even other data from the robot.

•rCommPort ne_PortNum {,ne_BaudRate {,ne_NumBits {,ne_Parity {,ne_StopBits {,ne_Protocol}}}}}

This command is exactly the same as SetCommPort above. It sets the com port number and parameters and opens the com port for communications. However, it also signals a flag that makes the simulator use the com port specified in place of the screen. To return back to using the screen issue the command again but with 0 as the com port number.

•rCommand(ne_Command,ne_Data)

This function will send the two bytes ne_Command and ne_Data over the serial comm. It will then wait for 5 bytes to be received over the serial comm. If the 5 bytes are received within the TimeOut limit (see above) then the function will return these 5 bytes in a string (byte buffer).

If the robot has not been initialized with an rLocate, or rCommport has not been issued, or the serial comms fail for any other reason or the 5 bytes are not received within the TimeOut limit then the function will return a blank string ("").

This function allows you to send a GENERAL command (with a parameter) to the real robot and to receive 5 bytes which you can use in any fashion. Use GetStrByte() to obtain the individual bytes from the string of 5 bytes.

•rLocate ne_X,ne_Y   (code 3)

You still need to issue this command before using the protocol just as in the simulator. This command initializes the real robot and starts the command process. No use is made of the second (and the others if you happen to be using them) parameters but they need to still be there because the command is the same as in the simulated one but does not use the numbers when the protocol is active. This means that you do not need to change your simulator program to make it work with the protocol. The protocol sends two bytes 03 and ne_X. It will expect to receive 5 bytes where the first three are as described above. The last two are not used.

•rForward ne_Amount   **(code 6 or 7)**

This command will send two bytes 6 (or 7) and Abs(ne_Amount). 6 is the code for going forward and 7 is for going backwards. ne_Amount is the distance required if it is positive then code 6 is sent and if it is negative then it is made positive and the code 7 is sent. The received data contains 5 bytes but only the first 3 are used. They are in the order described above for the status of the sensors.

•rTurn ne_Amount   **(code 12 or 13)**

This command will send two bytes 12 (or 13) and Abs(ne_Amount). 12 is the code for turning right and 13 is for left. ne_Amount is the required degrees, if positive then code 12 is sent and if negative then the number is made positive and code 13 is sent. If you specify a number greater than 180 then the turn is made into ne_Amount-360 and if it is less than -180 (i.e. more negative than -180 e.g. -190) then it is made into 360+ne_Amount. So if your simulator command says rTurn 190 then the value sent to the real robot will be 170 with code 13 (i.e. left turn of 170). The received data contains 5 bytes but only the first 3 are used. They are in the order described above for the status of the sensors.

•rCompass ()   **(code 24)**

This function will send two bytes 24 and 0. 24 is the code for the compass. The received data contains 5 bytes. The first 3 used are in the order described above for the status of the sensors. The last two bytes are the value returned by the compass on the real robot representing the heading (MSB first). This means that this function will return a number formed as a 16 bit number from the 4th byte of the received 5 bytes as the MSByte of the number and the 5th byte as the LSByte.

•rSpeed ne_Speed   **(code 36)**

This command will send two bytes 36 and ne_Speed. 36 is the code for setting a speed on the physical robot and ne_Speed is the required speed (0 to 255). The received data contains 5 bytes. The first 3 used are in the order described above for the status of the sensors. The last two bytes are not needed and are set to 0.

•rLook ({ne_Angle})   **(code 48 or 49)**

Will send two bytes 48 (or 49) and Abs(ne_Angle). 48 is the code for the camera sensors reading ne_Angle degrees to the right and 49 is to the left. If ne_Angle is negative it will be made positive and code 49 will be sent.. The received data contains 5 bytes. The first 3 used are in the order described above for the status of the sensors. The last two bytes are the value returned representing the color seen by the sensor. (MSB first). This means that this function will return a number formed as a 16 bit number from the 4th byte of the received 5 bytes as the MSByte of the number and the 5th byte as the LSByte

•rGPS vn_X,vn_Y   **(code 66)**

This command will send two bytes 66 and 0. 66 is the code for GPS sensors reading and vn_X will be set to the X pos and vn_Y to the Y position. The received data contains 5 bytes. The first 2 are the X position and the second two are the Y position. The fifth is not used and is set to zero. (MSB first).

This command is an exception to the 5 bytes received in all the other commands. The 5 bytes received after issuing this command are not used to update the Bumpers, Infrared, and Line sensors status. Instead the first 2 bytes are used to calculate the X-position and the second two bytes are for Y-position. The last byte is not used.

•rBeacon (ne_Color)   (code 96)

Will send two bytes 96 and ne_Color. 96 is the code for beacon sensors reading and ne_Color is the required color. The received data contains 5 bytes. The first 3 used are in the order described above for the status of the sensors. The last two bytes are the value returned by the beacon representing the distance measured to the found beacon or zero if beacon is not found. (MSB first). This means that this function will return a number formed as a 16 bit number from the 4th byte of the received 5 bytes as the MSByte of the number and the 5th byte as the LSByte.

•rChargeLevel ()   (code 108)

This function will send two bytes 108 and 0. 108 is the code for the battery charge level meter. The received data contains 5 bytes. The first 3 used are in the order described above for the status of the sensors. The last two bytes are the value returned by the battery charge meter on the real robot representing the battery charge level in percentage(MSB first). This means that this function will return a number formed as a 16 bit number from the 4th byte of the received 5 bytes as the MSByte of the number and the 5th byte as the LSByte. Since the value is a percentage value then it is not likely to exceed 100. However, you can use the number returned as you need and you may program the robot to return any number 0 to 0xFFFF if you wish.

•rPen ne_State   (code 129)

This command will send two bytes 129 and ne_State. 129 is the code for pen control. ne_State is either Up(0) or Down (not zero can be any number other than zero usually it is 1). The received data contains 5 bytes. The first 3 are in the order described above for the status of the sensors. The last two bytes are not needed and are set to 0.

•rRange ({ne_Angle})   (code 192 or 193)

Will send two bytes 192 (or 193) and Abs(ne_Angle). 192 is the code for range sensors reading at ne_Angle degrees to the right and 193 is to the left. If ne_Angle is negative it is made positive and code 193 is sent. The received data contains 5 bytes. The first 3 used are in the order described above for the status of the sensors. The last two bytes are the value returned by the rangers representing the distance measured. (MSB first). This means that this function will return a number formed as a 16 bit number from the 4th byte of the received 5 bytes as the MSByte of the number and the 5th byte as the LSByte.

Ports & Serial I/O

•General Information

The following commands allow for using direct port I/O where you can read/write a byte from/to a particular port on the PC. There is a set of special commands for I/O to the parallel port as a special case for ease of use. There is also a set of commands that allow for Serial I/O using either actual com ports on the PC or virtual com ports created by protocols such as Bluetooth devices or USB devices. These devices will create a virtual port number that can be used for all intents and purposes as if it were a physical serial com port.

The Robot Simulator has an extension that allows for the use of serial I/O to communicate to and from a real robot, effectively enabling programming of a real robot using the RobotBASIC language. The protocol extension will be explained in its own section below.

To facilitate serial com port setup there are a set of constants that are listed in Appendix B.7.6. The I/O commands ***are not*** case sensitive.

Note: See the notes at the top of the Standard User Interfacing section.

Note: The following functions and commands will help in manipulating the string buffer for sending or after receiving. ToByte(), PutStrByte(), GetStrByte(), BuffPrintT, BuffPrintB, BuffWrite(), BuffWriteB(), BuffRead(), BuffReadI(), BuffReadB(), BuffReadF() and of course all the string mainpulation functions as well as number conversion functions. Also see CrLf(), Substitute(), Extract(), NumParts(), mFromString and mToString().

•Serial I/O Commands

Note: The OnSerial statement will interrupt normal program flow and jump to a subroutine (event handler) that must handle the event and then return back to program execution. This occurs every time there are bytes in the serial buffer. Reading the buffer will clear it.

When sending data through the serial port you are sending a string. This string can be considered as one dimensional array of bytes. You can put data in the string in many ways. SerOut behaves like a print statement and will create a string that results from the list of expressions given as parameters to the command. This will also convert numbers to their string format. While SerialOut does not convert the numbers to their string format, rather it will treat numbers as one byte values and will send only the LSByte of the numbers given.

Another way you can create the string (byte array) to be sent is by using the String Buffer functions. See BuffPrint and BuffWrite() and BuffWriteB(). Also see PutStrByte(), toByte() and Char().

All of these would help in creating the byte array (string) to be sent through the serial port.

•SetCommPort ne_PortNum {,ne_BaudRate {,ne_NumBits {,ne_Parity {,ne_StopBits {,ne_Protocol}}}}}

This command sets the com port number and parameters and activates the port for communications.
- Port Number can be from 1 to 5000 .
- Baud Rate can be 0 to 14 (see the RobotBASIC Constants section for details of codes). Defaults to 6 i.e. 9600 baud.
- The number of Data Bits in the transmitted byte can be 4,5,6,7 or 8. Defaults to 8.
- The Parity check can be from 0 to 4 (see RobotBASIC Constants section). Defaults to 0 (no parity).
- Stop Bits in the transmission (see RobotBASIC Constants section) ranges from 0 to 2. Defaults to 1 i.e. 1 stop bit.
- Flow Control protocol (see RobotBASIC Constants section) ranges from 0 to 2. Defaults to 0 i.e. None.

To deactivate the communications port issue SetCommPort 0

•SerPorts vs_PortsList

This command checks the computer to see what Comm ports are available for use. It then creates a list of all the Comm Port numbers and assigns the vs_PortsList variable the list with CR/LF separating the numbers. This list can be assigned directly to a ListBox (see AddListBox) since it is a CR/LF separated list of strings. You also can use Extract() to extract a particular port number from the list and use ToNumber() to convert it to an actual Integer value to be used in SetCommPort or rCommPort.

•SerOut Expr {,Expr {; Expr ...}}

This command is similar to Print. The output of the command is sent to the serial port in place of the screen.

Outputs the values of *expr....* to the serial port. A **,** between the expressions makes them print with no space between them a **;** prints them with a tab space between them. You must specify at least one expression. The result of all the expressions is put together as specified by the commas and semicolons into one string and the string is outputted to the serial port as specified by SetCommPort. The total length of the resulting string will be truncated to 4095 bytes if it exceeds this amount.

If Expr results in a numeric it will be converted to the string format. DO if you say SerOut Alpha and Alpha contains the value 435 then the characters 4, 3 and 5 will be put out to the serial port.

SerOut behaves just like a Print statement but the resulting output is put out to the serial port instead of the screen. See SerialOut for more options in puting out numbers.

•SerialOut Expr {,Expr {, Expr ...}}

This command is different from SerOut above. Only commas are allowed to separate the various expressions. The expressions can result in numerical (float or integer) or string values.

If the expression results in a float value it will be rounded down to become an integer. If the resulting integer value is greater than 255 (0xFF or 0%11111111) then it will be made into a byte by zeroing all the other bytes other than the LSByte.

If the expression results in a string then the string will be treated as a one-dimensional array of bytes whose values are the values of the characters in the string.

The results of all the expressions will be accumulated into one array of bytes in the order they are specified and sent through the active comm port as specified by SetCommPort. The total length of the resulting array will be truncated to 4095 bytes if it exceeds this amount.

Also see BuffPrint and PutStrByte(), toByte(), BuffWrite() and BuffWriteB().

•SerIn vs_Bytes

This command reads the data that is currently in the serial communications buffer all in one go and puts it as a string in the variable vs_Bytes. You can use string manipulation commands and functions as well as conversion functions to make use of the data. The command will not cause a time out. If there are no bytes in the input buffer the string returned will be null. Use CheckSerBuffer to find out how many bytes (if any) of data are waiting on the buffer.

See GetStrByte(), BuffReadI(), BuffReadB() and BuffRead().

•SerBytesIn ne_NumOfBytesToRead,vs_BytesRead,vn_ActualNumberRead

This command attempts to read the required number of bytes from the serial input buffer and puts them in to the string variable vs_BytesRead. vn_ActualNumberRead is set to the number of bytes actually read before a time out occurred. The command will wait until the required number of bytes are read. If a time out occurs before all the characters are retrieved then what ever characters have been read are returned inside vs_BytesRead and vn_ActualNumberRead is set to the number actually read. See SetTimeOut and GetTimeOut below. The maximum amount for ne_NumOfBytesRequired is 4095 bytes and the minimum is 1. It will be set to the closest limit if it is outside the range 1 to 4095.

292

•SetTimeOut {ne_MilliSeconds}

This command sets the time out for the serial port reading commands. ne_MilliSeconds is the number of milliseconds to wait before a time out occurs. It is optional and if it is not given or is less than one then 5000 will be assumed (i.e. 5 seconds). 5000 is also the default upon program startup.

•GetTimeOut vn_TimeOutValue

This command reads the current setting for the time out for the serial port and puts the value in vn_TimeOutValue. The number returned is in milliseconds.

•CheckSerBuffer vn_NumOfBytes

This command set the value of the variable vn_NumOfBytes to the number of character in the serial input buffer. You can read them with the commands above.

•ClearSerBuffer {ne_Which}

This command clears the Input and Output serial buffers. If ne_Which is not given or is zero then both buffers will be cleared. A value of 1 will clear the Input buffer, a value of 2 will clear the output buffer. Any other values will be ignored.

•ReadSerSignals vn_Flags

This command checks the status of the CTS (clear-to-send), DSR (data-set-ready), Ring (ring indicator) and RLSD (receive-line-signal-detect) signals and puts them into the vn_Flags variable as a bit map. Any signal that is on will have a 1 in its corresponding bit and if it is off it will have a 0. The bits are in the order given above starting from the Least Significant Bit onwards. So CTS is bit 0 and RLSD is bit 3.

•SetSerDTR {on|off}

This command will set the DTR signal line to on or off. If no parameter is given then on is assumed.

•SetSerRTS {on|off}

This command will set the RTS signal line to on or off. If no parameter is given then on is assumed.

•Parallel Ports I/O Commands

These commands read and write byte values to the parallel port specified. These commands assume that your system has a bi-directional parallel port (ECP standard). If your system does not have this then only output will be possible and no input can occur. You can check if your system has this capability and set it using the BIOS setup upon starting your PC. If you have more than one parallel port you can specify which one to use by specifying its base address using

SetPPortNumber.

•PPortOut {ne_ByteValue}

Outputs the byte value to the parallel port If ne_ByteValue is greater than 255 only the lower byte will be outputted. If ne_ByteValue is not given it will be 0 and if it is a float it will be truncated to an integer then to one byte (LSB).

•PPortIn vn_ByteValue

Reads the data byte at the parallel port and assigns it to the variable vn_ByteValue.

•SetPPortNumber {ne_PortNumber}

This commands sets the base address of the parallel port to be used by all the parallel port commands including the virtual ones below. The system defaults to address 888 (hex 0x378) which is usually the first and only parallel port on most systems. If your system has more than one port and you wish to use other than the default first port use this command to specify the port number (in decimal). You can find the addresses of available ports from the BIOS setup upon starting your computer, or you can use the Windows System to do the same. ne_PortNumber is optional and if it is not given or it is less than one then the system will use port number 888 (0x378). **Beware that if you specify the wrong address the commands will not function and you may even damage your system**.

> **WARNING! Use these commands with care. Badly designed hardware connected to the parallel port can damage the port. If you are going to experiment with electronics and these commands do so at your own risk and know what you are doing. Failure to do the correct design will damage your port if not your whole computer.**

•*Virtual* Parallel Port I/O Protocol

This protocol is included as a convenience for extending the single byte parallel port to 4 input bytes and 4 output bytes. The protocol assumes there is multiplexing hardware connected to the parallel port. You can write your own protocol using InPort and OutPort but this protocol is provided for convenience and speed.

The protocol makes use of the control port on the parallel port to put the port number on the multiplexer hardware (3 bits) and then uses a fourth bit to clock the multiplexer and then reads the data or outputs the data depending on what port number is in use.

The result is that one parallel port with only 8 I/O pins can be expanded to 4x8 Input and 4x8 Output pins. The hardware will not be discussed here.

On the parallel port connector Pins 2 to 9 are the data pins. Pins 1, 14, and 16 will be used to set the address on the multiplexer. Where LSB is Pin 1. Pin 17 will be used to clock the Multiplexer (low is HiZ high is Clocked) assuming a rising edge trigger.

Addresses 0 to 3 will be input ports (to the PC) and 4 to 7 will be output ports (from the PC).

•VPPortOut ne_VirtualPortNo,ne_ByteValue

Outputs the byte value to the **virtual parallel port** number specified. If the byte value is greater than 255 only the lower byte will be outputted. The port number is limited to 1 to 4 if it is outside these limits then the closest limit will be set.

•VPPortIn ne_VirtualPortNo,vn_ByteValue

Reads the byte value at the **virtual parallel port** number and then puts it in the variable vn_ByteValue. The port number is limited to 1 to 4 if it is outside these limits then the closest limit will be set.

> **WARNING!** **Use these commands with care. Badly designed hardware connected to the parallel port can damage the port. If you are going to experiment with electronics and these commands do so at your own risk and know what you are doing. Failure to do the correct design will damage your port if not your whole computer.**

•General Ports I/O Commands

•OutPort ne_PortNumber,ne_ByteValue

Outputs the byte value to the PC port number. If ne_ByteValue is greater than 255 only the lower byte will be outputted. ne_PortNumber can be any valid port number.

> **WARNING!** **Beware of using this command incorrectly. You can damage your system if you write or read from a wrong port number.**

•InPort ne_PortNumber,vn_ByteValue

Reads the byte value at the PC port number and then puts it in the variable vn_ByteValue as a number. ne_PortNumber can be any valid port number.

> **WARNING!** **Beware of using this command incorrectly. You can damage your system if you write or read from a wrong port number.**

USBmicro U4x1 Functions

The USBmicro L.L.C. U401, U421, USBPIR, and other USBmicro devices are very effective I/O devices that provide a very convenient conduit for doing Digital I/O from the PC to electronics devices such as robots.

RobotBASIC provides many ways you can communicate from a PC to a digital electronic circuit. One very effective, convenient, safe and versatile method is to use the U4x1 USB devices from USBmicro. These devices have 16 digital I/O lines that can sink about 50 mA, and drive about 5mA. The device is powered from the USB port so it is very convenient for doing low powered I/O. If you need more current than can be provided by the U4x1 you can use it with an appropriate power isolation circuit.

The U4x1 is also a lot more than just 16 plain digital I/O lines - you can use these lines in a strait forward manner as 2x8 bit ports with individual lines being configurable as either Input or Output. But you can also have the device do SPI and 1-Wire serial communications to devices that support these protocols. Additionally, the U4x1 can be used to control an LCD and a Stepper motor (***control only - not a driver - you need to provide current driving separately***), or you can configure it to provide a parallel strobe signal.

For the SPI system you can configure the U4x1 to act as an SPI slave or SPI master. For the 1-Wire it acts as a Master. With these protocols you can easily interact with a plethora of devices like ADC, DAC, thermometers, compasses, GPSs, and much much more.

The functions (below) provide access to all the functionalities supported by the U4x1. All you need to do is have a U4x1 plugged into one (or more) USB port on your computer. The functions are divided into three types:

DLL Specific functions	provide information about the hardware driver software (DLL)
Device Information Functions	provide information about individual devices connected to any USB port.
Device I/O Functions	provide the I/O from and to any particular device.

The U4x1 has 16 I/O lines set out as two 8 bit Ports (A and B). You can set and reset each Output line individually or as an 8 bit group. You can configure each line as Input or as output. You read the lines as a group of 8 lines (Ports) but with the use of usbm_SetBit() and usbm_ResetBit() you can set individual bits.

To make proper use of the U4x1 devices and to get deeper

understanding of the operations of the function below and of the device's limitations and capabilities, you must read the USBmicro documentation and information. The information below relates to how to use the functions within RobotBASIC that reflect the LOW LEVEL functions within the device's ROM. To use the following functions correctly you have to understand how they are invoked by the U4x1 device. To do this you MUST read the documentation. Go to www.usbmicro.com and view the information in the section of the web site called the "ODN" or Online Development Notebook. In it is programming information that is kept up to date and some examples. For more examples of how to use the hardware – including examples written in RobotBASIC – read through the blog at www.circuitgizmos.com.

The RobotBASIC downloadable zip (www.RobotBASIC.com) has a folder called USBmicroDemos. In this folder there are 4 RB programs that demonstrate the use of the U4x1 with RB.

Note: See the notes at the top of the Standard User Interfacing section. In the following list ne_ means numerical expression, se_ means string expression.

Note: *In all indexing 0 is the first index and so on. So 1st bit in the port is bit 0. The first device is device 0 and so forth.*

Note: *In all the functions where a byte is required you use an integer but you must not exceed 0xFF (255). With many commands you pass an array of bytes or you get back an array of bytes. This array is really just a string. You can put data in it using the PutStrByte() and read data from it using GetStrByte(), when you use these functions you again use an integer but must not exceed 0xFF. Also see ToByte().*

Note: When specifying the device number (which U4x1 you want to control) for all the device specific function use 0 for the first device, 1 for the second device and so forth. In other words the device number list is a list that starts with 0. When either a parameter or the returned value is a string then the string must/will contain byte values of the data. Use GetStrByte() and PutStrByte() to extract the byte value from the returned string. Also see the Buffer manipulation functions BuffRead(), BuffWrite() etc. which manipulate a buffer as a one dimensional array of binary bytes.

Note: The following functions and commands will help in manipulating the string buffer for sending or after receiving. ToByte(), PutStrByte(), GetStrByte(), BuffPrintT, BuffPrintB,

BuffWrite(), BuffWriteB(), BuffRead(), BuffReadI(), BuffReadB(), BuffReadF() and of course all the string mainpulation functions as well as number conversion functions. Also see CrLf(), Substitute(), Extract() and NumParts().

•DLL Specific Functions

These functions let you find out information about the DLL that RobotBASIC uses to control the USBmicro hardware as well as some functions that deal with all of the U4x1 devices in general.

•usbm_DllSpecs()
Returns a string that contains information about the DLL. There are four sections separated by the | character. You can use Extract() to extract each section separately if desired. The sections are:

About | Copyright | Version Date | Version Number

If the USBm.Dll is not installed and running the returned string will be a blank string ("").

•usbm_ErrorSpecs()
Returns a string that contains information about the "recent error string and debug string" - if any - in the DLL. There are two sections separated by the | character. You can use Extract() to extract each section separately if desired. The sections are:

Recent Error | Debug String

•usbm_ClearRecentError()
Always returns -1. The function clears any recent error data in the DLL.

•usbm_FindDevices()
Returns -1 (true) if there are U4x1 devices connected to the PC. Returns 0 (false) otherwise. ***You must call this function before you do anything with devices***. This function must be the first function called before addressing any devices. It essentially finds all of the U4x1 devices connected to the computer.

•usbm_NumberOfDevices()
Returns the number of U4x1 devices connected to the PC (as found by usbm_FindDevices()). A value of 0 means there are no devices connected.

•usbm_SetReadTimeout(ne_Time)
Returns true if successful, false otherwise. This function sets the timeout for ***all*** the read commands. The value should be in milliseconds. The default is 1000 msecs = 1 sec. Rarely is this ever changed.

•Device Information Functions

These functions find out information about any selected device. ***Once again, usbm_FindDevices() must be called once at the beginning of a program before you can address any device.***

•usbm_DeviceSpecs(ne_DeviceNumber)
Returns a string that contains information about a specific device identified by its number. There are 7 sections separated by the | character. You can use Extract() to extract each section separately if desired. The sections are:

DID | PID | VID | Mfr | Prod | Serial Number | Firmware Version.

DID = Device ID, PID = Product ID, VID = Vendor ID, Mfr = Manufacturer's name, and Prod = Product name. The Serial Number is a unique 12 digit number for every U4x1 device. The Firmware Version value is the revision of the U4x1 firmware.

If the device referred to by ne_DeviceNumber is not a valid device, the returned string will be "NOTVALID".

•usbm_DeviceValid(ne_DeviceNumber)
Returns true if the device number refers to a connected and active device. False otherwise. This can be called periodically to detect whether a certain U4x1 has been unplugged.

•usbm_CloseDevice(ne_DeviceNumber)
Returns true if the device was successfully closed and false otherwise. It isn't strictly necessary to close a device – Windows takes care of that.

•Device I/O Functions

These functions directly control (or read from) devices. Again, the first U4x1 found is indexed as "0". ***Also, again, usbm_FindDevices() must be called once at the beginning of a program before you can address any device.***

•usbm_InitPorts(ne_DeviceNumber)
•usbm_InitPortsU401(ne_DeviceNumber)
•usbm_InitPortsU421(ne_DeviceNumber)
•usbm_InitPortsU451(ne_DeviceNumber)
Returns true if successful, false otherwise. On the U401 and U421 These function resets the A and B ports as Input Ports, which is the default state upon connecting the device to the PC. On the U451 will reset port A to input, port B to output and will clear the internal latches.

299

•usbm_DirectionA(ne_DeviceNumber,ne_PinsDirection,ne_PinsFormat)
•usbm_DirectionB(ne_DeviceNumber,ne_PinsDirection,ne_PinsFormat)

Returns true if successful, false otherwise. This function sets the direction of each specific pin in the port. A 1 in the bit position in ne_PinsDirection and ne_PinsFormat means output, a 0 is input.

If ne_PinsDirection and ne_PinsFormat are both set to 0%11111111 (the value 255), then the port is all output. If ne_PinsDirection and ne_PinsFormat are both set to 0%00000000 (the value 0), then the port is all input.

Pin numbering in the byte is from right to left i.e. LSBit is bit number 0 and MSBit is bit number 7. So if you want to set Port A on the first device to have pin 0 and pin 4 as inputs and the rest as outputs then use:

```
        n = usbm_DirectionA(0,0%11101110, 0%11101110)
or      n = usbm_DirectionA(0,0xEE, 0xEE)
or      n = usbm_DirectionA(0,238, 238)
```

Generally ne_PinsDirection and ne_PinsFormat are the same value. See USBmicro.com for other values.

•usbm_DirectionAIn(ne_DeviceNumber)
•usbm_DirectionAOut(ne_DeviceNumber)
•usbm_DirectionAInPullUp(ne_DeviceNumber)
•usbm_DirectionBIn(ne_DeviceNumber)
•usbm_DirectionBOut(ne_DeviceNumber)
•usbm_DirectionBInPullUp(ne_DeviceNumber)

Returns true if successful, false otherwise. These functions set the direction of *all the pins* on port A/B to either all as input or as output or as input with internal pull-up resistors. This is the same as using usbm_DirectionA/B() but is a shortcut to set *ALL* the pins.

•usbm_WriteA(ne_DeviceNumber,ne_ByteValue)
•usbm_WriteB(ne_DeviceNumber,ne_ByteValue)

Returns true if successful, false otherwise. The byte value is written to Port A/B to the lines that are set as outputs. The function writes the value to the entire port (A or B). Lines that are not set as output will not be affected.

•usbm_ReadA(ne_DeviceNumber)
•usbm_ReadB(ne_DeviceNumber)

Returns the byte value representing the states of the pins on Port A/B. The value returned is not a valid value if the device is not a validly active device, see usbm_DeviceValid(). The entire port (A or B) is read.

•usbm_ReadLatches(ne_DeviceNumber)
Returns a string that contains the values of the internal pin-change latches. After reading changed latches the latches are reset.

The first byte (byte 1) in the string (byte array) will always hold the value 0x0F. Byte 2 and 4 contain the latched value for a bit transition from 0xFF on port A (B) to any other value. If your port is pulled high with resistors (external or internal) and a button press pulls the pin low then these are the bytes to use. If your port is normally low and a button pres sets a line high, then the latch data returned in bytes 3 and 5 are the appropriate bytes to use.

•usbm_SetBit(ne_DeviceNumber,ne_PinNumber)
•usbm_ResetBit(ne_DeviceNumber,ne_PinNumber)
Returns true if successful, false otherwise. This function makes *high or low* a particular pin on any of the ports. The pin numbering is 0 for A0 1 for A1...7 for A7...8 for B0, ...15 for B7. This lets you set or reset any single bit out of all 16 port bits.

•usbm_WriteABit(ne_DeviceNumber,ne_AndingMask, ne_OringMask)
•usbm_WriteBBit(ne_DeviceNumber,ne_AndingMask, ne_OringMask)
Returns true if successful, false otherwise. This function reads the current status of the pins in the A/B port and then ANDs the value with the ANDing mask, then the new value is ORed with the ORing mask, then the result is written to port A/B.

•LCD Related Functions
•usbm_InitLCD(ne_DeviceNumber,ne_Sel, ne_Port)
Returns true if successful, false otherwise. It specifies the port to use for the data port and the pins to use for the R/W, RS, and E lines for controlling an LCD. The LCD commands are appropriate for HD44780 devices and devices that are compatible. Most common character LCD display modules will work. These LCDs can have 8 bit or 4 bit data lines and 4 bit control lines. The U4x1 can send data to and control such an LCD once set up to use the appropriate lines.

This function will set up I/O pins so that they are correctly configured to communicate with such LCDs.

See the USBmicro documentation for more details and also see the 1Wire_DS1820_LCD_LED_PushButton_Tests.BAS demo program in the downloadable zip file. This program communicates with a 1-Wire controllable thermometer (ds1820) and gets temperature data and *displays it on an LCD* and the PC screen simultaneously.

•usbm_LCDCmd(ne_DeviceNumber,ne_CommandByte)
Returns true if successful, false otherwise. Sends a command code to the LCD. This is a command from among a list of commands that an LCD accepts like clearing the screen or

setting up the display format (see the USBmisro_Test2.Bas demo).

•usbm_LCDData(ne_DeviceNumber,ne_DataByte)

Returns true if successful, false otherwise. Sends a data byte to the LCD. These are usually the characters that will be displayed on the LCD (see the USBmisro_Test2.Bas demo).

•1-Wire Related Functions

•usbm_Reset1Wire(ne_DeviceNumber,ne_Specs)

Returns the status of any devices on the 1-Wire line. Returns 0 if any device responded and 1 if none did. This function also sets up the 1-Wire line to be used.

The 1-Wire protocol is a serial communications protocol that uses, well, one wire....but not really since there has to be a ground line. The "1-Wire" line is both the power and the data line for 1-Wire devices. The U4x1 can be configured to automatically send and receive data from a 1-Wire device on any of the 16 pins. The U4x1 can only be a 1-Wire master, not a 1-Wire slave device.

For an example of the use of this system see the USBmisro_Test2.Bas demo program that communicates with a thermometer (ds1820) and gets temperature data and displays it on an LCD and the PC screen simultaneously.

•usbm_Write1Wire(ne_DeviceNumber,ne_Data)

Returns true if successful, false otherwise. Writes a byte to the 1-Wire device. The U4x1 will take care of shifting out the 8 bits of the byte all in the background (see the USBmisro_Test2.Bas demo).

•usbm_Read1Wire(ne_DeviceNumber)

Returns a byte value that is read from the 1-Wire device. The U4x1 takes care of shifting in the 8 bits all in the background (see the USBmisro_Test2.Bas demo).

•usbm_Write1WireBit(ne_DeviceNumber,ne_BitValue)

Returns true if successful, false otherwise. Writes a 0 or 1 to the 1-Wire device.

•usbm_Read1WireBit(ne_DeviceNumber)

Returns a bit value that is read from the 1-Wire device.

•2-Wire (e.g. I2C) Related Functions

•usbm_Wire2Control(ne_DeviceNumber,ne_Signal)

This function sends a specific signal to the 2-wire port setting the data and clock lines as defined by this command. Signals are specific patterns of setting the 2-wire clock and data lines high or low. For I2C this command is good for initialization of the clock and data lines, for generating a start sequence, and for making a stop sequence.

The function sends the ne_Signal value to the device and then returns an integer with only the LSByte set to the current value of either the 2-wire data line or the 2-wire clock line for the signals that return data. If the function fails it will return the value 0xFFFFFFFF.

PA.3 is the 2-wire data line, while PA.2 is the 2-wire clock line. For 2-wire communication these two lines are set to be open collector/drain lines. Since they are only able to be set to zero by the U4x1 device, they must be pulled high (to 5V) by an external resistor in order to have a high state. This is often called "active low and passive high." For typical 2-wire communication (such as I2C) a 4700 ohm (4.7 kohm) resistor will suffice. For I2C communication the first three signal types (0, 1, 2) are useful for generating the initial I2C state, the start condition, and the stop condition. For transfer of clocked bytes of data, use Wire2Data.

Signal types
  0 - Set clock and data to open-drain, set data high, set clock high. (Good for I2C initialization.)
   1 - Set data high, clock high, data low, clock low. (Good for I2C start signal.)
   2 - Set data low, clock high, data high. (Good for I2C stop signal.)
   3 - Set clock low, data low.
   4 - Set data high, clock high.
   5 - Set data high
   6 - Set data low.
   7 - Set clock high.
   8 - Set clock low.
   9 - Return data line.
  10 - Return clock line.

•usbm_Wire2Data(ne_DeviceNumber,se_DataBytes)
This function sends data to the 2-wire port. Eight bits of data are clocked out the 2-wire port. The 2-wire data line toggles to match the bits in the command as the clock line pulses high. Optionally a 9th data bit can be sent. For I2C this command is good for transmitting/receiving a byte (8 bits) of data, as well as an optional 'ACK' bit.

To see how the data bytes should be put in the byte array se_DataBytes read the USBmicro documentation. The function expects the data bytes to be sent to the device to be in the byte array (string) se_DataBytes but not the command code (just the data bytes). The function will then return a string (byte array) with the data returned as described in the USBmicro documentation. The first byte will be the value 0x19 always. The actual returned data starts at byte 2 in the returned string. See the USBmicro documentation.

303

•SPI Related Functions
•usbm_InitSPI(ne_DeviceNumber,ne_Specs)
Returns true if successful, false otherwise. It sets the attributes of the SPI system.

The SPI protocol is a 3 wire serial communications protocol (really 4 since a ground is needed). The communication lines are a clock line, a data line *from* the device, and a data line *to* the device. In this protocol there is always a Master and multiple Slaves. The U4x1 can act as a slave if needed but most devices like an ADC will be slaves. The U4x1 can be set up as a master to communicate with such devices and control them and send and receive data from them.

The U4x1 uses particular I/O lines to do the work. See the USBmicro documentation for details. Also see the USBmicro_Test4.Bas in the download zip file. This program communicates with the SPI slave 2-Chanel Analog to Digital 12 bit converter (LTC1298) and displays analog inputs from it on the PC screen. The demo also explains all connections.

Most often the U4x1 is used as a SPI master (talking to an EEPROM or an SPI A/D chip) and then only usbm_InitSPI() and usbm_SPIMaster() are used.

•usbm_SPISlaveRead(ne_DeviceNumber)
Returns a string of byte data from the Slave buffer (maximum 6 bytes). You can use GetStrByte() to extract the individual bytes.

•usbm_SPISlaveWrite(ne_DeviceNumber,se_DataBytes)
Returns true if successful, false otherwise. Writes 1 to 6 bytes to the SPI slave buffer. The length of the data string determines the number of bytes written. Use PutStrByte() to create the data string. Use this function to write data to an SPI Master when the U4x1 is the slave.

•usbm_SPIMaster(ne_DeviceNumber,se_DataBytes)
Returns a string of byte values input from the SPI slave after it has read the corresponding number of bytes from the data string. Use GetStrByte() to extract the byte values and PutStrByte() to create the data string. Use this function to send data to and receive data from an SPI slave when the u4x1 is acting as a master.

Note: The Bytes array se_DataBytes should contain a maximum of 6 data bytes, which are the data to be sent to the slave. The function will then return a string (byte array) that contains any data returned from the slave but the first byte in the string is *not* data. You should consider the data from the slave to be in the returned byte array as starting at the *second* character in the returned string.

•Stepper Motor Related Functions

304

•usbm_Stepper(ne_DeviceNumber,se_DataSpecs)

Returns true if successful, false otherwise. The byte data string specifies the channel and other details. This function gives access to a very powerful feature of the U4x1 devices -you can control the Stepping of two Stepper motors forward or backwards independently, all in the background so the PC can be doing other things while the stepper motors are being operated.

The U4x1 does the LOGIC of the 4-line stepping. These lines must be connected to further POWER DRIVER circuitry to do the actual driving of the motors. See the USBmicro documentation for detail of this function and how to use the U4x1 to drive up to two stepper motors.

•Strobe I/O Functions (See the USBmirco documentation for details of these functions)

•usbm_StrobeWrite(ne_DeviceNumber,se_ByteData)

Returns true if successful, false otherwise. Writes a byte to a port based on a strobe line and timing. The byte data string specifies the setup and so forth.

•usbm_StrobeRead(ne_DeviceNumber,se_ByteData)

Returns a byte value of data read from a port based on a strobe line and timing. The byte data string specifies the setup and so forth.

•usbm_StrobeWrites(ne_DeviceNumber,se_ByteData)

Returns true if successful, false otherwise. Writes multiple bytes (1 to 6) to a port based on a strobe line and timing. The byte data string specifies the setup and the data to be written.

•usbm_StrobeReads(ne_DeviceNumber,se_ByteData)

Returns a string of byte data read from a port based on a strobe line and timing. The byte data string specifies the setup and so forth.

•A General *HOOK* Function to future functionalities in the U4x1

•usbm_DeviceCmd(ne_DeviceNumber,se_Data)

Returns a string that contains the results of the response to the command specified in the se_Data string. The data string passed is a set of 8 bytes. The first byte specifies the command code and the next 7 bytes are any byte data required by the command. The returned string contains the first byte as the command number (again) and then the next 7 bytes are any data returned by the command. Not all the bytes may have significance in either the passed string or the returned string.

This function can be used to provide access to any functionality in the USBm.DLL that may be implemented in the future. It can also provide access to all the above functions, but it is easier to use the above formats of the functions. Details of how to access the additional functions will be spelled out at the USBmicro web site.

The passed string will be truncated to 8 bytes if it is longer. It can be shorter if not all the byte positions are required.
Use GetStrByte() function to extract the byte values from the string and PutStrByte() to put bytes into the passed string. If you wish to display the data as hexadecimal values use Hex().

When creating the string of byte values use the PutStrByte(string,byte position,desired byte numeric value) to place the byte value in the desired position in the string.

Internet Commands & Functions

•General Information

The following commands allow for using a WAN/LAN or INTERNET connection to send/receive bytes of data or send an email.

Note: See the notes at the top of the Standard User Interfacing section.

Note: The following functions and commands will help in manipulating the string buffer for sending or after receiving. ToByte(), PutStrByte(), GetStrByte(), BuffPrintT, BuffPrintB, BuffWrite(), BuffWriteB(), BuffRead(), BuffReadI(), BuffReadB(), BuffReadF() and of course all the string mainpulation functions as well as number conversion functions. Also see CrLf(), Substitute(), Extract() and NumParts(). Additionally, see mFromString and mToString().

•Email (SMTP) Commands

•SendEMail a_MessageSpecs,a_MessageBody {,ne_ShowProgress}
This command will send an email through the internet to a particular address. You can have multiple addresses and also attachments.

a_MessageSpecs is a one-dimensional array and has to have at least 8 elements. The elements are as described below. a_MessageBody is a one-dimensional array that holds the body of the email message. There can be as many elements as you need. Each element will be a line in the message. The elements can be numerical or string. If they are numerical they will be converted to strings.

If ne_ShowProgress is true or is not given, a Dialog Box will be shown that will show the progress of the operation of sending the email. If it is false then no dialog will be shown.

The program will not proceed to the next line after the SendEmail statement until the email has been successfully sent. If there is a problem then an Error message will be issued and the program will halt. If you wish you can use the OnError statement to trap errors and redirect the flow.

Once the email is successfully sent, program execution will proceed. If you specify ne_ShowProgress as false then you may want to display a message of your own design.

a_MessageSpecs[0] = The user ID of the email account. This is the name of the email account e.g. jimsmith

a_MessageSpecs[1] = The Host ID of the email account. This is the email server name e.g. mail.somehost.net

a_MessageSpecs[2] = The sender's email address. This is the address of the sender e.g. jimsmith@somehost.net

a_MessageSpecs[3] = The TO addresses. This is the addresses to send the email to. This can be many addresses separated with a Crl/Lf character pair (see CrlLf()). e.g. "rayd@yahoo.com"+crlf()+"marylew@hotmail.com"

a_MessageSpecs[4] = The CC addresses. This is the addresses to send a Carbon Copy of the email to. This can be many addresses separated with a Cr/Lf character pair. e.g. "rayd@yahoo.com"+crlf()+"marylew@hotmail.com"

a_MessageSpecs[5] = The BCC addresses. This is the addresses to send a Blind Carbon Copy of the email to. This can be many addresses separated with a Cr/Lf character pair.e.g. "rayd@yahoo.com"+crlf()+"marylew@hotmail.com"

a_MessageSpecs[6] = The Subject. This is the subject header of the email.

a_MessageSpecs[7] = Attachments. This is a list of files to be sent along with the email. The names of the files have to be full path and extension. Also the names of the files have to be separated with a Cr/Lf character pair. If a file does not exist the email will not be sent and an error will occur.

a_MessageSpecs[8] = This element is optional and if it is not given or is not an integer that is greater than 0 then it will be ignored. The email socket used will default to using port 25. With is optional element you can set a different port to send the SMTP data over. If it is given and is a valid integer greater than 0 and less than 0xFFFF then the port will be set to the value specified in the element.

Note: *The email socket utilizes port 25 to send the email and thus you have to have an ISP that allows SMTP email sending and it has to be over port 25. You can change the port by specifying its number in the 9th element of the parameters array (a_MessageSpecs). However, most SMTP servers that serve ports other than 25 also require some authentication hand shaking and this email socket does not have a provision for doing this.*

Example:
```
data a;"myname"                                      //User ID (account id)
data a;"mail.myserver.net"                           //Host ID (email server)
data a;"myname@myserver.net"                         //From Address  (sender's address)
data a;"myfriend1@somedomain.net"+crlf()+"myfriend2@hotmail.com" //To addresses
data a;""                                            //CC addresses
data a;""                                            //BCC addresses
data a;"test email from RB"                          //Subject
data a;"d:\FileName1.doc"+crlf()+"c:\Test\FileName2.Jpg" //Attachment files
data b;"Hello Guys,"+spaces(20)+DateStr(Now())       //message body
```

```
data b;"","This is a test email sent from RB"
data b;"These lines are to test math:"
data b;123+45,sin(23),"bbbbb"+3456,"",""
data b;"sam"
sendemail a,b                              //send the email
print "done"
```

•TCP Sockets Functions

There are **_two TCP sockets_** provided in RobotBASIC. A **_Server and a Client_** socket. Use the Server socket to accept connections from TCP Client sockets connecting to your application. Use the client socket to connect to a system that has a TCP Server socket. All the functions below have a prefix which is either TCPC_ to indicate functions that deal with the Client Socket, or TCPS_ to indicate functions that deal with the Server Socket.

The server socket can accept multiple clients. It can receive from any or all the clients and can BROADCAST to all the clients. Data received from clients connected to a server will be appended to a buffer (only one) as they are received. All clients will put data in the ONE buffer. When the server sends data it will be sent to ALL connected clients.

To start a server you must activate it using the TCPS_Serve(). To obtain the data received into the server receive buffer use the TCPS_Read() and to send data use TCPS_Send(). To terminate serving use TCPS_Close().

To use a client socket you must connect to a server socket using the TCPC_Connect() and you close a connection using TCPC_Close(). To send data use TCPC_Send() and to obtain the data in the receive buffer use TCPC_Read().

The client socket has a receive buffer where all data received from the server will be appended. Once you read the buffer it will be erased. You can find out how many bytes there are in the buffer before you read it using TCPC_BuffCount().

Once a client has established a connection to a server the link can be thought of as a Buffered Asynchronous Serial Link and for all intents and purposes it acts as so, except it is over the internet or LAN or WAN or WiFi.

To enable the server in identifying the data as being from one client or another you can send header data and likewise to identify data from the server as being targeted to a particular client then again you must add a header to indicate so.

Since there is only one server socket in RobotBASIC then you cannot create two server sockets simultaneously in the same program. However, it is possible to run two RobotBASIC programs or two instances of the same RB program on the same machine. If you do this you must ensure that none of these instances is serving on the same port. You will get an error if you do.

If you wish to change the port a server socket serves you must TCPS_Close() it and then TCPS_Serve() to open it again but with the new Port.

You must not have two instance of a server socket serving the same port on the same IP address. If you do you will get a Window system error and your program will halt.

There is only one client socket in RB and you can only connect to one server at a time. You can TCPC_Close() to disconnect the client from a server and then TCPC_Connect() to open it again but connecting to a different server IP or port. You can have multiple instances of the same program all connecting to the same server. However, when the server sends data they will *all* receive the same data. If you wish to target a particular instance you must establish a system of addressing and handshaking *programmatically* so that the server can target a particular client.

When data is received by the server it will be appended to a buffer. You can find out how much data there is in a buffer using TCPS_BuffCount(). You can have the server automatically append a header to all received packets that identify the client that sent the packet. This feature is off by default but can be turned on or off using TCPS_Header(). See the details of the header in the description of TCPS_Header().

When data is received by the client it will be appended to a buffer. You can find out how much data there is in a buffer using TCPC_BuffCount(). The client data does not have the option of a header since a client only receives data from the server it is connected to and this is known by the client already since it connected to the server.

<u>Note:</u> **The OnTCPC and OnTCPS statements will interrupt normal program flow and jump to a subroutine (event handler) that must handle the event and then return back to program execution. This occurs every time there are bytes in the receive buffer of the server (onTCPS) or the client (OnTCPC). Reading the buffer will clear it.**

Example: For a more complex example of how to use this facility see the TCP_Server_Demo.BAS and TCP_Client_Demo.Bas programs. You will find these in the RobotBASIC downloadable zip file from **www.robotBASIC.com**. The example below is a simple one that shows how to create two sockets that talk to each other.

```
MainProgram:
  addmemo "ss",10,40,350,250 \ addmemo "sr",10,340,350,250 \ readonlymemo "sr"
  addmemo "cs",380,40,350,250 \ addmemo "cr",380,340,350,250 \ readonlymemo "cr"
  addcheckbox "s",10,320,"Add Header",1
  xyText 120,10,"Server Send",,15,fs_Bold \ xyText 510,10,"Client Send",,15,fs_Bold
  xyText 120,310,"Server Receive",,15,fs_Bold \ xyText 510,310,"Client Receive",,15,fs_Bold
  n = tcps_serve() \n = tcps_header(on) \ delay 10 \ n = tcpc_connect(tcp_LocalIP())
  ontcps tcpsHandler \ ontcpc tcpcHandler \ onmemo mHandler \ oncheckbox cHandler
  while true
```

```
     wend
   end
 tcpsHandler:
   setmemotext "sr",tcps_read()
   setmemoselection "sr",memolinescount("sr")+1,1,1
   focusmemo "cs"
   ontcps tcpsHandler
 return
 tcpcHandler:
   setmemotext "cr",tcpc_read()
   setmemoselection "cr",memolinescount("cr")+1,1,1
   focusmemo "ss"
   ontcpc tcpcHandler
 return
 mHandler:
   lm = LastMemo()
   if lm == "ss" then n=tcps_send(getmemotext(lm))
   if lm == "cs" then n=tcpc_send(getmemotext(lm))
   onmemo mHandler
 return
 cHandler:
   lc =lastcheckbox()
   n = tcps_header(getcheckbox(lc))
   oncheckbox cHandler
 return
```

•General Functions
•TCP_LocalIP()
Returns the IP address of the machine the program is running on. This is useful for knowing the IP address of the local machine so as to enable remote clients (and UDP sockets) to identify the machine.

•Server Functions
•TCPS_Serve({ne_Port})
Activates the server and starts it listening on the given Port. If the Port number is not specified or is less than 1 or is greater than 65535 then 50000 is assumed. The function always returns 1.

If you attempt to activate the server on a port that is currently being used by another server on the same machine you will get a Window system error and your program will halt. You must not have two sockets (TCP or UDP) serving the same Port number on the same IP address. Whether they are from two RB programs or even non-RB programs.

•TCPS_Header({on|off})
Data received by the server can have a header added to it that says [From:IP:Port: N Bytes]. Where N is the number of bytes received and IP:Port is the IP address and port of the client

that sent the data. This is appended to every group of bytes received from a client sending to the server. By default there is no header, but you can turn on header appending using this function.

If you specify *on* the header appending is turned on. *Off* will turn it off. If you do not specify either, the state will not be changed. The function returns the current state of the header appending before changing it.

Note: This header is appended by the server when it receives the data. It is not part of the received data. The sender may put its own header information which is not under the control of the server.

•TCPS_BuffCount()
Returns the number of bytes in the server's receive buffer. You can obtain the bytes using TCPS_Read().

•TCPS_Read()
Returns a string which contains the bytes in the server's receive buffer at the time of reading and clears the buffer at the same time. If there is no data then a blank string will be returned "". You can treat the returned buffer as a string or you can use it with the BuffRead/Write() manipulation functions.

It is possible for the buffer to contain more bytes than is reported by TCPS_BuffCount() by the time you read it if a client is sending data at a rapid pace. The data is not lost since the buffer will continue to append it until you attempt to read the buffer. When you read the buffer the current data in it is returned by the function and is cleared at the same time. If data comes while this operation is occurring it won't be lost; it will be appended to the buffer after it is cleared.

To effect a controlled rate of sending and receiving you need to establish a sequencing protocol so as to prevent sending when the server does not want to receive and vice versa.

•TCPS_Peek()
Returns the bytes in the buffer at the time of peeking but *does not clear the buffer*. This is useful if you wish to see what data there is in the buffer before you read it and remove the data from it.

•TCPS_Send(se_Data)
Attempts to send se_Data to *all* the clients connected to the server. The function will wait until all the data has been sent or a time out has occurred.

The function will always return true. To check if the data has actually been sent you must

312

check the status string using TCPS_Status(). The string will contain the words 'Sent N Bytes' if successful or 'Error:N' if not. Where N is a code that indicates the nature of the error

•TCPS_Close()

Deactivates the server. All clients connected to it will be disconnected. If the server is not currently active there is no effect. The function always returns true.

You need to make sure you issue this function before terminating your program to effect a controlled disconnect from clients.

•TCPS_Status()

Returns a string that shows the status of the client socket. This can be one of the following:

Server Off	occurs when the socket is not activated.
Listening	occurs when the socket is activated and is ready to accept clients.
Accepted [IP:Port]	occurs when the socket has accepted and connected to a client. IP:Port is the client's address and port.
Received N Bytes [IP:Port]	occurs when the server receives data from a client. N is the number of bytes received and IP is the address of the sending client and Port is its Port number.
Error:N	occurs when any problem is encountered with the link to a client. N indicates the nature of the error.
Client Disconnected [IP:Port]	occurs when a client disconnects from the server. IP:Port is the client's address and port.
Sent N Bytes	occurs when the server has sent data. N is the number of bytes that where intended to be sent.

•Client Functions
•TCPC_Connect(se_ServerIPaddress{,ne_ServerPort})

Attempts to connect the client to the server with the desired IP address and Port number. If the port number is not given or is less than 1 or is greater than 65535 then it will be assumed to be 50000. If it is successful the status of the client will show 'Connected:IP' so to make sure the client is connected you must check the status string using TCPC_Status(). The function always returns true.

•TCPC_ConnectHost(se_ServerName{,ne_ServerPort})

Attempts to connect the client to the server with the desired Name Address and Port number. A Name Address can be an IP address or a name like "My Server Machine". The text format has to correspond to a valid name on the network that can be converted to an IP address by the router. If it is successful the status of the client will show 'Connected:IP' so to make sure the client is connected you must check the status string using TCPC_Status(). The function always returns true.

•TCPC_BuffCount()

Returns the number of bytes in the client's receive buffer. You can obtain the bytes using TCPC_Read().

•TCPC_Read()

Returns a string which contains the bytes in the client's receive buffer at the time of reading and clears the buffer at the same time. If there is no data then a blank string will be returned "". You can treat the returned buffer as a string or you can use it with the BuffRead/Write() manipulation functions.

It is possible for the buffer to contain more bytes than is reported by TCPC_BuffCount() by the time you read it if the server is sending data at a rapid pace. The data is not lost since the buffer will continue to append it until you attempt to read the buffer. When you read the buffer the current data in it is returned by the function and it is cleared at the same time. If data comes while this operation is occurring it won't be lost; it will be appended to the buffer after it is cleared.

To obtain a controlled rate of sending and receiving you need to establish a sequencing protocol so as to prevent sending when the client does not want to receive and vice versa.

•TCPC_Peek()

Returns the bytes in the buffer at the time of peeking but *does not clear the buffer*. This is useful if you wish to see what data there is in the buffer before you read it and remove the data from it.

•TCPC_Send(se_Data)

Attempts to send se_Data to the connected server. The function will wait until all the data has been sent or a time out has occurred.

The function will always return true. To check if the data has actually been sent you must check the status string using TCPC_Status(). The string will contain the words 'Sent N Bytes' if successful or 'Error:N' if not.

•TCPC_Close()

Disconnects the client from the server it is currently connected to. If the client is not currently connected to any server no action is taken. The function always returns true.

You need to make sure you issue this function before terminating your program to execute a controlled disconnect from a server.

•TCPC_Status()

Returns a string that shows the status of the client socket. This can be one of the following:

Disconnected	occurs when the socket is not connected to a server.
Disconnecting	occurs when the socket is in the process of disconnecting from the server.
Looking Up	occurs when the socket is looking up the IP address of the required server.
Connecting	occurs when the server has been found and the client is in the process of connecting to it.
Connected:IP	occurs when the client has established a link with a server. IP is the address of the server.
Error:N	occurs if the client is unable to find, connect or send data to a server. N is the number of the error and identifies what is the cause.
Received N Bytes	occurs when the client has received data from the server into its receive buffer. N is the number of bytes received.
Sent N Bytes	occurs when the client has successfully sent data to the server. N is the number of bytes sent.

•UDP Sockets Functions

RobotBASIC allows you to create ***multiple*** UDP sockets in the same program which can be used to Send and Receive data over the UDP protocol. This protocol does not require that you connect to a host and does not guarantee that any data you send to one are actually received by it. All it guarantees is that the host address (IP) you provided is a valid one and that the data was sent to it. No guarantee that it received the data fully or partially or not at all. It is up to you to provide some kind of handshaking.

When you start a socket you specify the port number it will serve (i.e. receive data from). You can have multiple sockets in the same program and multiple RB programs running on the same machine (i.e. IP) that create sockets. *However, you MUST NOT have two sockets (UDP or TCP) that serve the same Port number on the same IP whether they are running in the same program or in different programs on the same machine (i.e. same IP). Whether they are from two RB programs or even non-RB programs.*

When you use the socket to send data you must specify the IP address and the Port of the target socket which could be on a different machine, a different program or the same program. *However, you must not send data to a port on the same IP as the sender socket that is not being served by another socket. If you do you will get a Windows system error and your program will halt.*

When data is received by the socket it will be appended to a buffer. Each socket has its own receive buffer. You can find out how much data there is in a buffer using UDP_BuffCount(). You can have the socket automatically append a header to all received packets that identify the sender. This feature is off by default but can be turned on or off using UDP_Header(). See the details of the header in the description of UDP_Header().

The socket can receive and send simultaneously, so you can establish a buffered asynchronous serial communications system which happens to be over the Internet or LAN or WAN or WiFi.

Note: There is no UDP_Close function. Once a UDP socket is created and associated to a port it will be active until the program finishes. You will not be able to create another socket with the same port again during the life of the program. If you do, all you will be doing is renaming the same socket. You can, of course, send to different IP/Port addresses on the fly using the socket so there is no need for it to be closed (unlike a client/server socket).

Also see TCP_LocalIP().

Note: The OnUDP statement will interrupt normal program flow and jump to a subroutine (event handler) that must handle the event and then return back to program execution. This occurs every time there are bytes in the receive buffer of the UDP socket. Reading the buffer will clear it.

Example: For a more complex example of how to use this facility see the UDP_IO_Demo.BAS program. You will find this program in the RobotBASIC downloadable zip file from **www.robotBASIC.com**.

The example below is a simple one that shows how to create two sockets that talk to each other.

```
MainProgram:
  addmemo "u1s",10,40,350,250 \ addmemo "u1r",10,340,350,250 \ readonlymemo "u1r"
  addmemo "u2s",380,40,350,250 \ addmemo "u2r",380,340,350,250 \ readonlymemo "u2r"
  addcheckbox "u1",10,320,"Add Header",1 \addcheckbox "u2",380,320,"Add Header",1
  xyText 120,10,"UDP 1 Send",,15,fs_Bold \ xyText 510,10,"UDP 2 Send",,15,fs_Bold
  xyText 120,310,"UDP 1 Receive",,15,fs_Bold \ xyText 510,310,"UDP 2 Receive",,15,fs_Bold
  n = udp_start("u1",4000) \ n = udp_start("u2",5000)
  n = udp_header("u1",on) \ n = udp_header("u2",on)
  onudp udpHandler \ onmemo mHandler \ oncheckbox cHandler
  while true
  wend
end
udpHandler:
  if udp_buffcount("u1")
    setmemotext "u1r",udp_read("u1")
    setmemoselection "u1r",memolinescount("u1r")+1,1,1
    focusmemo "u2s"
  endif
  if udp_buffcount("u2")
    setmemotext "u2r",udp_read("u2")
    setmemoselection "u2r",memolinescount("u2r")+1,1,1
```

316

```
      focusmemo "u1s"
    endif
    onudp udpHandler
  return
  mHandler:
    lm = LastMemo()
    if lm == "u1s" then n=udp_send("u1",getmemotext(lm),tcp_LocalIP(),5000)
    if lm == "u2s" then n=udp_send("u2",getmemotext(lm),tcp_LocalIP(),4000)
    onmemo mHandler
  return
  cHandler:
    lb =lastcheckbox()
    n = udp_header(lb,getcheckbox(lb))
    oncheckbox cHandler
  return
```

•UDP_Start(se_Name{,ne_ListenPort})

This function will create a UDP socket and give it the name se_Name which is the name you must use with all the other UDP functions.

ne_ListenPort is optional and if not specified or is less than 1 then 50001 will be assumed.

You must not try to create more than one socket on the same port either in the same program or in distinct programs that run simultaneously on the same machine (i.e. same IP). If you create a socket with the same listening port as another socket on the same machine both sockets may not receive data or one will get all the data while the other would not; there is no guarantee to the behavior except that problems will arise.

In the same program if you try to start more than one UDP socket serving the same IP you will just be renaming the socket and you will not be able to access the previous socket.

Once created a port can only listen on the specified port upon creation (or 50001 if not specified). However it can send to *any* port and IP address any time, so it can send to one machine some moment and another later. ***However you must not send to a port on the same IP as the sending socket that does not have an associated socket. This will cause a Windows system error and your program will halt.***

If you wish to run two instances of the same program on the same machine then you must not have the two instances use the same port for listening simultaneously. You can get around this by providing a means for setting the listening port before starting the socket for each instance of the program.

Each socket you create will have its own status and data receive buffer and count value.

•UDP_BuffCount(se_Name)

317

Returns the number of bytes in the receive buffer of the UDP socket. The socket will continue to receive data from any sender and will append them to a buffer as they are received. The buffer will continue to grow until you read it. When you read a buffer it will be also cleared at the same time.

•UDP_Read(se_Name)
Returns the bytes in the buffer at the time of reading and clears the buffer at the same time. If there is no data then a blank string will be returned "". You can treat the returned buffer as a string or you can use it with the BuffRead/Write() manipulation functions.

It is possible for the buffer to contain more bytes than is reported by UDP_BuffCount() by the time you read it if a sender is sending data at a rapid pace. The data is not lost since the buffer will continue to append it until you attempt to read the buffer. When you read the buffer the current data in it is returned by the function and it is cleared at the same time. If data comes while this operation is occurring it won't be lost; it will be appended to the buffer after it is cleared.

To effect a controlled rate of sending and receiving you need to establish a sequencing protocol so as to prevent sending when the receiver does not want to receive and vice versa.

•UDP_Peek(se_Name)
Returns the bytes in the buffer at the time of peeking but ***does not clear the buffer***. This is useful if you wish to see what data there is in the buffer before you read it and remove the data from it.

•UDP_Send(se_Name,se_Data,se_TargetIP{,ne_TargetPort})
Will send the buffer se_Data to a target machine with UDP support. The machine is identified with the se_TargetIP and ne_TargetPort combination.

The function will wait until all the data has been sent or a time out has occurred. If a time out occurs then the status string will be set to "Bad Address [IP]" and the function will return 0. If the function succeeds then the status string will be set to "Sent N Bytes [IP:PORT]" and will return the number of bytes actually sent. Check the status string using UDP_Status() and also check the value returned in comparison to the number of bytes in the sent buffer.

Note: *The UDP socket is limited to sending only <u>a maximum of 2048</u> bytes in one go. So you must not send a buffer longer than this number. If se_Data is longer than 2048 it will be shortened to that length and any data beyond 2058 bytes will be lost. If you need to send more than 2048 bytes you must send them over multiple sends.*

•UDP_Header(se_Name{,on|off})
Data received by the socket can have a header added to it that says [From:IP:N Bytes]. Where

N is the number of bytes received and IP is the IP address of the sender. This is appended to every group of bytes received from a sender sending to the socket. By default there is no header, but you can turn on header appending using this function.

If you specify *on* the header appending is turned on. *Off* will turn it off. If you do not specify either, the state will not be changed. The function returns the current state of the header appending before changing it.

Note: This header is appended by the receiver socket when it receives the data. It is not part of the received data. The sender may put its own header information which is not under the control of the receiver socket.

•UDP_Status(se_Name)
This function returns a string that describes the status of the UDP socket. The status can be one of the following:

Received N Bytes [IP]	occurs when data is received. N is the number of bytes received and IP is the IP address of the sender.
No Activity	occurs when there is no activity and also when the socket is first started.
No Data Sent	occurs if you try to send an empty string.
Bad Address [IP]	occurs when the send IP address is a bad address and IP is the bad address.
Sent N Bytes [IP:PORT]	occurs after a UDP_Send() succeeds. N is the actual number of bytes sent and IP is the destination IP address and PORT is the destination PORT.

Other messages are also possible depending on certain situations.

Commands & Functions Alphabetically

•<u>The Commands List</u> (350)

<u>Note:</u> See notes at the top of the Standard User Interfacing section

AbortMethod {ne_AbortCode}
AddButton se_Name,ne_X,ne_Y{,ne_W{,ne_H{,se_Hint}}}
AddCheckBox
se_Name,ne_X,ne_Y{,se_Caption{,ne_Checked{,ne_LeftOrRight{,se_Hint}}}}
AddEdit se_Name,ne_X,ne_Y{,ne_W{,ne_H{,e_Text{,se_Hint}}}}
AddListBox se_Name,ne_X,ne_Y{,ne_Width{,se_Items{,se_Hint}}}
AddListBoxItem se_Name{,e_NewItem}
AddMemo se_Name,ne_X,ne_Y{,ne_W{,ne_H{,se_Text{,se_Hint}}}}
AddMemoLine se_Name{,e_Text}
AddRBGroup
se_Name,ne_X,ne_Y{,ne_Width{,ne_Height{,ne_Columns{,se_Buttons{,se_Caption{,se_Hint}}}}}}
AddRBGroupButton se_Name{,e_ButtonCaption}
AddSlider
se_Name,ne_X,ne_Y{,ne_Width{,ne_Min{,ne_Max{,ne_Vertical{,ne_TickFreq{,ne_BigIncr{,se_Hint}}}}}}}
AddSpinner
se_Name,ne_X,ne_Y{,ne_W{,ne_H{,ne_Min{,ne_Max{,ne_Incr{,ne_Vertical{,ne_Wrap{,se_Hint}}}}}}}}
AddTimer se_Name{,ne_Period}
AllowEvents {on|off}
Arc
ne_X1,ne_Y1,ne_X2,ne_Y2{,ne_StartAngle{,ne_ArcLength{,ne_PenWidth{,ne_PenColor}}}}
Beep {ne_Count}
BmpChangeClr se_SourceFile,ne_FromColor,ne_ToColor{,ne_Tolerance}
BmpCompare se_SourceFile{,se_CompareFile{,se_ToFile{,ne_Tolerance}}}
BmpContrast se_SourceFile,ne_Ratio{,ne_Threshold{,se_ToFile}}
BmpEdges se_SourceFile{,ne_Threshold{,se_ToFile{,ne_EdgeType}}}
BmpFindClr
se_SourceFile,ne_Color,vn_Result{,vn_Confidence{,ne_ClrTolerance{,ne_ConfidenceTolerance{,ne_GridSize{a_SectorsCount}}}}}

BmpNegative se_SourceFile{,se_ToFile}

BmpRGB se_SourceFile,ne_Rratio,ne_Gratio,ne_Bratio{,se_ToFile}

BmpStats a_Stats{,se_FileName}

BmpToBW se_SourceFile{,ne_Threshold{,se_ToFile}}

BmpToCb {se_FileName{,ne_X{,ne_Y{,ne_Width{,ne_Height}}}}}

BmpToGray
se_SourceFileName{,se_ToFileName{,ne_RedRatio{,ne_GreenRatio{,ne_BlueRatio}}}}

BorderEdit se_Name{,true|false}

BorderMemo se_Name{,true|false}

BuffPrintB vs_BuffString{,Expr,Expr,Expr...}

BuffPrintT vs_BuffString{,Expr,Expr;Expr...}{;|,}

CbFitBMP {se_FileName{,ne_Width{,ne_Height}}}

CbToBMP {se_FileName}

CheckSerBuffer vn_NumOfBytes

Circle ne_X1,ne_Y1,ne_X2,ne_Y2{,ne_PenColor{,ne_FillColor}}

CircleWH ne_X1,ne_Y1,ne_Width,ne_Height{,ne_PenColor{,ne_FillColor}}

ClearListBox se_Name

ClearMemo se_Name

ClearRBGroup se_Name

ClearScr {ne_Color}

ClearSerBuffer {ne_Which}

ClrCB

CommaTab {true|false}

CopyFitScr {ne_CopyNumber{,ne_X{,ne_Y{,ne_Width{,ne_Height}}}}}

CopyScr {ne_CopyNumber{,ne_X1{,ne_Y1{,ne_Width{,ne_Height}}}}}

CopyToScr
{ne_CopyNumber{,ne_ScreenX{,ne_ScreenY{,ne_Width{,ne_Height{,ne_MapX{,ne_MapY}}
}}}}}

Data a_Name;Expr{,Expr....}

Debug {Expr1,Expr2;Expr3...}

DebugOff

DebugOn

Declare v_Name {{=}e_InitialValue}{, ...}

Delay {ne_Milliseconds}

DeleteListBoxItem se_Name{,ne_Index}

DeleteMemoLine se_Name{,ne_LineNumber}

DeleteRBGroupButton se_Name{,ne_Index}

Dim a_Name1[ExprN{,ExprN...}]{ , a_Name2[ExprN{,ExprN...}] {, ...}}}...

DrawShape se_Shape,ne_X,ne_Y{,ne_Scale,ne_Color}

EnableButton se_Name{,true|false}

EnableCheckBox se_Name{,true|false}

EnableEdit se_Name{,true|false}

EnableListBox se_Name{,true|false}

EnableMemo se_Name{,true|false}

EnableRBGroup se_Name{,true|false}

EnableSlider se_Name{,true|false}

EnableSpinner se_Name{,true|false}

eRectangle ne_X1,ne_Y1,ne_X2,ne_Y2{,ne_PenWidth{,ne_PenColor}}

eRectangleWH ne_X1,ne_Y1,ne_Width,ne_Height{,ne_PenWidth{,ne_PenColor}}

FilePrintB vn_FileHandle{,Expr,Expr,Expr...}

FilePrintT vn_FileHandle{,Expr,Expr;Expr...}{;|,}

FitBMP {se_FileName{,ne_X{,ne_Y{,ne_Width{,ne_Height}}}}}

FitCb {ne_X{,ne_Y{,ne_Width{,ne_Height}}}}

Flip {on|off}

FlipBMP
{se_FileName{,ne_ScreenX{,ne_ScreenY{,ne_Width{,ne_Height{,ne_MapX{,ne__MapY}}}}
}}}

FlipCb

FloatEdit se_Name{,true|false}

FloodFill {ne_X{,ne_Y{,ne_NewColor{,ne_OldColor}}}}

FloodFill2 {ne_X{,ne_Y{,ne_NewColor{,ne_BorderColor}}}}

FocusButton se_Name

FocusCheckBox se_Name

FocusEdit se_Name

FocusListBox se_Name

FocusMemo se_Name

FocusRBGroup se_Name

FocusSlider se_Name

FocusSpinner se_Name

ge3Dto2DA a_3dPoints,a_CameraSpecs

ge3Dto2DV
ne_X,ne_Y,ne_Z,ne_Rho,ne_Theta,ne_Phi,ne_Dist,ne_CenterX,ne_CenterY,vn_ScrX,vn_ScrY

ge3Dto2DVA ne_X,ne_Y,ne_Z,a_CameraSpecs,vn_ScrX,vn_ScrY

geCentroids a_3DPoints,a_SurfacesSpecs,a_Centroids

gePlotEdges a_3DPoints,a_Edges{,ne_LineWidth{,ne_LineWidth{,ne_Color}}

gePlotSurfaces
a_3DPoints,a_SurfacesSpecs{,ne_DoFilling{,ne_LineWidth{,ne_OnlyVisible{,ne_CentroidAll}
}}}

geRotateA a_3DPoints,ne_RotAngle,ne_AxisCode{,ne_From{,ne_To}}

geRotVx ne_X,ne_Y,ne_Z,ne_RotAngle,vn_X',vn_Y',vn_Z'

geRotVy ne_X,ne_Y,ne_Z,ne_RotAngle,vn_X',vn_Y',vn_Z'

geRotVz ne_X,ne_Y,ne_Z,ne_RotAngle,vn_X',vn_Y',vn_Z'

GetButton vs_Name

GetColor vn_PenColor,vn_BkgrndColor

GetCursor vn_Code
GetError vn_ErrNo{,vs_ErrMessage{,vn_LineNo{,vn_CharNo}}}
GetKey vn_KeyCode
GetKeyE vn_ScanCode
GetLineWidth vn_Width
GetTimeOut vn_TimeOutValue
GetXY vn_X,vn_Y
geVisibles a_3DPoints,a_CameraSpecs,a_SurfacesSpecs{,a_Edges{,ne_ColorFactor}}
GotoXY {ne_X{,ne_Y}}
HideButton se_Name{,true|false}
HideCheckBox se_Name{,true|false}
HideEdit se_Name{,true|false}
HideListBox se_Name{,true|false}
HideMemo se_Name{,true|false}
HideRBGroup se_Name{,true|false}
HideSlider se_Name{,true|false}
HideSliderDial se_Name{,true|false}
HideSpinner se_Name{,true|false}
HonorCrLf {true|false}
#Include "FileName.Ext"{,...}
InlineInputMode {on|off}
InPort ne_PortNumber,vn_ByteValue
Input {e_Prompt,}v_Name | a_Name[,,,] {,...}
IntegerEdit se_Name{,true|false}
Joystick ne_JoystickNo,vn_XAxisPos,vn_YAxisPos,vn_ThrottlePos,vn_Buttons
JoystickE ne_JoystickNo,a_ReturnedData
Line ne_X1,ne_Y1,ne_X2,ne_Y2{,ne_PenWidth{,ne_PenColor}}
LineTo ne_X,ne_Y{,ne_PenWidth{,ne_PenColor}}
LineWidth {ne_Width}
mAdd a_Sourced,a_Destination
mAND a_Source,ExprN
mBezier a_Vertices{,ne_PenWidth{,ne_PenColor}}
mCombineClr a_RedValues,a_GreenValues,a_BlueValues,a_RGBvalues
mConstant a_Source,Expr
mCopy a_Source,a_Destination
mDet a_Source,vn_Determinant
mDFT a_Samples{,ne_WindowFunction}
mDiagonal a_Source,Expr
MediaGetPosition {vn_X{,vn_Y{,vn_Width{,vn_Height}}}}
MediaPause ne_DeviceNumber{,on|off}
MediaPlay ne_DeviceNumber,se_FileName{,ne_Loop}
MediaRecord ne_DeviceNumber,se_FileName

MediaReposition {ne_X{,ne_Y{,ne_Width{,ne_Height}}}}
MediaSave ne_DeviceNumber
MediaShow ne_DeviceNumber{,true|false}
MediaStop ne_DeviceNumber
MediaVideoSize DeviceNumber{,vn_Width{,vn_Height}}
mExpFit a_XYdata,vn_Exponent,vn_Factor
mFFT a_Samples{,ne_WindowFunction}
mFromString a_TextLines,se_String{,se_Separator}
mGraphPaper a_Specs
MicroDelay {ne_Amount}
mInvert a_Source,a_Destination,vn_Determinant
MirrorBMP
{se_FileName{,ne_ScreenX{,ne_ScreenY{,ne_Width{,ne_Height{,ne_MapX{,ne__MapY}}}}
}}}
MirrorCb
mLogFit a_XYdata,vn_Factor,vn_Translation
mmAND a_Source,a_Destination
mmOR a_Source,a_Destination
mmShiftL a_Source,a_Destination
mmShiftR a_Source,a_Destination
mMultiply a_Left,a_Right,a_Result
mmXOR a_Source,a_Destination
mNOT a_Name
mOR a_Name,ExprN
mPlotXY a_Specs,a_Xvalues,a_Yvalues   **OR**   **mPlotXY** a_Specs,a_XYvalues
mPolyFit a_XYdata,a_Specs
mPolygon a_Verices{,ne_FillColor}
mRead a_Name,se_FileName
mReadBMP a_Pixels{,se_FileName{,ne_ClrCode}}
mRegression a_XYData,vn_Slope,vn_Intercept
mScale a_Name,ExprN
mScrFitArray a_Pixels{,ne_X{,ne_Y{,ne_Width{,ne_Height}}}}}
mScrFromArray
a_Pixels{,ne_ScreenX{,ne_ScreenY{,ne_Width{,ne_Height{,ne_ArrayX{,ne_ArrayY}}}}}}
mScrToArray a_Pixels{,ne_X{,ne_Y{,ne_Width{,ne_Height}}}}
mShiftL a_Name,ExprN
mShiftR a_Name,ExprN
mSortR a_Name{,ne_OnRowNumber{,ne_Descending}}
mSortC a_NAme{,ne_OnColumnNumber{,ne_Descending}}
mSub a_Source,a_Destination
mTextFR a_TextLines,se_TextFileName
mTextFW a_TextLines,se_TextFileName

mTranspose a_Source,a_Destination

mWrite a_Name,se_FileName

mWriteBMP a_Pixels{,se_FileName}

mXOR a_Name,ExprN

ngc_DistanceHeading ne_LatA,ne_LonA,ne_LatB,ne_LonB,vn_Distance,vn_Heading

ngc_FractionDistancePoint
ne_LatA,ne_LonA,ne_LatB,ne_LonB,ne_FractionalDistance,vn_Lat,vn_Lon

ngc_LatFromLonCrossing ne_LatA,ne_LonA,ne_LatB,ne_LonB,ne_Lon,vn_Lat

ngc_LonFromLatCrossing ne_LatA,ne_LonA,ne_LatB,ne_LonB,ne_Lat,vn_Lon1,vn_Lon2

ngc_RadialIntersection
ne_LatA,ne_LonA,ne_LatB,ne_LonB,ne_HeadingFromA,ne_Heading,FromB,vn_Lat,vn_Lon

ngc_RadialPoint ne_LatA,ne_LonA,ne_Distance,ne_Heading,vn_Lat,vn_Lon

ngc_TrackPointsFromPoint
ne_LatA,ne_LonA,ne_LatB,ne_LonB,ne_LatD,ne_LonD,ne_DstnceFrmPnt,vn_Lat1,vn_Lon1,vn_Lat2,vn_Lon2

ngc_XTrackError
ne_LatA,ne_LonA,ne_LatB,ne_LonB,ne_LatD,ne_LonD,vn_XTrackDistance,vn_AlongTrackDistance

nrl_DistanceHeading ne_LatA,ne_LonA,ne_LatB,ne_LonB,vn_Distance,vn_Heading

nrl_RadialPoint ne_LatA,ne_LonA,ne_Distance,ne_Heading,vn_Lat,vn_Lon

nwt_GSpeedCourse
ne_WindSpeed,ne_WindDirection,ne_TrueSpeed,ne_Heading,vn_GrndSpeed,vn_CourseHeading

nwt_GSpeedHeading
ne_WindSpeed,ne_WindDirection,ne_TrueSpeed,ne_CourseHeading,vn_GroundSpeed,vn_Heading

nwt_TSpeedHeading
ne_WindSpeed,ne_WindDirection,ne_GrndSpeed,ne_CourseHeading,vn_TrueSpeed,vn_Heading

nwt_TSpeedWSpeed ne_V1,ne_V2,ne_V3,vn_TrueSpeed,vn_WindSpeed

nwt_WSpeedDirection
ne_GroundSpeed,ne_CourseHeading,ne_TrueSpeed,ne_Heading,vn_WindSpeed,vn_WindDirection

nwt_XWind ne_WindSpeed,ne_WindDirection,ne_RunwayHeading,vn_XWind,vn_HeadWind

ObjectGet a_ObjectArray,ne_ObjectNumber

ObjectPut a_ObjectArray,ne_ObjectNumber

OutPort ne_PortNumber,ne_ByteValue

OverlayText
{ne_X{,ne_Y{,e_Text{,se_FontName{,ne_FontSize{,ne_FontStyle{,ne_PenColor}}}}}}

Pie
ne_X1,ne_Y1,ne_X2,ne_Y2{,ne_StartAngle{,ne_ArcLength{,ne_PenColor{,ne_FillColor}}}}

PlaySong {se_Notes}

PlayWav {se_FileName{,ne_Mode{,ne_Loop}}}

PPortIn vn_ByteValue

PPortOut {ne_ByteValue}

Print {Expr,Expr;Expr...}{;|,}

PrinterSetup

PrintScr

rCharge {ne_Value}

rCommPort ne_PortNum {,ne_BaudRate {,ne_NumBits {,ne_Parity {,ne_StopBits {,ne_Protocol}}}}}

ReadBMP
{se_FileName{,ne_ScreenX{,ne_ScreenY{,ne_Width{,ne_Height{,ne_MapX{,ne_MapY}}}}}}
}}

ReadMouse vn_X,vn_Y{,vn_Buttons}

ReadOnlyEdit se_Name{,true|false}

ReadOnlyMemo se_Name{,true|false}

ReadPixel ne_X,ne_Y,vn_Color

ReadScr {se_FileName}

ReadSerSignals vn_Flags

RecordGet a_DataBaseArray,ne_RecordNumber

RecordPut a_DataBaseArray,ne_RecordNumber

Rectangle ne_X1,ne_Y1,ne_X2,ne_Y2{,ne_PenColor{,ne_FillColor}}

RectangleWH ne_X,ne_Y,ne_Width,ne_Height{,ne_PenColor{,ne_FillColor}}

RemoveButton se_Name

RemoveCheckBox se_Name

RemoveEdit se_Name

RemoveListBox se_Name

RemoveMemo se_Name

RemoveRBGroup se_Name

RemoveSlider se_Name

RemoveSpinner se_Name

RemoveTimer se_Name

RenameButton se_CurrentName,se_NewName

ResizeBMP {se_SourceFileName{,ne_Width{,ne_Height{,se_ToFileName}}}}

RestoreScr {ne_X{,ne_Y}}

rFloorColor {ne_Color}

rForward {ne_Pixels}

rGps vn_X,vn_Y

rHeading {ne_Degrees}

rIgnoreCharge {true|false}

rInstError {ne_PercentageLevel}

rInvisible ne_Color1 {,ne_Color2...}

rLocate
ne_X,ne_Y{,ne_Heading{,ne_Size{,ne_BorderColor{,ne_InsideColor{,ne_ObeyFlip}}}}}

RotateBMP
{se_FileName{,ne_Angle{,ne_ScreenX{,ne_ScreenY{,ne_Width{,ne_Height{,ne_MapX{,ne_MapY}}}}}}}}}

RotateCb {ne_Angle}

rPen ne_State {,ne_Color}

rRelocate {ne_X{,ne_Y{,ne_Heading}}}

rSenseType {ne_NumSensors}

rSensor ne_SensorNo,ne_Range,vn_Color,vn_Distance,vn_Found

rSensorA ne_Angle,ne_Range,vn_Color,vn_Distance,vn_Found

rSlip {ne_PercentageLevel}

rSpeed {ne_Speed}

rTurn {ne_Degrees}

SaveScr {ne_X1{,ne_Y1{,ne_X2{,ne_Y2}}}}

SaveScrWH {ne_X1{,ne_Y1{,ne_Width{,ne_Height}}}}

ScrFromCb {ne_ScreenX{,ne_ScreenY{,ne_Width{,ne_Height{,ne_MapX{,ne_MapY}}}}}}

ScrLimits vn_XLimit,vn_YLimit

ScrSetMetrics
{ne_X{,ne_Y{,ne_Width{,ne_Height{,ne_PanelVisible{,ne_AllowResize}}}}}}

ScrGetMetrics
{vn_X{,vn_Y{,vn_Width{,vn_Height{,vn_PanelVisible{,vn_AllowResize}}}}}}

ScrToCb {ne_X{,ne_Y{,ne_Width{,ne_Height}}}}

SeedRandom {ne_Seed}

SendEMail a_MessageSpecs,a_MessageBody {,ne_ShowProgress}

SerBytesIn ne_NumOfBytesToRead,vs_BytesRead,vn_ActualNumberRead

SerialOut Expr {,Expr {, Expr ...}}

SerIn vs_Bytes

SerOut Expr {,Expr {; Expr ...}}

SerPorts vs_PortsList

SetButtonCaption se_Name{,e_Caption}

SetButtonDim se_Name{,ne_X{,ne_Y{,ne_W{,ne_H}}}}

SetButtonFont se_Name{,se_FontType{,ne_FontSize{,ne_FontStyle{,ne_FontColor}}}}

SetCBText {se_Text}

SetCheckBox se_Name{,true|false}

SetCheckBoxCaption se_Name{,e_NewCaption}

SetCheckBoxColor se_Name{,ne_Color}

SetCheckBoxDim se_Name{,ne_X{,ne_Y}}

SetColor {ne_PenColor{,ne_BackGroundColor}}

SetCommPort ne_PortNum {,ne_BaudRate {,ne_NumBits {,ne_Parity {,ne_StopBits {,ne_Protocol}}}}}

SetCursor {ne_CursorShapeCode}

SetEdit se_Name{,e_Value}

SetEditColor se_Name{,ne_Color}

SetEditDim se_Name{,ne_X{,ne_Y{,ne_W{,ne_H}}}}

SetEditFont se_Name{,se_FontType{,ne_FontSize{,ne_FontStyle{,ne_FontColor}}}}

SetEditMask se_Name,se_MaskSpecs

SetInputArea {se_Text}

SetListBox se_Name{,ne_Index}

SetListBoxColor se_Name{,ne_Color}
SetListBoxDim se_Name{,ne_X{,ne_Y{,ne_W}}}
SetListBoxFont se_Name{,se_FontType{,ne_FontSize{,ne_FontStyle{,ne_FontColor}}}}
SetListBoxItems se_Name{,e_ItemsList}
SetMemoColor se_Name{,ne_Color}
SetMemoDim se_Name{,ne_X{,ne_Y{,ne_W{,ne_H}}}}
SetMemoFont se_Name{,se_FontType{,ne_FontSize{,ne_FontStyle{,ne_FontColor}}}}
SetMemoScrollBars se_Name{,ne_Value}
SetMemoSelected se_Name{,ne_StartCharPosition{,ne_NumCharacters}}
SetMemoSelection
se_Name{,ne_LineNumber{,ne_CharacterNumber{,ne_SelectionLength}}}
SetMemoText se_Name{,e_Text}
SetMousePos {ne_X{,ne_Y}
SetPixel {ne_X{,ne_Y{,ne_Color}}}
SetPPortNumber {ne_PortNumber}
SetPromptArea {se_Text}
SetRBGroup se_Name{,ne_Index}
SetRBGroupButtons se_Name{,e_ButtonsList}
SetRBGroupColor se_Name{,ne_Color}
SetRBGroupColumns se_Name{,ne_NumColumns}
SetRBGroupDim se_Name{,ne_X{,ne_Y{,ne_W{,ne_H}}}}
SetRBGroupFont se_Name{,se_FontType{,ne_FontSize{,ne_FontStyle{,ne_FontColor}}}}
SetSerDTR {on|off}
SetSerRTS {on|off}
SetSliderBarEnd se_Name{,ne_Value}
SetSliderBarStart se_Name{,ne_Value}
SetSliderDim se_Name{,ne_X{,ne_Y{,ne_W}}}
SetSliderMax se_Name{,ne_NewValue}
SetSliderMin se_Name{,ne_NewValue}
SetSliderPos se_Name{,ne_PositionValue}
SetSpinner se_Name{,ne_Position}
SetSpinnerDim se_Name{,ne_X{,ne_Y{,ne_W{,ne_H}}}}
SetSpinnerIncr se_Name{,ne_Value}
SetSpinnerMax se_Name{,ne_NewValue}
SetSpinnerMin se_Name{,ne_NewValue}
SetSpinnerWrap se_Name{,true|false}
SetTextBuff {se_Text}
SetTimeOut {ne_MilliSeconds}
SetTimer se_Name{,true|false}
SetTimerPeriod se_Name{,ne_Period}
SetTimerTicks se_Name{,ne_Count}
ShowSliderBar se_Name{,true|false}

SizeBMP se_FileName,vn_Width,vn_Height
SizeCb vn_Width,vn_Height
SortListBox se_Name{,true|false}
Sound ne_Frequency,ne_Duration{,ne_Mode}
Speaker {on|off}
Stepping {On|Off}
Swap v_Left | a_Left[...] ,v_Right | a_Right[...]
TextBuffToCB
ToBMP se_SourceFile{,se_ToFile}
Transparent {on|off}
Undeclare
VarSet se_VarName,e_Value
VPPortIn ne_VirtualPortNo,vn_ByteValue
VPPortOut ne_VirtualPortNo,ne_ByteValue
WaitKey {e_Prompt,}vn_KeyCode
WaitNoKey {ne_MillisWait}
WaitNoKeyE ne_ScanCode{,ne_MillisWait}
WrapMemo se_Name{,true|false}
Write {Expr,Expr;Expr...} {;|,}
WriteBMP {se_FileName{,ne_X{,ne_Y{,ne_Width{,ne_Height}}}}}
WriteScr {se_FileName}
xyInput v_Input{,ne_X{,ne_Y{,e_Title{,e_Default{,ne_BoxLength}}}}}
xyString ne_X,ne_Y,Expr{;expr,expr;...}
xyText
{ne_X{,ne_Y{,Expr{,se_FontName{,ne_FontSize{,ne_FontStyle{,ne_PenColor{,ne_BackgroundColor}}}}}}}}

•The Functions List (475)

Note: See notes at the top of the Standard User Interfacing section

AbortFlag()
Abs(ExprN)
ACos(ExprN)
ACosH(ExprN)
Ascii(se_Text)
ASin(ExprN)
ASinH(ExprN)
ATan(ExprN)
ATan2(ne_X,ne_Y)
ATanH(ExprN)
Average(a_Data)

329

Bin(ExprN{,ne_NumBits})
BinToInt(e_BinaryValue)
BitSwap(ne_Number{,ne_NumberOfBits})
BlueValue(ne_Color)
BuffRead(se_Buffer,ne_Position,ne_NumBytes)
BuffReadB(se_Buffer,ne_Position)
BuffReadF(se_Buffer,ne_Position)
BuffReadF32(se_Buffer,ne_Position)
BuffReadI(se_Buffer,ne_Position)
BuffWrite(se_Buffer,ne_Position,e_Value)
BuffWriteB(se_Buffer,ne_Position,ne_Value)
BuffWriteF32(se_Buffer,ne_Position,ne_Value)
ButtonEnabled(se_Name)
ButtonHasFocus(se_Name)
ButtonHidden(se_Name)
CaptureDlg({se_FileName})
CaptureImage({se_FileName})
CaptureRdy()
CaptureSrc()
CartX(ne_Radius,ne_ThetaRadians)
CartY(ne_Radius,ne_ThetaRadians)
CbRt(ExprN)
Center(se_Text,se_PadChar,ne_NumChars)
Char(ne_AsciiCode)
CheckBoxEnabled(se_Name)
CheckBoxHasFocus(se_Name)
CheckBoxHidden(se_Name)
ClrBit(ne_Number,ne_BitPosition)
ClrByte(ne_Number,ne_BytePosition)
CommandsList()
ConstantsList()
ConsToClr(ne_ColorConstantValue)
Contains(se_Text,se_CharList)
Convert(ne_ValueToConvert, ne_ConversionTypeCode)
CorrCoef(a_Data)
Cos(ne_Radians)
CosH(ExprN)
Count(a_Data)
CrLf()
Date({ne_Type})
DateStr(ne_DateTimeValue)
DateTime(ne_DateTimeValue{,se_Format})

DateTimeStr(ne_DateTimeValue)
DateTimeVal(se_DateTimeString)
DateVal(ne_Year,ne_Month,ne_Day)
Day(ne_DateTimeValue)
DayOfWeek(ne_DateTimeValue)
Degrees({ne_Degrees{,ne_Minutes{,ne_Seconds}}})
Degrees(se_FormattedDegrees)
DeskTopHeight()
DeskTopWidth()
DFtoSF(ExprN)
DirCount()
DirCreate(se_DirPath)
DirCurrent()
DirExists(se_DirPath)
DirList()
DirPrompt()
DirRemove(se_DirPath)
DirSet(se_DirPath)
DiskFree(ne_DiskNumber)
DiskSize(ne_DiskNumber)
DtoR(ne_Degrees)
EditBorder(se_Name)
EditChanged(se_Name)
EditEnabled(se_Name)
EditHasFocus(se_Name)
EditHidden(se_Name)
EditReadOnly(se_Name)
Encrypt(se_Text,se_Key)
ErrMsg(se_MessageText{,se_BoxTitle{,ne_Style}})
Evaluate(se_Expression)
Exp(ExprN)
Exp10(ExprN)
Extract(se_Text,se_SeparatorChars,ne_Part)
FactorColor(ne_Color,ne_Factor)
Factorial(ExprN)
ff_CIFV(PV,INTR,TERM)
ff_CII(PV,FV,TERM)
ff_CIT(PV,INTR,FV)
ff_FV(PMT,INTR,TERM,TYPE)
ff_FVP(FV,INTR,TERM,TYPE)
ff_FVT(PMT,INTR,FV,TYPE)
ff_PV(PMT,INTR,TERM,BAL,TYPE)

ff_PVP(PV,INTR,TERM,BAL,TYPE)
ff_PVT(PMT,INTR,PV,BAL,TYPE)
ff_SLN(COST,SALVAGE,LIFE)
ff_SYD(COST,SALVAGE,LIFE,PERIOD)
FileChangeExt(se_FileName,se_NewExtension)
FileDelete(se_Name)
FileDir(se_Name)
FileDrive(se_Name)
FileClose(ne_FileHandle)
FileCopy(se_SourceFile,se_DestinationFile{,ne_Mode})
FileCreate(se_FileName)
FileDate(se_FileName)
FileEnd(ne_FileHandle)
FileOpen(se_FileName,ne_Mode)
FilePrompt({Expr})
FileRead(ne_FileHandle{,ne_ByteCount)
FileReadB(ne_FileHandle)
FileReadF(ne_FileHandle)
FileReadField(ne_FileHandle{,se_Separator})
FileReadI(ne_FileHandle)
FileSave({Expr})
FilesCount({se_Filter})
FileSeek(ne_FileHandle,ne_FromWhere,ne_OffsetCount)
FileSize(ne_FileHandle)
FileSize(se_Name)
FilesList({se_Filter})
FileWrite(ne_FileHandle,e_Value)
FileWriteB(ne_FileHandle,e_Value)
FileExists(se_FileName)
FileExt(se_Name)
FileName(se_Name)
FilePath(se_Name)
FileRename(se_OldName,se_NewName)
FileSearch(se_FileName,se_DirList)
Format(ExprN,se_FormatSpecifier)
Frac(ExprN)
FunctionsList()
GetBit(ne_Number,ne_BitPosition)
GetButtonCaption(se_Name)
GetButtonFont(se_Name)
GetButtonH(se_Name)
GetButtonW(se_Name)

GetButtonX(se_Name)
GetButtonY(se_Name)
GetByte(ne_Number,ne_BytePosition)
GetCBText()
GetCheckBox(se_Name)
GetCheckBoxCaption(se_Name)
GetCheckBoxColor(se_Name)
GetCheckBoxX(se_Name)
GetCheckBoxY(se_Name)
GetEdit(se_Name)
GetEditColor(se_Name)
GetEditFont(se_Name)
GetEditH(se_Name)
GetEditUnmasked(se_Name)
GetEditW(se_Name)
GetEditX(se_Name)
GetEditY(se_Name)
GetListBox(se_Name)
GetListBoxColor(se_Name)
GetListBoxFont(se_Name)
GetListBoxItem(se_Name,ne_ItemIndex)
GetListBoxList(se_Name)
GetListBoxText(se_Name)
GetListBoxW(se_Name)
GetListBoxX(se_Name)
GetListBoxY(se_Name)
GetMemoCharNo(se_Name)
GetMemoCharPos(se_Name)
GetMemoColor(se_Name)
GetMemoFont(se_Name)
GetMemoH(se_Name)
GetMemoLine(se_Name,ne_LineNumber)
GetMemoLineNo(se_Name)
GetMemoSelection(se_Name)
GetMemoText(se_Name)
GetMemoW(se_Name)
GetMemoX(se_Name)
GetMemoY(se_Name)
GetRBGroup(se_Name)
GetRBGroupButton(se_Name,ne_Index)
GetRBGroupCaption(se_Name)
GetRBGroupColor(se_Name)

GetRBGroupFont(se_Name)
GetRBGroupH(se_Name)
GetRBGroupItems(se_Name)
GetRBGroupText(se_Name)
GetRBGroupW(se_Name)
GetRBGroupX(se_Name)
GetRBGroupY(se_Name)
GetSliderBarEnd(se_Name)
GetSliderBarStart(se_Name)
GetSliderMax(se_Name)
GetSliderMin(se_Name)
GetSliderPos(se_Name)
GetSliderW(se_Name)
GetSliderX(se_Name)
GetSliderY(se_Name)
GetSpinner(se_Name)
GetSpinnerH(se_Name)
GetSpinnerIncr(se_Name)
GetSpinnerMax(se_Name)
GetSpinnerMin(se_Name)
GetSpinnerW(se_Name)
GetSpinnerWrap(se_Name)
GetSpinnerX(se_Name)
GetSpinnerY(se_Name)
GetStrByte(se_String,ne_ByteNumber)
GetTextBuff()
GetTimerPeriod(se_Name)
GetTimerTicks(se_Name)
GreenValue(ne_Color)
Hex(ExprN{,ne_NumBytes})
HexToInt(e_HexValue)
Hour(ne_DateTimeValue)
Insert(se_Text,se_Insert,ne_CharNum)
InString(se_Main,se_Sub{,ne_StartFrom})
IsNumber(Expr)
IsString(Expr)
JustifyL(se_Text,se_PadChar,ne_Len)
JustifyR(se_Text,se_PadChar,ne_Len)
KeyDown({ne_ScanCode})
LastButton()
LastCheckBox()
LastEdit()

LastKey()
LastListBox()
LastMemo()
LastMouse()
LastRBGroup()
LastSlider()
LastSpinner()
LastTimer()
Lat_DM(ne_Degrees)
Lat_DMS(ne_Degrees)
Left(se_Text,ne_NumChars)
LeftTrim(se_Text)
Length(se_Text)
Limit(ne_Value,ne_LowerLimit,ne_UpperLimit)
ListBoxEnabled(se_Name)
ListBoxHasFocus(se_Name)
ListBoxHidden(se_Name)
ListBoxItemsCount(se_Name)
ListBoxSorted(se_Name)
Log(ExprN)
Log2(ExprN)
LogB(ne_Base,ExprN)
Lon_DMS(ne_Degrees)
Lon_DM(ne_Degrees)
Lower(se_Text)
MakeBit(ne_Number,ne_BitPosition,on|off)
MakeByte(ne_Number,ne_BytePosition,ne_ByteValue)
Map(ne_FromValue, ne_FromMin, ne_FromMax, ne_ToMin, ne_ToMax)
mAverage(a_Data)
Max(a_Data)
MaxDim(a_Name{,ne_Dimension})
MaxFloat()
MaxInteger()
MaxV(ExprN1,ExprN2)
mCount(a_Data)
mDim(a_Name)
Median(a_Data)
MediaIsVideo(ne_DeviceNumber)
MediaState(ne_DeviceNumber)
MemoBorder(se_Name)
MemoChanged(se_Name)
MemoEnabled(se_Name)

335

MemoHasFocus(se_Name)
MemoHidden(se_Name)
MemoLinesCount(se_Name)
MemoReadonly(se_Name)
MemoScrollBars(se_Name)
MemoWrap(se_Name)
Millisecond(ne_DateTimeValue)
Min(a_Data)
MinFloat()
MinInteger()
Minute(ne_DateTimeValue)
MinV(ExprN1,ExprN2)
mMax(a_Data)
mMin(a_Data)
Mod(ne_Numerator,ne_Denominator)
Month(ne_DateTimeValue)
mRange(a_Data)
MsgBox(a_TextLines{,e_Title{,ne_X{,ne_Y{,ne_W{,ne_H{,ne_DoWrap}}}}}})
mStdDev(a_Data)
mSum(a_Data)
mToCommaText(a_TextLines)
mToString(a_TextLines{,se_Separator})
mType(a_Name[...])
mVariance(a_Data)
nCr(ne_NumElementsAvailable,ne_NumElementsToSelect)
NLog(ExprN)
NoSpaces(se_Text)
NotContains(se_Text,se_CharList)
Now()
nPr(ne_NumElementsAvailable,ne_NumElementsToSelect)
NumParts(se_Text,se_Separator)
Pi({ne_Multiplier})
PixelClr(ne_X,ne_Y)
PolarA(ne_X,ne_Y)
PolarR(ne_X,ne_Y)
ProbG(ne_Element,ne_Mean,ne_StdDev)
ProbGI(ne_Probability,ne_Mean,ne_StdDev)
ProgName()
PromptBMP({se_Filter})
PromptColor({ne_DefaultColor})
Proper(se_Text)
PutStrByte(se_String,ne_ByteNum,ne_Val)

Random(ExprN)
RandomG(ne_Mean,ne_StdDev)
Range(a_Data)
rBeacon(ne_Color)
RBGroupEnabled(se_Name)
RBGroupHasFocus(se_Name)
RBGroupHidden(se_Name)
RBGroupItemsCount(se_Name)
RBGroupNumColumns(se_Name)
rBumper()
rChargeLevel()
rCommand(ne_Command,ne_Data)
rCompass()
rDBumper({ne_Color})
rDFeel({ne_Color})
re_End({ne_GroupNumber})
re_GrpNumber(se_GroupName)
re_Match(se_Text)
re_NumOfGrps()
re_Replace(se_Text{,se_ReplaceWith{,ne_SartFromPositionNumber{,ne_NumberOfMatchesT
oReplace}}})
re_Search(se_Text{,ne_SartFromPositionNumber})
re_Setup(se_Template{,ne_Mode})
re_Start({ne_GroupNumber})
RedValue(ne_Color)
Replace(se_OriginalString,se_NewSubString,ne_StartingAt)
rFeel()
RGB(ne_RedValue,ne_GreenValue,ne_BlueValue)
rGpsX()
rGpsY()
rGround(ne_SensorNo)
rGroundA(ne_Angle)
Right(se_Text,ne_NumChars)
RightTrim(se_Text)
rLook({ne_Angle})
RotShape(se_ShapeString,ne_Direction)
Round(ExprN)
RoundDN(ExprN{,ne_Type})
RoundUP(ExprN{,ne_Type})
rPoints()
rRange({ne_Angle})
rSense({ne_Color})

RtoD(ne_Radians)
Second(ne_DateTimeValue)
SetBit(ne_Number,ne_BitPosition)
SetByte(ne_Number,ne_BytePosition)
SFtoDF(ExprN)
Sign(ExprN)
SignExtend8(ExprN)
SignExtend16(ExprN)
Sin(ne_Radians)
SinH(ExprN)
SliderBarHidden(se_Name)
SliderDialHidden(se_Name)
SliderEnabled(se_Name)
SliderHasFocus(se_Name)
SliderHidden(se_Name)
Soundex(se_Text{,ne_Length})
Spaces(ne_NumOfSpaces)
Spawn(se_ProgramName,se_Parameters,ne_Mode)
Spell(ExprN)
SpinnerEnabled(se_Name)
SpinnerHasFocus(se_Name)
SpinnerHidden(se_Name)
SqRt(ExprN)
sRepeat(se_RepeatChars,ne_NumTimes)
StatementsList()
StdDev(a_Data)
StringBox(se_Text{,e_Title{,ne_X{,ne_Y{,ne_W{,ne_H{,ne_DoWrap}}}}}})
StrInput({e_Caption{,e_Prompt{,e_Default}}})
StrOfBytes(Expr{,Expr{,....}})
Substitute(se_Text,se_TextToReplace,se_ReplaceWith)
Substring(se_Text{,ne_StartChar{,ne_NumCharacters}})
Sum(a_Data)
Tan(ne_Radians)
TanH(ExprN)
TCP_LocalIP()
TCPC_BuffCount()
TCPC_Close()
TCPC_Connect(se_ServerIPaddress{,ne_ServerPort})
TCPC_ConnectHost(se_ServerName{,ne_ServerPort})
TCPC_Peek()
TCPC_Read()
TCPC_Send(se_Data)

TCPC_Status()
TCPS_BuffCount()
TCPS_Close()
TCPS_Header({on|off})
TCPS_Peek()
TCPS_Read()
TCPS_Send(se_Data)
TCPS_Serve({ne_Port})
TCPS_Status()
TextBox(se_FileName{,e_Title{,ne_X{,ne_Y{,ne_W{,ne_H{,ne_DoWrap}}}}}})
TextHeight(se_Text{,se_FontName{,ne_FontSize{,ne_FonctStyle}}})
TextWidth(se_Text{,se_FontName{,ne_FontSize{,ne_FonctStyle}}})
Time({ne_Type})
Timer( )
TimerIsOn(se_Name)
TimeStr(ne_DateTimeValue)
TimeVal(ne_Hour,ne_Minute,ne_Second,ne_Milliseconds)
ToByte(Expr)
ToCommaText(se_Text)
ToNumber(Expr{,ne_Default})
ToString(Expr)
ToTime(ne_Seconds)
Trim(se_Text)
UDP_BuffCount(se_Name)
UDP_Header(se_Name{,on|off})
UDP_Peek(se_Name)
UDP_Read(se_Name)
UDP_Send(se_Name,se_Data,se_TargetIP{,ne_TargetPort})
UDP_Start(se_Name{,ne_ListenPort})
UDP_Status(se_Name)
Upper(se_Text)
usbm_ClearRecentError()
usbm_CloseDevice(ne_DeviceNumber)
usbm_DeviceCmd(ne_DeviceNumber,se_Data)
usbm_DeviceSpecs(ne_DeviceNumber)
usbm_DeviceValid(ne_DeviceNumber)
usbm_DirectionA(ne_DeviceNumber,ne_PinsDirection,ne_PinsFormat)
usbm_DirectionAIn(ne_DeviceNumber)
usbm_DirectionAInPullUp(ne_DeviceNumber)
usbm_DirectionAOut(ne_DeviceNumber)
usbm_DirectionB(ne_DeviceNumber,ne_PinsDirection,ne_PinsFormat)
usbm_DirectionBIn(ne_DeviceNumber)

usbm_DirectionBInPullUp(ne_DeviceNumber)
usbm_DirectionBOut(ne_DeviceNumber)
usbm_DllSpecs()
usbm_ErrorSpecs()
usbm_FindDevices()
usbm_InitLCD(ne_DeviceNumber,ne_Sel, ne_Port)
usbm_InitPorts(ne_DeviceNumber)
usbm_InitPortsU401(ne_DeviceNumber)
usbm_InitPortsU421(ne_DeviceNumber)
usbm_InitPortsU451(ne_DeviceNumber)
usbm_InitSPI(ne_DeviceNumber,ne_Specs)
usbm_LCDCmd(ne_DeviceNumber,ne_CommandByte)
usbm_LCDData(ne_DeviceNumber,ne_DataByte)
usbm_NumberOfDevices()
usbm_Read1Wire(ne_DeviceNumber)
usbm_Read1WireBit(ne_DeviceNumber)
usbm_ReadA(ne_DeviceNumber)
usbm_ReadB(ne_DeviceNumber)
usbm_ReadLatches(ne_DeviceNumber)
usbm_Reset1Wire(ne_DeviceNumber,ne_Specs)
usbm_ResetBit(ne_DeviceNumber,ne_PinNumber)
usbm_SetBit(ne_DeviceNumber,ne_PinNumber)
usbm_SetReadTimeout(ne_Time)
usbm_SPIMaster(ne_DeviceNumber,se_DataBytes)
usbm_SPISlaveRead(ne_DeviceNumber)
usbm_SPISlaveWrite(ne_DeviceNumber,se_DataBytes)
usbm_Stepper(ne_DeviceNumber,se_DataSpecs)
usbm_StrobeRead(ne_DeviceNumber,se_ByteData)
usbm_StrobeReads(ne_DeviceNumber,se_ByteData)
usbm_StrobeWrite(ne_DeviceNumber,se_ByteData)
usbm_StrobeWrites(ne_DeviceNumber,se_ByteData)
usbm_Wire2Control(ne_DeviceNumber,ne_Signal)
usbm_Wire2Data(ne_DeviceNumber,se_DataBytes)
usbm_Write1Wire(ne_DeviceNumber,ne_Data)
usbm_Write1WireBit(ne_DeviceNumber,ne_BitValue)
usbm_WriteA(ne_DeviceNumber,ne_ByteValue)
usbm_WriteABit(ne_DeviceNumber,ne_AndingMask, ne_OringMask)
usbm_WriteB(ne_DeviceNumber,ne_ByteValue)
usbm_WriteBBit(ne_DeviceNumber,ne_AndingMask, ne_OringMask)
Variance(a_Data)
varsList({ne_Global})
varType(se_VarName)

varValue(se_VarName)
vType(v_VarName)
WavBusy()
Within(ne_Value,ne_LowerLimit,ne_UpperLimit)
Year(ne_DateTimeValue)

•The Simulator Commands (18)

Note: See notes at the top of the Standard User Interfacing section

rCharge {ne_Value}
rCommPort ne_PortNum {,ne_BaudRate {,ne_NumBits {,ne_Parity {,ne_StopBits {,ne_Protocol}}}}}
rFloorColor {ne_Color}
rForward {ne_Pixels}
rGps vn_X,vn_Y
rHeading {ne_Degrees}
rIgnoreCharge {true|false}
rInstError {ne_PercentageLevel}
rInvisible ne_Color1 {,ne_Color2...}
rLocate ne_X,ne_Y{,ne_Heading{,ne_Size{,ne_BorderColor{,ne_InsideColor}}}}
rPen ne_State {,ne_Color}
rRelocate {ne_X{,ne_Y{,ne_Heading}}}
rSenseType {ne_NumSensors}
rSensor ne_SensorNo,ne_Range,vn_Color,vn_Distance,vn_Found
rSensorA ne_Angle,ne_Range,vn_Color,vn_Distance,vn_Found
rSlip {ne_PercentageLevel}
rSpeed {ne_Speed
rTurn {ne_Degrees}

•The Simulator Functions (16)

Note: See notes at the top of the Standard User Interfacing section

rBeacon(ne_Color)
rBumper()
rChargeLevel()
rCommand(ne_Command,ne_Data)
rCompass()
rDBumper({ne_Color})
rDFeel({ne_Color})

rFeel()
rGpsX()
rGpsY()
rGround(ne_SensorNo)
rGroundA(ne_Angle)
rLook({ne_Angle})
rPoints()
rRange({ne_Angle})
rSense({ne_Color})

Customized Help

This section is available from within RobotBASIC's help system as a jumping point. You can add your own text to replace this text and be able to jump to it any time you wish from within the RB help system. Just maintain the heading above intact and RB will be able to locate it within the help file to direct you immediately to this area any time you need it.

The help system utilizes a customizable separate file called RobotBASIC_HelpFile.RTF. This is an RTF formatted file that has to reside inside the same folder where the RobotBASIC.exe is contained. The file can be modified to include special help catered to your requirements in this section.

This feature can be of utility to teachers. A teacher may customize the help file to the needs and level of the students. Moreover, the help file may be used to give extra information to students regarding coursework materials.

Note: This file is best modified using the WordPad program provided in all MSWindows systems. It must be saved as an RTF format file. MSWord can read and write RTF format files but it may not save using the version of the RTF format required by RobotBASIC. If you find that the file is garbled when you read it in the RobotBASIC help screen, then load and save the file again using the WordPad program. The headings in the file have the character • before or surrounding all headings (no space after it). This is important and the headings must remain as is for RB to be able to locate them within the help file.

www.ingramcontent.com/pod-product-compliance
Lightning Source LLC
Chambersburg PA
CBHW080152060326
40689CB00018B/3948